# FIELD & STREAM
## The Complete Fisherman

Book One: Fish Finding, copyright © 1978, 1999 by Leonard M. Wright Jr. An earlier version of this book was published in 1978 by New Century Publishers under the title *Winchester Press Fish-Finding Guide.*

Book Two: Fishing Knots, copyright © 1999 by Peter Owen; design and illustration by Peter Owen.

Book Three: Baits and Rigs, copyright © 1999 by C. Boyd Pfeiffer

Book Four: Bass Fishing, copyright © 1974, 1999 by Mark Sosin and Bill Dance. Originally published as *Practical Black Bass Fishing* in 1974 by Crown Publishers, Inc. The text has been updated and condensed.

Book Five: Fly Fishing, copyright © 1987, 1999 by Leonard M. Wright Jr. Originally published as *First Cast: The Beginner's Guide to Fly Fishing* in 1987 by Fireside, a division of Simon & Schuster, Inc., by arrangement with Nick Lyons Books.

Book Six: Tackle Care and Repair, copyright © 1987, 1999 by C. Boyd Pfeiffer

The Lyons Press is an imprint of The Globe Pequot Press.

Library of Congress Cataloging-in-Publication Data is available.

Manufactured in Canada
First edition/Second printing

# FIELD & STREAM
# The Complete Fisherman

**Leonard M. Wright,**

**Peter Owen, C. Boyd Pfeiffer,**

**Mark Sosin & Bill Dance,**

**and the Editors of *Field & Stream***

**THE LYONS PRESS**
**GUILFORD, CONNECTICUT**
**AN IMPRINT OF THE GLOBE PEQUOT PRESS**

# Contents

## Book Five:   Fly Fishing

## Book Six:   Tackle Care and Repair

# FIELD& STREAM

# The Complete Fisherman

## Book One

### Fish Finding

Leonard M. Wright

# Brooks, Streams, and Rivers

RUNNING WATER differs from still water in one important way: It brings the food to the fish like an endless belt conveyor, while lake or pond fish have to cruise around and find their meals. As a result, most fish in flowing water tend to stay in or near one chosen place for days, weeks, even months, because their food travels to them.

3

However, most fish make short trips several times a day from their secure resting places to areas where food is more plentiful. These journeys may be only several feet and are seldom more than 100 yards. Then, too, most river fish move slightly upstream as the season advances, seeking temperatures more to their liking. Running water not only gets bigger as it progresses downstream; it gets warmer, too.

Most river fish stake out a territory and defend it from all smaller or weaker rivals. Despite this, fish are constantly seeking to better their lot, and steadily challenge their betters for choicer quarters. So if you catch a good trout, for example, from a deep cut under a root tangle one evening, fish it carefully on your next outing. Another good fish is almost certain to move into this choice vacancy—often within a few hours.

Fish living in running water are usually somewhat smaller than specimens of the same species that inhabit lakes and ponds. Floods and droughts reduce their food supplies. And it takes energy that would otherwise go into growth to battle the current. But river fish undergo tougher training and usually fight harder than their still-water brethren. And perhaps even more important, there's a special charm to flowing-water fishing that has convinced many anglers that this is the choicest fishing of all.

## 1. OUTSIDES OF BENDS

Wherever running water changes direction, both the main thread of the current and the deeper water will be near the outside edge of the turn. This concentration of food-carrying current, plus the security of deeper water, make the outsides of bends prime fish-holding places.

## 2. MERGING CURRENTS

Where two currents come together, twice as much food is carried to the fish. Wherever you find this condition, along with reasonable depth or protective cover, you will also find fish. In fact, fish often feed at shallow current junctions when they feel protected by the dim light of dawn or dusk.

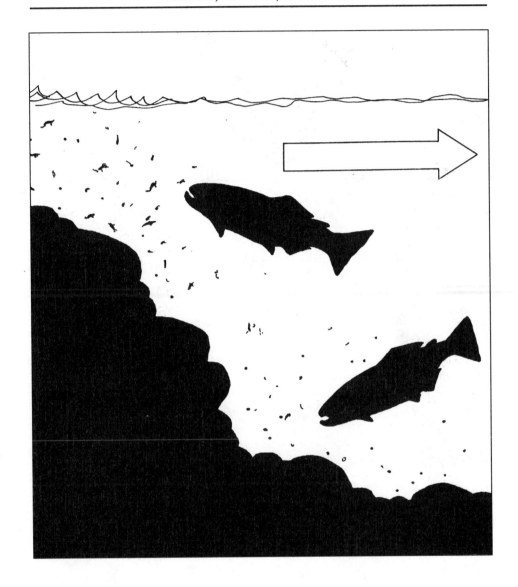

## 3. Drop-Offs

Where water suddenly deepens—as at the heads of most pools—the current slows down and the food carried by the flow begins to settle to the bottom, making easy pickings for fish. Such places have everything: easy food, the safety of depth, and the comfort of a moderate current.

## 4. EDDIES

Water rushing into a pool faster than it can escape tends to form a large, slow whirlpool. Fish will often position themselves where the upstream flow starts to slow down as well as in the main downstream current. Again, they have the benefits of food, comfort, and safety.

## 5. DAMS AND FALLS

In places where water drops vertically over an obstruction, it digs a deep, safe hole for fish. In addition, such places are difficult for fish to climb over, so that fish moving gradually upstream to cooler water or to spawn tend to bunch up just below dams and falls.

## 6. Big Rocks and Boulders

Not only do these break the current—giving fish resting places—but there are also deep holes just below them and often undercuts on their sides. Both of these offer fish safety. Places studded with big rock slabs and boulders are always prime sections of any stream.

## 7. OVERHANGING BUSHES OR TREES

Since most river fish's enemies attack from above, the fish prefer some overhead cover. Then, too, overhanging foliage or deadfalls give shade as well as protection—a condition most fish seek on bright, sunny days. Even where the water may appear shallow, such places are always worth trying.

## 8. UNDERCUTS

Another, and often more productive, form of cover is created where currents undercut banks or rock ledges. Such places, especially cuts under the roots of big, bankside trees, are the safest of all in the river. The biggest fish like to take over these lairs and repel all intruders.

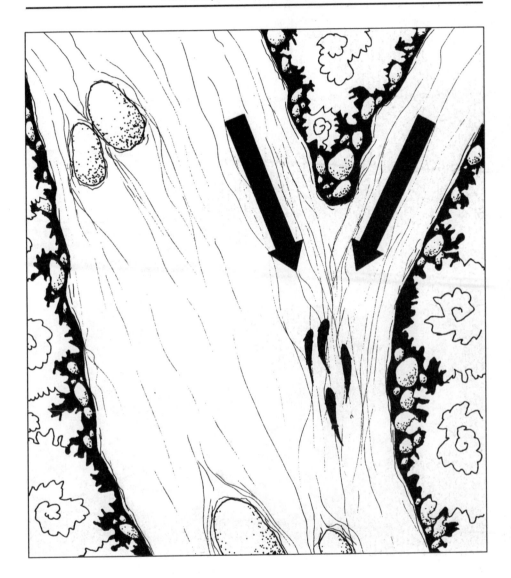

## 9. Feeder Brooks

The junction of a small stream with a larger one is often a top spot—provided there's reasonable depth and cover nearby. Here, not only do you have the advantage of two currents funneling food to the fish, but you also have the cooler water to attract fish in hot summer weather.

## 10. SPRINGS

Not all additions to streams come from visible brooks. In some places, water wells up into the stream from underground sources. Again, the fish-comfort factor comes into play. Such water is much cooler than river water in midsummer, yet warmer in winter and in early spring.

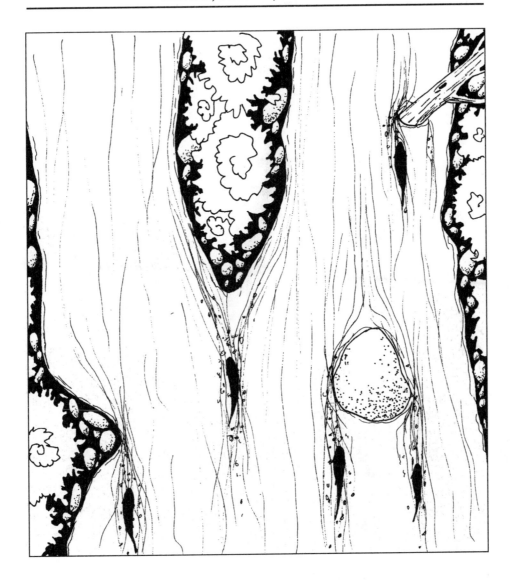

## 11. CURRENT EDGES

Wherever a rock, small island, piece of debris, or any other object pokes through the surface or out into the flow, a short drift line is created. You can often spot them by lines of drift matter or bubbles. Given enough depth or nearby cover, fish will work these natural food funnels.

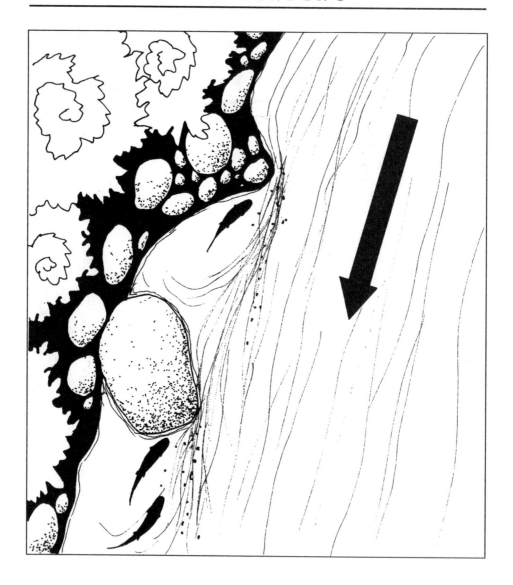

## 12. Mini Eddies

Shoreline clumps of sedge grass, rocks, and small indentations in cliff faces create small eddies downstream that break the current and collect food. Fish often hang out in such places for both comfort and food. Such places can be hard to spot, but keep your eyes open for them.

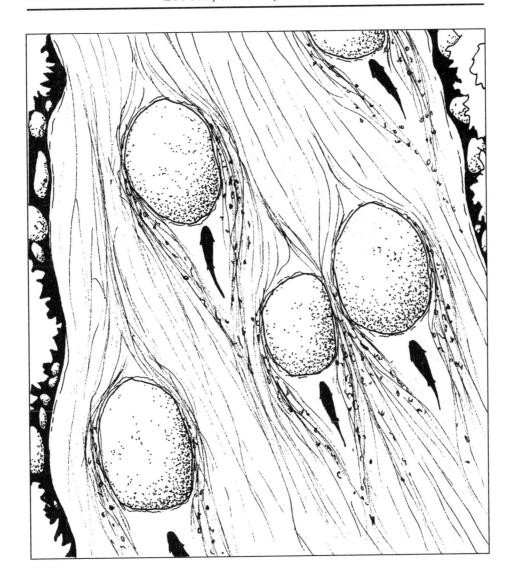

## 13. POCKETS

Large rocks or boulders emerging, or almost emerging, from rapids cause the current to dig downstream holes, creating mini pools. These can be surprisingly productive, despite their small size— especially during midday or in hot weather.

## 14. SHADY SPOTS

On summer afternoons, when the rest of the river seems dead, you can often get interesting fishing early in the afternoon by fishing north-south sections with high, shading hills to the west of them. By using a map or by exploring, you can often find such sections and extend your fishing day.

## 15. TAILS OF POOLS

Late in the evening, often just before it gets too dark to see, fish will drift down the pool and feed at the lip where it breaks out into the next rapids. This is seldom a good location early in the day, but it can offer the best sport of the day on a late-summer evening.

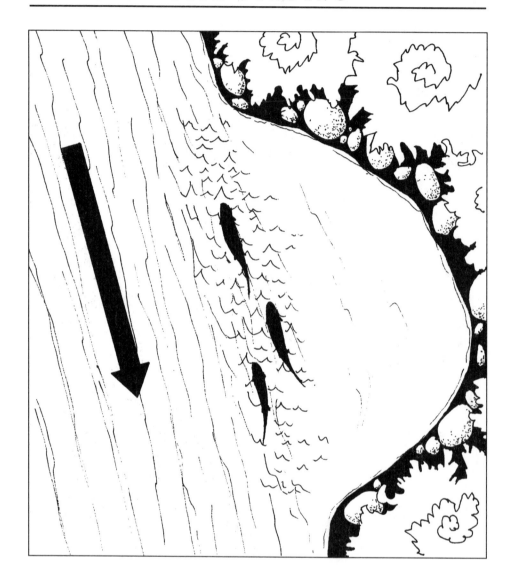

## 16. DANCING PYRAMIDS

Where slow water meets fast, a series of small, stationary, dancing waves will occur. Food drops to the bottom here, and large, lazy fish will take over these patches—if there's enough depth. Even if depth and cover are lacking, fish are still likely to feed in such places at dusk.

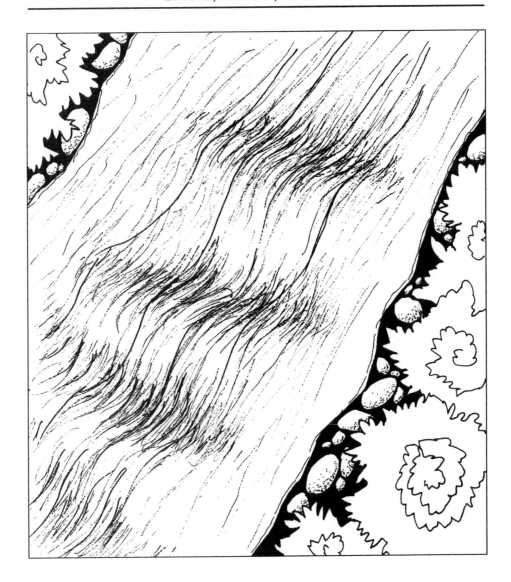

## 17. STANDING WAVES

When you see one or a series of stationary "bumps" or waves in a fast
run or a rapid, you can be sure there's an obstruction—probably a
submerged boulder—directly upstream. Trout, especially rainbows,
like such lies—so give them extra attention.

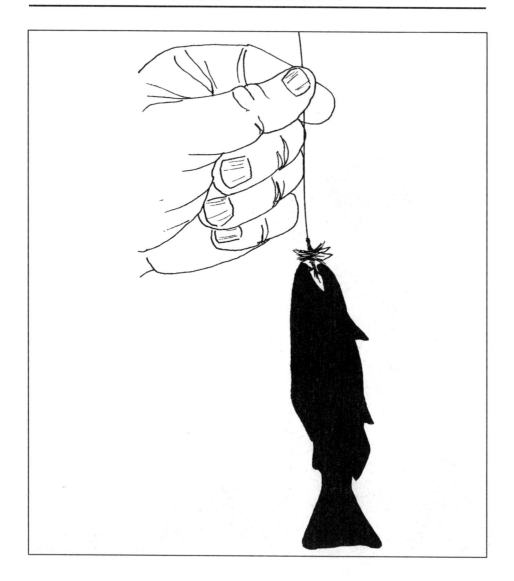

## 18. LITTLE FISH

If you take a small fish from a place that looks like a choice big-fish
spot, move on. Something's wrong. The place just isn't as good as it
looks. There are probably no big fish there, because large specimens
do not allow small ones within 5 or 10 feet of their lies.

## 19. CHECK IT OUT

During midday—especially on warm, sunny days—it pays to walk through water you expect to fish that evening. You will discover fish lies you would never have noticed by looking at the surface. If you wade in swimming trunks, you can feel the colder water from springs, too.

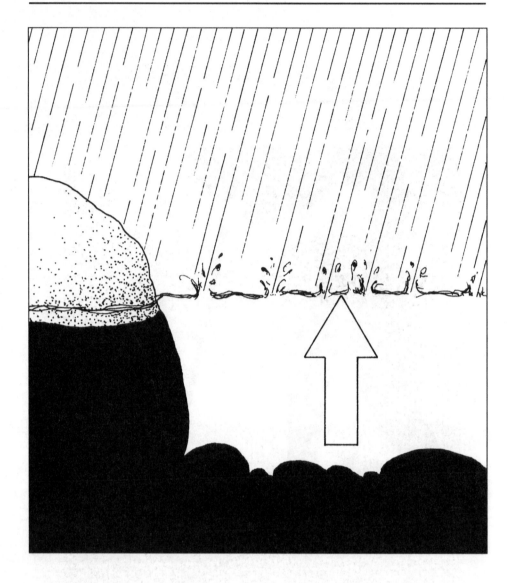

## 20. RISING WATER

Many streams and rivers seem to go dead during low water and hot weather. However, if you time your trip to arrive right after a good rain when the water is rising and cooling, you can often enjoy fishing that rivals the best you had in springtime.

CHAPTER

# Ponds and Lakes

S TILL WATERS are harder to "read" than flowing waters. There are
no telltale currents to help you discover where the food is concentrated. Then, too, lakes and ponds are usually quite deep,
making it harder to pick out fish-holding places.

Another problem is that since there are no currents to bring food to the fish, still-water species have to cruise around to find food, and moving targets are notoriously harder to hit. Therefore, it's particularly important to learn all you can about the habits and habitat preferences of the type of fish you are after.

The majority of still-water fish, like the smallmouth bass, feed in fairly shallow water early and late in the day, retreating to deeper water as the sun and temperature get higher. Some, like pike and pickerel, spend most of their time hiding in the shallows waiting for their prey to come to them. And a few members of the trout family spend most of the summer in the cool depths feeding on schools of deep-water baitfish.

The successful pond and lake fisherman, no matter where he travels, is the one who knows the territorial and temperature preference of the fish he's after, figures in the time of day or year, and, above all, uses his eyes. There are always a surprising number of clues to show him the secrets of the flat and baffling sheet of water in front of him. You will find some of the most important of these on the following pages.

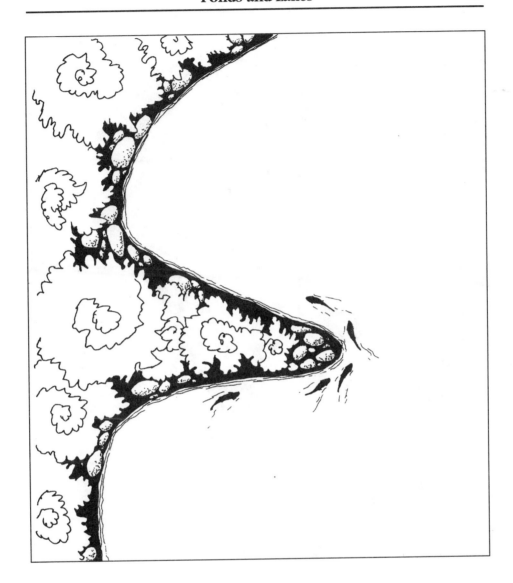

## 1. POINTS OF LAND

A peninsula jutting into the water offers you two benefits. First, it gives you larger areas of the depth that fish prefer along both of its sides. Second, and equally important, fish cruising the shoreline will tend to pass through a small area off the underwater tip.

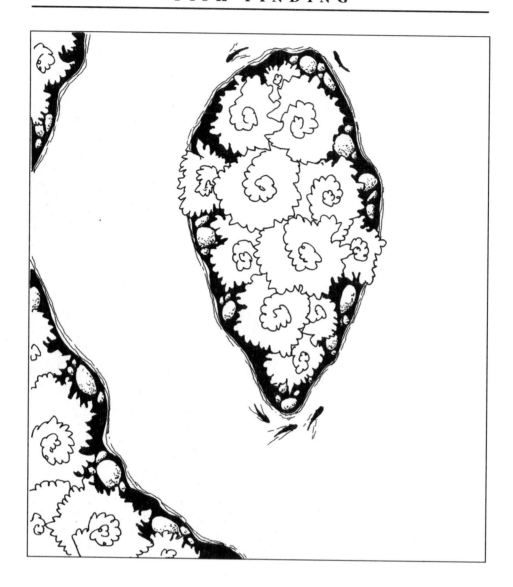

## 2. ISLANDS

Like points of land, islands give you increased areas of fish-holding and fish-feeding territory. Fish tend to remain near such places in good quantities. Clues to underwater contours and depths are given by the above-water terrain as described in other parts of this section.

## 3. Cliffs

Like steep banks, cliffs tell you to expect deep water below them. And one thing more: It is also fairly certain that pieces of rock have crumbled off the cliff over the years, building up a productive area of rubble and boulders along the bottom.

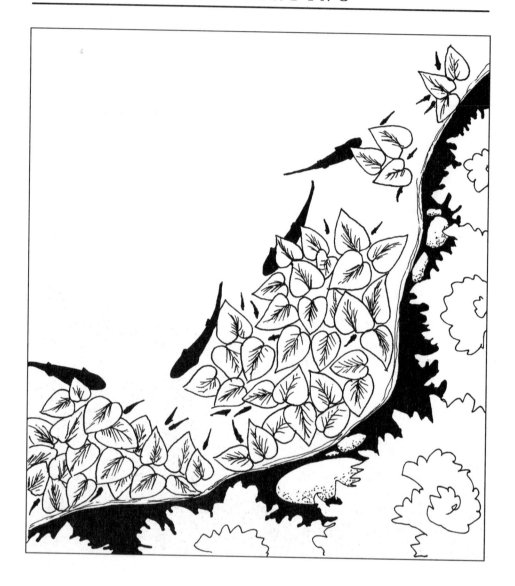

## 4. EDGES OF PADS

Small fish, which feed on the insects that live on stems of lily pads and weeds, attract hungry big fish. The shade created by dense patches of pads is also an attraction. Fish along the outside edges and in the larger openings so your line will not get fouled so often.

## 5. UNDERWATER WEED BEDS

Shallow weed beds can often be seen below the surface; deeper ones have to be located by trolling. Weeds give food and protection to small fish that are sought after by big predators like pike and bass. Work weed beds carefully and thoroughly—especially the edges.

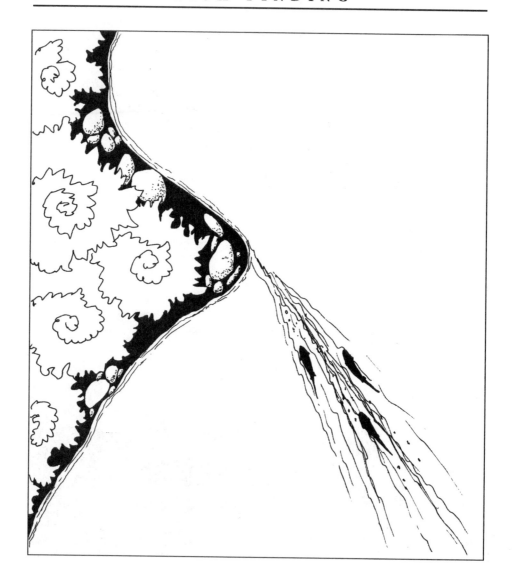

## 6. Drift Lines

On windy days, you will often notice distinct lines on the water's surface. These are caused by fast-drifting surface water, and are most often downwind—sometimes extending several hundred yards—from points or islands. The surface food concentrated in these lines attracts fish.

## 7. Coves

With their long shorelines, extensive shallows, and protection from most winds and waves, coves are top food-producing areas. Shallow sections should produce warm-water fish, and the deep water off the points is a good bet for big fish waiting to make nightly raids for food.

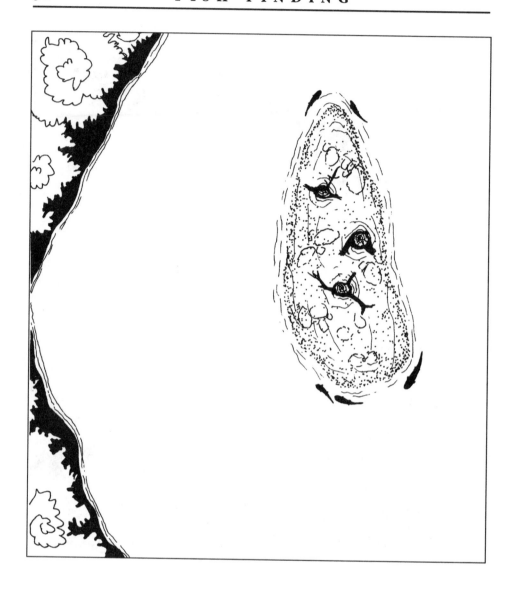

## 8. Sunken Islands

Reefs and underwater bars are really islands that did not quite make it. They offer the same fishing advantages as true islands and should get extra attention. Some are marked by buoys. Others can be found on charts or by searching on sunny, windless days.

## 9. SPRING HOLES

Where cool water boils up from the bottom, it will attract deep-water fish during the summer—even if the depth is not great. Such places are usually well-kept local secrets, but you may find some by testing temperatures while swimming or by exploring with a mask.

## 10. INLET STREAMS

Inflowing water brings extra food, but just the flow itself seems to
attract some fish. Many species, such as smelt in the spring and trout
and salmon in the fall, spawn in running water; look for concentrations at stream mouths in the appropriate seasons.

## 11. STEEP BANKS

Where the land pitches steeply into the water, you can expect good depth very close to shore. Fish that prefer deep water, or those driven deep by summer heat, are likely to be in such places. Various depths along the slope should be tested carefully for different species of fish.

## 12. Gradual Shores

Where the land slopes gently into the water, look for shallows well out into the lake. Such water, especially if the bottom is sandy, is often unproductive. But if there are boulders or weed beds, give them extra attention, for they may hold most of the fish in that area.

## 13. BAITFISH

You will often notice that schools of minnows, small sunfish, or perch tend to hang out in a certain area. Big fish that like to feed on them may not be nearby during the bright hours of the day, but be sure to fish such areas carefully at both dawn and dusk.

## 14. BOULDERS

Big, roundish underwater rocks—especially those over a yard in diameter—provide shade and hiding places for fish both large and small. Crawfish like such places, too. Fish every sunken boulder carefully and, if you find a cluster of them, you have hit a hot spot.

## 15. Deeper Does It

If you are fishing what appear to be the best places and still are not catching any fish, try farther out from shore. The fish are usually deeper, rather than shallower, than you would expect—especially at midday or during summer, when the surface water gets hot.

## 16. TRY NIGHTS

During midsummer, when most vacations take place, fish often bite poorly. If working deeper, cooler water does not produce, try fishing at night. This tactic can be especially effective with largemouth and smallmouth bass. Surface lures are usually best.

## 17. GET A FISH'S-EYE VIEW

It's a smart idea to explore a clear-water lake or pond with swimsuit and mask at midday during warm weather. You will not only locate some unnoticed sunken weed beds, reefs, rocks, and drop-offs, but you are also apt to spot many fish for a later try.

# Bays and Estuaries

THESE ARE THE areas where fresh and salt water usually meet. Estuaries certainly are a first mixing point of the two types of water; but many, or even most, bays have a touch of freshwater influence.

How does this affect the fishing—and the fishermen? In several ways.

Let us take estuaries first. The strong influence of fresh water here has a great attraction for some fish. Tarpon, snook, striped bass, to name a few, have a well-known urge to enter brackish, or mixed, waters. These waters are also, in spawning season, concentration points for anadromous species: saltwater fish that spend most of their lives in the ocean, but must spawn in sweet water. Some of these are shad, herring, salmon, and sea-run trout.

Surprisingly, some purely freshwater species such as the largemouth bass can tolerate quite a bit of salt water. There are estuaries in the South where you can catch largemouths and snook on successive casts.

Bays, with or without pronounced freshwater influence, have a few extra things in common. Mainly, they are protected from the ravages of storms and pounding waves. This makes them ideal nurseries for many species of fish and crustaceans—all of which are fodder for bigger and better fish. Also, their shallower waters warm up more quickly in the spring or during summer days, raising the metabolism rate—and feeding needs—of many warm-water species.

By all means, read the next section of this book, "Surf and Shore." A few of the tips in that section can also be helpful to bay and estuary fishermen—and every angler these days needs all the help and advice he can get.

## 1. NARROWS

Currents speed up where the water is pinched. This digs a deeper channel for fish protection and concentrates the food moving through into a narrower, easier-to-get-at area. Except at dead-high or dead-low tides when water movement ceases, these are hot spots.

## 2. PIERS AND PILINGS

With their weed attachments they not only provide food for small fish and crabs, but also create protective eddies when currents are running. Small fish plus barnacles, periwinkles, mussels, and oysters that often grow on piers and pilings make these structures choice spots.

## 3. MOVING PATCHES

Schools of fish like mackerel and a few others can be so tightly packed that they actually color the water—even when they are a few feet below the surface. Some baitfish do this also. Always follow and cast to such places until you are sure your eyes are playing tricks.

## 4. STRANGE RIPPLES

These can also be created by school fish, but only when they are very close to the surface. Even when the light is bad, you can spot these slight surface disturbances. Ripples can be caused by a school of baitfish or by predators. Get to such suspicious breaks fast and start fishing.

## 5. BIRDS

Wherever baitfish are pushed to the surface or boil up wounded from deep water, seabirds will gather quickly. Fishermen who follow close behind should do well. If the minnows seem frightened to the surface, fish shallow. If they're boiling up wounded, fish deep.

## 6. BRACKISH PONDS

These may hold significant quantities of catching-sized fish only occasionally, but they are important as nurseries and as food supplies. Where they empty into bay, ocean, or tidal river, you can expect fish to be positioned for easy pickings—especially at low tide.

## 7. CHANNELS

Fish often follow channels in and out with the tide, not only because the water is deeper, but because the food-bearing currents are stronger. Anchor just off the edge and fish into deeper water. Buoys often mark channels. It's illegal to tie up to them, but smart to fish near them.

## 8. OTHER BOATS

One of the surest ways to find good fishing spots is to watch where other boats go. Anglers who fish an area regularly know where the fish are—or where they *usually* are. Nobody can complain if you follow their example. But you can become unpopular if you crowd in too close.

## 9. BENDS

Tidal rivers, like freshwater rivers, dig deep and tend to undercut their banks on the outside portions of bends. Most food will funnel through such places, and their extra depth and overhead cover make them choice holding places for many types of gamefish.

## 10. BACKWATERS

Where tidal currents flow in a direction that is opposite to the main flow—as they often will for short distances just below sharp points or obstructions—food will tend to drop to the bottom. Schools of baitfish tend to gather here, attracting bigger predators.

## 11. JUMPING BAITFISH

Whenever you see a shower of minnows in the air, get to the area and start fishing quickly. Baitfish don't jump because they need the exercise. They are trying to escape from danger—usually big fish that are lurking below and are actively feeding.

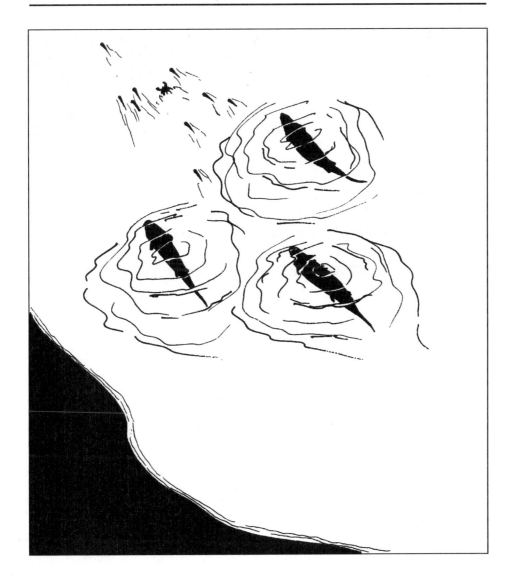

## 12. SWIRLS

On calm days or in the evening, you will often see a boil or boils on the surface. This usually means that a fish has taken a shrimp, swimming crab, or minnow just below the surface. The bigger the swirl, the bigger the fish, so fish the larger boils first.

## 13. Bay Entrances

Where bays empty into the ocean—often through a narrow cut or channel—there will be a strong current to pull food in and out, according to the tide. The biggest fish in the bay, including some visitors from the ocean, are likely to hang out here.

## 14. CHUM

When fishing is poor or slackens off, even though you are in a choice spot, it often pays to try to attract fish and start them feeding again. Extra bait or crushed clams, mussels, crabs, and so on, parceled out downcurrent, will usually start the action.

## 15. Stir Things Up

Even if you have no chum or spare bait aboard, you can often attract fish—especially bottom-feeding types—by dragging your anchor in a small area. This works best over a sand or mud bottom. It uncovers bottom food, and the clouded water itself will usually draw some fish.

# CHAPTER 4

# Surf and Shore

HERE, YOU ARE on the rim of a vast ocean. There is no influence of fresh water. Nor are the relatively shallow inshore stretches protected from surf or storms.

And this, perhaps, is what makes fishing from beaches and rocky shores so exciting. On all but rare calm days, waves created hundreds, even thousands, of miles away hammer away at the shoreline.

It is the power of these waves that creates a special type of fish feeding. It sets up powerful currents. It churns up the sand temporarily, exposing crabs, sand eels, sand bugs, shrimp, and so on, giving feeding fish sudden targets of opportunity.

Whether you fish from the shore itself or offshore from a boat, there is one important fact to remember. Many types of small fish migrate up the coastline in spring and down again toward warmer water in fall. This creates a "river" of fish—some earlier in the season than others—up and down the coastline for most of the year. Newspaper and radio reports will usually tell you what part of this migration, and how concentrated, is in your area.

The ocean can be dangerous to waders and boaters, so be careful, be watchful, and be prepared. You are trespassing on the edge of an area where even large ships have disappeared. But this is also the place where the biggest fish of all live, and that adds an extra zest to fishing.

## 1. OFFSHORE BREAKERS

Where waves break a good distance offshore and there is a relatively calm patch of water between them and shore, you can be sure there is some relatively deep water between the breakers. Here is a natural place for food, baitfish, and gamefish to collect.

## 2. THROATS OF TIDAL PONDS OR CREEKS

At ebb or low tide, salt creeks and ponds pour strong currents into the ocean—carrying a stream of crabs, shrimp, and minnows with them. At times like these, such places are hot spots, but at a high, or flooding, tide they may provide only so-so fishing.

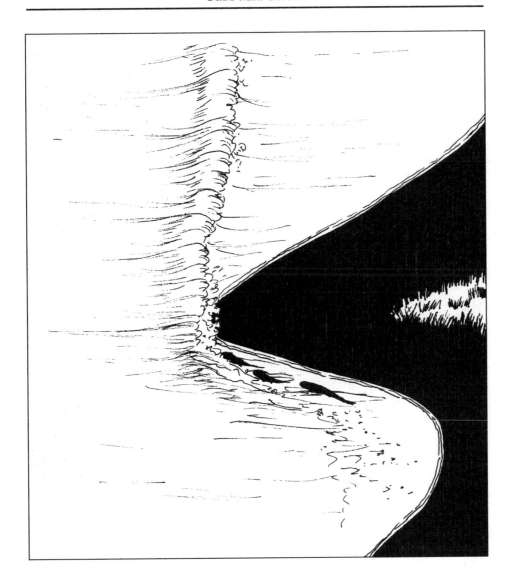

## 3. POINTS

These are natural fish concentrators because schools, or single fish, cruising the coastlines tend to pass by just off the point. And when tides are running slightly crossways to points, you get an extra bonus: They tend to create big eddies that hold baitfish, drift food, and gamefish.

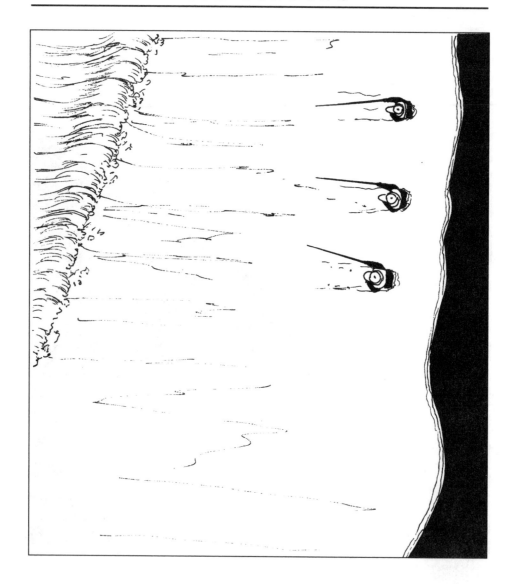

## 4. OTHER FISHERMEN

Many other fishermen you see are locals with local knowledge and experience. Fish near them (observing a decent interval) or where you have seen them fish, and you will cash in on old-timer's knowledge. (You will also find most of them fishing in places described in this section!)

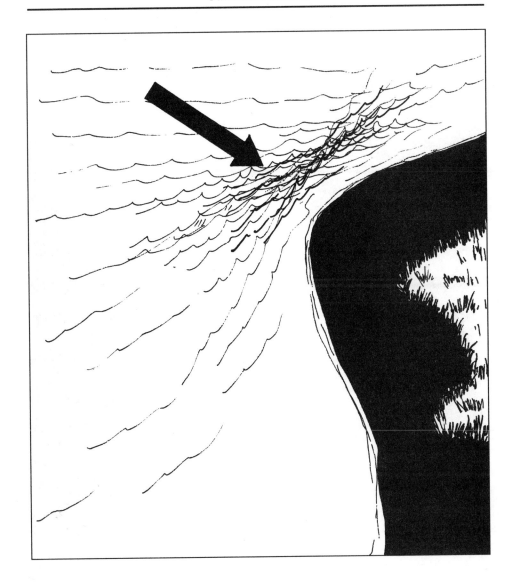

## 5. DANCING WAVES

Where two currents—even light ones—collide, a stationary patch or strip of small dancing waves will occur. Food will tend to collect or drop to the bottom in such places, attracting feeding or just lazing baitfish, which in turn will attract the hungry predators you are after.

## 6. Dark Patches

These usually mean weed patches or clumps of rocks with weeds attached. Rocks hold crabs, mussels, barnacles, and so on, while weeds offer protection for minnows and other types of food. If there are only a few of these in a sandy area, fish them hard and pay special attention to the edges.

## 7. LINES OF SPUME OR FLOTSAM

These visible trails usually mean the edge of a tidal current—often one so slight that it leaves no other traces. Debris attracts baitfish and smaller marine organisms. Bigger fish are attracted in turn. And some fish, like dolphinfish, lie in the shade that is created.

## 8. JETTIES AND BREAKWATERS

These structures not only give shore anglers access to deeper water, but also have special fish-attracting qualities of their own. Their rock structure offers hiding places for crabs and fish, and they create currents and eddies that bunch baitfish and other food.

## 9. CLIFFS

There are almost always boulders and rock slabs on the ocean bottom below rock cliffs—whether you can see them or not. Years of storms and surf have quarried these from the rock face. Such places are favorite haunts of striped bass, tautog, and many other species.

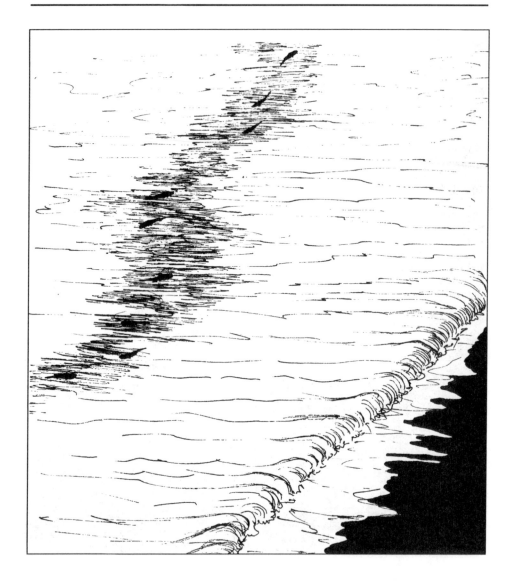

## 10. DARK WATER

Deep water is a different color from shallow water. It is usually a darker green or deeper blue. Many fish—especially during daylight hours—hang out in deeper water than you would expect, so give the deeps extra attention if the shallows are not producing any action.

## 11. ROILY WATER

Some portions of the shoreline are more susceptible to erosion than others, and here the surf stirs up bottom silt and food while nearby areas remain clear. Fish the edges, not the centers, of such patches. Fish enjoy the extra food here, but dislike getting sand in their gills.

## 12. TIDAL RIPS

Points of land, sunken sandbars, underwater channels, and the like
can funnel tidal flow into easily seen temporary "rivers." Their faster
flow and usually greater depth attract fish looking for either food or
safety. Fish find such places quickly, so fish them carefully.

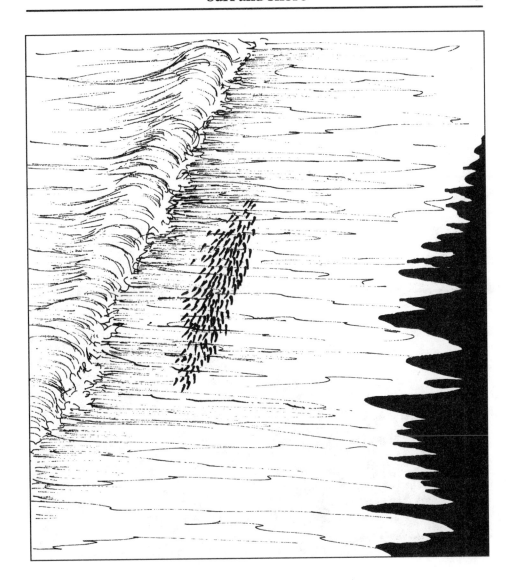

## 13. BAIT SCHOOLS

Wherever you notice a concentration of small fish—whether in an eddy, off a jetty, or seen through a wave in the surf—cast quickly. Fish eat fish. If you want to do the same, give extra attention and effort to places where bite-sized specimens gather.

## 14. INCOMING TIDES

If you have a choice of fishing time, take the flood tide. This does not hold true in all situations, but fish usually feel bolder, feed more heavily, and work in closer to shore when the water is getting deeper.

## 15. TRY NIGHTS

Most hospitable and accessible shorelines attract so many bathers and boaters during the summer that gamefish are commonly driven off into deeper water. All this changes after dark when the crowds are gone. Big fish often raid the shallows for food after dark.

## 16. AFTER A BLOW

Major storms can often muddy the inshore water so badly that fishing is ruined. But a good blow or mild storm, in most areas, quickens the surf and stirs up extra food. If the water remains reasonably clear, this is a prime time for the surf caster.

# FIELD& STREAM

# The Complete Fisherman

## Book Two

## Fishing Knots

Peter Owen

# 1

# HOOK AND TACKLE KNOTS

The knots in this section are for attaching hooks and flies to a leader or tippet, and attaching various items of tackle— lures, swivels, and sinkers—to a line.

An important aspect of choosing which knot to use is to feel fully confident with that knot. The knot you eventually choose will be a vital link between you and your quarry, so practice and experiment with it until you feel confident.

# ARBOR KNOT

This strong but simple knot, also known as the **reel knot,** is used to secure one end of the line to the spool arbor of the reel, hence the name.

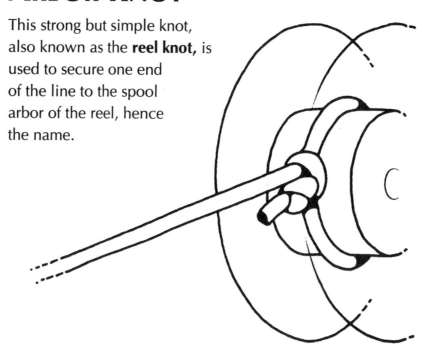

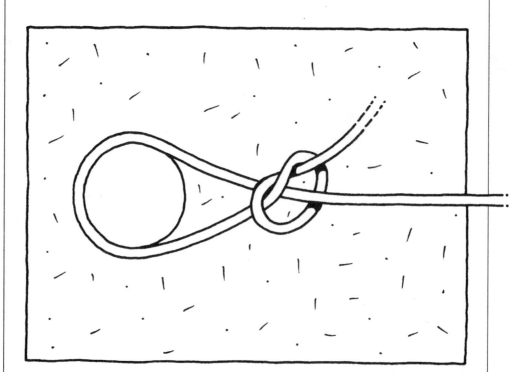

**1** Take the line around the spool arbor of the reel. Then take the tag end around the standing part and tie an overhand knot.

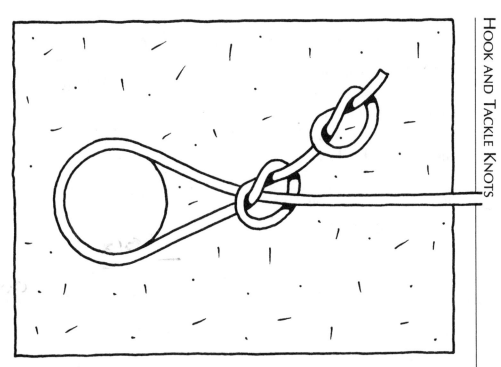

**2** Tie a second overhand knot in the tag end as close as possible to the first overhand knot.

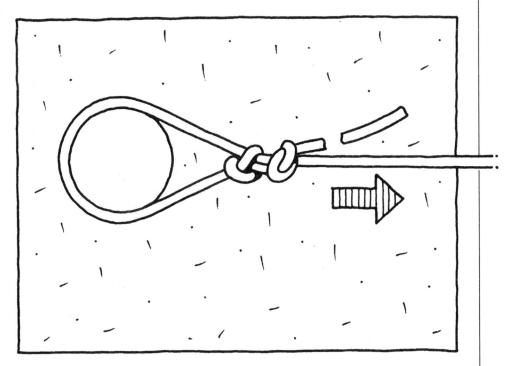

**3** Pull on the standing part of the line, and the two overhand knots will jam together against the spool. Trim the knot end.

**83**

# IMPROVED CLINCH KNOT

This is one of the most popular knots for tying line to a hook, fly, swivel, or lure. It is known by some fishermen as the **tucked half blood knot.** It is quick and easy to tie, and it's particularly effective with fine monofilament.

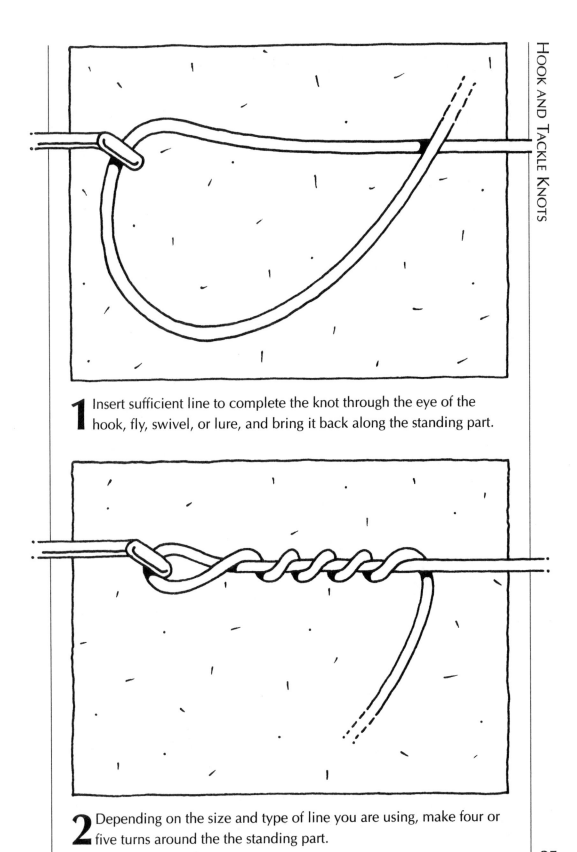

**1** Insert sufficient line to complete the knot through the eye of the hook, fly, swivel, or lure, and bring it back along the standing part.

**2** Depending on the size and type of line you are using, make four or five turns around the the standing part.

**85**

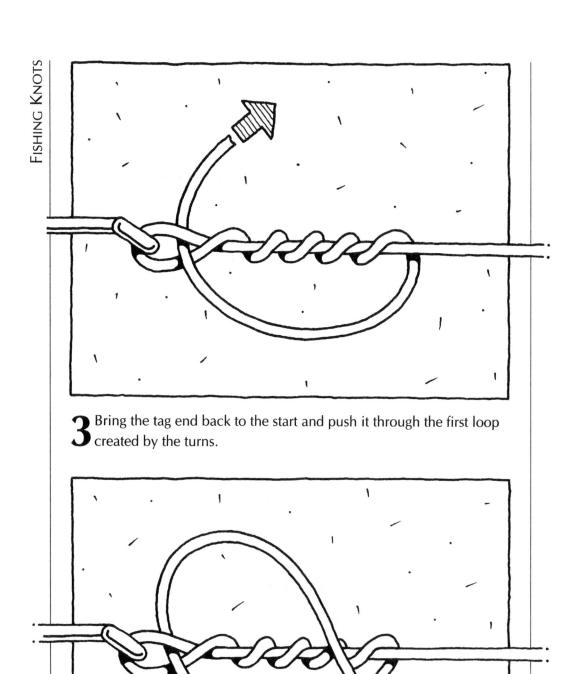

**3** Bring the tag end back to the start and push it through the first loop created by the turns.

**4** Bring the tag end back over and then push it down through the large loop.

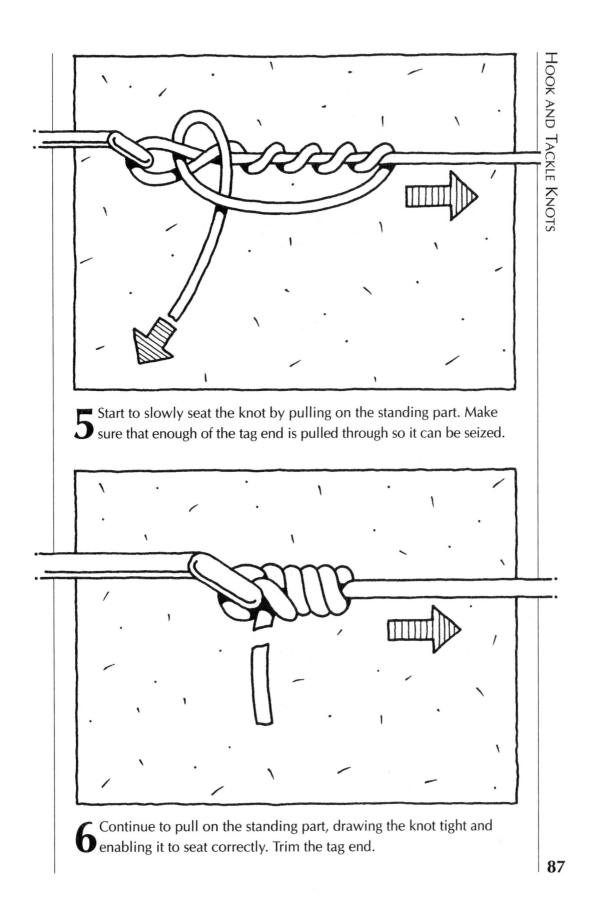

**5** Start to slowly seat the knot by pulling on the standing part. Make sure that enough of the tag end is pulled through so it can be seized.

**6** Continue to pull on the standing part, drawing the knot tight and enabling it to seat correctly. Trim the tag end.

# UNI-KNOT

This knot, also known as the **grinner knot,** is one of the most reliable knots for tying an eyed hook or fly to a leader or tippet. It can also be used to tie line to a swivel, sinker, or lure, and is effective with most types and sizes of line.

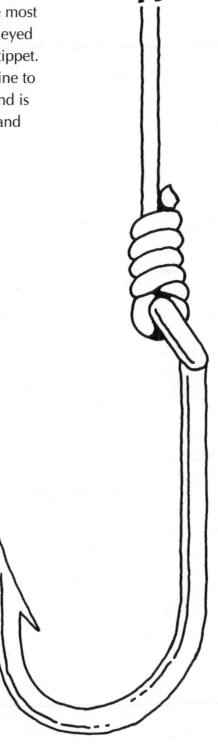

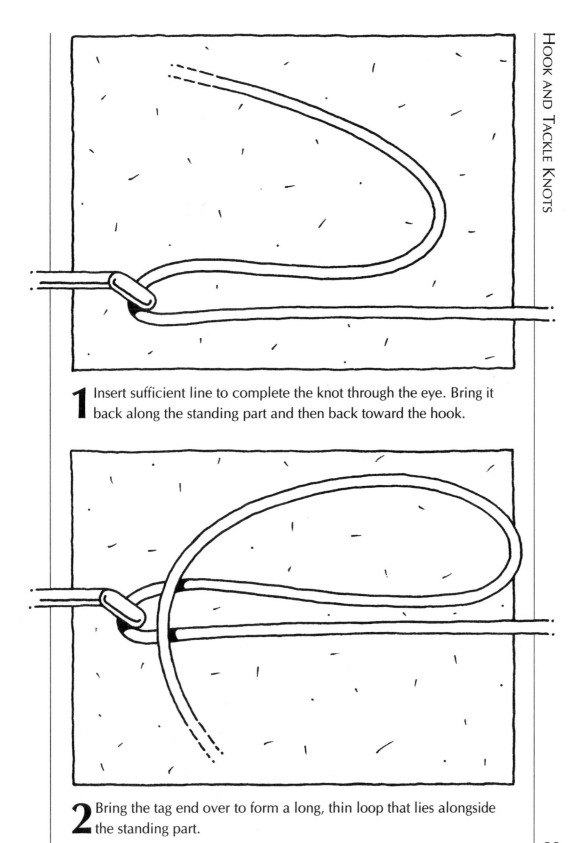

**1** Insert sufficient line to complete the knot through the eye. Bring it back along the standing part and then back toward the hook.

**2** Bring the tag end over to form a long, thin loop that lies alongside the standing part.

**89**

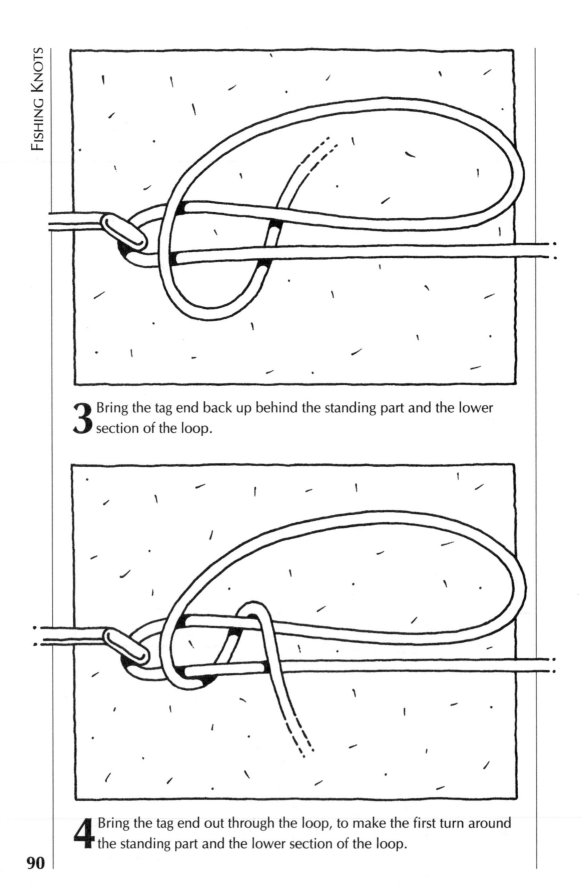

**3** Bring the tag end back up behind the standing part and the lower section of the loop.

**4** Bring the tag end out through the loop, to make the first turn around the standing part and the lower section of the loop.

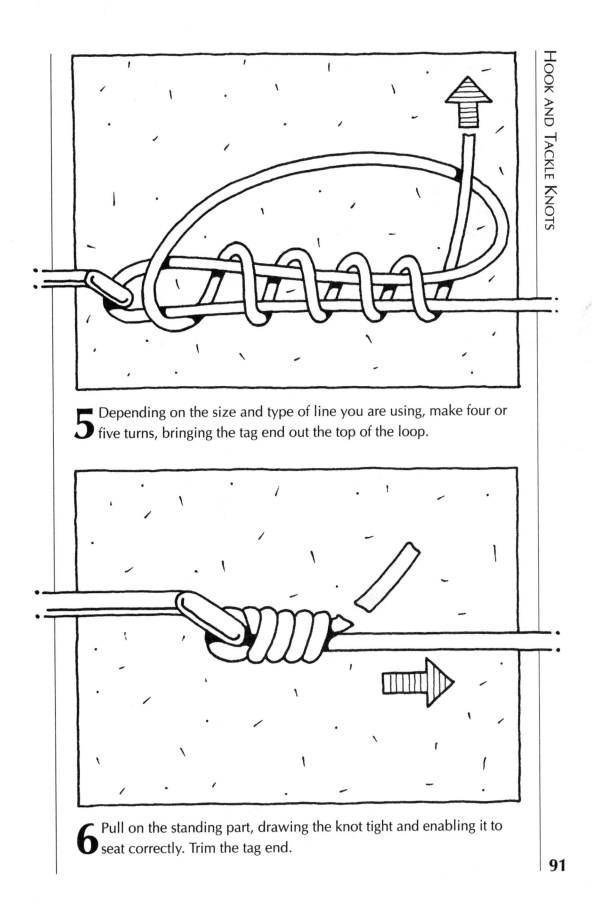

**5** Depending on the size and type of line you are using, make four or five turns, bringing the tag end out the top of the loop.

**6** Pull on the standing part, drawing the knot tight and enabling it to seat correctly. Trim the tag end.

**91**

# DOUBLE TURLE KNOT

This knot is used exclusively for tying flies with up- or downturned eyes to tippets. It is not suitable for straight-eyed hooks. It is designed to allow an excellent fly presentation by keeping the fly in line with your cast.

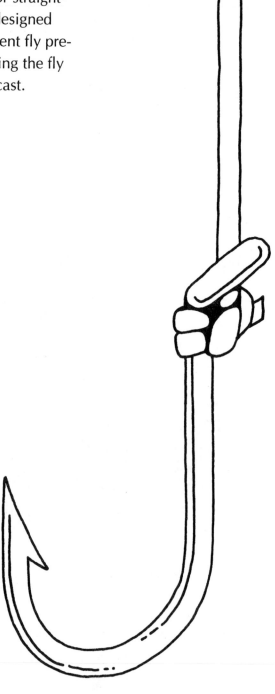

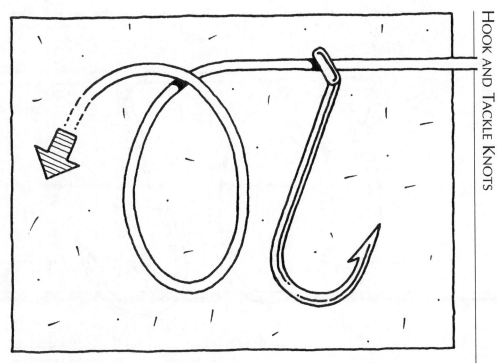

**1** Insert sufficient line to complete the knot through the eye of the hook. Form a small loop.

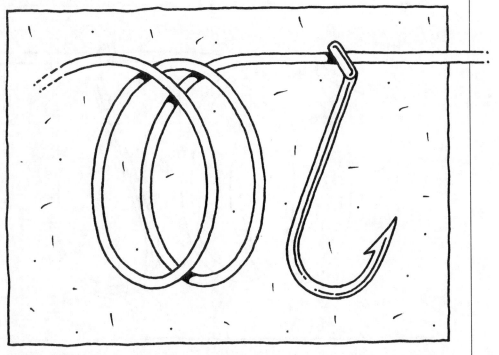

**2** Bring the tag end around to create another, identical loop. This loop sits on top of the first one.

**93**

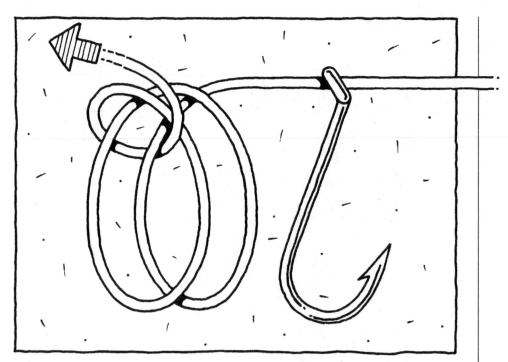

**3** Continue bringing the tag end around, taking it through both loops and bringing it out at the top of the loops.

**4** Tie an overhand knot around the the two loops, but don't tighten it completely. (This will allow for final adjustments.)

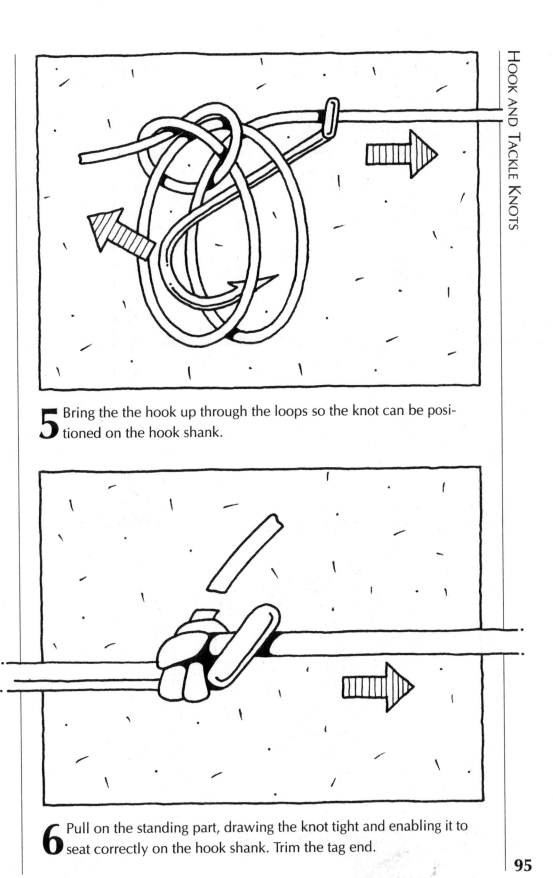

**5** Bring the the hook up through the loops so the knot can be positioned on the hook shank.

**6** Pull on the standing part, drawing the knot tight and enabling it to seat correctly on the hook shank. Trim the tag end.

**95**

# GEORGE HARVEY DRY-FLY KNOT

Developed by fly-fishing
expert George Harvey, this
knot is specifically designed
for attaching a dry fly to a
tippet. Tied correctly, it is a
very secure knot that will
help you make a precise
and delicate dry-fly
presentation.

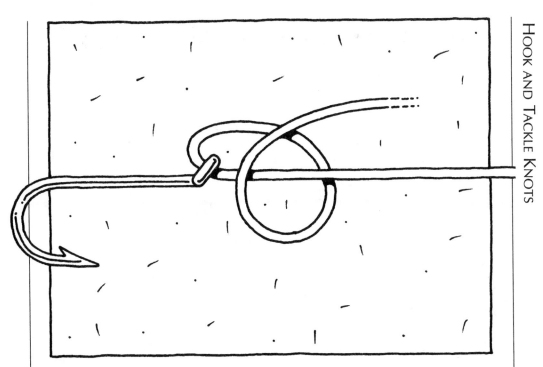

**1** Insert sufficient line through the eye, and form a small circle around the standing part; the tag end should finish in front of the standing part.

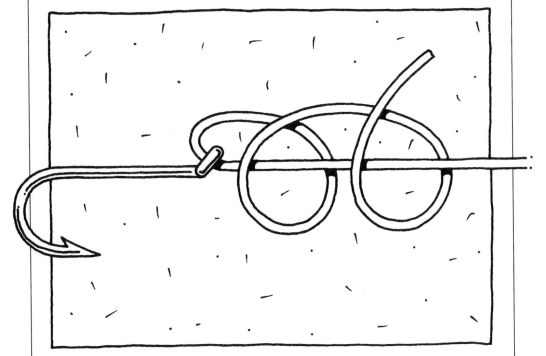

**2** Create a second small circle of the same size around the standing part, again with the tag end finishing in front.

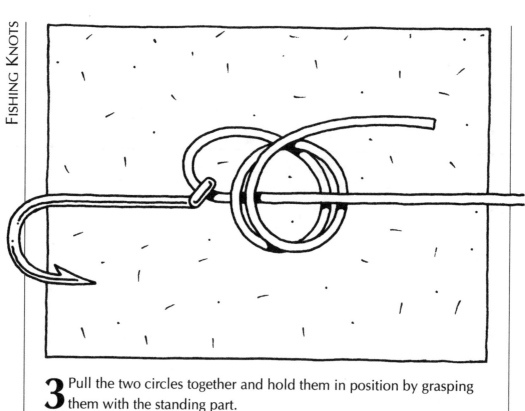

**3** Pull the two circles together and hold them in position by grasping them with the standing part.

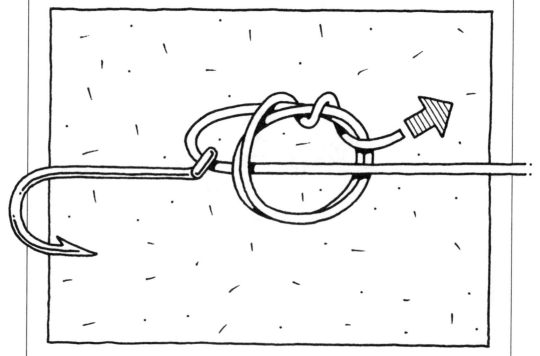

**4** Loop the tag end over and through the two circles twice, bringing the tag end out in the opposite direction to the hook.

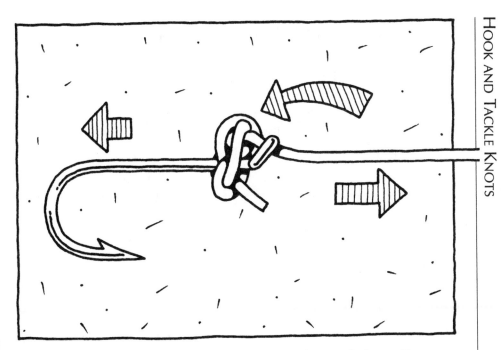

**5** Hold the hook and slowly start to draw the knot tight by pulling on the standing part. If the knot is tied correctly, the loops will slide back and jump over the eye of the hook as it is drawn up.

**6** Continue to pull on the standing part, drawing the knot tight and enabling it to seat correctly. Trim the tag end.

**99**

# NONSLIP MONO KNOT

This knot is designed to give artificial lures a more attractive action in the water. The knot forms a loop that doesn't slip, and allows the lure to move around more. The number of turns required when tying this knot will differ with various types and sizes of line. Try seven turns for fine monofilament, fewer turns with heavier line.

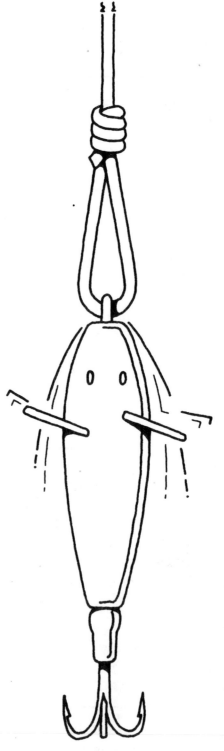

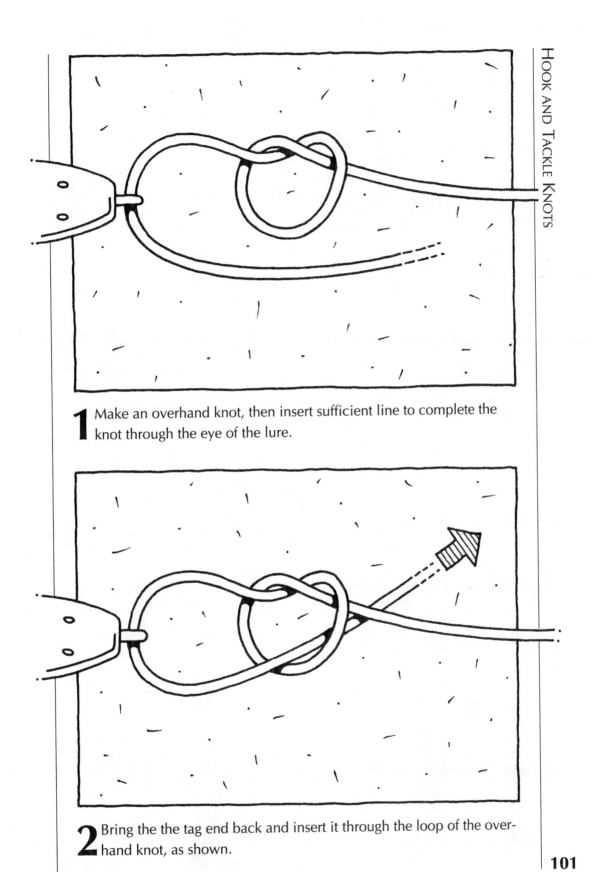

**1** Make an overhand knot, then insert sufficient line to complete the knot through the eye of the lure.

**2** Bring the the tag end back and insert it through the loop of the over-hand knot, as shown.

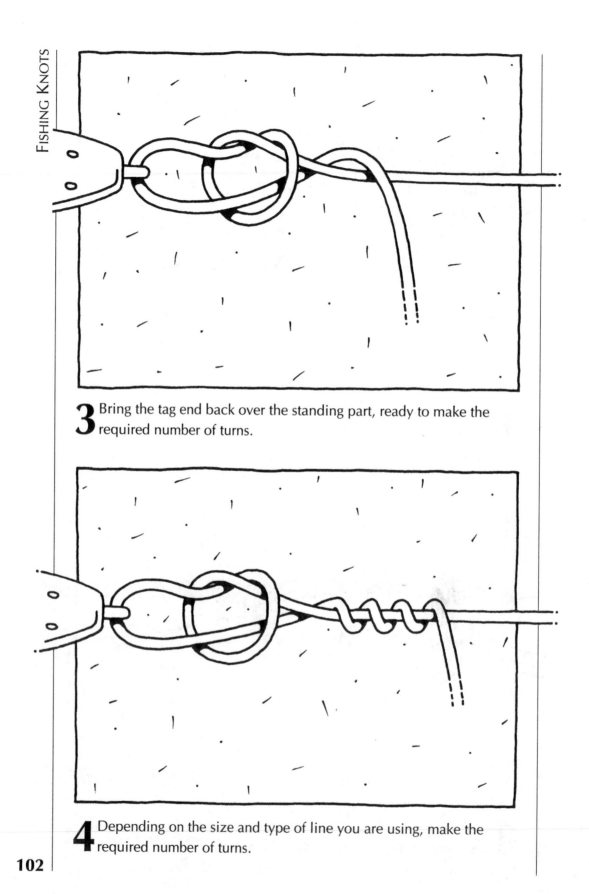

**3** Bring the tag end back over the standing part, ready to make the required number of turns.

**4** Depending on the size and type of line you are using, make the required number of turns.

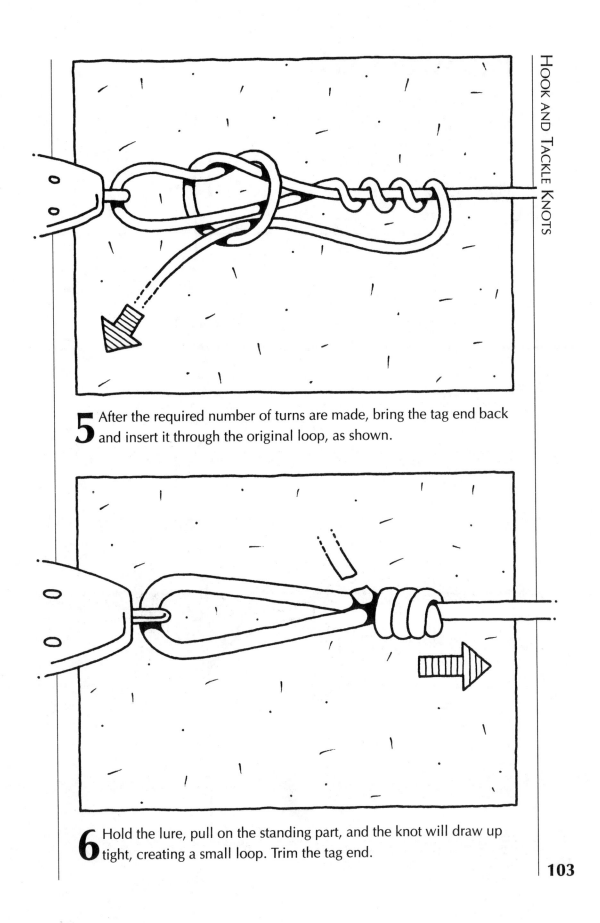

**5** After the required number of turns are made, bring the tag end back and insert it through the original loop, as shown.

**6** Hold the lure, pull on the standing part, and the knot will draw up tight, creating a small loop. Trim the tag end.

# PALOMAR KNOT

This is a quick and effective knot for tying onto swivels, lures, and sinkers. It uses more line than other knots; allow for this when tying.

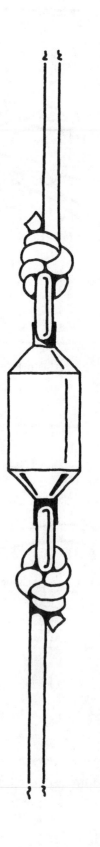

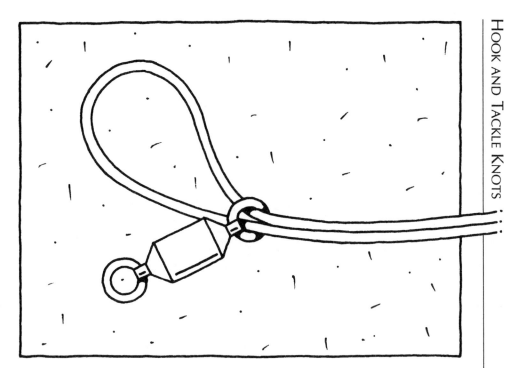

**1** Insert a loop of sufficient double line to complete the knot through the eye of the swivel, lure, or sinker.

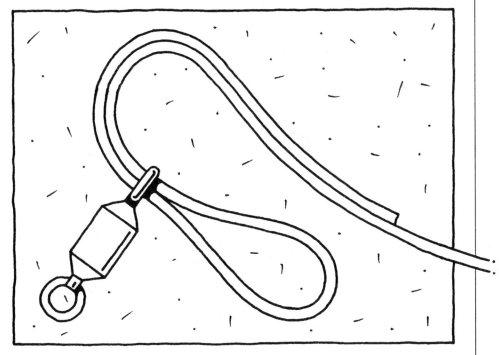

**2** Bring the loop and swivel, lure, or sinker back alongside the standing part.

**105**

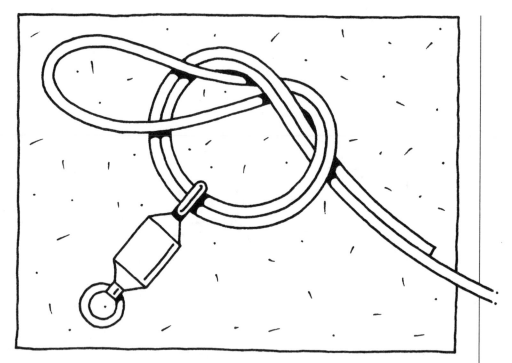

**3** Bring the loop around and make an overhand knot, as shown above.

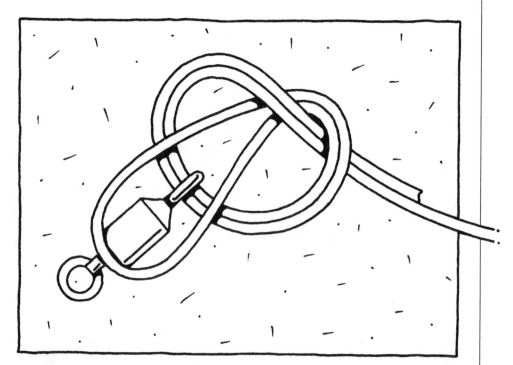

**4** Bring the loop back down and position it over the top of the swivel, lure, or sinker.

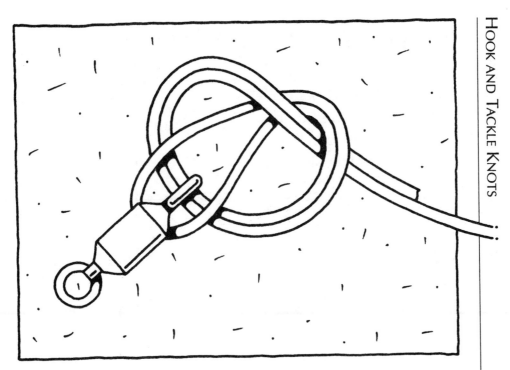

**5** Hold the tag end and the standing part together, and pull the swivel, lure, or sinker out through the loop.

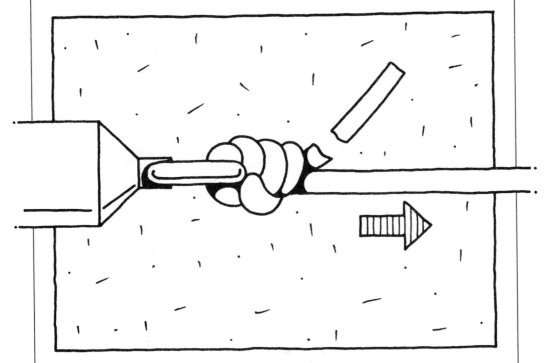

**6** Pull on the standing part and the tag end together, drawing the knot tight and enabling it to seat correctly. Trim the tag end.

# SNELLING AN EYED HOOK

The snell is still widely used by saltwater fishermen, but is often overlooked by other anglers. Tied correctly, it is a very secure knot for attaching an eyed hook to a line.

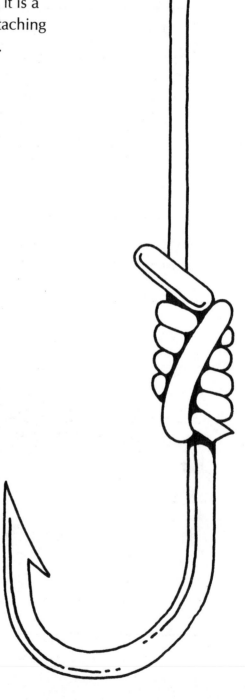

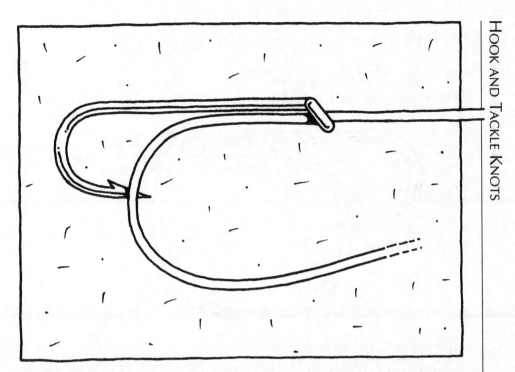

**1** Insert sufficient line to complete the knot through the eye, and then turn it back in the direction of the standing part.

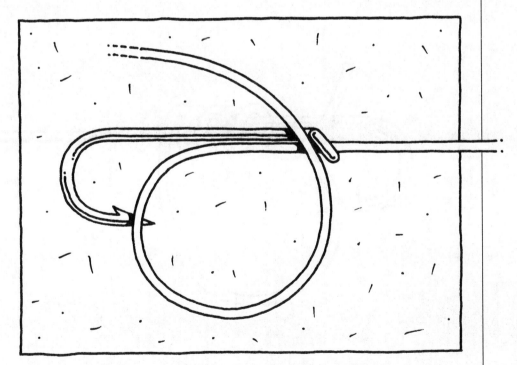

**2** Bring the tag end up to form a large loop. This loop needs to lie along the hook shank.

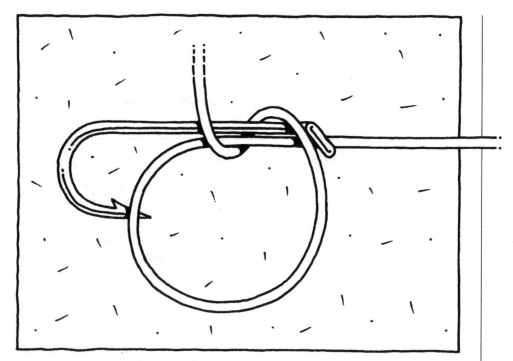

**3** Bring the tag end down to create the first turn around the loop and the hook shank.

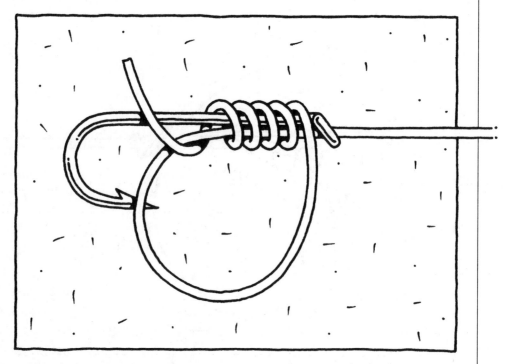

**4** Depending on the size and type of line you are using, make five or six turns away from the hook eye toward the hook point.

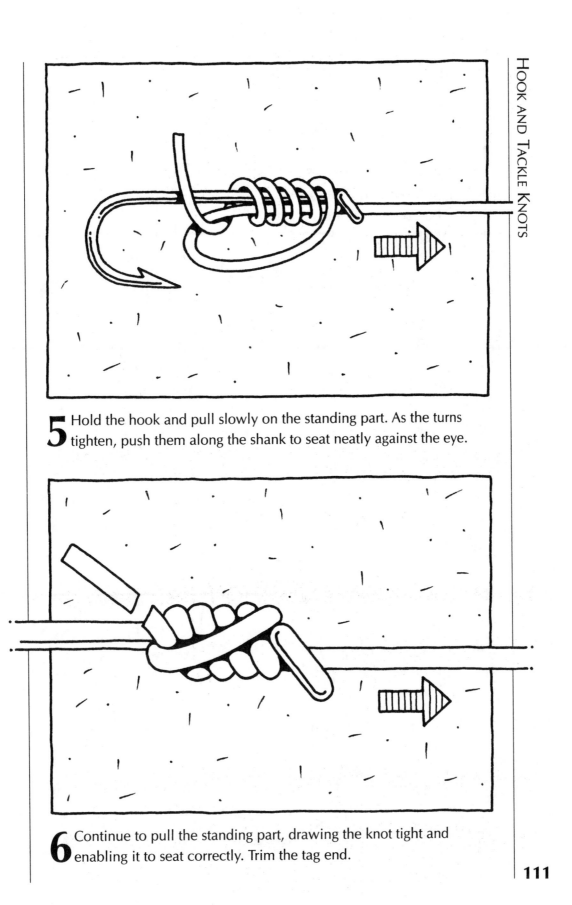

**5** Hold the hook and pull slowly on the standing part. As the turns tighten, push them along the shank to seat neatly against the eye.

**6** Continue to pull the standing part, drawing the knot tight and enabling it to seat correctly. Trim the tag end.

**111**

# SPADE-END KNOT

Still a popular alternative to an eyed hook is the spade-end hook. This knot is designed specifically for tying this type of hook to a line. Take care to seat the knot correctly around the hook shank.

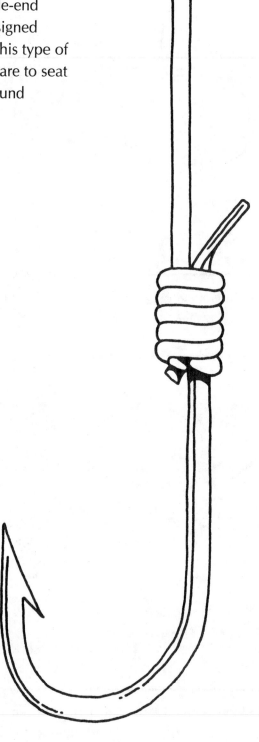

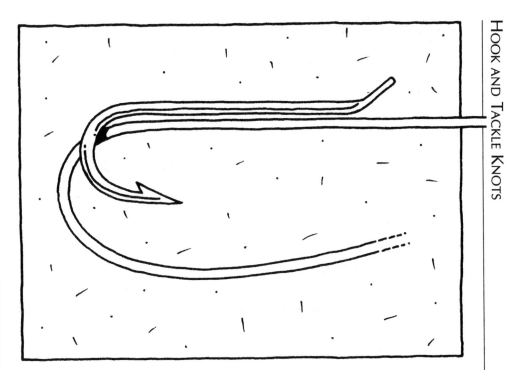

**1** Place sufficient line to complete the knot alongside the shank of the hook, and bring the tag end back toward the standing part.

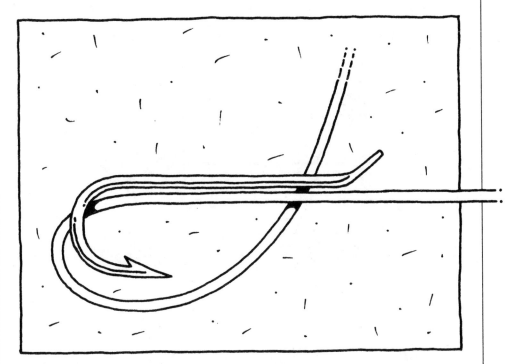

**2** Bring the tag end up and behind the hook shank and standing part to form a large loop.

**113**

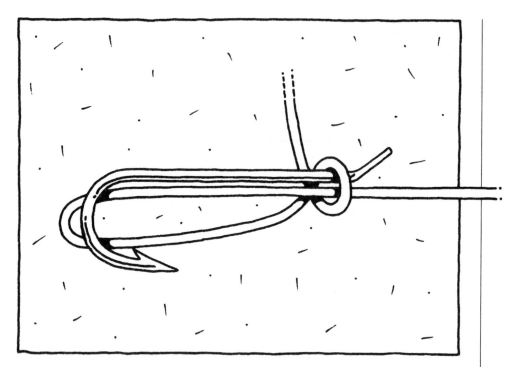

**3** Bring the tag end over to form the first turn. This first turn also tightens the standing part and the loop against the hook shank.

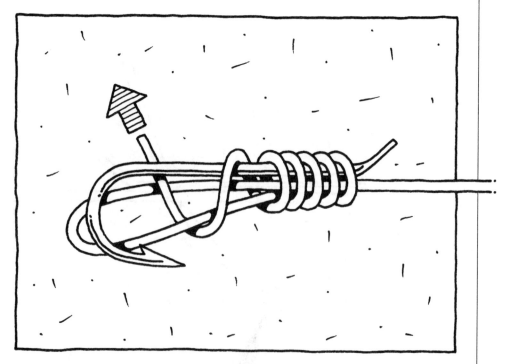

**4** Depending on the size and type of line you are using, make five or six turns away from the spade end, and bring the tag end out of the loop.

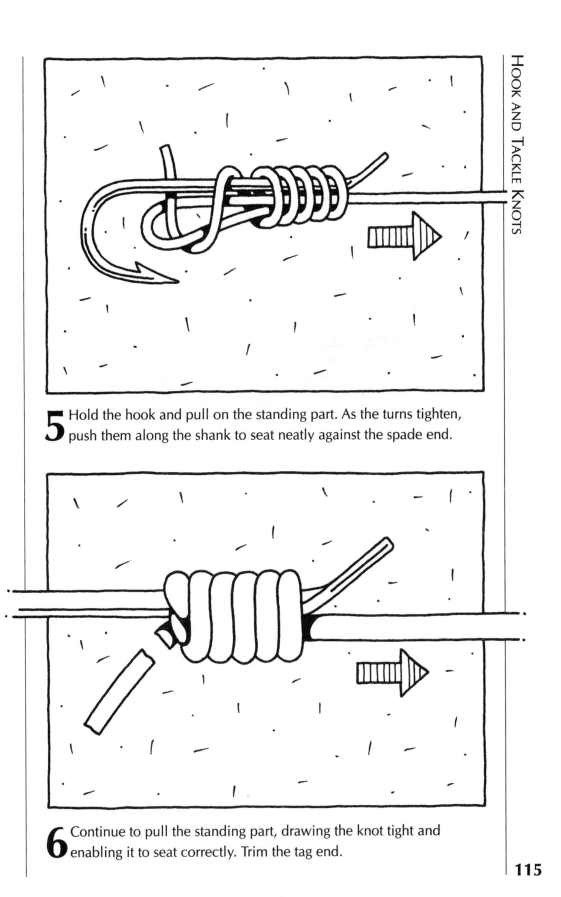

**5** Hold the hook and pull on the standing part. As the turns tighten, push them along the shank to seat neatly against the spade end.

**6** Continue to pull the standing part, drawing the knot tight and enabling it to seat correctly. Trim the tag end.

**115**

CHAPTER

# JOINING LINES

The joining of two lines is one of the most important connections in a tackle system.

The four tested and reliable knots in this section, when correctly tied, will provide secure connections. Because of the wide variety of line materials and sizes available, the number of turns required in each knot will differ. A general guideline is given, but a certain amount of experimentation may be required for you to achieve the optimum number of turns.

# BLOOD KNOT

This longtime favorite fishing knot is still one of the most effective ways to join two lines, especially monofilament lines that are of the same or similar diameters. Having an equal number of turns on both sides of the knot helps absorb strain and shock.

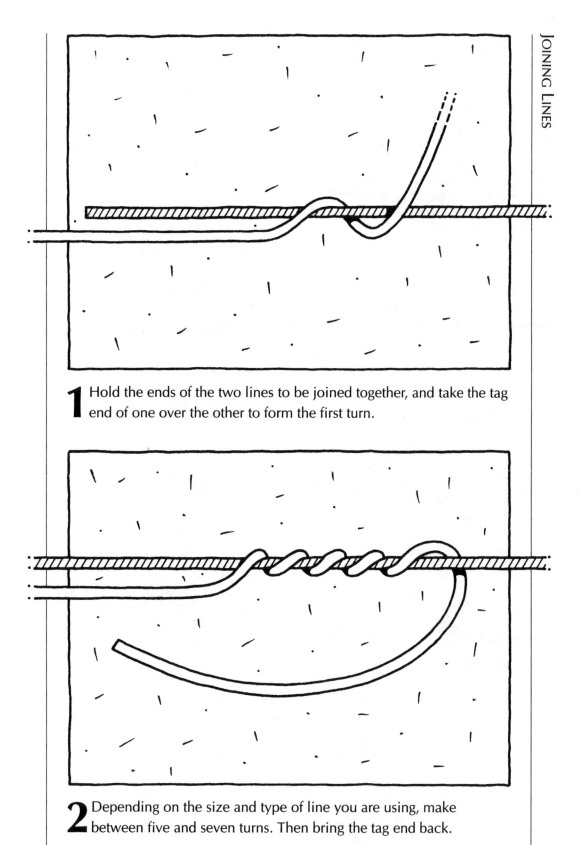

**1** Hold the ends of the two lines to be joined together, and take the tag end of one over the other to form the first turn.

**2** Depending on the size and type of line you are using, make between five and seven turns. Then bring the tag end back.

**119**

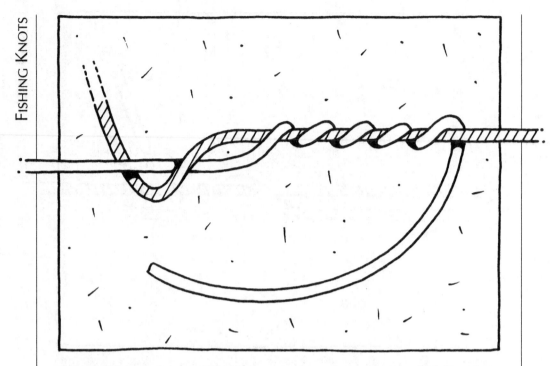

**3** Holding the lines and turns in position, take the tag end of the other line and start to make a turn, as shown.

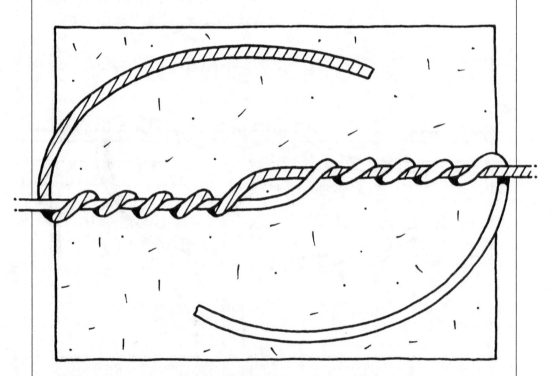

**4** Make an equal number of turns, taking care to leave a clear division between the two sets of turns.

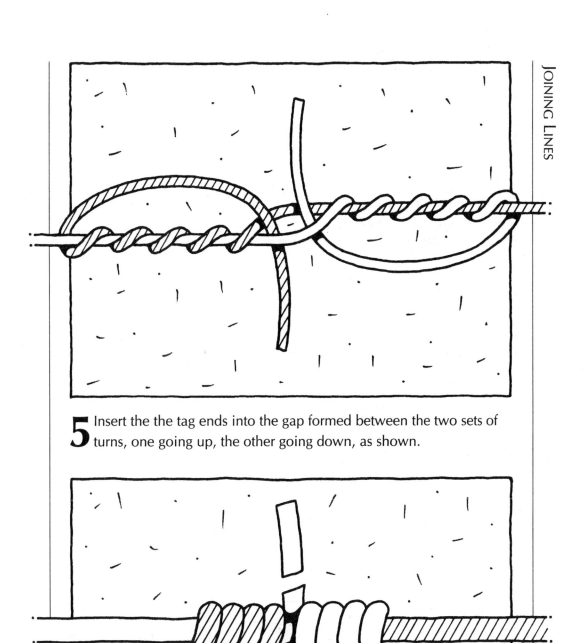

**5** Insert the the tag ends into the gap formed between the two sets of turns, one going up, the other going down, as shown.

**6** Slowly pull the two standing parts and tag ends until the knot seats correctly with the tag ends seized in the center. Trim the tag ends.

**121**

# DOUBLE UNI-KNOT

Also known as the **double grinner knot,** this knot uses the tying principle of two knots tied back to back and then seated together to form a strong connection. With practice, it is easy to tie and very effective.

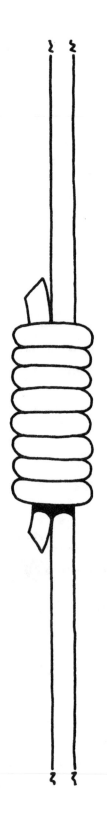

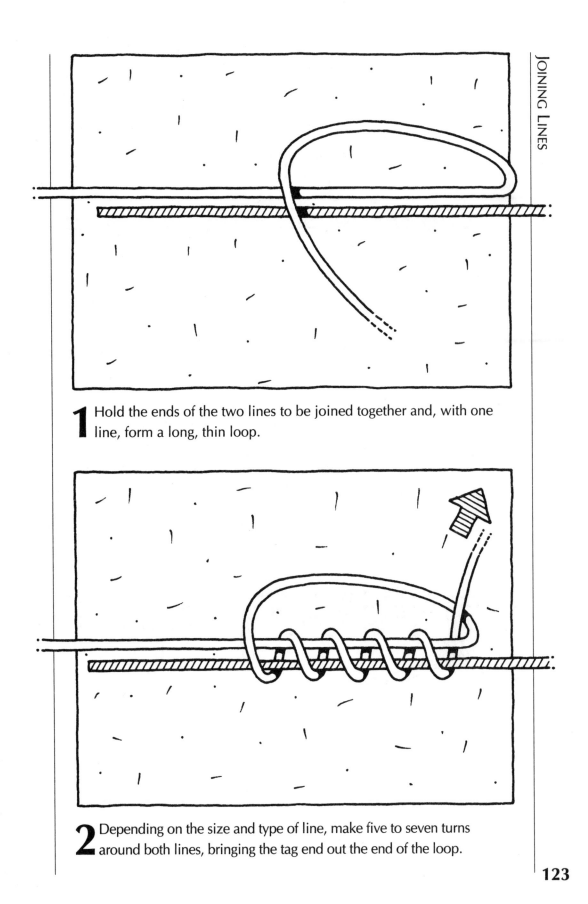

**1** Hold the ends of the two lines to be joined together and, with one line, form a long, thin loop.

**2** Depending on the size and type of line, make five to seven turns around both lines, bringing the tag end out the end of the loop.

**123**

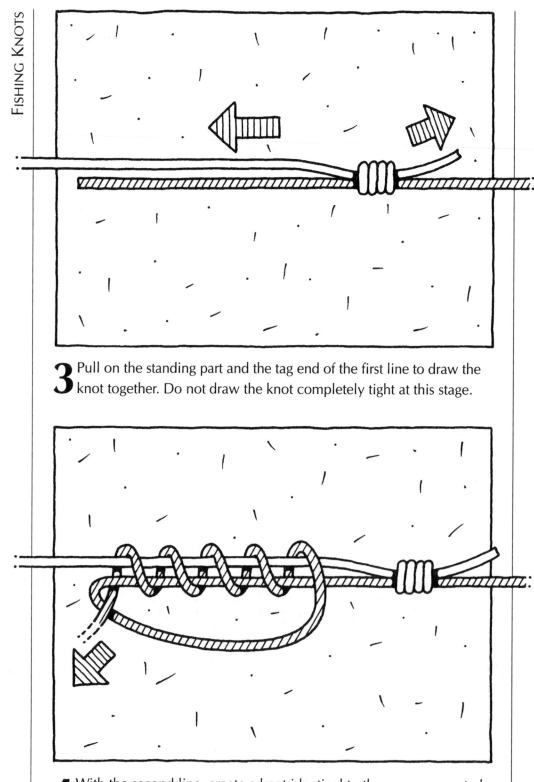

**3** Pull on the standing part and the tag end of the first line to draw the knot together. Do not draw the knot completely tight at this stage.

**4** With the second line, create a knot identical to the one you created with the first line, except the other way around.

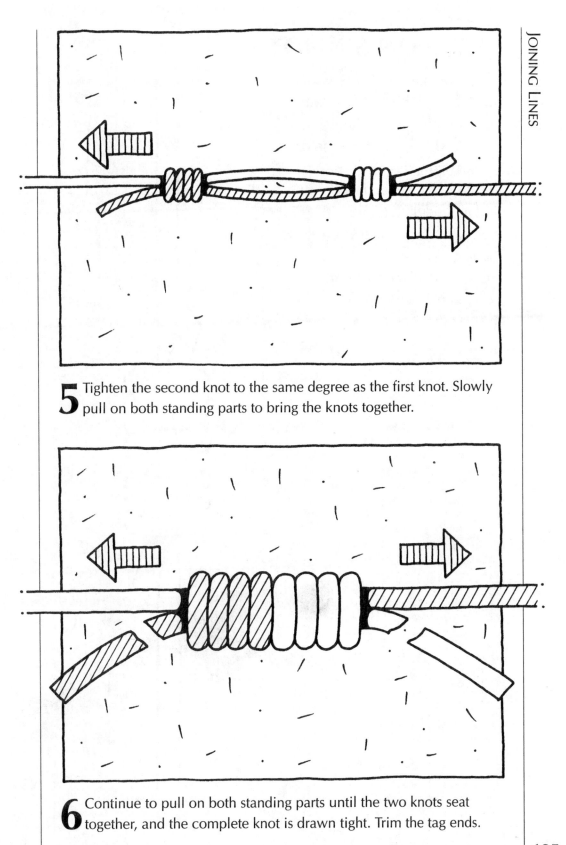

**5** Tighten the second knot to the same degree as the first knot. Slowly pull on both standing parts to bring the knots together.

**6** Continue to pull on both standing parts until the two knots seat together, and the complete knot is drawn tight. Trim the tag ends.

**125**

# SURGEON'S KNOT

Also known as the **water knot,** this is one of the best all-around knots for joining two lines. The lines need to be of the same or similar diameters and types for this knot to be effective. If you find it difficult to tie from the diagrams, just remember that one of the lines—in most cases the leader—needs to be short enough to pass through the loop.

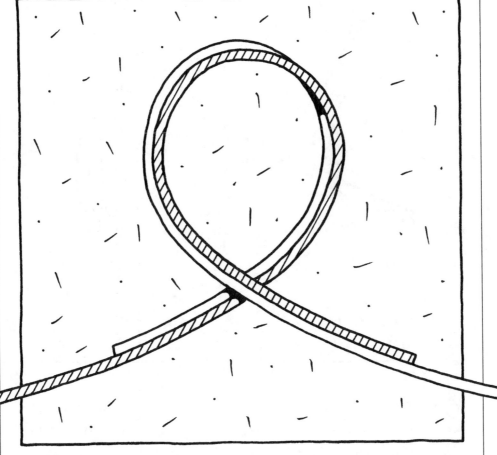

**1** Hold sufficient lengths of the two lines side by side. In the illustration above, the unshaded clear line is the shorter one.

**2** Hold both lines together and twist them over to form an open loop, as shown above.

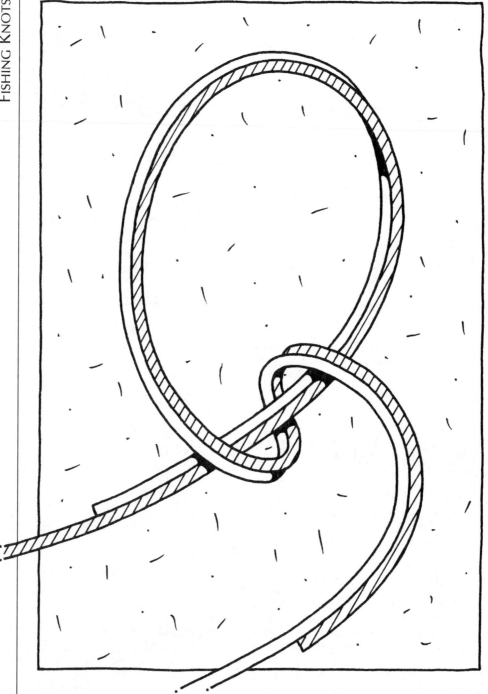

**3** Make a first turn as shown. The unshaded clear line is short enough to pass through the loop. It is important to keep the loop open at this stage in order to make more turns.

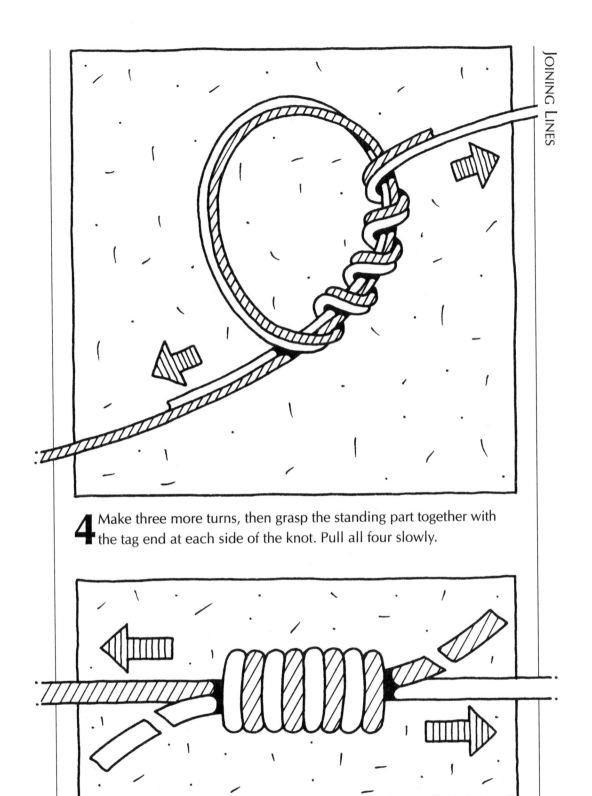

**4** Make three more turns, then grasp the standing part together with the tag end at each side of the knot. Pull all four slowly.

**5** Continue to pull the standing parts and the tag ends, drawing the knot tight and enabling it to seat correctly. Trim the tag ends.

**129**

# ALBRIGHT KNOT

This is one of the most reliable fishing knots for joining two lines of unequal diameters and different materials. A good time to use this knot, for example, is when you're connecting monofilament backing to a fly line.

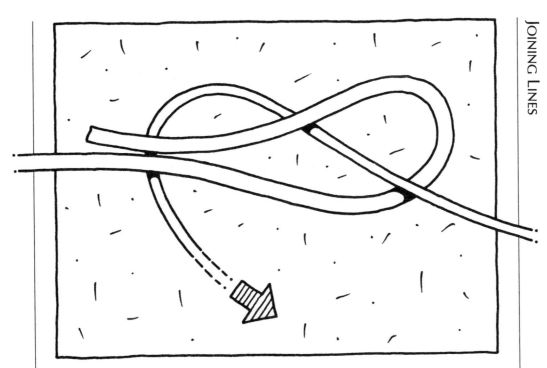

**1** Create a loop in the tag end of the heavier line, then feed the tag end of the lighter line through the loop.

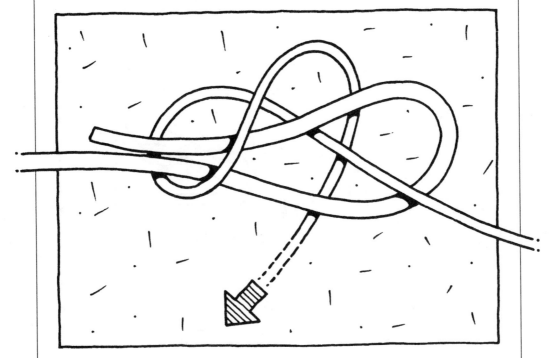

**2** Bring the tag end up and over the loop to create the first turn, as shown above.

**131**

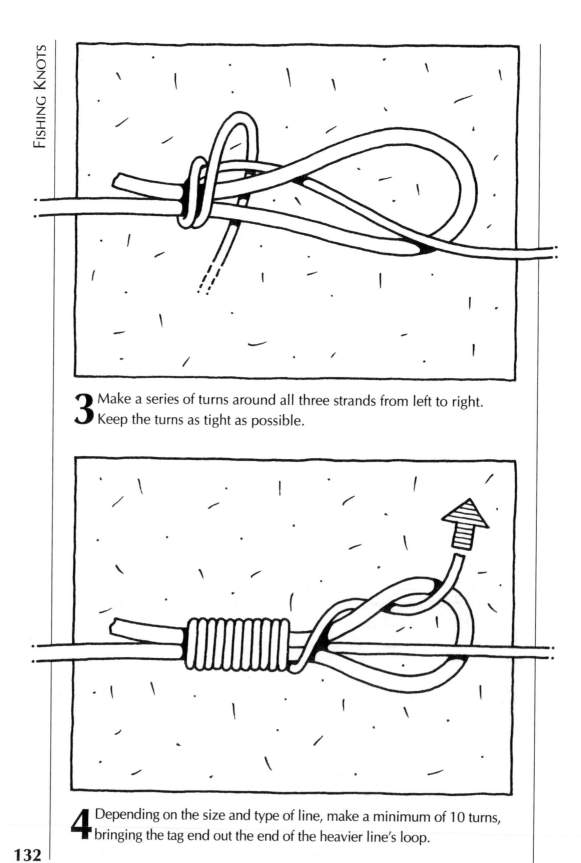

**3** Make a series of turns around all three strands from left to right. Keep the turns as tight as possible.

**4** Depending on the size and type of line, make a minimum of 10 turns, bringing the tag end out the end of the heavier line's loop.

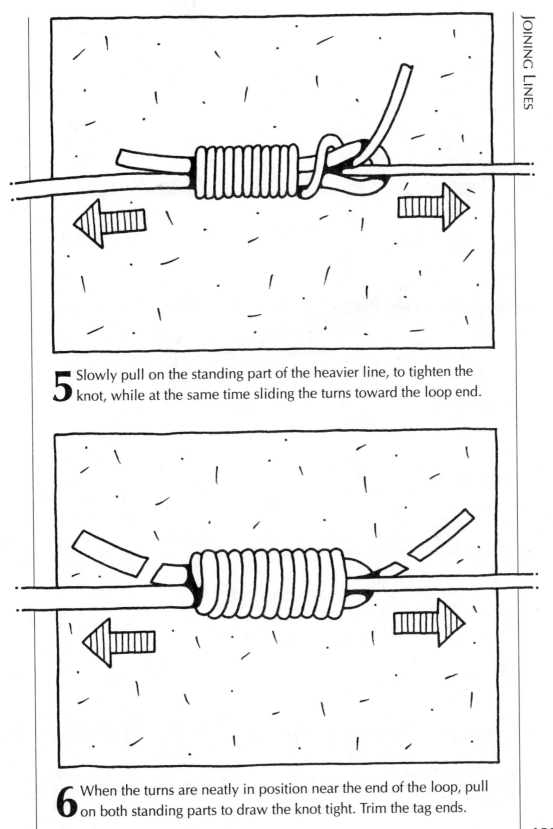

**5** Slowly pull on the standing part of the heavier line, to tighten the knot, while at the same time sliding the turns toward the loop end.

**6** When the turns are neatly in position near the end of the loop, pull on both standing parts to draw the knot tight. Trim the tag ends.

**133**

CHAPTER

# LOOPS

Correctly tied loops are exceptionally strong, and for many anglers the interlocking-loop system (see page 136) is an integral part of the tackle system.

Loops have a wide range of fishing applications, and the interlocking-loop system provides the perfect answer for any line connection that needs to be changed frequently. A good example is being able to change a premade leader quickly and efficiently while fishing. Because no actual knot tying is involved, this can be a real advantage in adverse weather conditions or poor light.

# SURGEON'S LOOP

This reliable and widely used loop uses the same tying method as the surgeon's knot (see page 126), except it is constructed from a single length of line. It is also known as the **double loop.**

*An interlocking-loop system created with two surgeon's loops.*

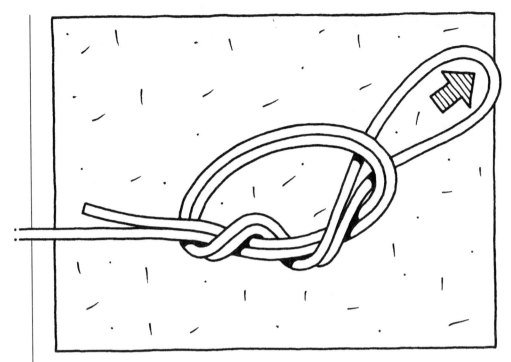

**1** Double the tag end of a length of line, create a double overhand knot as shown above, and then slowly pull the loop through.

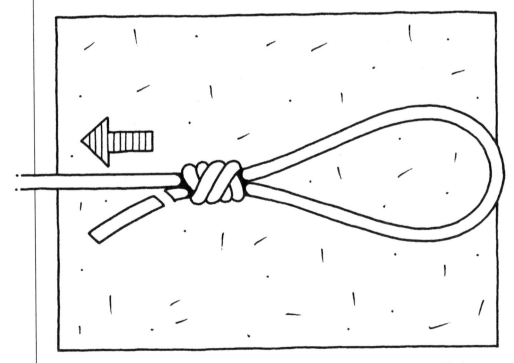

**2** Finalize the size of the loop required, then draw the knot tight by holding the loop and pulling the standing part. Trim the tag end.

# DROPPER LOOP

This extremely useful loop is used by a wide range of anglers; to many, it is known as the **blood loop.** It creates a loop at right angles to the main line. Fly fishermen use it to attach additional flies, known as droppers, while other anglers use it to attach sinkers and extra hooks to a line.

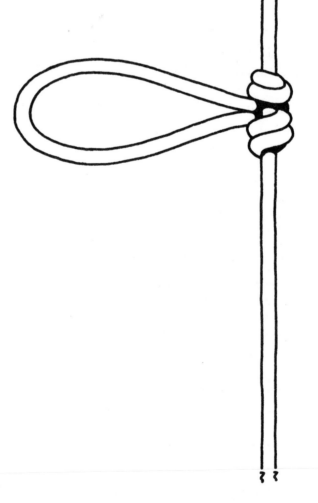

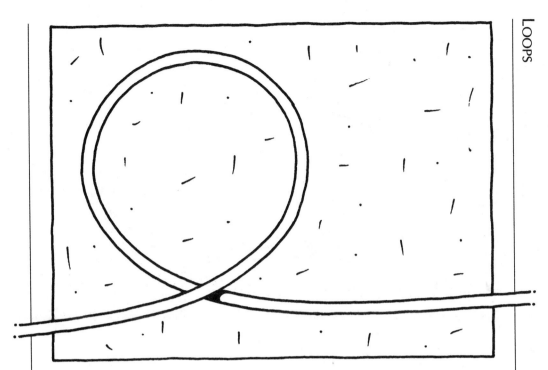

**1** Choose the point in the line at which you want to position your dropper loop, and form a circle.

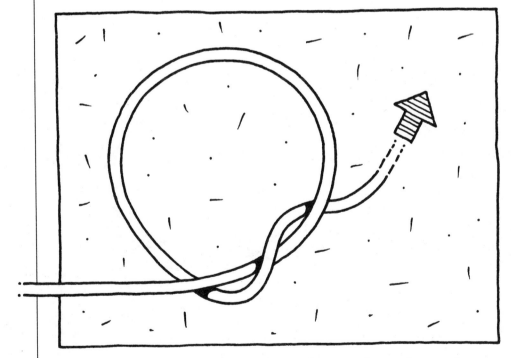

**2** The size of the circle will determine the size of your dropper loop. Create the first turn with an overhand knot.

**139**

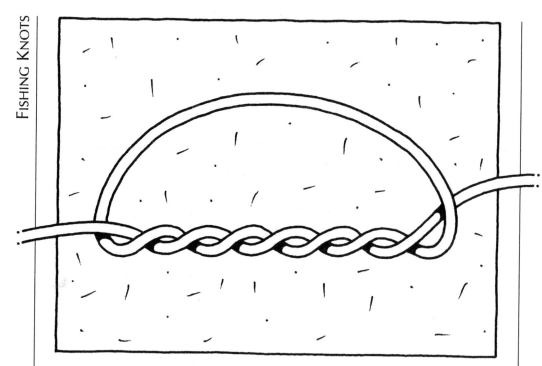

**3** Depending on the size and type of line, make three or four turns in total, and position the knot as shown above.

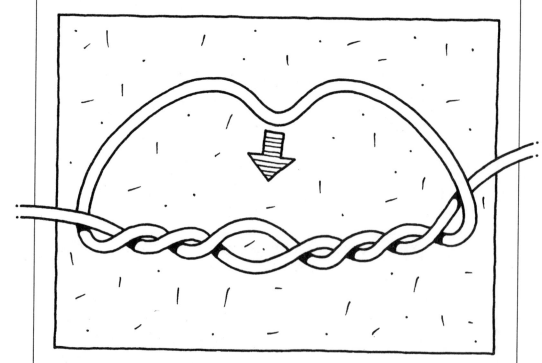

**4** Create a slightly larger gap in the center of the turns, and bring the top of the main loop down to form the dropper loop.

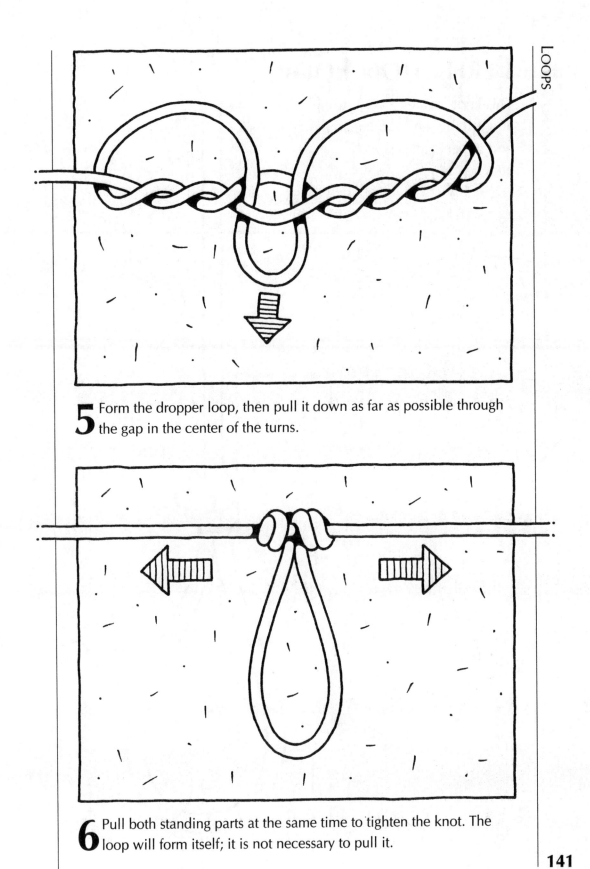

**5** Form the dropper loop, then pull it down as far as possible through the gap in the center of the turns.

**6** Pull both standing parts at the same time to tighten the knot. The loop will form itself; it is not necessary to pull it.

# PERFECTION LOOP

This knot creates a very strong
and reliable end loop; leaders
and tippets can be easily
attached to it.

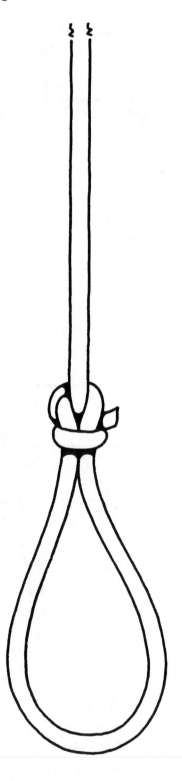

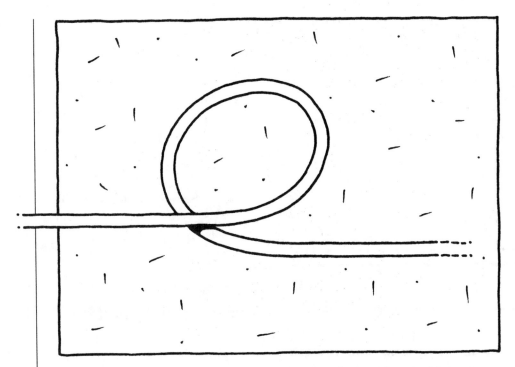

**1** Create a loop near the end of the line, as shown, then hold that loop in position.

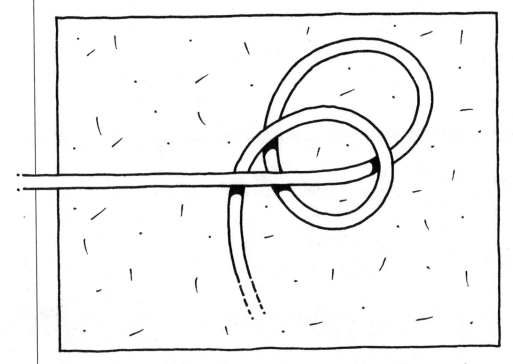

**2** Bring the tag end back over to form a second loop. The tag end should now be positioned behind the standing part.

**143**

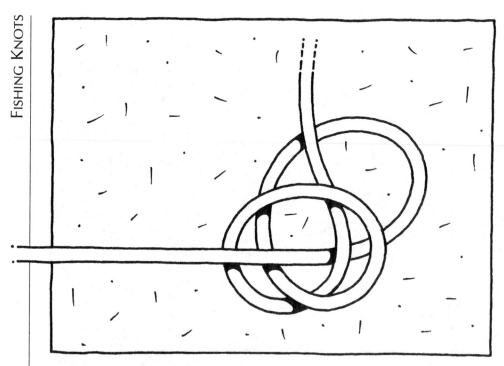

**3** Bring the tag end back up and position it between the two loops, as shown above.

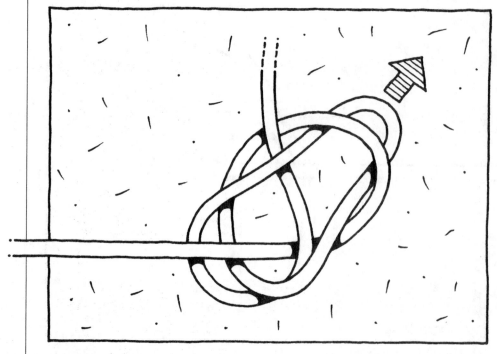

**4** Grasp the front loop, form it into a narrower loop, and then push it through the rear loop.

144

**5** Pull the loop through as far as possible. You can still adjust the size of the loop at this stage, if desired.

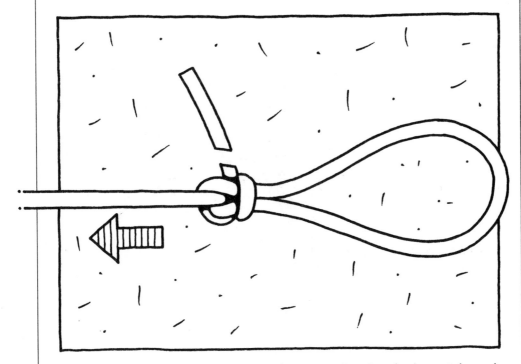

**6** Hold the loop and pull the standing part, drawing the knot tight and enabling it to seat correctly. Trim the tag end.

# BIMINI TWIST

This knot creates a loop that will give 100 percent knot strength. It is tied at the tag end of the line to form a main connection that other line or tackle can be secured to. It may take a little time to perfect, but once mastered, it provides one of the most secure loops possible.

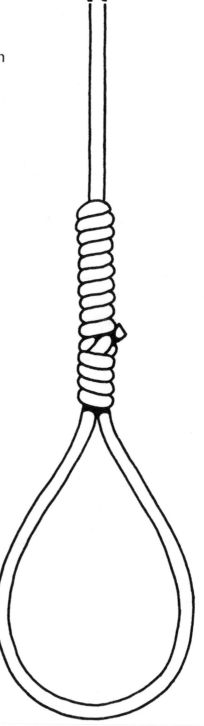

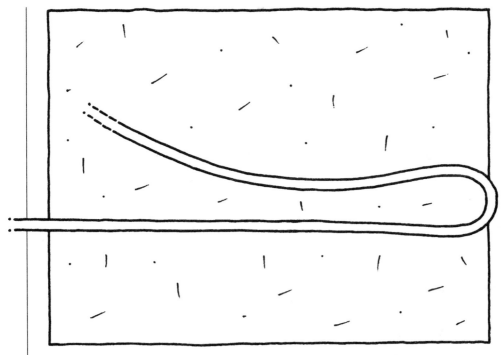

**1** Double the line back against the standing part. Depending on the number of turns used, this knot will require a long length of line.

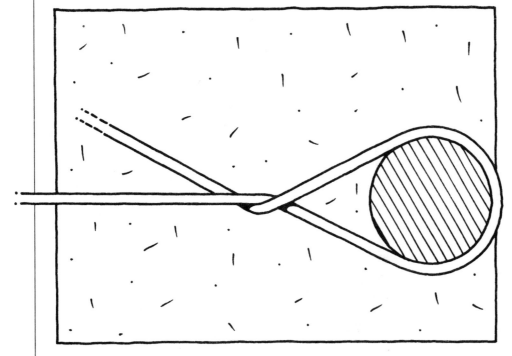

**2** The first stage of this knot is best tied around a solid object. Take the line around the object and create the first turn, as shown.

**147**

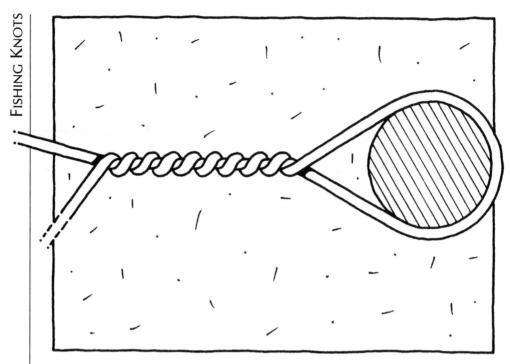

**3** Depending on the line you're using, make between 8 and 20 turns. Fifteen turns are recommended for regular monofilament.

**4** It is very important to keep pressure on both the standing part and the tag end, to keep the turns as tight as possible.

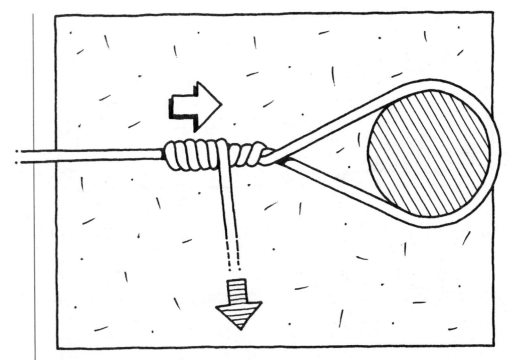

**5** Make approximately the same number of turns back over the original turns in the direction of the solid object.

**6** At this point, remove the loop from the solid object, and create a holding knot with the tag end.

**149**

**7** Still keeping pressure on the standing part and the loop, tighten the holding knot and bring the tag end out.

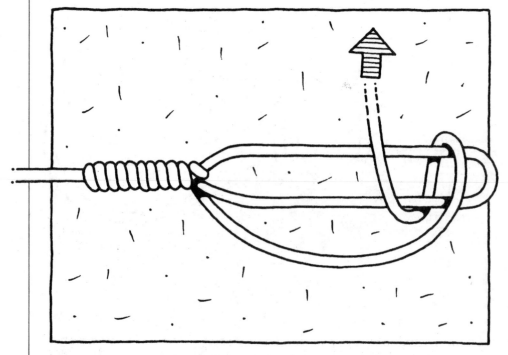

**8** Holding the knot in the position shown above, make a turn around the narrowed loop with the tag end.

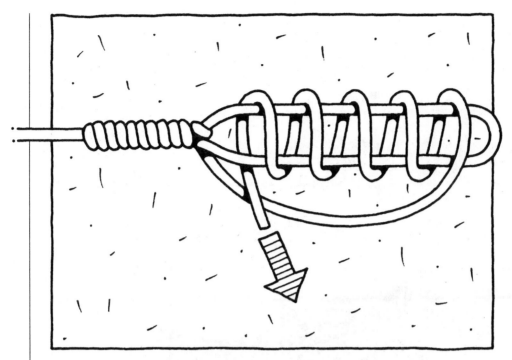

**9** Make four or five turns, and then pull slowly on the tag end to seat this series of turns back against the original turns.

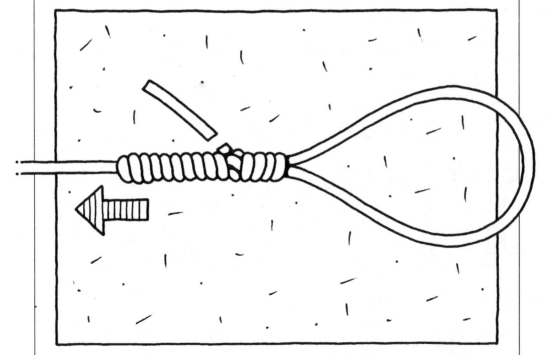

**10** With the second series of turns seated correctly, hold the loop and pull the standing part to finalize the knot. Trim the tag end.

CHAPTER 4

# FLY-LINE
# KNOTS

A fly line requires a secure knot at both ends—to attach the backing line at one end, and to attach the butt section of the leader at the other.

This section covers various methods of tying these knots, some of which can initially prove difficult. Follow the instructions closely and practice before tying the final knot. If you are not totally confident with your knots, seek help from your local tackle store. In most cases, the owner will be only too pleased to help out.

# NAIL KNOT

This knot is used to attach backing line or a leader to a fly line. It is tied with assistance of a small-diameter nail or needle. The nail or needle acts to stiffen the fly line and help form the knot.

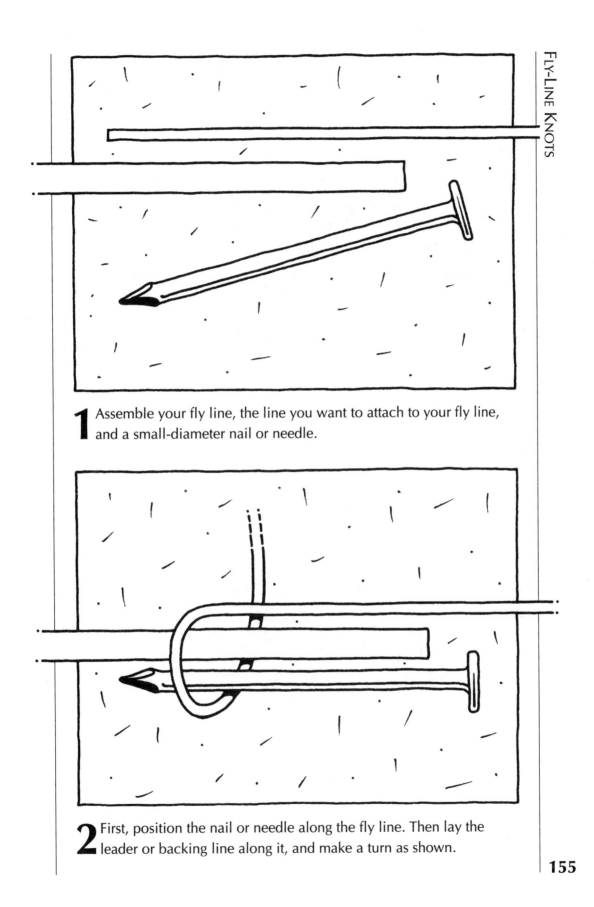

**1** Assemble your fly line, the line you want to attach to your fly line, and a small-diameter nail or needle.

**2** First, position the nail or needle along the fly line. Then lay the leader or backing line along it, and make a turn as shown.

**155**

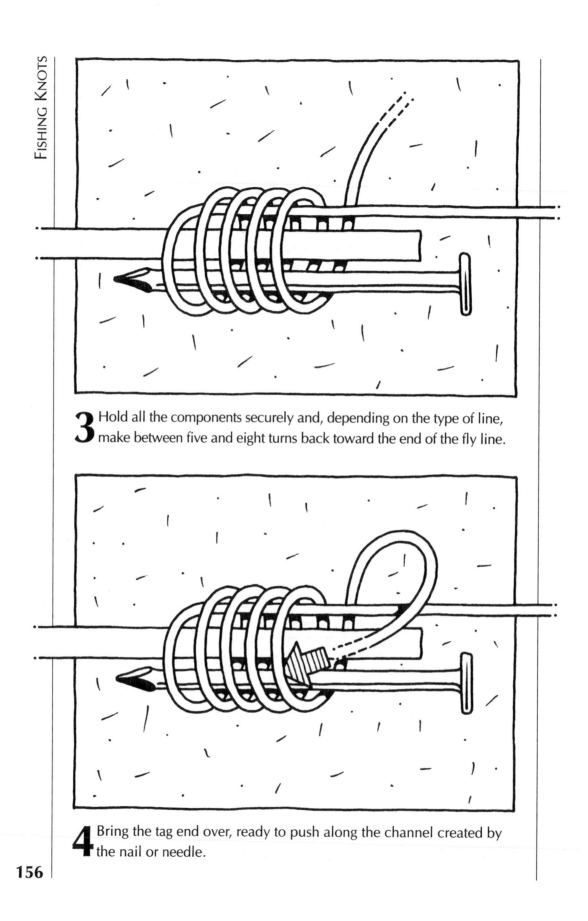

**3** Hold all the components securely and, depending on the type of line, make between five and eight turns back toward the end of the fly line.

**4** Bring the tag end over, ready to push along the channel created by the nail or needle.

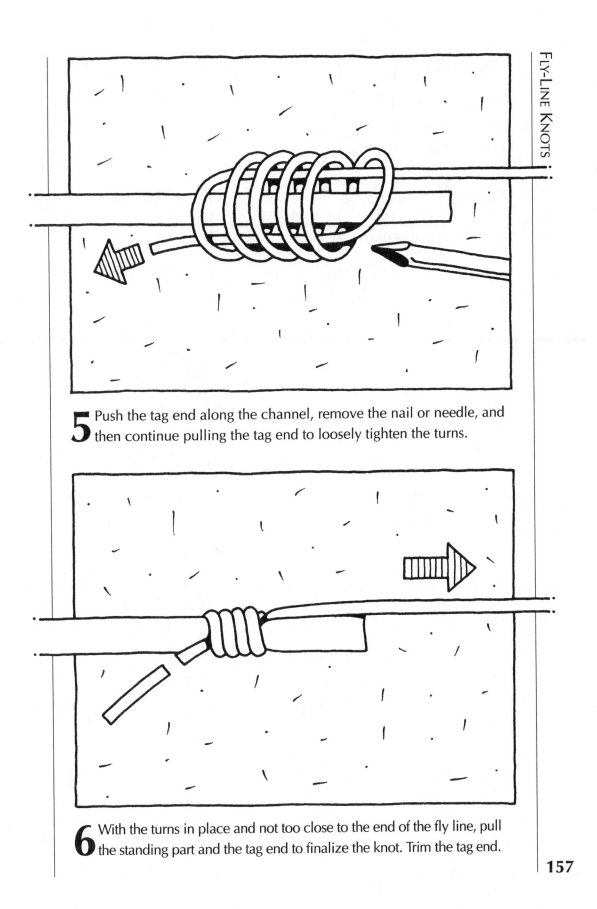

**5** Push the tag end along the channel, remove the nail or needle, and then continue pulling the tag end to loosely tighten the turns.

**6** With the turns in place and not too close to the end of the fly line, pull the standing part and the tag end to finalize the knot. Trim the tag end.

**157**

# NEEDLE KNOT

This knot creates the best solution for joining a monofilament leader to a fly line. It is a very neat and smooth connection that is extremely strong. It will not snag on rod guides or pick up debris in the water.

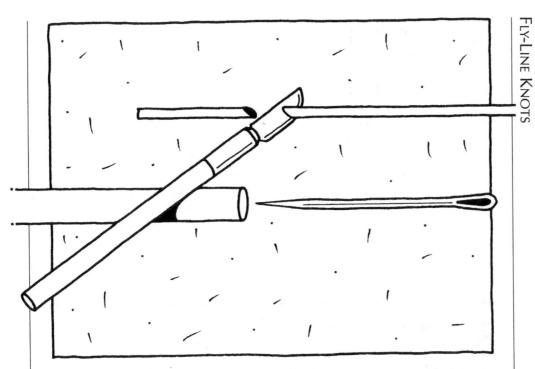

**1** Assemble the fly line, a needle, and the line you want to attach to the fly line; this line should have its end cut at an angle, as above.

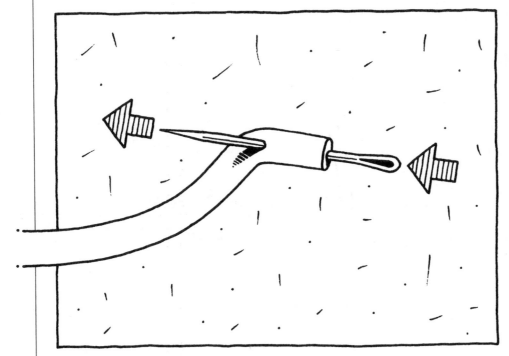

**2** Push the needle along the center of the fly line, and then bend the fly line to allow the needle to exit.

**159**

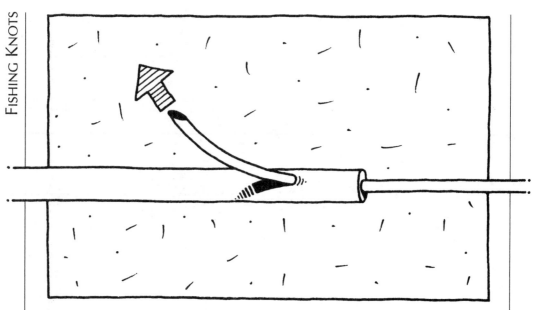

**3** Insert the leader or backing line into the hole created by the needle and then out the hole in the side of the fly line. Should it prove difficult to insert the leader or backing line, replace the needle, heat its point, and then remove. The heated needle point will open the hole; take care to not damage the lines with excess heat.

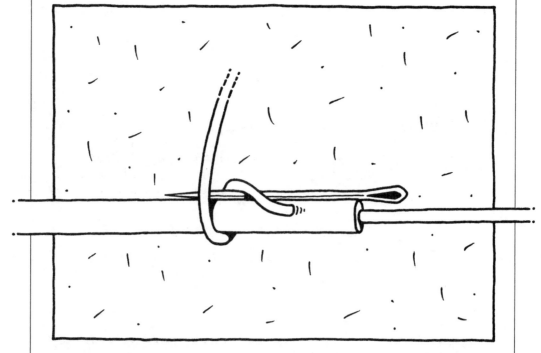

**4** Position the needle along the side of the fly line, and make a turn with the tag end of the leader or backing line.

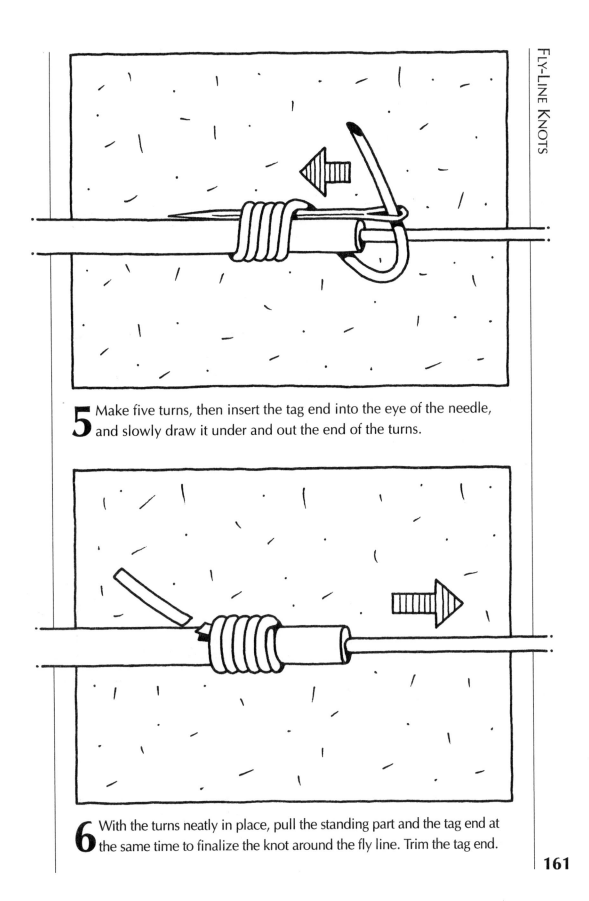

**5** Make five turns, then insert the tag end into the eye of the needle, and slowly draw it under and out the end of the turns.

**6** With the turns neatly in place, pull the standing part and the tag end at the same time to finalize the knot around the fly line. Trim the tag end.

# NEEDLE MONO LOOP

This is a good alternative to the needle knot (see page 158) if you prefer a loop at the end of your fly line to make interlocking-loop connections. The tying method is the same as for the needle knot, except you use a doubled monofilament line.

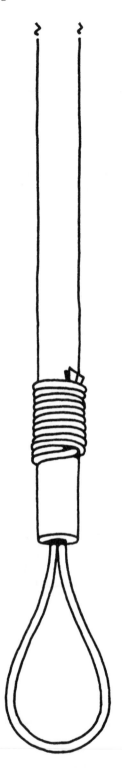

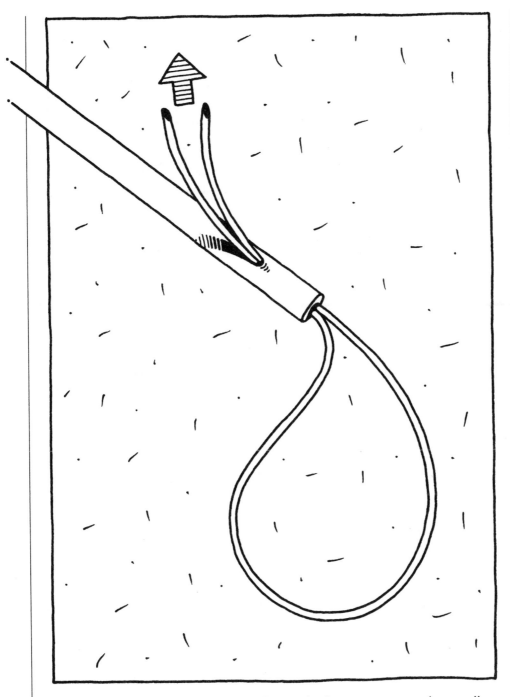

**1** Create the hole in the fly line in exactly the same way as the needle knot (see pages 159 and 160). But instead of inserting a single piece of line, insert a piece of line that has been doubled to form a loop at the end of the fly line. Determine the size of loop you require at this stage.

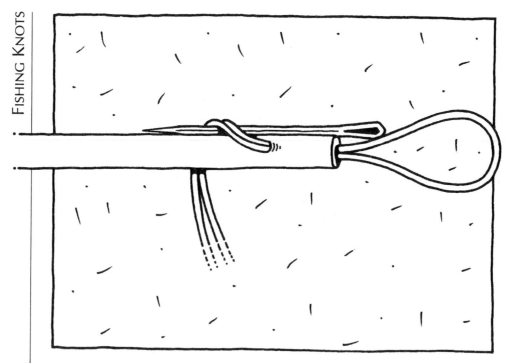

**3** With the size of the loop determined, lay the needle along the fly line and start to make the first turn with the two strands of line.

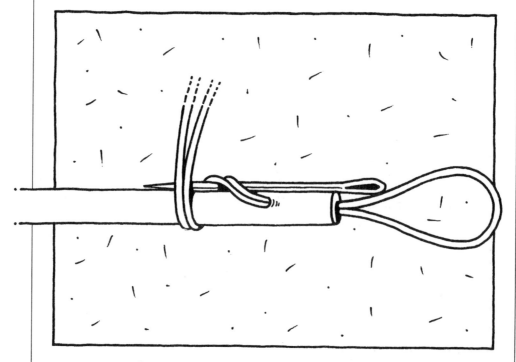

**4** Continue the first turn. Because two strands of line are being used, it is important that all the strands seat tightly against each other.

164

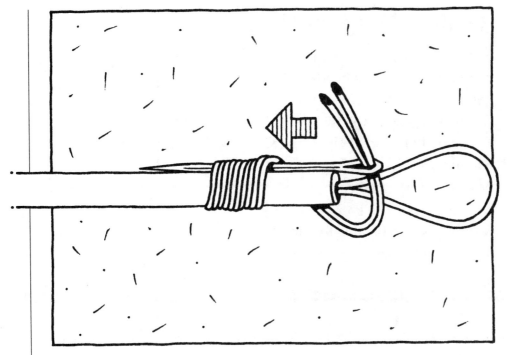

**5** Make three to five turns, then insert the tag ends into the eye of the needle, and slowly draw them under and out of the end of the turns.

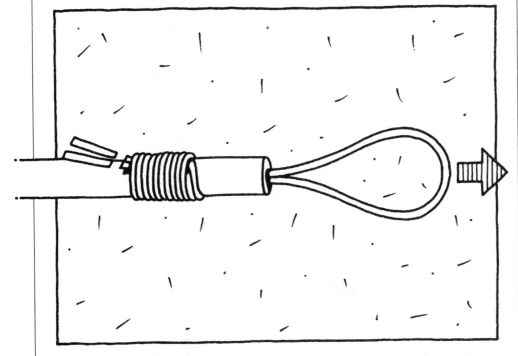

**6** With the turns neatly in place, pull the loop and the tag ends at the same time to finalize the knot around the fly line. Trim the tag ends.

**165**

# TUBE NAIL/NEEDLE KNOT

If you find tying the nail knot
(see page 154) or the needle
knot (see page 158) difficult,
substitute a small, hollow tube
for the nail or needle. The tube
will need to be stiff enough to
provide support to the fly line
while you form the knot, and
wide enough to be able to pass
the line through.

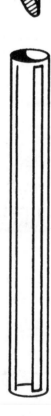

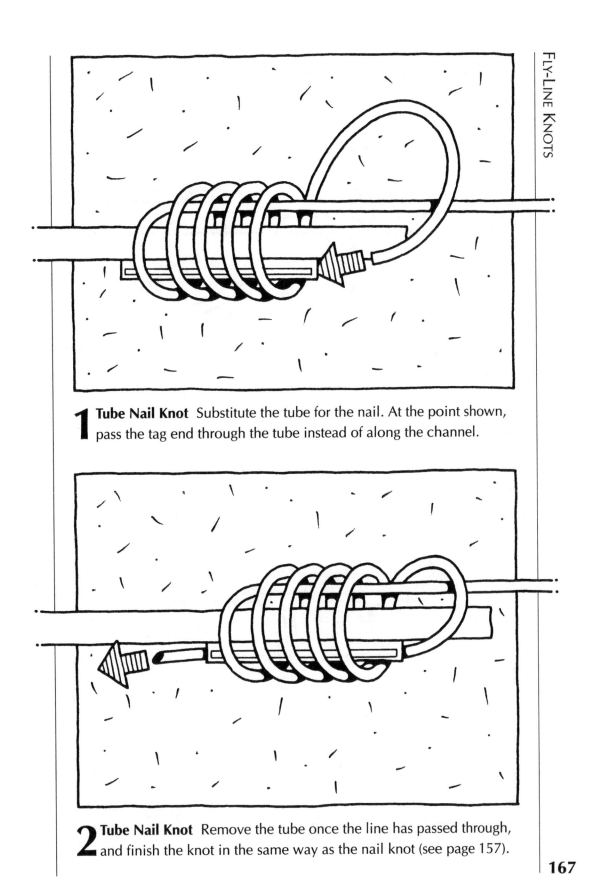

**1** **Tube Nail Knot** Substitute the tube for the nail. At the point shown, pass the tag end through the tube instead of along the channel.

**2** **Tube Nail Knot** Remove the tube once the line has passed through, and finish the knot in the same way as the nail knot (see page 157).

**167**

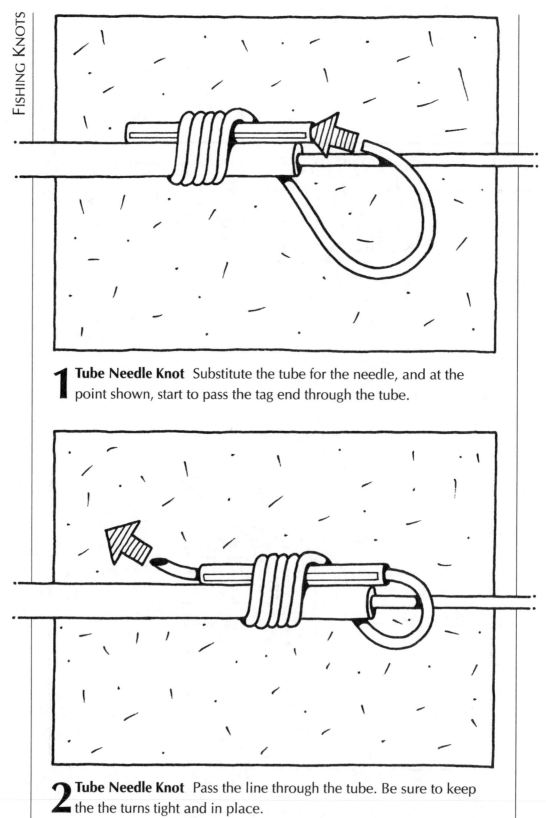

**1** **Tube Needle Knot** Substitute the tube for the needle, and at the point shown, start to pass the tag end through the tube.

**2** **Tube Needle Knot** Pass the line through the tube. Be sure to keep the the turns tight and in place.

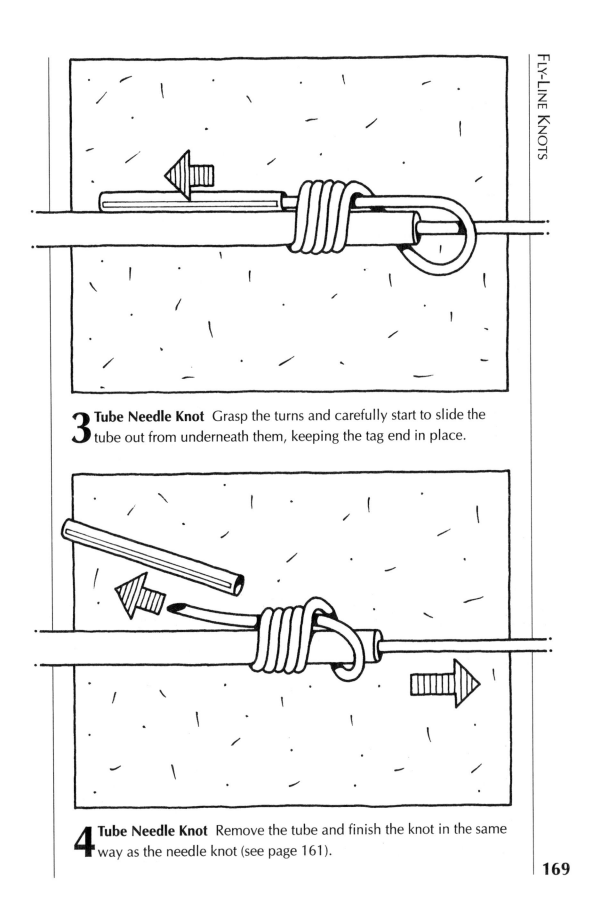

**3 Tube Needle Knot** Grasp the turns and carefully start to slide the tube out from underneath them, keeping the tag end in place.

**4 Tube Needle Knot** Remove the tube and finish the knot in the same way as the needle knot (see page 161).

**169**

# EMERGENCY NAIL KNOT

If your nail or needle knot breaks while you are fishing, it is possible to solve the problem by creating an emergency nail knot with a strong piece of monofilament.

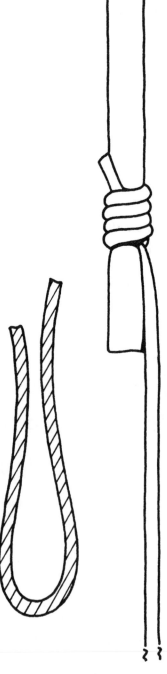

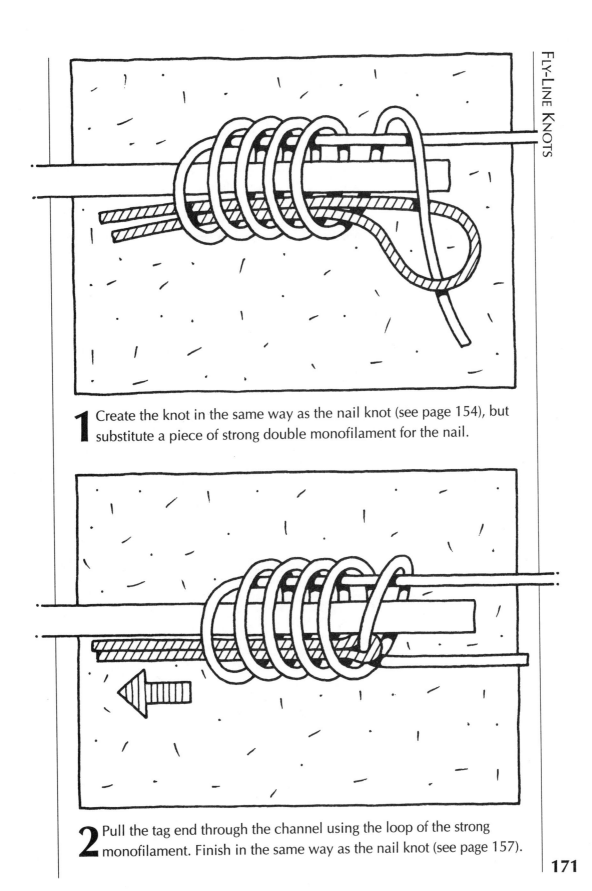

**1** Create the knot in the same way as the nail knot (see page 154), but substitute a piece of strong double monofilament for the nail.

**2** Pull the tag end through the channel using the loop of the strong monofilament. Finish in the same way as the nail knot (see page 157).

**171**

# FIELD& STREAM

# The Complete Fisherman

## Book Three

## Baits and Rigs

C. Boyd Pfeiffer

# Freshwater and Saltwater Baits

**B**EFORE YOU USE any bait, always check local regulations. Some areas prohibit the use of goldfish (carp), for example, because they can easily take over prime bass waters. To increase survival among released fish, many trout waters prohibit the use of baits (which the fish tend to swallow along with the hook), and restrict fishing to flies or lures. Check local restrictions about gathering baits as well; taking baits from trout streams is prohibited in many areas.

Many baits are used in both freshwater and saltwater fishing. Here are some examples.

Chunks of fish can be cut into strips, fillets, or bite-size pieces for bait.

Here a small chunk of baitfish is threaded onto a hook with the point of the hook showing.

Strips of bait are ideal when chumming or fishing the mid-depths. The thin, cigar-shaped strip will sink more readily than the wide fillet, thus allowing adjustment for current or tide.

- **Cut baits:** Chunks or slices of fish make good baits for still fishing, drift fishing, or bottom fishing. Small fish are often cut into pieces and hooked through the skin to help keep them in place. Larger fish are sometimes filleted first (leaving the skin on, but removing the scales), then cut into smaller chunks. Long, thin, tapered strips cut from a fillet or section of the belly work well for many species. Hook them through the skin at the thick end of the triangle.

- **Prepared baits:** Commercially available baits include paste-like concoctions that are specially formulated for carp, catfish, crappies, and other popular species. These baits are often scooped directly from the tin and molded onto a bait hook, which may be a single hook with barbs or a treble with a spring baitholder attachment. You can prepare simple home-made baits using cheese, dough, or blood-based formulas. Prepared baits are widely used in both fresh and salt water, primarily for bottom-feeding species.
- **Doughballs:** A type of prepared bait, easily made at home. They are a favorite of carp but also useful for other bottom-feeding fish, such as suckers or catfish. Doughballs are made of bread dough or a similar tough, doughy mix that can be easily molded onto a hook and will hold up when continually soaked.

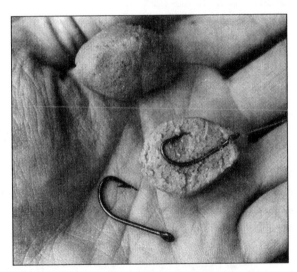

A doughball, cut open to show the hook. The dough hides the hook so that the fish will more readily take it.

Commercial dough is available for making doughballs, but here are two easy and effective formulas. The first is for strawberry-flavored carp dough, since carp seem to like strawberries. Dissolve 2 or 3 tablespoons of strawberry gelatin in 2 cups of boiling water (sugar can also be added to sweeten). Mix 2 cups of dry cornmeal and 1 cup of flour, add to the water-flavor solution, and mix well until it reaches a tough, doughy consistency.

Another favorite is Champion carp dough. Mix 1 cup each of Wheaties cereal, flour, oatmeal, and molasses. Add 1 cup of hot water and a small amount of vanilla extract. Mix thoroughly, once again aiming for a tough, moldable consistency. (One way to keep dough from breaking down is to carefully add bits of raw cotton balls to the mix to give it strength and body.)

Each fishing region seems to have its own slightly different version of the doughball. Some of the more exotic flavors include anise, beer, crushed canned corn, raspberry, licorice, cheese, and honey. They can all be stored in zipper-lock plastic bags or aluminum foil, and most of the fishing techniques are similar. Simply place the dough on the hook in grape-size balls, using a single hook or a treble hook with a spring (baitholder).

- **Shrimp:** Shrimp are an all-purpose bait for salt water and fresh water. Even if unavailable from inland baitshops, they can be purchased at most food markets. Small shrimp can be used whole, with live ones hooked through the forward part of the tail so the vital parts are not pierced. They can also be hooked through the middle of the tail. Dead shrimp, if small enough, can be threaded completely onto a hook, the point running out through the tail so the tail curves naturally. You can hook

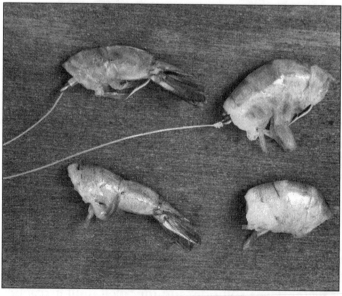

Shrimp can be cut up into bait sections, using chunks or the tail, as shown here.

the tails of larger shrimp the same way, first removing the shell or slightly crushing the body to release its scent and increase its attractiveness in the water. Or you can cut the tails into smaller chunks and impale them on the hook.

Shrimp chunks and tails are often used to "sweeten" lures used in both fresh- and saltwater fishing. Here, shrimp is being added to a jig.

- **Grass shrimp:** These small shrimp are found inshore and in brackish water, and are available from bait dealers or by seining them from shallow shoreline areas. They are used live and whole; thread one or more through the body or tail onto a hook for perch, striped bass, and other inshore species.
- **Worms:** Earthworms, manure worms, and red worms are commonly used in freshwater and sometimes in saltwater fishing. Live worms are hooked whole or broken into smaller bits and threaded onto a hook; two or three small worms may also be threaded through the thicker collar on the body. You can use larger worms such as nightcrawlers with a two- or three-hook gang rig, threading one large worm onto all the hooks. Bass and catfish are often caught by using a mass of wriggling worms threaded onto one hook. Earthworms will not last as long in salt water as in fresh water, but they are a popular substitute for the more expensive bloodworms and sandworms available in coastal baitshops.

Small grass shrimp.

Simple worm riggings can include threading the hook through the length of the body, or through one or two spots, as shown here.

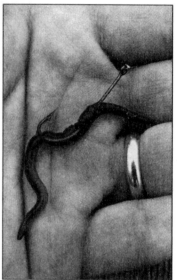

To completely hide a hook, thread several worms onto the shank and cover the point as much as possible.

- **Freshwater minnows:** Almost any type of freshwater minnow or small fish can be used as bait. Minnows, chubs, dace, shiners, and other species are sold in baitshops, and minnows can be netted from ponds or small streams. (In most cases you will need a fishing license, so check local restrictions.) Ways to gather minnows include minnow traps baited with crumbs and grain, dip nets baited the same way, or seines run by one or two anglers through the water and then lifted to capture the contents.

  The best way to hook minnows depends on how you are going to fish them. For casting and retrieving, trolling, or drifting minnows, hook them vertically through both lips. For drifting, also try hooking through the tail. When you are fishing a minnow under a bobber, hook through the back, just forward of the dorsal fin, but take care not to damage the spinal cord.

  Minnows can also be hooked onto some lures, such as jigs. One trick is to lip-hook a minnow upside down on a lightweight jig so the bait constantly struggles to regain an upright position. This struggle is sure to attract gamefish and provoke strikes.

Three ways to hook minnows (top to bottom): through the back for still fishing with a bobber, through the tail to allow the minnow to swim and attract fish, and through the lips when trolling or casting.

An upside down lip-hooked minnow on a jig will constantly try to right itself, making for more strikes.

Eels can be used fresh or salted and preserved, rigged whole through the lips or eyes or cut into chunks for still fishing and bottom fishing.

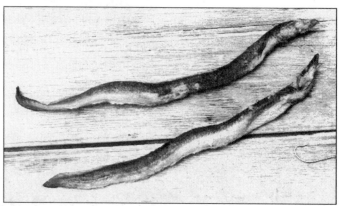

Live baitfish are often used to attract large salt-water gamefish. This bait has been hooked through the forward back, taking care not to damage the spinal cord.

- **Saltwater minnows:** Mullets, herring, menhaden, sardines (West Coast), candlefish (West Coast), spearing (Northeast Coast), killifish, anchovies, alewives, pinfish, smelt, silversides, sand eels, and similar baitfish are popular in coastal waters. Most are available from live-bait dealers or can be caught using a dip net, short seine, or cast net.

  Typical hooking methods are similar to those for freshwater minnows: through the lips in a vertical plane (trolling, deep jigging, or casting), through the back (drifting and still fishing, but be careful to avoid the spine to keep the bait lively), and through the wrist of the tail for drifting and fishing tides.

  Another method is hooking the bait through the side. For this technique, run a long-shank hook through the mouth, out the gill, and into the side of the fish near the tail. Or run a double hook, eye-first, up through the vent and out the mouth, where you tie or connect it to a line or leader. For trolling, use a large hook and attach the minnow side to side through the eyes or securely through the top and bottom lips. Use dead minnows with these methods.

In both freshwater (catfish) and much saltwater fishing, a good way to hook dead minnows is to run a double hook through the vent and out the mouth, then attach a leader or tie on the line.

- **Adult insects:** These are good baits if they are easy to catch, are large enough to be impaled onto a hook, and are local food that fish would normally eat. Good examples include crickets, grasshoppers, beetles, leafhoppers, dragonflies, damselflies, dobsonflies, and crane flies. Crickets, grasshoppers, and beetles are relatively easy to catch; dragonflies and damselflies may require nets and some ingenuity. Hook insects through the abdomen to hide the hook, or through the back of the thorax with an exposed hook. This keeps the insect living longer and acting naturally. Occasionally a very light split-shot sinker is helpful when you fish with insects.

Crickets and other insects can be threaded individually (top) or in multiples (bottom) onto a light-wire hook, as shown, for catching trout and panfish.

- **Immature insects:** Aquatic, immature (nymphal) forms of insects are also useful as baits. Large nymphs of mayflies, stone-flies, and caddis (the insects that form cases of wood or stone) make ideal baits. Hellgrammites (larvae of the dobsonfly) are preferred by smallmouth bass and large trout. Hook these insects through the back of the thorax. Immature terrestrial insects (beetles, crickets) can also be effective baits.
- **Frogs:** Frogs and toads are now thought to be threatened by ultraviolet light from a thinning ozone layer, as well as by acid precipitation. We therefore do not recommend wild specimens

as baits. However, if a bait dealer can *verify that they were raised, not captured in the field,* then frogs are suitable bait for bass and pike. Hook them through the lip if casting or trolling; through the leg if drifting or still fishing.

Mealworms, available from bait-shops, can be threaded individually and lengthwise onto a hook; or thread them through the body, as shown, for multiple hooking and a large bait.

- **Salamanders:** These and other amphibians also suffer a threatened existence, so only commercially raised baits should be used. Hook them through the lips. Small sizes are often used for trout, while larger specimens such as mud puppies or hellbenders are used for bass and walleyes.

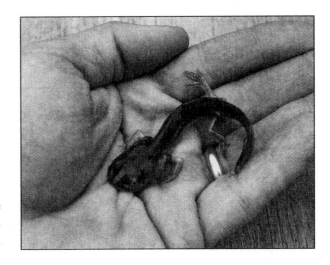

A salamander may be hooked through the lips or a front leg.

- **Leeches:** These are ideal baits, especially for walleyes and smallmouth bass. Where they are abundant, they can be caught in streams and ponds; or buy them from a bait dealer. Hook them through the front (head), or by threading the hook through the body. Leeches are effective on lures or on a single hook while drifting or using a bait-walking rig.

Leeches are best hooked through the forward part so that they swim naturally in the water.

- **Crawfish:** These are great baits for almost all freshwater fish, including trout, smallmouth and largemouth bass, panfish, walleyes, and catfish. Crawfish can be used whole or in parts. Hook whole crawfish through the back of the thorax or by threading the hook through the tail, with the bend of the hook following the natural bend of the tail. To use parts (for small-mouthed fish, or from large crawfish), cut the tail into short pieces and use as you would shrimp, threading a small chunk onto a hook. The entire tail can also be used; thread it onto a suitable hook. A light in-line sinker is sometimes helpful to get the crawfish down to where the fish are feeding.
- **Marshmallows:** A simple and effective bait for trout, panfish, carp, and catfish. Most anglers use the "mini" or marble-size marshmallows, but the large standard size can also be cut into chunks. Thread one onto a hook, burying all of the shank and point. Or slice halfway through a marshmallow, slip it over the line and hook shank, then slide it down to bury all three points of a treble hook.
- **Cheese:** Cut into chunks, this is an ideal bait for many species, including panfish, catfish, carp, and even trout. Kraft's Velveeta brand is preferred by many anglers, since it has a smooth consistency, cuts easily, and threads well onto hooks. However, some cheeses with a similar consistency work equally well.

One or more chunks of bait can be placed on a hook, depending on the size of the hook.

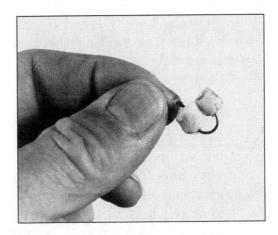

- **Clams:** A wide variety of clams is found along saltwater and freshwater shores. They are most effective when you are bottom fishing with a single- or double-hook bottom rig. Whole clams can be used, or small parts can be cut up and threaded onto a hook (make sure that as much of the shank and point are covered as possible). Clams are often difficult to hold on a hook; it helps to remove the bait from the shell to let it harden and toughen in the sun and air for a few minutes. However, do not allow it to dry out completely or become brittle.

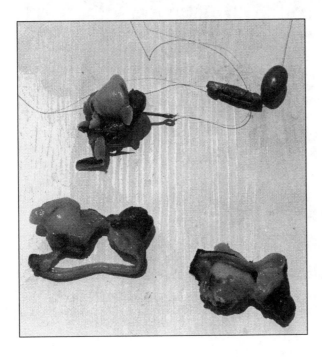

Clams are ideal for saltwater fishing and freshwater bottom fishing (using freshwater mussels), and are best hooked by threading the hook several times through the body of the clam.

- **Mussels:** Usually found on pilings, bridge abutments, jetties, rock piles, or similar inshore and tidal structures, mussels can be used the same way as clams. Thread the entire mussel onto the hook or cut it up into smaller pieces to thread onto small hooks.

- **Bloodworms and other sea worms:** Bloodworms, sandworms, pile worms, clam worms, cinder worms, and others can bite and pinch, so beware of the front end of these creatures. They should be handled carefully and placed whole or in pieces on a hook. Several can be threaded onto one large hook to make a mass of worms, which will attract larger fish. Or use a single-worm rig with a series of three hooks on a leader, each hook an inch or so apart, and impale the worm by its tail, head, and middle onto the three hooks.

- **Sand fleas:** Sometimes called sand crabs or mole crabs, these small, shell-backed, crablike creatures are usually found right at the surf line. Sand fleas are easily captured by digging along

Bloodworms are a saltwater bait used for bottom fishing and still fishing in salt water; cut them into pieces, as shown here, or thread them completely onto a hook.

this wash line, and are good baits for surf fishing. They can be threaded singly or in multiples onto a hook.

- **Strip baits:** These are nothing more than strips of fish, often from those caught but not wanted, or from the belly of fish that have been filleted or cleaned. The best strips are from small fish. Fillet out each side and trim into a long triangle. Remove the scales to make it easy to hook once through the skin, or back and forth several times on long strips with long-shank hooks. Such strips can be made in any size to suit the fishing—as small as ¼ inch wide and 1 inch long, and up to an inch or more wide and 4 to 6 inches long. Ideal for trolling, and bottom rigs or dropper rigs.

Strips from the belly of a caught fish (top) or a chunk with the tail intact (bottom).

- **Squid:** A popular saltwater bait, squid can be used whole by running the line through the mantle (use a bait-threading nee-dle) and hooking in the head. Larger squid can be cut into crosswise circles; these can then be made into tapered pieces as strip baits. A squid's head can also be used on a larger rig by hooking it through the eyes. Squid are popular for trolling, as well as any bottom rig, float rig, or basic rig.

Squid are best fished by cutting into chunks for threading onto a hook or making strips for trolling.

- **Octopi:** Like squid, octopi can be used whole in small sizes, or you can cut the tentacles into sections to use as chunk bait or into long sections for use as strip baits. Octopi are tough and an ideal saltwater bait.
- **Conches and whelks:** These large shellfish are good eating for humans but can also be used as bait. Cut the tough bodies into chunks for small fish, or use the bait whole and thread it onto a hook for larger fish.
- **Eels:** Ideal baits for a number of inshore and coastal species, they can be used whole and live for trolling for striped bass and other coastal species: Simply hook them through the eyes or lips. Chunks of eel are also a tough and useful bait for bottom fishing. Cut the eel into suitable-size pieces and thread them through the skin onto a hook. (Eels also make ideal crab baits in traps, in pots, or on trotlines.)
- **Crabs:** Hard-shell, soft-shell, and peeler crabs are all good saltwater baits. Hard-shell crabs are best fished by cutting them into pieces. First twist the legs off at the body; each leg can then be further broken or cut into small sections for bait. Next, pull up the apron and peel off the back at the same time. Cut the crab in half, then cut each half into smaller sections. Soft-shell and peeler crabs are better for baits, since they

are easier for most fish species to eat. They are cut and hooked the same way as hard-shell crabs. Crabs, like a number of other fragile baits, are not suitable for trolling. Similarly, use care when casting, since these baits do not stay on the hook well. Use a gentle, loblike cast, or try rigging the bait with a rubber band or string.

Crabs can be torn apart and cut into chunks for still fishing.

# Bait Rigs

ALMOST ANY BAIT RIG can theoretically be used for any kind of fishing, but some are obviously intended for fresh water and some for salt water. As a result, there many variations in hooks, leader lengths and styles, sizes and positions of sinkers, and so on. However, our focus here is on basic rigs. The main concerns in choosing any rig are whether you will be casting and retrieving, drifting a bait, fishing with a float, bottom fishing with a sinker, or trolling.

CLICKING
NOISE

SPLIT-SHOT →

NEEDLE-NOSE
WORM WEIGHTS

18 INCHES

HOOK

BAIT

Sometimes several sinkers are better than one, such as when you are using several small sinkers, or using a sinker with a series of beads that will clatter or click to make noise as you hop and bounce a bait along the bottom.
*Cliff Shelby.*

All bait rigs incorporate a line or leader, a hook or hooks, and often a sinker and/or float (bobber). Some rigs also require a separate line or leader (dropper) to hold a hook coming off the main line. All rig components, however, need to be joined using one of the common methods described below.

Use a three-way swivel by tying the line to one of its eyes, the leader with the hook (or snelled hook) to its second eye, and a snap with a sinker to its third eye. A variation of this method is to tie a short leader to the third eye that is tied to another three-way swivel. This creates a second hook rig. Three- and even four-hook rigs can be made this way. A standard swivel (with two eyes) can be used to tie the line and the hook snell (leader) to one eye, and the sinker or a second line to the other.

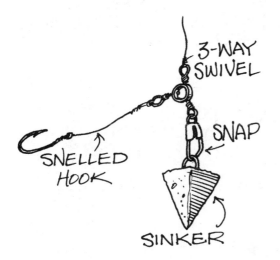

A simple bottom rig can be made with a three-way swivel, tying the line to one eye, adding a snap that opens on both ends to the second eye, and tying or looping a snelled hook to the third eye. *Cliff Shelby.*

To make a two-hook bottom rig, string together several snaps, swivels, and snelled hooks, and add a sinker to the bottom. *Cliff Shelby.*

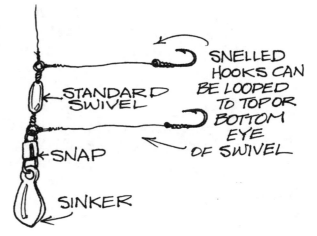

For example, you can tie an in-line dropper loop in the line wherever you want, pull it tight, and clip one end of the loop close to the knot. This becomes a separate leader for a hook attachment. Or tie an in-line dropper loop but, instead of clipping the line, loop the end through the hook eye and around the hook to attach it. (To keep the hook straight with the line, you must use one with a turned-up or turned-down eye.)

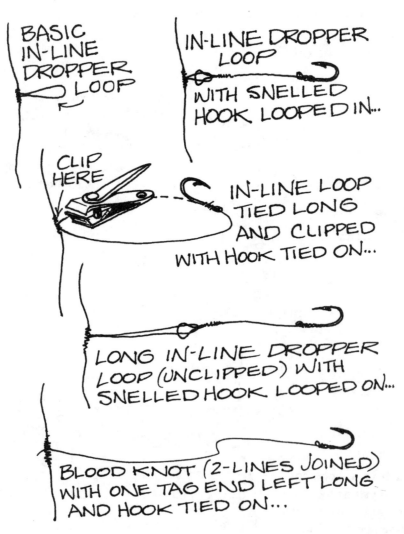

BASIC IN-LINE DROPPER LOOP

IN-LINE DROPPER LOOP WITH SNELLED HOOK LOOPED IN...

CLIP HERE

IN-LINE LOOP TIED LONG AND CLIPPED WITH HOOK TIED ON...

LONG IN-LINE DROPPER LOOP (UNCLIPPED) WITH SNELLED HOOK LOOPED ON...

BLOOD KNOT (2-LINES JOINED) WITH ONE TAG END LEFT LONG AND HOOK TIED ON...

In-line dropper loops.
*Cliff Shelby.*

Here are two other possibilities. Tie an in-line dropper loop as above, but use it to interlock with the loop of a snelled hook instead of threading through the eye of a hook. Or tie a blood knot, leave one of its tag ends very long, and attach a hook to it.

Hook lears or spreaders are wire forms that you can buy or make; they extend the hook leader or snell out from the main line. A simple one can be made from light spring wire in the shape of an L on its side, with an eye formed at each end and at the bend in the L. Attach the line to the eye at one end of the L, the sinker or continuing line to the eye at the bend, and the hook leader or snell to the eye at the end of the second arm.

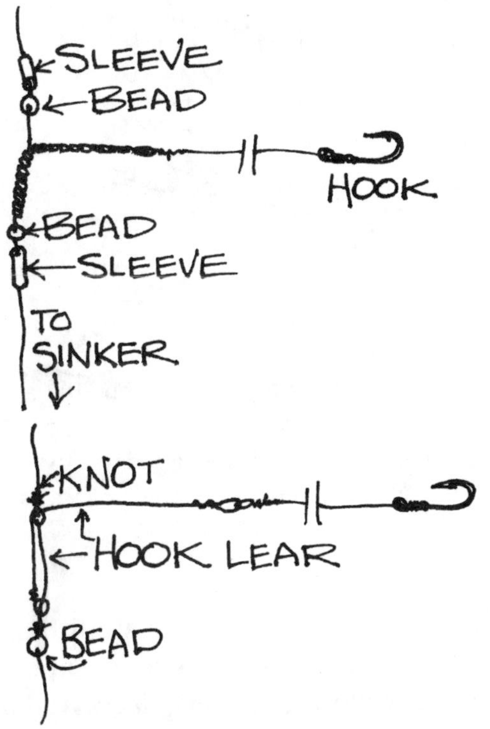

SLEEVE
BEAD
HOOK
BEAD
SLEEVE
TO SINKER
KNOT
HOOK LEAR
BEAD

Commercial hook lears, available at tackle shops, allow you to make up your own rigs by adding lears to the line to form single- or multiple-hook rigs. Hook lears are extensions that help keep the snelled hooks away from the line and prevent tangling.
*Cliff Shelby.*

Float rigs use a float to suspend the baited hook at the desired depth above the bottom. The float, a sinker to submerge the bait, and the hook can all be in a straight line, or dropper leaders off the main line between the float and sinker can hold the hook and bait. This second method, preferred by many, also lets you use several droppers to fish at different depths or to try different baits.

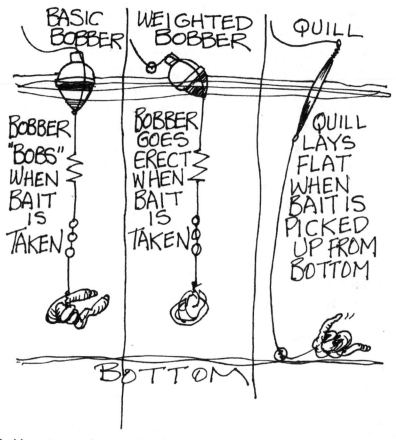

Basic bobber rigs can be varied as follows: Left, a basic bobber that "bobs" up and down as the bait is taken; center, a weighted bobber that springs up from lying on its side when the bait is taken or moved; and right, a quill float that is rigged to sit vertically with a suspended bait and will lie on its side when the bait is picked up by a fish. *Cliff Shelby.*

Float rigs can be awkward or dangerous to cast if you are fishing with line going more than about 3 feet deep. In these instances, a bobber stop will allow you to use a float while fishing very deep. Add a small stop to the line; you can reel this in with your line on most tackle. The stop can be as simple as a rubber band tied onto the line, or a small spring or rubber bead (available through tackle dealers) that is threaded onto it. The line is also threaded through a small sliding bead big enough to block the sliding float. The bead and float slide to the end of the line before your cast. When you do cast this outfit, the weight of the sinker and the baited hook pull the line through the float and bead until both are halted by the small bobber stop.

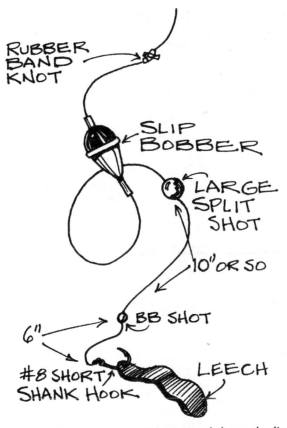

RUBBER
BAND
KNOT

SLIP
BOBBER

LARGE
SPLIT
SHOT

10" OR SO

BB SHOT

6"

#8 SHORT
SHANK HOOK

LEECH

Slip bobber rigs consist of a sinker that slides up and down the line, ending with a sinker and bait rig, as shown. A rubber band knotted or tied to the line, or a commercial bobber stop rig, will prevent the bobber from sliding all the way up the line yet still make casting possible when you are fishing deep.
*Cliff Shelby.*

Systems such as this allow you to use a wide variety of floats, from simple round plastic devices to the longer and more sensitive European-type floats. The best bobber systems use just enough weight to sink the bait and allow casting, and a bobber with just enough buoyancy to keep it floating. Both allow for maximum sensitivity to the feel when a fish takes the hook. Such rigs are used mostly for fishing with baits. However, they are also excellent for fishing with such lures as jigs or bait-tipped jigs at a certain depth, particularly for crappies or perch.

Bottom-fishing rigs (similar to float rigs but without the float) can be fished right on the bottom or suspended vertically from a boat, bridge, pier, jetty, or other structure to fish the mid-depths. In its simplest form, a bottom-fishing rig consists of an in-line sinker, such as a rubber core or pinch-on, with the end of the line tied to a hook. The bait rests on the bottom, unless you add a float to the end of the line (next to the hook) to suspend the bait.

A simple one-hook bottom rig can be made by tying a hook to the end of the line, then adding a pinch-on or rubber-core sinker anywhere along the line.
*Cliff Shelby.*

Many bottom rigs use droppers off the main line to hold the hook, with a sinker tied to the end of the main line. Such rigs can be bought or made using three-way swivels, standard swivels, or knots.

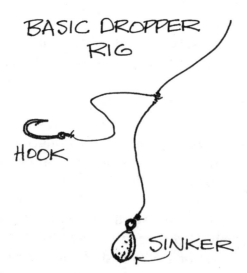

Cutting the line allows you to tie a blood knot with a long tag end for tying on a hook, while tying the sinker to the end of the line.
*Cliff Shelby.*

A two-hook bottom rig adds a second dropper or leader above the first. Three hooks are sometimes fished this way, but rarely more. To avoid tangling the hooks, keep the upper dropper line shorter than the distance between the line connection and the lower hook connection.

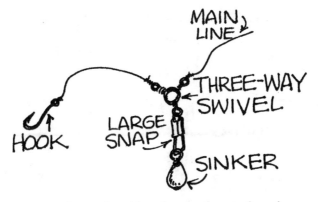

Simple bottom rigs can be made with a three-way swivel, as shown.
*Cliff Shelby.*

Which sinker to use in a bottom rig depends on the type of bottom, as well as the weight required to hold the rig and counteract the tide or current. Similarly, hooks vary in size and type with the species sought.

Here are five simple possibilities for bottom rigs.

- Tie a hook to the end of the line, and add a pinch-on or rubber-core sinker 12 to 24 inches above it. The sinker will keep the hook on the bottom. When fished above the bottom, the bait will drift with the current or tide.
- Tie a sinker to the end of the line, then tie in an in-line dropper loop. Add the hook by running the loop through the hook eye, interlocking it with a loop-eye snelled hook, or cutting one end of the loop and tying it to the hook.
- Make a two-hook bottom rig as above, but with two dropper loops in the line.
- Buy single- or two-hook bottom rigs for your fishing. These consist of a swivel or eye to which you tie the line, a snap on the bottom to hold a sinker, and two arms or hook lears to hold hooks or snells.

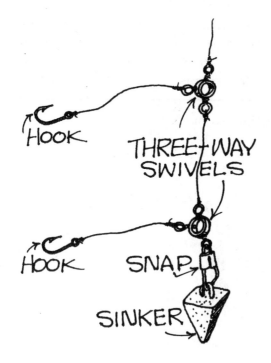

Using two three-way swivels and a double-ended snap enables you to make up simple two-hook bottom rigs with any desired spacing between the hooks. They can be tied with regular monofilament line, or heavier monofilament for increased strength and durability.
*Cliff Shelby.*

- Spreader rigs are used primarily for shallow saltwater flounder fishing, as well as freshwater perch and panfish. These usually consist of a center line-tie, a snap for a sinker directly under the line-tie, and two to four arms on which leaders or snelled hooks can be added. They are usually fished to hold baits where the fish are located—either on the bottom for flounder, or at mid-depths for perch, panfish, and crappies.

Spreader rigs, available from coastal tackle shops, are widely used to fish several baits for bottom species such as fluke, flounder, and sea bass. Snelled hooks are added to the end of the wire frame arms.
*Cliff Shelby.*

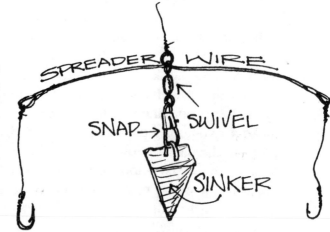

Drift-fishing rigs are similar to bottom rigs but have no weight— or less weight—to allow a bait to drag along behind a drifting boat. This allows you to cover more water when fishing and also helps you locate schools or pockets of fish. Drift-fishing rigs may also be used from an anchored boat in a current or tidal flow; the technique is to drift a bait by slowly releasing line from the reel. A light sinker will help get the bait down, and the multiple hooks help present the bait over a larger area.

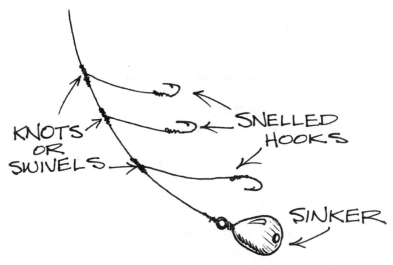

Drift-fishing rigs, in which the rig is not fished on the bottom, still require sinkers to keep the baits down. Here the snelled hooks can be attached using swivels or in-line dropper loops.
*Cliff Shelby.*

Another type of drift rig uses a sinker designed to drag along the bottom, pulling a bait or lure as the boat drifts. The weight is usually tapered or fixed to a long wire that slides along the bottom. Many anglers use V-shaped or safety-pin-type wires that allow them to tie the line to the apex of the V, and then tie the leader and lure or bait to the unweighted end of the V.

Trolling with bait usually involves strip baits, whole fish, or minnows that are lip-hooked or sewn onto a hook so they track well through the water without twisting line. Some trolling rigs are designed so the bait actually skips on the surface (as in big-game fishing), but most are fished deep. Trolling rigs are also used with lures such as spoons, jigs, crankbaits, and soft plastics.

Bait-walking sinkers can be used to drift or slow-troll a bait along the bottom for species such as walleyes. The lead sinkers are designed to slide over most obstructions.
*Cliff Shelby.*

Other bait-walking rigs can include a T style or three-way swivel with a rubber-hose sleeve attached to one eye to hold pencil lead. The length and diameter of the lead can be varied to adjust for the desired weight. Bottom-fishing sinkers molded onto a wire (sometimes straight, sometimes like a safety pin, as shown) allow you to fish the bottom with minimal chance of hanging up.
*Cliff Shelby*

Planers—sometimes called diving planes, because of the way they dive in the water—are also used to fish both baits and lures. Tie the line to the front end of the plane, and the leader (ending with the lure or bait) to the back end. Various triggering devices release the plane when a fish hits.

Some rigs keep a bait down with a sinker. This is positioned either in-line between the line and long leader, or suspended a few inches to a few feet off the third eye of a three-way swivel tied between the line and leader. The length of leader between the hook and sinker varies with fishing conditions. For freshwater fishing, only a few feet of leader is needed. For some types of saltwater fishing, up to 30 feet or more of leader is sometimes necessary. Rigs with long leaders require handlining to land the fish, since it is usually impossible to reel in past the sinker fixed to the rig.

Some baitfish-trolling rigs require special rigging of the bait. A good example is the ballyhoo rig commonly used for trolling this long-beaked baitfish. A wire leader is attached to the hook with a haywire twist, the end of the haywire ending with a straight "pin" or right-angle projection. A separate wire—often copper—is wrapped to the hook eye and used to secure the bait.

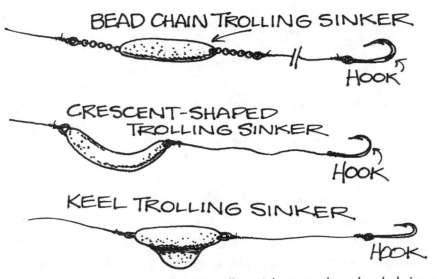

To reduce rotation and line twisting, trolling sinkers can have bead chains, as with the cigar sinker (top); or they can be specially shaped, as with the crescent sinker (middle) and keel-trolling sinker (bottom).
*Cliff Shelby.*

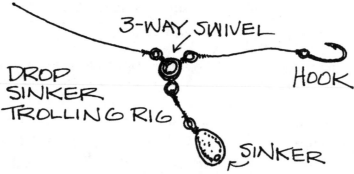

One way to keep a lure or bait at a given depth right off the bottom is to use a drop sinker rig, in which a sinker is tied to a line that in turn is tied to a three-way swivel. Line length for the sinker can range from a few inches to 5 or more feet. *Cliff Shelby.*

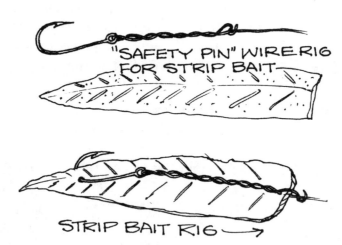

To troll strip baits, use a wire leader in which the wire is twisted together to hold a hook, then the end is used to attach the upper end of the strip bait. The hook is placed through the tail of the bait.
*Cliff Shelby.*

The ballyhoo is actually hooked through the gills, then down into the belly, and out the belly or vent. On other species, hook through the mouth and out the belly. The leader's right-angle pin impales the head of the bait; you then use the copper wire to wrap the nose or beak of the baitfish to the wire leader. After you have secured the head, finish the rig by wrapping the wire around the forward part of the wire leader.

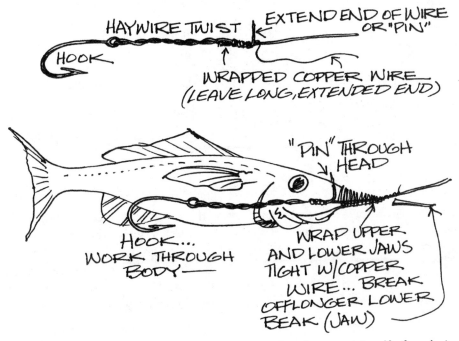

HAYWIRE TWIST — EXTEND END OF WIRE OR "PIN"

HOOK

WRAPPED COPPER WIRE (LEAVE LONG, EXTENDED END)

"PIN" THROUGH HEAD

HOOK... WORK THROUGH BODY —

WRAP UPPER AND LOWER JAWS TIGHT W/COPPER WIRE... BREAK OFF LONGER LOWER BEAK (JAW)

Wire leaders with a haywire twist (wire twisted around itself after being threaded through the hook eye) are also used to hold trolling baitfish, with the hook worked through the body or out through a gill and hooked into the side, then the head of the bait wrapped with the tag end of the wire. This is ideal for slim-headed baitfish such as balao (ballyhoo).
*Cliff Shelby.*

Another way to rig a free-swimming bait is to use heavy thread and a needle. Secure the thread to the hook with a series of half hitches, then run the needle and thread alternately through the lips and eyes of the baitfish, securing it with half hitches to the hook. Your sewing thread thus forms a sling through the front of the bait, with its ends attached to the bend of the hook on each side of the baitfish's head. Eels are often hooked this way, or by hooking straight through the eyes or lips.

Surf fishermen can use single- or two-hook bottom rigs as described above, or a different and useful rig called the "fish-finder." This rig uses a sliding sinker connector, which allows a fish to take the bait without detecting the weight. To make this rig, run the line through the sliding sinker connector, then tie the line to a standard swivel. Tie a 24- to 30-inch leader with hook to the second eye of the swivel. The swivel will stop the sliding sinker (usually a pyramid or bank sinker), allowing smooth casting.

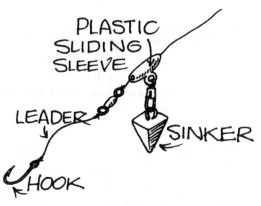

To allow fish to take a bait without dragging the sinker and perhaps dropping the bait, use a fish-finder rig. This employs a special sinker sleeve through which the line slides, as shown. These are widely available in coastal surf shops. For freshwater fishing, you can use the same rig with a snap swivel; the line goes through the eye of the swivel and the sinker attaches to the snap. Most rigs also use a swivel in the line to prevent the sinker from sliding down and tangling with the bait.
*Cliff Shelby.*

A similar rig for freshwater fishing (most often for catfish and carp) uses the same arrangement. Run the line through an egg sinker, tie the line to a swivel, and end with a 3-foot leader and a single hook.

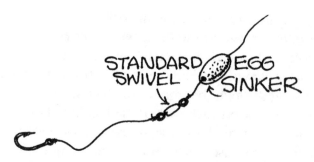

Here a simple freshwater sliding-sinker rig uses an egg sinker. The line runs through the egg sinker then is tied to a swivel; next comes a length of leader, before you tie on the hook and add bait.
*Cliff Shelby*

# Lure Rigs

LURES CAN BE CAST or trolled at the end of your fishing line, and often no other rigging is required. Whether you are fishing for freshwater or saltwater species, simply use your favorite line-to-lure knot. However, it is essential to work or retrieve all lures so that they resemble live, injured bait, or have an erratic action that singles them out from other baitfish. Such erratic action alerts gamefish to the lure, making strikes more likely. Try a mix of twitches, jerks, pauses, swimming motions, jigging actions, and similar movements.

Some lures are sold in bulk without any hook or other tackle and must be rigged before use. This is true of most soft-plastic lures. The Texas rig is basic to fishing any worm, lizard, crayfish, or other soft plastic for largemouth bass, smallmouth bass, walleyes, panfish, perch, trout, or catfish. The technique consists of tying the worm hook to the end of the line, threading the hook point straight into the head of the lure, bringing it out the side, then repositioning the hook point in the body of the worm.

The secret of an effective rigging is to make sure that the worm or lizard is straight on the hook, with no bends, kinks, or stretching. This is an ideal basic rig, but especially so for fishing in weeds or around snags and underwater structure. (A tapered worm weight can also be used to provide casting weight or to help sink the worm to where the fish are feeding.)

The Florida rig is much like the Texas rig, but the hook is threaded farther into the head of the worm so that it is kinked. The result is a worm that twists and swims in the water, although it can also twist the line unless you attach a swivel. A variation uses a

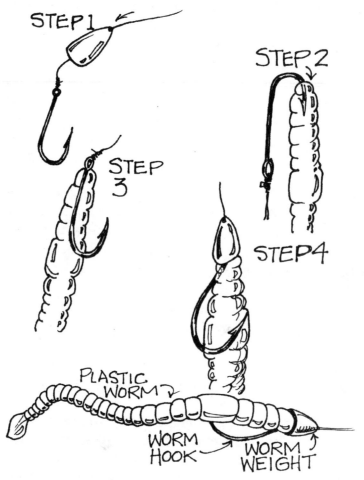

Basic plastic-worm rigging for bass:

1. Run line through tapered worm sinker and tie on hook.
2. Run point of hook straight into head of worm.
3. Bring point of hook out of worm's side so that only end of hook shank remains in the worm.
4. Insert point of hook back into worm's body to make it weedless.

*Cliff Shelby.*

barbed-shank, baitholder hook, with the point exposed and the worm extending partway down the hook bend to create the kink and the swimming motion. A ball-bearing swivel can be used to reduce line twist. This rig is best for open water, where the twisting, swimming motion will draw fish out and provoke strikes.

The rear-hook Texas rig is a variation, with the hook placed in the tail of the worm. One way is to tie the hook to the line, run the hook through and out the head of the worm, then into the body, repeating this several times as necessary, before turning it and sinking the point into the tail end of the worm.

An alternative is to run a very long needle (available from clothing and upholstery stores) eye-first up from the worm's tail and out the head, thread the line through the needle eye, and pull it back through the worm before tying on the hook. This is the best rig when fish are striking short—not taking the whole worm, or striking and running without getting a head-hooked worm in their mouth.

The Carolina rig uses either an exposed hook or a weedless hook rig (Texas rig) with a sliding bullet sinker on the line; you then tie the line to a swivel, and tie the swivel to a leader (often 24 to 30 inches long) that ends with the worm. It is difficult to cast and must be lobbed, but it is good for fishing deep in large lakes. It will take fish from deeper waters than any crankbait.

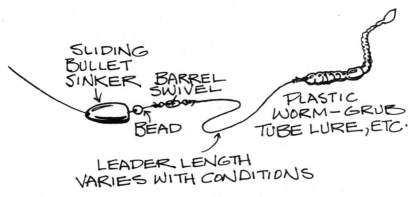

A basic Carolina rig can use a Texas-rigged (weedless) worm, or one with an exposed hook point. It is ideal for fishing deep, open water.
*Cliff Shelby.*

The wacky worm rig is fished most often around structure or in open water for suspended bass. When it moves through the water, it looks a lot like a live, writhing worm. Achieve this action by burying a lead worm weight or a small nail body in the head of the worm, then hooking the worm through the center with the point exposed. The weight causes the head of the worm to sink; when jigged, it will have a wacky up-and-down movement. This is an ideal rig for spotted bass or any fish that hold in deep, open water, along water edges, or near break lines.

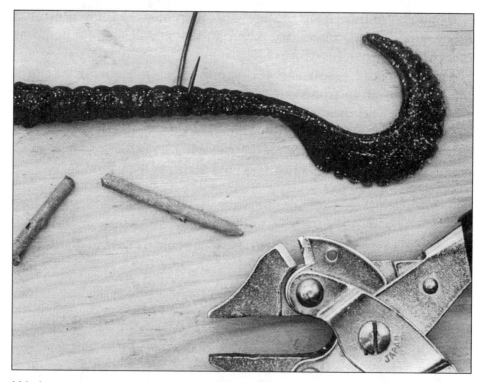

Wacky worm rigs are made by hooking a plastic worm in the middle and adding a weight to the head to give it an erratic action in the water. Lead inserts are available commercially, or you can use a length of nail (shown here).

Any of the above rigs can be fished alone, or rigged with a tapered worm weight to get the lure down to the fish and to help penetrate weeds. Plastic worms sometimes require special tricks to rig correctly. Here are two tips that make worms easier to fish, regardless of the rig you use. First, peg the worm to the line by running a toothpick into the hole in the weight after threading it onto the line and tying and rigging the worm hook. Break off the toothpick to prevent snags. The peg will hold the weight in place and allow it to pound through weeds and sink the worm rapidly. The second tip is similar: To keep fish from taking a worm or soft-plastic lure and sliding it down the hook, hold the worm in place with a toothpick threaded through the head of the worm and the eye of the hidden hook.

Some lures require added weight or rigging to be cast properly or trolled at the correct depths. There are a number of solutions, including an in-line sinker positioned between the rod and the lure to help

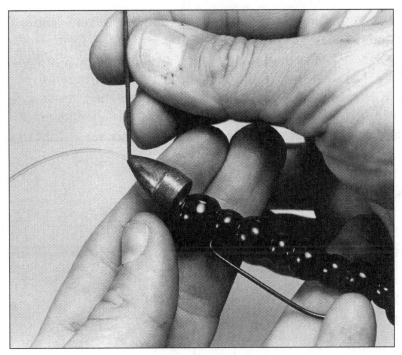

To hold a worm weight in place ahead of the worm, peg it with a toothpick. Pegs are also available commercially.

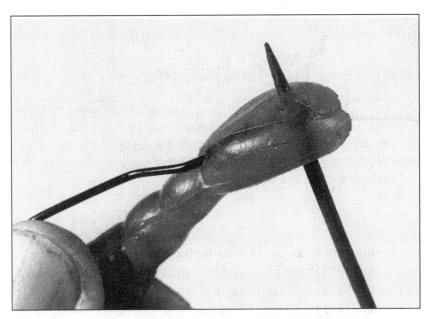

To prevent a worm from sliding down on a hook, peg the worm to the eye of the hook (as shown) after you thread the worm onto the hook. Break off ends of the toothpick before fishing.

get lures deep. If you are trolling, sinkers can be 30 feet or more ahead of the lure in salt water, but usually only a few feet in fresh water. With rigs designed for casting, such as the Carolina, the sinker should be carefully positioned: no closer than about 1 foot in front of the lure to prevent slowing the lure action, and no more than about 2 ½ feet ahead of it to allow for casting. Cast slowly and carefully, and make sure that you have complete clearance for the lure rig.

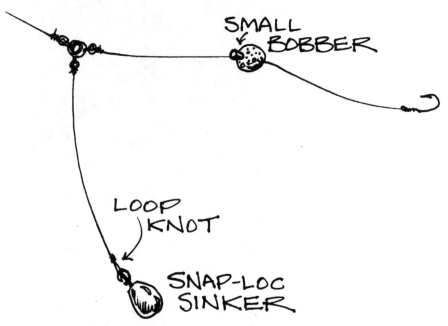

Bottom rigs that have the line, bait or lure leader, and sinker leader tied to separate eyes of a three-way swivel are effective and easy to make. The length of the leader from the swivel to the sinker controls the depth of the rig. Some bait rigs, especially when very slowly trolled, use a small bobber (as shown) to keep the bait visible to the fish and off the bottom.
*Cliff Shelby.*

Drop sinkers are used only in trolling, not casting, to keep the lure close to the bottom. Rig them by using a three-way swivel with the line tied to one eye, the lure tied by a leader to the second eye, and the sinker tied to a 1- to 3-foot leader to allow it to bounce along the bottom. (Note that fish caught on trolled lures with long leaders must be handlined to the boat, since the swivel cannot be reeled through the guides or onto the spool.)

Bait-walker rigs are similar to the drop-sinker rig, with a short leader and a special sinker that drags along the bottom during slow trolling or drifting. Bait-walker rigs are most often used in fresh water, with the lure close to the bottom.

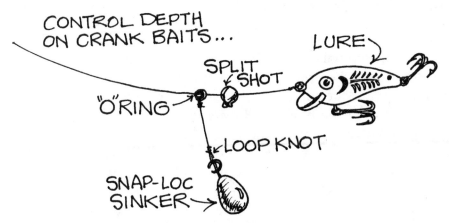

Sinkers, either in-line or drop-style off a leader, can be used to control the depth of a running lure that might otherwise float, never reaching the desired depths. A swivel or split shot, as shown, is used to keep the sinker away from the line-tie to the lure, and to make sure that the lure action is not compromised by the weight.
*Cliff Shelby.*

One way to make bottom rigs in snaggy water is to use a series of split shot on a separate leader off a swivel or tied from a dropper loop. Then, if the sinkers get caught, they will pull off so that the bait/hook or lure is not lost. Use a lighter-test sinker leader than you do in the main line.
*Cliff Shelby*

Deep-water trolling the mid-depths—for fish such as salmon and trout—is easy when you use a heavy sinker that stays deep when slow-trolled, combined with one or more lures fished off droppers that are several feet long. Attach them to the main line above the sinker using three-way swivels, blood knots, or dropper loops. This type of rig is often used to fish the thermocline—the layer of water separating the warmer upper waters and the colder, oxygen-poor depths.

Planers, used only for trolling, work similarly to the diving planes on submarines. When rigged between the rod and the lure, the planer and lures or bait are forced by the pressure of moving water deeper than they would ordinarily track. Most planers are equipped with a mechanical or magnetic catch that trips when a fish strikes. The planer then loses its diving capability until the fish is landed and the planer reset. Divers are similar to planers but feature an erratic side-to-side motion that gives the lure more action in the water.

Side planers are little floating "sleds" attached by a heavy line to a fixed point on the boat. Clips that release on a strike allow the planer to hold fishing line and trolling lures. Side planers are used primarily in large freshwater lakes for trolling multiple lines, or to get lures close to a shallow, rocky shoreline.

It is often effective to fish two lures in tandem on one line. Rig the added lure from a dropper, or from a leader running from the main lure to a trailing lure. The two lures are generally separated by a foot or two. Here are some possible combinations.

- A small jig behind a topwater (cupped-face) chugger or a floating-diver plug.
- Two jigs, one on the main line and one on a dropper.
- A small jig on a dropper in front of a diving crankbait—as if the crankbait were chasing the smaller jig.
- A small spoon on a dropper in front of a larger spoon.
- A large streamer fly followed by a nymph.
- A small nymph on a dropper in front of a streamer fly.
- A Texas-rigged plastic worm or grub on a dropper ahead of a jig.
- A small and large lure, or two same-size lures in different colors.

Lures are often "sweetened" with bait to increase strikes and catches. The bait should enhance the lure and not interfere with any built-in lure action. Some typical lure-and-bait combinations are:

- Spinners are often tipped with a piece of worm, bloodworm, small minnow, or strip bait cut from caught fish.
- Weedless spoons need thin baits such as strip baits, pork rinds, minnows, or leeches to avoid interfering with the spoon's side-to-side action.
- Trolling spoons are often tipped with strip baits or minnows.
- Soft plastics, such as the grubs often fished on jigs in salt water, can be tipped with a shrimp, shrimp tail, or bloodworm.
- Spinnerbaits and buzzbaits are commonly tipped with pork rinds or strip baits.

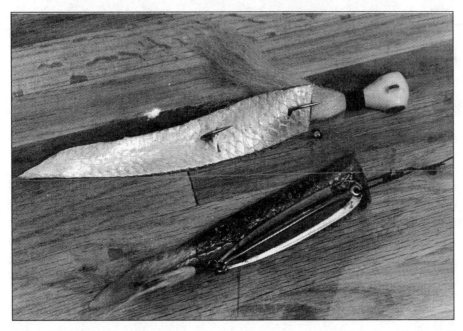

Strips of fish can be used to "sweeten" lures, such as the strip baits used on this jig and metal casting spoon.

- Heavy-structure spoons dropped to deep structure are often sweetened in salt water with shrimp, clams, clam snouts, strip baits, shiners, or bloodworms; in fresh water, with earthworms, small minnows, or leeches.
- In salt water, jigs are tipped with shrimp, bloodworms, minnows, strip baits, or clam snouts. In fresh water, they are tipped with earthworms, strip baits, salamanders, crayfish, or leeches.

Here, shrimp is added to a jig as an enticement.

- Offshore-trolling lures are frequently rigged with whole bait-fish, specially rigged to troll at relatively high speeds. Strip baits cut from the belly of a fish may be substituted.

Taste and smell attractants have become popular with some anglers. However, they are best used with lures that are fished slowly and deliberately, such as jigs and soft plastics. Attractants are seldom effective when used with trolled lures or lures that are cast and retrieved at high speed, since the scent dissipates too rapidly for a fish to find or follow the lure.

CHAPTER

# Basic Lures and How to Use Them

**T**HERE IS AN ENORMOUS variety of lures, each designed to catch specific fish in particular situations. Here is a broad cross section of the many types of lures and their uses.

Surface plugs come in the chugger style (cupped face, makes a splash); cigar style (makes a wake but no splash); and cigar with propellers (make lots of bubbles and noise). Large and small sizes are available for both fresh water and salt water. Use them when you are fishing shallows, for any surface-feeding fish, or when fish are breaking the surface. A tip about buying these lures: Check the belly color, since this is what the fish mostly sees. Most are white, yellow, or black. Use white for bright days, yellow for overcast days, and black for dull days or night fishing.

Some saltwater surface lures actually sink. Their heavy weight helps you cast them on stout tackle, and also creates a wake and noise on your retrieve; the slanted face combined with a fast retrieve keeps them on or near the surface. They are fished by casting to schools of fish that are breaking the surface, or in areas where you suspect the fish to be close to the top.

Floating-diving plugs and crankbaits are similar—since you cast them out and reel (or crank) them back in. The former group may be designed to always stay on the surface, or they may dip down when retrieved quickly. Both can be used for trolling in fresh and salt water, but usually crankbaits are more popular for this purpose. Crankbaits can be designed as shallow, medium, and deep runners. The longer the lip and the closer it is to parallel with the lure body, the deeper the plug will run.

217

Topwater plugs are similar for both freshwater and saltwater fishing. These freshwater plugs include (top to bottom rows) wobble-type lures, chuggers or poppers, propeller baits, and plain stick baits.

Floating-diving crankbaits can vary in body shape, lip length, and lip position.

Long lips will cause crankbaits to dive deep; short lips will cause crankbaits to run shallow. Here, a variety of lip styles is shown.

The best lures to troll offshore from a large boat are skipping lures—large skirted lures designed to skip and bounce across the surface. Usually made of vinyl, wood, metal, and hard plastic, many are also brightly colored and sport large eyes to look like baitfish. The head of the lure has a center hole through which a heavy wire or monofilament leader runs; this is then cinched or snelled to a large ocean hook.

Skipping lures are primarily used offshore, but smaller versions are used inshore for coastal species such as bluefish, dolphinfish, and striped bass. The lures are trolled skipping on the surface, usually in the first or second wave behind the boat. You can use several designs or colors, fishing each from a different rod. With outriggers extended from the side of the boat, you can troll as many as eight lures at the same time.

Jigs and bucktails can be bare and plain to hold a soft plastic grub or worm, or they can be dressed with hair, synthetics, or feather tails. Replaceable rubber or plastic skirts are also popular in both fresh and salt water. Often tipped with bait or a soft plastic trailer, jigs are available in sizes ranging from $\frac{1}{80}$ ounce through 20 ounces. Most freshwater jigs weigh from about ¹⁄₃₂ ounce through ½ ounce; most saltwater, from ¼ ounce through several ounces. They can be cast or trolled (there are specific designs for each use), fished close to the surface, or dropped straight down to catch bottom fish.

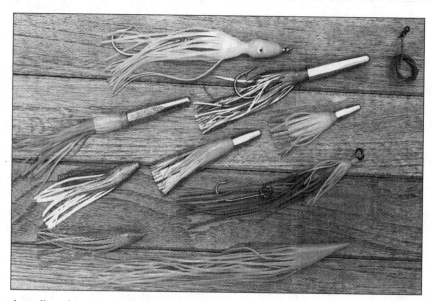

Vinyl trolling lures are designed mostly for saltwater fishing, and are made so that the line or leader runs through the lure before a hook is tied on.

In saltwater fishing, jigs can be used for deep jigging (as over structure or wrecks), casting, or trolling.

Structure spoons are thick metal lures used in deep jigging over reefs in salt water, surf casting along coasts, and deep fishing over structure in fresh water. Many styles, sizes, and finishes are available, but most tend to be bright and flashy, and to employ treble hooks. The addition of a swivel to this rig will often prevent the line from twisting as a result of the spoon's action in the water.

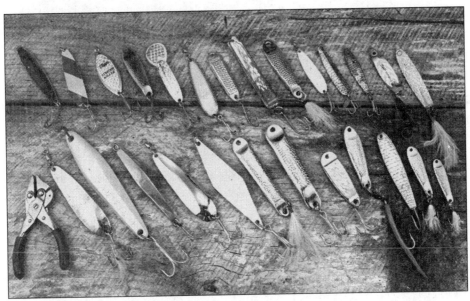

Structure or jigging spoons can be used for casting or for vertical jigging, since they are heavily weighted and will sink rapidly.

Casting spoons are curved to make them wobble when trolled or retrieved. Often they are fished around weeds, so they require a wire weedguard. Casting spoons with free-swinging hooks are used mostly in salt water; those with a fixed hook, more often in fresh water.

Trolling spoons are much like casting spoons, but are generally larger. Some use a single hook fastened to the spoon; others have a free-swinging single or treble hook. To take them deeper, trolling spoons are sometimes rigged with an in-line or drop sinker.

Spinners have a central shaft with a rotating blade that flashes and attracts fish. They are primarily used for casting and retrieving in fresh water. Sizes to catch everything from trout to muskies are available, in many styles, finishes, and colors. Spinners tend to twist line, so a good swivel is essential.

Casting spoons are often made in weedless styles (as shown in these examples), for fishing in weeds for bass, pike, and walleyes.

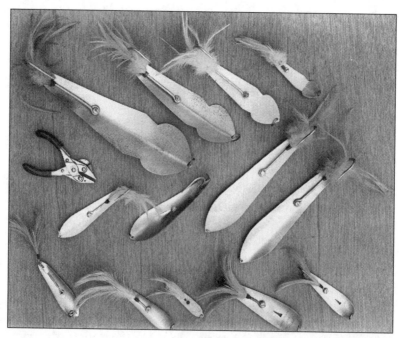

Trolling spoons are used in open water, and thus seldom have weedguards. Since they are made of thin metal and designed for a lot of wobble in the water, they are difficult to cast.

Spinners are among the most popular of lures for all freshwater fishing, since many styles are available for everything from trout to muskies.

Spinnerbaits look like jigs, but have a safety-pin-like arm that extends from the leadhead. At its end are one or two blades that rotate and flash; a skirt just behind the head covers the hook. Spinnerbaits are designed for freshwater fishing at a variety of depths, but primarily for bass and walleyes using weight-forward spinnerbaits.

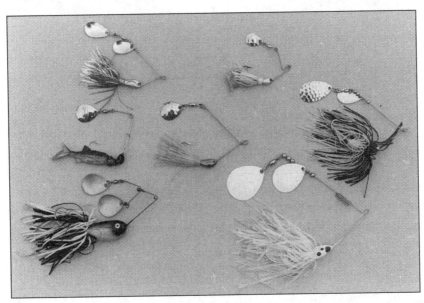

Spinnerbaits are ideal for bass, walleyes, and pike. They are worked under the surface.

Buzzbaits slightly resemble spinnerbaits, but use a wire form bent in a J shape. One or two propeller blades are then attached onto the end of the short upper arm of the J. As with spinnerbaits, a skirt covers the head. Buzzbaits are most effective when worked on the surface for bass.

Buzzbaits can come in safety-pin-arm or straight styles, but all are designed to be worked on the surface, where the blades churn the water and attract fish

Soft plastics comprise a large arsenal of lures for fresh and salt water. Many are close imitations of natural baits, such as worms, crayfish, lizards, slugs, shrimp, or baitfish. Others resemble nothing in nature and rely on their color, shape, and action (from arms, skirts, or other features) to attract fish. Soft plastics may be trolled, cast, deep-jigged, and fished in a wide variety of other ways for all freshwater and saltwater fish.

Trolling skirts are usually made of thin vinyl cut into slits. They are rigged with a leader through the body of the lure and a weight (usually an egg sinker) in the head to keep the lure skipping and swimming properly. They are also used as an additional skirt attractant in front of a trolled baitfish or strip bait. You can fish trolling skirts on the surface or deep by adjusting the trolling speed and/or sinker weight.

Tube lures are like small trolling skirts with a short skirt section. They are generally made in smaller sizes for freshwater fishing and rigged like plastic worms. Larger sizes are also available for saltwater fishing.

# FIELD& STREAM

# The Complete Fisherman

## Book Four

## Bass Fishing

Mark Sosin & Bill Dance

# 1

# Understanding Your Quarry

THE BLACK BASS are probably the most glamorous species in the fresh waters of the world today. They have a high intellect and a strong instinct for survival, but, like all other animals, bass have cycles through their lives that cause them to react in a particular manner. Both the largemouth and the smallmouth approach the physical configuration of the perfect predator, with broad, powerful tails, excellent vision, superb hearing, and the ability to maneuver under water quickly and effectively.

Unlike members of the pike or trout family, the bass is built to probe and forage around logs, rocks, and other forms of protective cover. Sometimes these fish will strike their prey from ambush and other times they'll simply cruise along looking for food. On the other hand, a bass is not tailored to long pursuit, and the chances of a largemouth or smallmouth running down a lure over a considerable distance are slim. Their preferred feeding strategy is to strike instantly when the prey (or lure) passes within range. Burst swimming speed of a bass is about 12 miles per hour, but the sustained swimming speed is much less.

A bass can suspend 2 inches off the bottom or 60 feet off the bottom without expending any more energy. The secret is its swim bladder, an airtight sac that can be inflated or deflated to help maintain a neutral buoyancy. Without it, a bass would sink to the bottom. The swim bladder means that a bass can be at any level, and, as we'll explore in the next chapter, depth is the primary consideration in locating bass.

Being the perfect predator, a bass feeds primarily by sight and sound. Its eyes are well developed, and through a system of orientation to the coming of daylight and darkness, the bass takes full advantage of periods of subdued light. That's one reason bass fishing is often good early in the morning and late in the afternoon. The bass can get closer to its prey and expend less energy in capturing its victim.

As in all fish, the iris in a bass's eye is fixed and cannot open or close down to adjust to the amount of light. This causes the bass to seek shade on a bright day, but there's more to that story. Any predator prefers to remain in darker waters, where it is afforded a certain amount of protection against its enemies while giving it the advantage in the strategy of feeding. It is far easier to see prey swimming by in better-lit water while remaining in semidarkness. And the prey cannot see the bass as well as the bass can see the prey.

Vision, of course, is affected by water clarity. The more turbid the water, the shorter the range of vision and the less time a bass has to decide about striking an offering. Fish know instinctively that once their prey escapes beyond the range of vision, it is gone forever. In clear water, a bass can take more time, but in murky water, it is now or never.

Anglers are always puzzled how a bass can clobber a black lure on a pitch-black night. They can understand the effect of a vibrating lure because they reason that the bass hears it, but something as mundane as a plastic worm raises a question. The answer centers on the lateral line on a bass. This lateral line, which extends from behind the gills to the tail on each side of the fish, is as accurate as radar in pinpointing the presence of an object. It is a hearing organ designed for sounds close to the fish.

Anything moving through the water must displace water molecules. It is precisely this displacement that is picked up by the lateral line, and the fish can strike the source of that sound as effectively as if it were seen with the eyes. The lateral line works only with near-field sounds—those that are within a few feet of the bass—but it is a deadly system. That's how a bass can hit a black plastic worm in deep water on a dark night.

In addition to the lateral line, bass also have ears inside their heads, although they do not have external earflaps as we do. Their bodies act as a sounding board, and they can hear and react to sounds a long distance away. The gentle *plop* of a lure on the water will get their attention, but too loud a disturbance could have the reverse effect, and warning sounds such as a tacklebox scraping on the deck can send a bass scurrying for cover. Sometimes, something as simple as squeaky oarlocks can keep an angler from catching a limit of bass. Simply being aware of what sound can do is half the battle.

## COLOR

You bet bass can see color, and even distinguish between various shades. Researchers have concluded that bass see color better than most other fish. The clue to color vision comes from the eye. If a fish has both cone and rod receptors in its eye, you can assume it sees color. The cone receptors are for periods of bright light and mean color vision. The rod receptors are used at night and during periods of low visibility, and basically provide black-and-white vision.

Extensive experiments have been performed on the largemouth to test its color perception. Conclusions point to the fact that the bass sees colors as if it were looking through a pair of yellow glasses. It has difficulty distinguishing yellow from gray, and both yellow and blue are less distinct than other colors. On the other hand, bass see red and violet best and green second best.

Not only can bass discern colors in the water, but they can identify colors and shades in the air before the object touches the water. And their perception is so keen that they can distinguish among 24 different shades.

From an angler's standpoint, bass have been taken on lures of practically every color and shade imaginable. On given days they may show a marked preference for one color. Yet each fisherman has his own favorites, and we certainly suggest experimentation. You have to determine what the fish will strike right now rather than what they hit yesterday.

## WATER TEMPERATURE

Fish are cold-blooded creatures and thus their temperatures are governed by those of the surrounding water. Each species exhibits specific temperature preferences, but also has temperature tolerances that cover a much wider range. The largemouth, for example, seems most comfortable when the water is between 65° and 75° F, while the smallmouth likes slightly cooler water (60–70° F). On the other hand, northern anglers often catch largemouths through the ice, which means that the water temperature is between 32° and 39.2° F.

Temperature affects both the occurrence and the well-being of fish, and bass are no exception. As the water chills, their metabolism starts to slow down, and in cold water, bass are very sluggish. They require much less oxygen and food, their digestive rate is very slow, and they don't exert much energy in chasing a lure. If you can find a spot where the water is slightly warmer than the surrounding area (such as the presence of a spring), you can bet there will be a concentration of fish right there.

At the other extreme, bass become uncomfortable when water temperatures rise above 80° F. With higher temperatures, fish require much more oxygen and will usually seek this oxygen above all other considerations. That's when you'll find them along windy shorelines, where a spring enters a lake, or among aquatic plants that produce oxygen.

From an angling standpoint, you must be alert to temperature changes and the response you can expect from bass. Remembering that bass are cold-blooded and take on the temperature of the surrounding water, you can gain some instant intelligence the moment you land a bass. If you have a temperature gauge with you, slip the thermistor into the fish's mouth and down into its stomach. Take a reading. Then lower the thermistor over the side until you find water of the same temperature. That's the depth at which the fish was before you hooked it.

## OXYGEN

Without oxygen, fish don't survive. It's as simple as that. To breathe, fish glean dissolved oxygen from the water through their gills. Compared to air, there's so little dissolved oxygen in the water that it is expressed in parts per million. A change of only one part per million can spell the difference between survival and death; it's that critical.

The main source of oxygen in a lake comes from photosynthesis, a process whereby aquatic plants produce oxygen. For that reason, lakes with good vegetation are often rich in oxygen. However, there is another aspect that must be considered: Oxygen is also a vital ingredient in the decomposition of dead plants, phytoplankton, and zooplankton. Too much decomposition and the water becomes oxygen depleted.

There is also an exchange of oxygen between water and air. Flowing water tends to pull oxygen with it, and if the water tumbles over rocks or cascades over a dam or spillway, it picks up oxygen in the process. At times when the oxygen content of a lake is particularly low, look for bass at these oxygen-rich points.

## STRATIFICATION

If it weren't for a complete turnover twice a year, most lakes and ponds would become stagnant because of a continued buildup of oxygen-depleted water. As water temperatures drop, water becomes heavier and more dense. Maximum density is reached when the water is 39.2° F. Colder than that, water becomes lighter. That's why ice floats on the surface. If water didn't become less dense as it freezes, the ice would settle to the bottom of northern lakes and destroy all aquatic life.

To trace the cycle: In the fall of each year, water temperatures drop and the heavier water falls to the bottom. This forces the bottom waters to the top, where they once again become reoxygenated; when this happens, the lake is said to "turn over." During this brief period, all levels of the lake have enough oxygen to support life, and bass could be scattered throughout any of the levels.

If the lake is far enough north for the water to reach 39.2° or colder, the 39.2° water will remain on the bottom and ice might coat the lake. The water in the intermediate levels will range between 39.2° and 32°.

In the spring, the process reverses itself. The ice melts, and as the surface waters warm to 39.2°, they become heavier than the water below them and sink to the bottom, once again forcing the bottom water to the top. The sun continues to warm the water and many lakes then become stratified.

On the basis of water temperature, three distinct layers form in a lake. The cold bottom layer is known as the hypolimnion. The warmer surface region is called the epilimnion, and there is a transitional zone between the two called the thermocline. By definition, water temperatures in the thermocline change 0.5° for every foot of depth. The thermocline is a relatively narrow band of water and can be found easily with a thermometer because of this rapid temperature change.

During the summer, the hypolimnion or bottom layer becomes devoid of oxygen, and therefore fish cannot penetrate this zone; that means that all the fish in the lake will be in the upper surface zone (epilimnion) or in the transitional zone (thermocline). Temperature causes this phenomenon, but oxygen is the governing factor concerning the distribution of fish.

## FEEDING FACTORS

In order to survive, a fish soon learns to measure the amount of energy it expends in relation to the rewards received. If a bass must expend more energy to catch its prey than the nourishment the prey will bring, it isn't worth the effort. That's why lunker bass often seem extremely lazy, and many knowledgeable anglers counter this trait by working a lure for only a short distance around structure.

When you cast around a stump, you realize that the bass will strike the lure close rather than chase the bait right up to the boat. There are exceptions, of course, but you can waste a lot of time fishing for the exception. A better approach is to fish the structure carefully and then retrieve rapidly for your next cast.

All predators exhibit a number of general tendencies. Two of the most important involve feeding in a school of bait. Contrary to the belief of some fishermen, a bass does not merely open its mouth and swim through baitfish in a random manner. In order to strike, a fish must isolate a specific victim and then pursue it. At the same time, a fish is more prone to select a prey that appears disabled or that looks different from the others.

These principles are particularly significant when bass are feeding on a school of baitfish; they help to explain why bass will strike a lure that lands amid the baitfish and then is retrieved out of the school. The instant the lure clears the school, it is easy for a bass to isolate it and attack; and it looks somewhat different from the other fish in the school.

Bass can be considered general predators and prefer live food or artificials that look alive. Their diet varies, but at times they will specialize for feeding efficiency. As an example, if a lake is loaded with 4-inch shad, the bass may prefer to feed on these, ignoring other foods in the process. In most situations, though, they feed on a variety of baits.

Research has shown that the mature smallmouth bass shows a decided preference for crawfish. For good reason. Smallmouths feeding on crawfish grow much faster than those that don't live where crawfish are abundant. If you're looking for good smallmouth habitat, the first clue is the number of crawfish present. Find crawfish and the smallmouth should be there. You should also recognize that crawfish normally hug the bottom, and smallmouths favoring a crawfish diet would prowl close to the bottom in search of food. To be effective, lures must be fished in this feeding zone.

## THE LIFESTYLE OF BASS

Both the largemouth and smallmouth bass spawn in the spring as the water temperature moves from cold to warm. Spawning is triggered by a number of factors and generally takes place when the water is somewhere between 60° and 70° F. At that time, the male bass will move into the shallows and fashion a nest in the bottom. Smallmouths prefer a gravel bottom, while largemouths use either gravel or sand bottoms for nests.

Largemouths nest in about 1 to 3 feet of water within 10 feet of shore, and the nests are spaced at least 20 feet apart as a rule. Smallmouths seem to be more concerned with cover and will build a nest in water ranging from 3 to almost 25 feet in depth. The exact spot is determined by water clarity, and you can assume that the clearer the water, the deeper the nest.

Once the nest is built, the male bass will seek a mate, luring or driving the female over the nest. When she has dropped eggs in the nest, the male will broadcast his milt over the eggs to fertilize them. Each female is capable of producing 2,000–7,000 eggs per pound of body weight, but all the eggs are not spawned at one time. In fact, a male usually spawns with several females, and the same female could spawn with a number of males.

When it's all over, there could be almost 2,000 eggs in a nest. The female then moves into deeper water, and the male remains to guard the nest. It takes between a week and 10 days for the eggs to hatch under normal conditions, but exceptionally warm water temperatures will speed the process. The bass fry are hatched with a yolk sac attached under their gills; the yolk sac supplies food for the first days of life.

A male on guard duty over a nest is particularly aggressive and will strike at anything that comes close to his charges. Bass during this period are very easy to catch if you can find them on the nests, but it also begs the question of how the removal of the male guard (or the female that is about to spawn) will affect the bass population in that particular body of water.

Smallmouths leave the nest before largemouths do, and the tiny fry may be only ½ inch in length when they strike out on their own.

Largemouths may be an inch long when they go it alone. In the process, however, one or both parents might turn on their offspring and attempt to consume them. At times, Papa Bass might devour 80 or even 90 percent of his brood.

Once the yolk sac is absorbed, the baby bass start to feed on live food and will move into the protective cover of the shallows. Until the bass are a couple of inches long, their main diet is composed of tiny crustacea. Then they switch to smaller fish, crawfish, and larger crustacea.

## HATCHERY BASS

If you've ever visited a trout hatchery, you were no doubt impressed with the efficiency of technique and the method used to artificially propagate the species. In fact, since trout spawning is directly related to the photo period (amount of daylight), artificial lights can be used to trigger the spawning much sooner than nature gets around to it.

Anglers who have watched biologists "strip" the eggs and milt from trout often harbor the belief that bass can be handled the same way. Bass cannot be "stripped"; they must be allowed to spawn naturally. Perhaps the best explanation of the procedure comes from the Pennsylvania Fish Commission, which tells us that brood stocks of bass must be kept in large ponds. When they build their nests and spawn, biologists must watch the nests closely. After the yolk sac is absorbed, the tiny fry will rise to the surface one time as a group and then settle back into the nest. When this happens, the fish culturist must be waiting with a fine-meshed net to scoop them up. The next time the fry rise from the nest, they disperse and are impossible to catch.

Once the fry are captured, the problems really begin. Unlike trout, which can be fed a diet of commercially available pellets, bass require live food. For the first five weeks—until they reach a length of 2 to 3 inches—the tiny bass are fed a diet of daphnia, a crustacean about the size of a pinhead.

In a hatchery, the young bass must be taught to eat a mixture of finely ground liver and saltwater fish. This is accomplished by mixing the fish meal with the daphnia and then decreasing the amount of daphnia while the fish meal increases. But eventually, the bass want live food again, and they must be fed minnows and crawfish.

You can imagine the problems of obtaining live food. Consider also that it takes much longer to raise bass to stockable size than it does trout, and that Pennsylvania can raise 97,000 pounds of trout per surface acre of raceway in a hatchery; if the same raceways are used for bass, 200 pounds per surface acre is an excellent crop.

For that reason, the few hatchery bass that are produced are earmarked for stocking in new impoundments. Besides, bass in the wild are very prolific spawners.

## THE RIDGE LAKE STUDY

In 1941, Dr. George Bennett of the Illinois Natural History Survey began a series of experiments with largemouth bass in an 18-acre impoundment. The impoundment is known as Ridge Lake and the study, which is almost legendary, is still being continued today. A total of 435 largemouth bass (335 of them yearling bass) were stocked in Ridge Lake by Dr. Bennett back in 1941. Three years later, 129 bluegills were stocked.

Fishing was permitted in Ridge Lake on a controlled basis, and a biologist checked the results of each angler. There was no charge for the boats, but all fish caught had to be kept by the angler for the survey. In addition, the water was completely drained out of the lake nine times between 1941 and 1963. Specially constructed weirs were used to capture all the fish in the lake, and the largemouths were kept in special holding pens until the lake refilled. Except for returning the bass that were in the lake at the time of a drawdown, no additional bass were ever stocked.

During the 23rd year of the study, Dr. Bennett calculated that more than 30,000 bass had been removed from Ridge Lake by angling or by scientific culling since the inception of the program. He quickly added that draining censuses confirmed that there were always between 1,500 and 6,000 largemouths in Ridge Lake. All that from the original stocking of 435 fish.

# The Confidence Game

BLACK BASS FISHING is changing. At one time, it was strictly a contemplative sport in which the angler silently rowed or paddled along the shoreline, tossing a hunk of wood, plastic, hair, or feathers toward a likely-looking pocket couched in shade or semi-darkness. In some parts of the country, bass fishing still follows this pattern almost exclusively; it's a delightful way to fish *providing* you fully understand that, when you face the shoreline, 90 percent of the fish are behind you in deeper water.

The realization that bass spend a significant portion of their lives away from the shoreline spawned a new breed of bass angler and encouraged the development of new techniques and modified tackle. This recent awareness has often been referred to as the scientific approach, particularly since it encompasses electronic aids such as depthsounders, temperature gauges, oxygen meters, and even instruments to measure the amount of turbidity in the water.

New words entered the vocabulary of every serious bass fisherman. Suddenly there was talk about structure and patterns, and bass fishing in general entered a competitive phase that replaced the contemplative aspects in many sections of the nation. Competition produces benefits. For one thing, it enables an individual to determine how he stands in comparison to other fishermen. And it provides the impetus to learn the latest approaches to bass fishing.

Equally important, competition gives birth to new techniques. There is always someone probing current methods and attempting to come up with a better approach, if for no other reason than to be a better competitor. Competition needs a vehicle where information can be exchanged and results measured. The local bass club was formed to satisfy this need, and it provides the mechanism by which sportsmen can formalize their fishing. At the same time, the formation of the national Bass Anglers Sportsman Society (BASS) did a great deal to help disseminate information on a national scale and even keep the isolated bass angler aware of the latest techniques.

Consider, also, that there is more bass water today in the United States than there was in the days of the pioneers. Most of this water has been created by man through the construction of impoundments and reservoirs. Fortunately, black bass are well suited to the maze of flood-control and water-storage projects that have pockmarked the face of our land. With more habitat and more fish, it is only logical that more people will accept the challenge of our greatest game-fish—the black bass.

## THE BEST BASS LURE

Confidence in your ability to locate bass and catch them is by far the greatest lure you have in your tacklebox. You must have complete confidence in what you are doing and the lure you are using. It's a mental attitude, to be sure, but it can make all the difference in the world in catching or not catching fish.

Unfortunately, the majority of bass fishermen pay only lip service to this vital ingredient. Yet if you were given the opportunity to chat with the top tournament bass fishermen, you would quickly realize that every one of them exudes confidence in his approach to the sport. The fact that one man might swear by spinnerbaits while another favors the plastic worm doesn't detract from this confidence. Neither does it matter whether the angler chooses to fish submerged treetops or search for a creek saddle. Each believes honestly that what he is doing will produce bass for him.

To be successful at bass fishing, you have to work at it. There are no miracle methods, no secret lures, and no shortcuts to the thrill of a strike. That's why your attitude must always be positive. You must believe that the next move you make will be the correct one. It's not easy to have confidence all the time, because you can't really fool yourself into thinking you have it. Instead, it is vital that you work at developing the mental attitude that is so important. The ultimate is never to get discouraged and to continue to believe that your approach is the best one for you.

If you fail on a given day, review the procedures you used and the places you fished. Go through a mental exercise and profit from your experience. Tell yourself that next time will be different. Above all, never lose sight of the fact that the reason you love bass fishing is that your quarry is so unpredictable. There will be times when you can't get the lure in the water fast enough and other times when you can't buy a strike regardless of what you do. If bass fishing were routine, you would soon tire of it.

At the end of the day—whether you were successful or not—it's a good idea to check with local guides and marina operators to find out what other anglers did that day. This comparison can add immeasurably to your knowledge. Perhaps you'll learn that no one else caught any fish or that someone mohawked bass on a particular lure or at a specific depth. File the information away in your computer or keep a log and make a note of it. You'll find it could provide the answer on another day when conditions seem similar.

Confidence also extends to the lure you are using. To fish a lure efficiently and effectively, you must first believe in your own mind that the lure you are fishing is the right one. Obviously, if you don't have faith in your lure, your casts are going to be less than accurate and your retrieves mechanical. Chances are that you'll change lures quickly and continue to change.

You gain confidence through experience and understanding. It starts with a comprehension of the habits and habitat of your quarry, which in turn dictates how and where you should fish and the tackle you should use. This book has been tailored to help you learn more about bass fishing and to instill in you the confidence that is so crucial. In many instances you'll discover that your approach is the preferred one, and we hope there will be other suggestions that will lead you to explore bass hideouts and techniques that you haven't tried before.

## Casting Accuracy

Every competent bass fisherman we've ever had the pleasure of meeting and observing on the water proved to be an extremely accurate caster. He could place a lure exactly where he wanted it time after time. And he exhibited superb familiarity with the tackle he was using, whether it was spinning or bait-casting gear, or a fly rod.

You'll discover that the ability to drop a bait on a precise spot will mean more fish on a consistent basis. Nothing destroys confidence faster than the frustrating tendency to hang a lure in the bushes or let it fall in a brush pile instead of alongside the brush. By the time you retrieve your lure, you might as well look for another spot.

Casting is a learned routine, and anyone can perfect his accuracy. All it takes is practice and more practice. The best time to improve your accuracy is when you are on dry land. If you wait until you're fishing, you'll end up wasting precious time. Simply set aside a few minutes each day and practice in the backyard or at a nearby park. Always select a target whenever you cast and try to put the lure on the mark.

## How Long Should You Fish Each Spot?

Beginning bass fishermen seem to be plagued by the question of how long they should work each location. In time, the answer becomes very apparent, but since the question does harbor importance for many anglers, let's tackle it right away. Again, confidence is the key. The moment you have lost confidence in the location, it's time to move on—or at least try to regain the confidence. Otherwise, you'll be going through the motions, but you won't have the concentration and thought behind your technique.

Normally, you should fish a spot until you have worked it thoroughly at all depths with an assortment of good lures in several colors, using variations in your retrieve. That might mean a few casts or it could dictate a couple of hours. Remember that even the correct lure fished at an incorrect depth or with the wrong retrieve might mean that you are doing nothing more than enjoying the great outdoors.

We're not trying to sidestep this question, but are simply pointing out the many variables in the answer. As an example, if you fish a particular spot regularly, you soon gain a feel for exactly where the fish should be, the lure to use, the type of retrieve, and even the direction of the retrieve. In that type of situation, you would probably have a pretty good idea whether fish were there or not on a given day. You wouldn't be probing, because experience has given you a great deal of information about that single spot. Under those circumstances, a spray of fan casts could tell the story.

Picture yourself, however, on an unfamiliar lake working a similar location. You have some thoughts on where the fish should be, but you'll have to work longer to determine if they are there or not. And you must also consider the degree of confidence and experience you have acquired. The veteran angler can cover an area somewhat more quickly than the neophyte and know that he has done the job thoroughly.

## Being Observant

Your degree of alertness and powers of observation are excellent indicators of the amount of concentration and confidence you have at the moment. If you persist in worrying about what happened at the office, at home, or somewhere else, you might as well put the boat back on the trailer and pick another day to fish. Bass fishing requires complete concentration.

When we discuss the establishment of a pattern, you'll see how important observation can be; but even in general bass fishing the ability to know what is taking place around you can tip the scales toward success. Bass fishing is often opportunity fishing. You must recognize a set of circumstances and then take advantage of them.

A good angler hears as well as sees, and his mind registers the impressions. If, for example, a bass slaps a baitfish on the surface behind you, your ears should convey the message, even though you are concentrating on casting to a target. The trick is to train your senses to accept the commonplace in nature and seek out the unusual. Let's carry the question of sound a step farther. Perhaps shad are frolicking on the surface. Your ears register and accept this sound as normal. But a deeper splash that signals a predator feeding on a minnow should attract immediate attention.

Top-ranking bass fishermen are forever able to recall the circumstances surrounding the catching of bass after bass. They seem to remember water depth, type of lure, speed of retrieve, and a host of other variables. They have total recall of these facts even years later. If we can interpret this uncanny ability, it boils down to concentration and observation. Nothing they do is haphazard. Each piece of the puzzle fits into place in their minds. When you train yourself to concentrate as thoroughly as they do, you're well on your way to becoming a top bass angler.

# Establishing a Pattern

BASS, LIKE ALL other animals, are creatures of habit and exhibit a lifestyle tailored to optimize food, protection, and comfort. The name of the game is survival and both the largemouth and the smallmouth play it well. Although there are exceptions to every generality, for purposes of discussion we can conclude that the majority of the bass in a given lake will be doing relatively the same thing at the same time.

*Pattern* is a word used to describe what a proportion of the bass are doing at a specific instant in time or what stimulus these fish might respond to. We can also define pattern as the type of place beneath the surface that a great many bass are using at the same time. To fully understand the concept, you must recognize that there could be several patterns in effect at the same time. Not all bass will be following the same one, but for you to be effective, you need only uncover a single pattern.

A pattern is often dictated by food supply, oxygen content, water temperature, time of day, and even time of year. The key to successful bass fishing is the ability to locate a pattern quickly and then stick to it until it fails to produce fish. Patterns take many forms and can even be said to include the type of lure and the speed of retrieve.

Let's concentrate most of our efforts on the *type* and *depth* patterns.

## TYPE PATTERN

The need to be alert and observant is the single key to finding pattern. The typical fisherman is so busy fishing that he often overlooks the signs of a pattern. He may be on the best pattern the lake has to offer, yet fail to recognize it as such. Top bass fishermen will amaze you with their ability to tell exactly what they did when they hooked a bass. They have an idea of the type of terrain, speed of retrieve, depth position of the lure, and a host of other factors. This ability is learned and developed, and we suggest that you work at honing your own powers of observation toward this goal.

Let's assume the average fisherman is casting a shoreline and suddenly hooks a bass. He continues working the shoreline and a little farther down hooks another bass. The tendency is simply to assume that he happened on a spot or two that held a bass. What he may very well have overlooked was that his first 50 casts were made at the bases of cypress trees and the 51st cast, which took the bass, happened to land alongside a willow tree. If the angler noted this mentally, then he would have become excited when the second bass struck, because that was also at the base of a willow tree.

Knowing this, our angler could then concentrate his energies on skimming the shoreline and looking for willow trees. There is every indication that a willow tree in the same depth of water would hold a bass.

We had a similar experience one day while fishing Sam Rayburn Reservoir in eastern Texas. The fish were in 17 to 20 feet of water, and every time we spotted an ironwood bush and the depth was right you could bet your rod and reel that a fish would hit. That's pattern fishing.

The more you fish a particular lake, the more you know about it and the easier it is to find a pattern. You also have the advantage of knowing similar spots the moment you do find a pattern. The reason for searching for a pattern is that fishing time is short; to maximize the utilization of the limited time all of us have, it makes sense to catch fish, and finding the pattern is the easiest way.

In searching for a type pattern, you must be alert to types of bottom. A bank may run from mud to rock to gravel. You catch a bass at the spot where rock turns to gravel; you continue moving down the bank and it happens again where rock turns to gravel. That's your pattern, and you immediately concentrate on those spots where rock turns to gravel. Bypass the other types of shoreline and jump from place to place that meets these conditions.

## DEPTH PATTERN

You can almost determine the skill of a bass fisherman by the second question he asks you. If you pass someone on a lake, he might ask how fishing is. You reply by showing him a couple of lunkers or by telling him you managed to fool a couple of bass. The most important question he can ask you is to tell him the depth at which you caught your fish.

Beginners have a tendency to begin a line of questioning about what lure you were using, how fast you worked it, or even where you caught the fish. But a knowledgeable bass master need only know the depth at which the fish were taken and he can put every piece of the puzzle together.

The single most important factor in bass fishing is finding the right depth. If you are not fishing the right depth, you're wasting your time. The best fisherman can fish the best lure in the world, but if he's fishing the wrong depth, he won't catch fish. At the right depth, almost anyone can catch fish.

We were fishing a lake in Florida that has any type of vegetation you could ask for. After spending a great deal of time fishing various places without enjoying a single strike, we pulled into a spot that had a small patch of lily pads about 20 feet square. After tossing a worm, spoon, and spinnerbait without a hit, we were about to seek greener pastures when we noticed three small lily pads isolated from the others. Each pad was about 6 inches in diameter. Easing over with the electric motor, we made a cast, let the worm sink into the grass, and started the retrieve. As the worm passed the clump of three lily pads, a bass picked up the worm and we set the hook. It wasn't a big bass, but on a fishless day, anything is greatly appreciated.

After landing that bass, a few more casts proved that it was a lone fish, so we eased over to the pads and found that the water was 2½ to 3 feet deep. Visions of a pattern raced through our heads as we began to search for isolated clumps of lily pads. The next bunch of pads didn't produce fish, and when we measured the water depth we found it was 1½ to 2 feet. We then edged the boat into slightly deeper water and discovered that when we found a few lily pads in 3 feet of water, we took a bass. If the pads were in 2 feet of water, they would be fishless. These weren't trophy bass, but they did provide plenty of action.

## FINDING THE RIGHT DEPTH

The better you know a lake, the easier it is to determine the correct depth on a given day. You already know a number of spots, and chances are that at least one of them will produce a fish or two, thus giving you depth information. There really isn't an easy way to find the right depth, but there are a few tips that might shorten the time.

Before you crank the engine on your boat, you should have been talking to the boat dock operator, any of the local fishing guides around, and even anglers who have just come back to the dock. Remember that right after you ask them how the fishing has been, inquire about the depth. They can give you some vital information.

Depth, of course, is directly related to temperature, and bass have a preferred comfort zone even though they are not always within that zone. Experience has shown that bass often hang out near the bottom in temperatures between 65° F and 75° F. It's easy enough to run the boat into deep water, drop a thermometer over the side, and read the depths at which this temperature range occurs. Then look for bottom structure within that preferred depth zone. Work different areas within that depth until you catch a fish. Note the depth and the type of place, so you can begin to establish a pattern.

We cannot overemphasize the importance of being observant. If you have difficulty in remembering, a notebook will solve that problem. Write it down and then keep the information in your tacklebox so you can refer to it constantly.

## Long, Sloping Points

Veteran bass anglers have discovered that if they must find the pattern depth quickly, long, sloping points extending out into the lake are the answer. They can work from the shallow beginning of the point, moving deeper and deeper until they find a fish. Usually, the better points for this type of exploring taper gradually rather than drop off abruptly.

To be productive, these points should have deep water on both sides, and if a submerged creek channel swings close by, so much the better. A narrow point extending into the lake is better than a very wide point, because you can cover it in fewer casts and the fish will be more concentrated if they are somewhere along that point.

Bass, and especially lunkers, demand plenty of deep water nearby. A point that meets this requirement should be a feeding station, and if bass are on it, you should find them. A creek channel adds spice to the terrain, but it is not really necessary (see illustration 1 on page 248). Work the point carefully, fanning your casts until you cover both sides. Then move down about a half cast and repeat the procedure.

Most of these points are really part of the secondary bank of the lake and may slope on one side and drop off abruptly on the other (see illustration 2). If these underwater points have brush or other cover close by, they will be even better.

During the spring and fall, one of the best places for big bass on a lake at home looks like illustration 3. Ninety percent of the time, the bass are taken along the three points with deep water on both sides. They are actually tiny peninsulas extending into the deeper water. Without a depthsounder, you would be hard pressed to locate these points.

In the spring, as water temperatures begin to warm, most of the fish hug the upper point where the water drops from 12 to 20 feet. During the fall, the other two points are usually more productive.

## Casting a Point

The normal tendency when fishing a point is to start shallow and continue working into deeper and deeper water. This method is generally productive, but you should be aware of other ways to fish the same area. Instead of starting along the shallow base of the point and fishing deeper, you may want to start in deep water and make your casts into shallower and shallower water.

It goes without saying that if you want to keep your lure along the bottom, it is much easier to fish from the shallows to the deep. But fish won't always hit a lure in that direction. That's why you want to vary your approach. If you don't take a fish from shallow to deep, reverse the procedure and fish from deep to shallow.

A third way of fishing the same area is to keep the boat parallel to the drop-off and use a series of fan casts to move the lure right along the drop-off. By paralleling, you can work the lure up the slope for a short distance or drag it down the slope, depending on your angle of cast.

The important consideration is the realization that lure direction is another variable that should be considered in determining pattern. On some days the fish will clobber a bait from shallow to deep and other days from deep to shallow. Try all approaches before you convince yourself that it's time to move to another point.

## The Countdown Method

It's one thing to be over the right depth of water and quite another to have your lure at the right depth. If you were to talk to a top-rated bass angler right after he made a cast, chances are that he wouldn't hear you or at least wouldn't take the time to give you an answer. The reason is that he's too busy counting.

Unless you are using a lure that floats on the surface, the trick is

**I. An ideal secondary point**

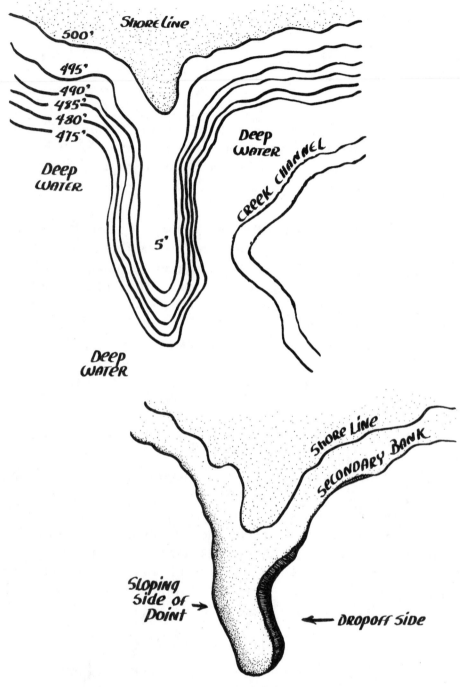

**2. A long, sloping underwater point**

to count as the lure sinks so that you have a reference point for depth. Each angler has his own counting method, which could be a rhythm such as "1 a-n-d 2 a-n-d 3 . . ." or "1,000 and 1, 1,000 and 2,

### 3. Typical lunker bass locations

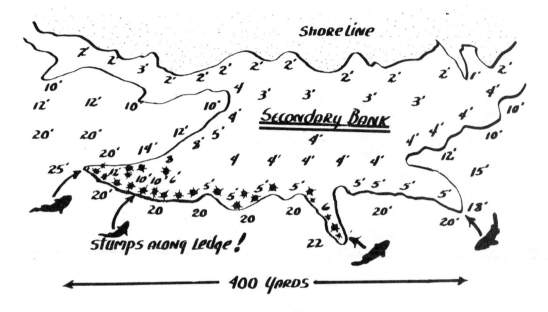

Shore Line

Secondary Bank

Stumps along Ledge !

◀—— 100 Yards ——▶

1,000 and 3 . . ." What you say to yourself is unimportant as long as you can approximate seconds of time.

The countdown method lets you know the depth of your lure at a given instant in time. You cannot fish scientifically without using the countdown method—it's that important. As an example, you could be working a sloping point and would have no way of knowing where your lure was unless you counted. Your cast may have been a shade too far and you could have dropped the lure over the edge of the drop-off. By counting down, you can tell this instantly. Perhaps there's a sudden drop-off that you didn't know existed. The countdown method will tell you that your lure is still falling even though it should have hit bottom. The corollary is also vital. A lure that stops too soon might have hit a ledge, but a better alternative is that a bass grabbed it as the lure was falling.

It's all part of the total picture you must maintain at all times. You must be mentally oriented by remembering the configuration shown on a contour map and orienting it through a depthsounder to the water below you. As the boat drifts or turns, the countdown method will tell you if you are casting the area you should be. After all, it looks so nice and neat in diagrams or on a topo map, but on the water you just don't have the reference points.

Above all, the countdown method helps you to concentrate and keeps you alert. Instead of permitting your mind to wander and perhaps miss an important concept, it forces you to count and think about what you are doing.

## WATER CLARITY

Even before you begin fishing a particular lake, you can gain some clues about preferred depth for bass. As a general rule, the clearer the lake, the deeper the fish will be. Of course, if the lake has a thermocline in the summer, the fish will not be below this depth, because there is no oxygen below it.

In dingy or muddy water, the fish will be much shallower, even on a bright sunny day. If the water is particularly muddy, the bass may be within 15 feet of the surface, since a muddy lake might not have any appreciable visibility below that level. Bass would find it difficult to feed below this minimal light level. Without cover, bass in lakes such as Ouachita, Bull Shoals, and Table Rock—all clear lakes— would be relatively deep. In muddy lakes such as the flat southern lakes, 15 feet might be a working bottom limit.

If you can see a white lure down to a depth of 3 feet under water, the bass in that lake are probably no deeper than 15 feet. But if you can see a white lure down to 12 feet, the bass could be as deep as 30 feet or more.

## THE DEEP, CLEAR LAKE MYSTIQUE

Even some of the best bass fishermen go to pieces if they are forced to fish a deep, clear lake. Thermoclines and other fishing limitations to the contrary, these anglers are overwhelmed by the mere thought that a lake might be 200 feet deep out in the center and plummet to 60 or 80 feet near some shorelines. They have visions of fish being at any depth and roaming all over the lake vertically and horizontally.

If you are faced with this situation, think through the problem. You'll soon realize that most of the fish in the deep lake will be between the surface and 35 feet or perhaps 40 feet. It's really no different than fishing a lake that is only 40 feet deep. Of course, because the lake is clear you could assume that the fish would be a little deeper than if they were in dingy water, but you're not going to fish very effectively below 40 feet, so concentrate between 15 and 35 feet and you should find all the fish you need.

Should a deep lake still prove troublesome, try to relate to a favorite lake back home. Scout the terrain until you find something that resembles a home-lake hot spot. Then start fishing it. Chances are you'll begin to catch fish.

## Contour Maps

Contour or topographic maps have become as useful to the modern bass fisherman as treasure maps were to the pirates of the 18th century. Without these magical guides, locating pay dirt can be a difficult task.

Recognize, however, that *not all* topographic maps contain depth information, and this is particularly true of natural lakes. If you plan to fish a man-made impoundment, the oldest map available might be the best one because it shows the area before it was flooded. Sometimes the newest map will do the job for you. The point to remember is that there are differences in topographic maps, and not all of them have the necessary contour information for fishermen.

When you receive your topographic map of the area you want to fish, you may discover that the reservoir or impoundment is not shown. The map may have been drafted before the reservoir was built, and this is precisely what makes it so valuable. Your first job is to outline the reservoir. Anyone who has fished impoundments knows that the water level varies with the season of the year and the amount of rain in the area or throughout the drainage basin. Water level is known as pool stage or pool elevation, and it can also be adjusted by opening or closing the floodgates on the dam.

Your initial interest is in normal pool elevation—the amount of water the reservoir was designed to hold. This is always expressed in feet above sea level. It is usually noted on the topographic map, but you can either ask the Geological Survey to note it for you or check with the Corps of Engineers for the information.

A contour map is a maze of lines connecting areas of the same elevation. There are different-scale maps, and the one you want is the map with the smallest intervals between contour lines. Standard intervals are 5 feet, 10 feet, and 20 feet of elevation. Five-foot intervals show much more detail for the fisherman than 10- or 20-foot intervals.

For purposes of illustration, let's assume that the normal pool elevation is 500 feet above sea level. Take a felt-tip marker and trace the 500-foot elevation lines wherever they appear on the map. This will be the normal shoreline of the impoundment. A transparent marker can then be used to color in the area of the impoundment.

If you are using a map with 5-foot intervals, you know that each succeeding line inside the reservoir represents 5 feet of depth (see illustration 4 on page 254). By subtracting the elevation shown on a

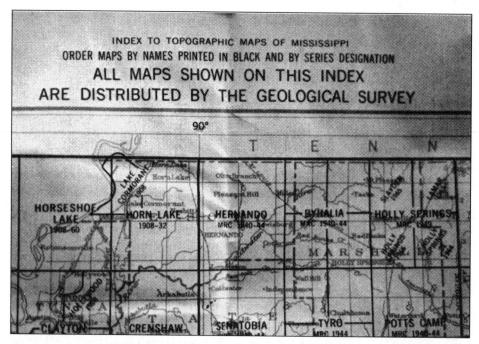

To order topographic maps you must first obtain an index and then request maps by name and series designated. If you are not certain which maps to order, write for a free index to: USGS Information Center, Box 25286, Denver, CO 80225.

specific contour line from the pool elevation of 500 feet (in this case), you can also arrive at the depth of any area.

Since most bass fishing is done from the shoreline to depths of 35 or 40 feet, you can see the need for 5-foot intervals on a map. When these interval lines are very close together, you can tell at a glance that there is a rapid drop-off. The tighter the lines, the sharper the drop-off.

To compensate for winter and spring rains, some lakes are drawn down from a high pool to a low pool. Pool elevation may be 500 feet in June and only 480 feet in September. In determining depth, you simply subtract elevations from the new pool stage. Most local newspapers provide daily lake readings so that you know the exact pool stage.

Underwater real estate is seldom flat and level. Usually, there are humps and rises that reach toward the surface, and many of these are good places to fish, especially when there is deep water nearby. The current depth of any rise in the bottom can be determined by subtracting that elevation from the height of the pool stage (see illustration 5); and the closeness of interval lines will tell you if it slopes upward or rises sharply.

## Triangulation

Once you begin studying your contour map, you'll quickly become convinced that it can be the best fishing partner you ever had. Recognize that it will take practice to read it effectively and that you will need a little experience to relate the map to the actual physical terrain. Everything on a map can appear neat and clean, yet when you're on the water, you have to orient the map to the landscape and your depthsounder.

The technique of triangulation will help you to locate spots that are out in the middle of the lake and not on the shoreline. Remember that 90 percent of the fish are usually in deeper water around some type of underwater structure. Your job is to find these places, and once you do, you want to be able to return to them easily. That's where triangulation comes in.

You can triangulate without the use of any sighting devices, but it is often much easier if you carry a small sighting compass with you. These are available at most outdoor stores and fit neatly in your tacklebox. You should always carry a compass on the water anyway, in addition to the one on your boat, and a sighting compass will serve both purposes.

If you use a sighting compass to triangulate, position the boat over the spot and select a prominent object on shore. It could be a tree, a house, a notch in a bluff, or any one of a thousand things. Chances are it appears on your contour map. If it doesn't, mark it in. Use your sighting compass to take the compass bearing of this object. In nautical terms, this gives you a line of bearing. Let's assume you picked a smokestack that was due east or 090° on the compass.

Now you must select a second object at approximately right angles to the first. You pick a water tower that is almost due south or 178°. Mark the object and its bearing on the chart. To find this exact spot again, you run on one of the lines of bearing. That is, you would start with the smokestack bearing 090° (due east) and run directly toward it on this bearing. Keep checking the cross bearing until the water tower is exactly 178°. You are now directly over the spot.

In selecting objects, make sure that they will look the same at all seasons of the year. Too often, an angler will select a tree that has unique foliage and then discover that in the late fall when the leaves are on the ground, he can't find his marker. (Speaking of markers, if you leave a buoy over the spot it might get moved or serve as an invitation to others to concentrate on this spot.)

**4. Pool elevation**

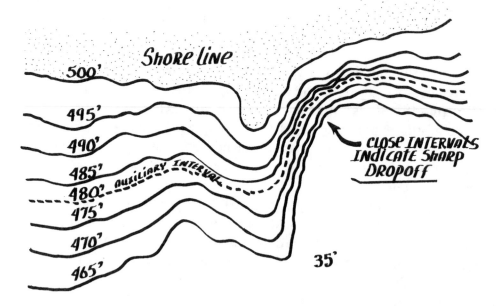

**5. The depth of humps**

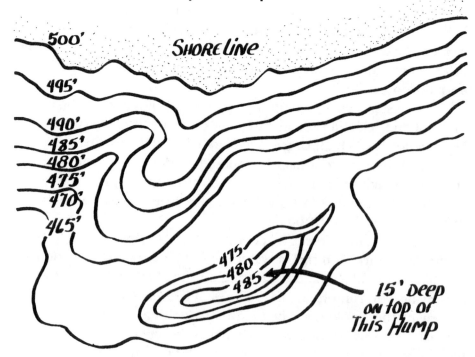

If there are enough prominent features around a lake or features that you can distinguish easily, you can use another method of triangulation. Instead of a compass, you can use a range to locate a line of bearing. A *range* is the nautical term to describe two objects on shore in direct line with each other. If you were to select a prominent tree

## 6. Triangulation

on the shoreline and line this up with a shoreline rock in front of the tree, you would create a range. Establish a second range at approximately right angles to the first—a dock with a cabin, for example—and you have triangulated your fishing spot.

To return to the spot, you simply run one of the ranges and keep checking until the second range forms. As an example, line up the rock with the prominent tree and run directly toward it. When the other two objects you have selected at right angles are in line, you're over the spot you want to fish.

In the course of time, you'll locate a multitude of places in a particular lake and you'll soon start to forget some of them unless you use a system for remembering. The best system we have found is to give each spot a name. Select a name that is seemingly ridiculous, but easy to remember. You might call it Lunker Haven, Honey Hole, Animal Farm, Jewelry Store, or any other name that comes to mind. You can also record the name in your notebook. It will probably come in handy when you're trying to figure out where to fish next someday in the future.

CHAPTER 4

# Locating Structure

IT IS IMPOSSIBLE to tell when the first bass fisherman turned his back on the shoreline and decided that most bass spend the major part of their adult lives in deeper water. Possibly the early beginnings of fishing for bass in deeper water happened more by accident than by design.

Structure fishing is the modern bass angler's cornerstone of success. With the ability to locate structure comes a working knowledge of the black bass, its habits, and its habitat. Consider that many of the large reservoirs across our country offer hundreds of miles of shoreline and thousands of acres of open water. That's a lot different from the tiny farm pond or tank out behind the barn where you can cast the shoreline a couple of times each evening, covering every foot of it.

If you're going to find fish on big water, you have to know where they are most likely to appear and then concentrate your efforts on only those spots that offer the greatest promise. You won't be right every time you launch your boat, but the law of averages is tipped heavily in your favor.

## WHAT IS STRUCTURE?

Consider structure to be the floor of the lake extending from the shallows to the deeper water. More precisely, it is unusual or irregular features on the lake bottom that are different from the surrounding bottom areas. A stump tipped on its side in a foot or two of water along the shoreline would be structure, and a creek bed meandering along the bottom of the lake at a depth of 25 feet is also structure.

Structure comes in all sizes and shapes. It can be straight or crooked, contain dents and depressions, or be flat. Some structure is long while other is short. Some is steep, sloping, barren, brushy, grassy, stumpy, rocky, mossy, or stepped. It can be shallow or deep—on the shoreline or offshore in open water.

One of the best ways to grasp the concept of structure is to use your imagination when you're driving along a highway. Look at the surrounding countryside and picture what it would look like if the entire area were suddenly inundated with water. Start trying to pick the places where bass would be most likely to hang out. You might start with the drainage ditch alongside the road you're driving on and around the culvert you just crossed.

As you go through these mental gyrations, you will start to associate stands of trees along the field perimeters as a specific type of structure. Some fields will slope and others will be flat, perhaps with a drop-off on one side. The idea is to be able to visualize what your favorite lake might look like if the water were suddenly drawn down. Most anglers find it difficult to picture the physical features of a lake bottom once it is covered with water. You know that there's a roadbed or ditch down below the surface, but unless you train yourself, you don't always visualize it when you are fishing.

A map and depthsounder can help you to gain the necessary mental picture, but if you also associate features with those you can see above the ground, it becomes a lot easier. Then, the next time you fish a creek bed shouldering into a point, you might be able to compare it with one you've seen on the way to the lake.

## THE GOLDEN RULE

For any type of structure to be productive, it must have immediate access to deeper water. This rule applies regardless of whether the structure sticks up out of 3 feet of water near the shoreline or happens to be a stand of trees in 35 feet of water in the center of the lake.

Bass consider the quick passage to deep water an escape route from predators or any type of danger. Call it instinct or habit, but bass won't wander very far from that escape route. Like submarines, the bass want the option of crash diving when they feel it necessary.

The same largemouths and smallmouths need a route to travel from their home in deep water to shallower areas for feeding. We believe that creek or river channels moving under a lake are in reality highways for bass, and that bass move up and down the creek channels just as a car moves along a road. There are other routes, to be sure, but creek channels are one of the best.

Another theory says that bass don't simply swim from deep water to shallow water without pausing along the way. Usually the fish will hesitate at natural breaks, which might be the edge of the drop-off or some kind of object at that junction. Some anglers believe that they may rest in these areas for periods of from a few minutes to a few hours. At any rate, keep in mind that not all bass move into the shallows at the same time, so there are always some fish along the deeper structure.

## A BUOY SYSTEM

Someone once said that a picture is worth a thousand words, but when you're trying to imagine what underwater structure looks like, a picture may be worth ten thousand words. The only way to capture the picture is to drop marker buoys in a pattern designed to trace out the structure. It's going to take a little time to do it right and it may require a dozen marker buoys or more, but it also could lead to the largest stringer of bass you've ever taken.

We believe it is worth the extra effort to catch fish. When you have planned and plotted your search for bass and are successful, it is the greatest feeling in the world. There's nothing comparable with finding something you cannot see.

It almost goes without saying that you must carry a good supply of buoys aboard your boat. We prefer to carry ours in two distinct colors so that we can mark either side of a channel or deep and shallow water. You can fashion your own buoys in a variety of ways. A piece of Styrofoam with some line wrapped around it and a weight works fine. Buoys are also available commercially and can be purchased individually or in kits of a half dozen or more.

Dropping buoys is pretty much a matter of common sense. Your goal is to outline the structure so that you can find the exact location of a drop-off or follow a curve or bend in a creek channel. In buoying a drop-off (illustration 7), you must work the boat back and forth, using your depthsounder to select each point where water depth begins to drop. Note that we would start in one corner and follow an in-and-out path (dotted line), tracing the entire point. If you find that one area has a particularly sharp drop-off or some irregular feature, you can use a different-colored buoy to mark it.

Once you have finished dropping the buoys, the underwater picture begins to come into focus. The best approach is to take out your

### 7. Buoying a drop-off

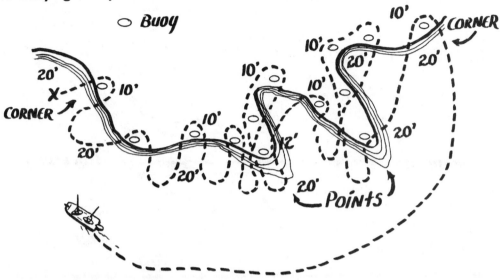

### 8. Dropping buoys along a creek channel

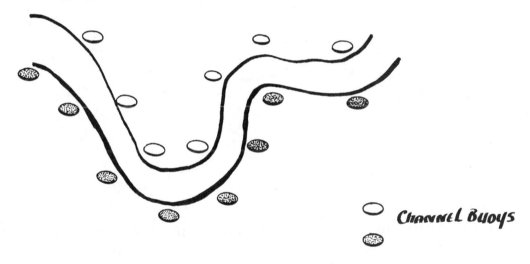

Channel Buoys

notebook and sketch the outline of the structure, using reference points where possible to orient it.

After you have recorded your find, you're ready to fish it, and you'll discover that the buoy system will guide each cast and help you to cover the area thoroughly. When you have fished the spot completely, ease through it again and retrieve your buoys.

When you are marking a creek channel, use two separate colors to denote each side of the creek, and follow the bends in the creek carefully. If you drop buoys at closer intervals, you'll trace a better outline. As you become more experienced, you won't need as many buoys to tell you how the creek meanders (illustration 8).

**9. Marking a ridge**

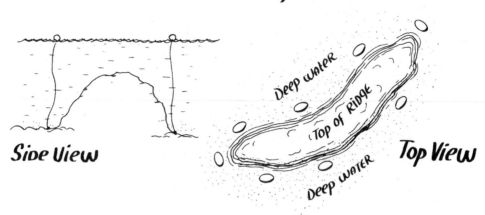

**10. Marking a hump**

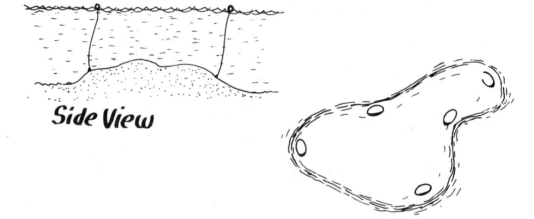

An underwater ridge can be fished by sitting over deeper water and casting into it or by sitting over the ridge and working your lure from deep to shallow. A third option is to sit off one of the points and cast parallel to it. No matter how you plan to fish it, your buoys should mark both ends of the ridge and both sides (illustration 9).

A hump or sheepback should be buoyed on all sides (illustration 10), and the number of buoys again depends on the area involved. Don't skimp when you drop buoys. It's better to use an extra one or two than to become confused on the structure shape. The side of the hump closest to deeper water will be the best, and you might want to mark this with buoys of a different color.

Don't fall into the trap of laziness. It's easy to convince yourself that you don't have to mark out a new spot before fishing it, but you must also accept the risk of not fishing it properly.

## CREEK BED POINTS

If you were to limit an experienced structure fisherman to one type of underwater terrain, his first choice would undoubtedly be a creek channel. Channels wind their way across and around the lake floor in every man-made reservoir or impoundment, and they are present in a number of natural lakes. As we mentioned earlier, bass use these creek channels as highways, and there are times when they will use the channels for shade and cover.

Anytime a creek channel runs in close to the bank or a point, it has to be a good place for bass. You may not always find the bass in residence, but sooner or later they should be there. These creek bed points, however, are always worthy of your attention, and if you're going to fish points, pick the ones where a creek is nearby.

In illustration 11 (see page 262), we show a typical shoreline that might occur in any type of lake—lowland, midland, or highland. This classification is primarily based on elevation, and each type of lake exhibits certain typical characteristics. Highland lakes are in hilly country and are usually deep and clear. Lowland lakes are shallow, flat lakes at low elevations that have a minimum of structure because the surrounding terrain is relatively flat. Midland lakes are found at intermediate elevations and exhibit characteristics of the other two.

All three points in the illustration (#1, #2, and #3) look as if they would hold fish, and they very well might, but Point #2 would obviously be the most productive. The reason is that #2 is a creek bed point—that is, the creek coming out of the cove moves right alongside this point of land.

Throughout this book we will continually try to make you aware of the fact that you have only a limited amount of time to fish, and that time should be spent on places offering the greatest potential. We'll suggest you pass up other places that might look good in favor of those that experience demonstrates to be the best. Here is a typical example:

The creek bed point is an excellent place to find and catch bass. Let's assume you have located a school of largemouths at daybreak one morning on the inside cove end of Point #2 (marked Spot A). It's a great beginning and you pick up a few fish, or perhaps you take your limit right there.

The next morning you can't wait for the alarm clock to ring; you rush through breakfast and hurry right back to Spot A. You're using the same lure and technique you employed yesterday, but this morn-

## 11. Creek bed point

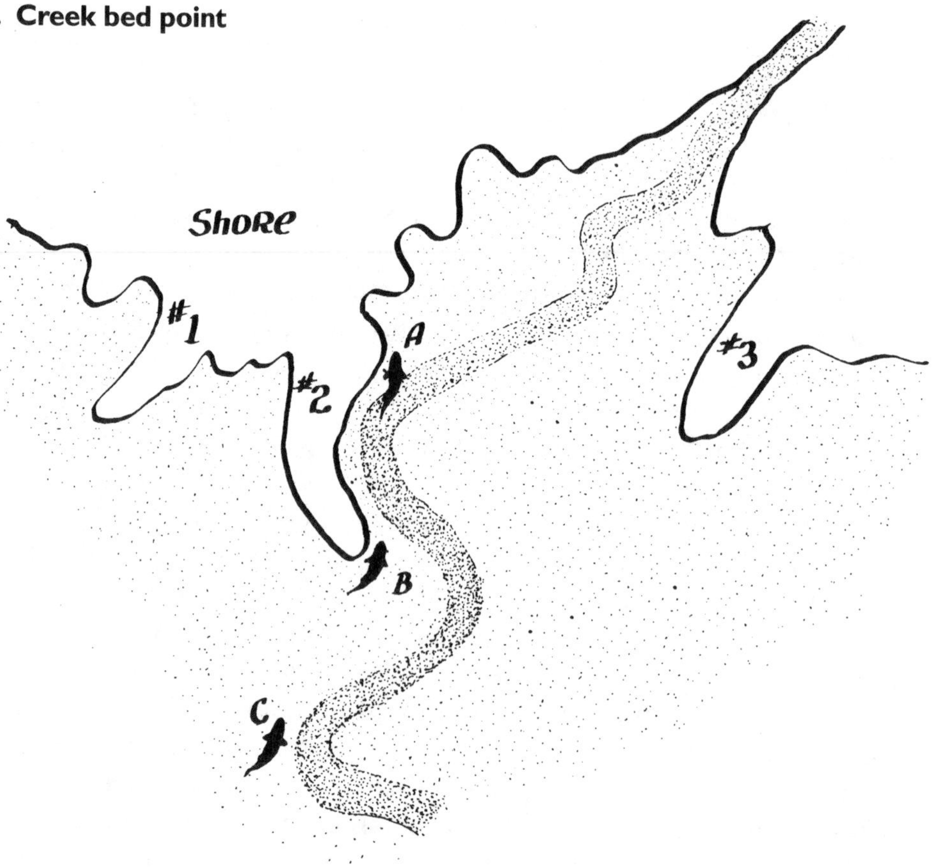

Shore

#1

#2

A

B

C

#3

ing you draw a blank. That's when you start analyzing the situation. There could be several reasons, and it's your job to find the right one.

Your first two impressions would be that the fish either have moved or for some unknown reason aren't hitting. These mental exercises may pacify the mind, but they are not going to catch fish for you until you begin to experiment. The bass may not prefer yesterday's lure, so you had better get busy trying a variety of other offerings. Possibly it's the retrieve that is bothering them. Yesterday they wanted the lure slow, but today they want it fast or they want it with a stop-and-start motion. Maybe they are a little deeper than yesterday, so you try that, too.

When you have gone through the routine and still haven't produced results, you must assume that the fish aren't there. That's a far better option than throwing in the sponge and convincing yourself that they are there but won't hit. This is where a good contour map pays dividends. If you know the area well, your options are apparent.

You then assume that the fish have moved from Spot A to Spot B (illustration 11). They could very easily be at Spot B hitting exactly the way they were yesterday on the same lure and same retrieve. If that doesn't work, you go through the routine a second time before you conclude that they may not have moved into the point but are hanging around the creek bend at Spot C. By knowing an area, you always stand a much better chance of catching fish.

It is equally important to remember that the bass might not be feeding, but remain schooled at Spot C because the water temperature is more to their liking or they just decide they don't want to move into shallower water to feed. There's no reason you can't catch fish at Spot C if they are there, even though the water is much deeper.

Another way to think about this hypothetical case is to consider that you caught fish early in the morning at Spot A or B. The fish were along the drop-off, but suddenly the action stopped. That's when you might want to give Spot C a try. The fish could have moved down the creek channel and right back to the U bend in the creek.

On other days, they may not be at Spot A or B at all, but you know that when they do move into shallower water, the odds are that they'll follow their own underwater highway down the creek channel.

Finally, if you find fish at a certain depth in Spot A, B, or C, you can assume that fish will also be in similar places around the lake. Check your contour map, select similar spots, and give them a thorough workout.

## CREEK CHANNEL POINTS IN COVES

You already know that creek channel points are among the best places to fish, and you know that coves can also be productive. Take a close look at illustration 12 (see page 264) and study it for a few moments. The first thing you should notice on this drawing of a typical cove in a lowland- or midland-type lake is that this particular cove has six points in it. The cove also has a creek that starts back in the right-hand corner and works its way out of the cove and into the main lake.

Again, it is possible that the fish could be at any one of the points, but we're going to play the odds to maximize our fishing. That means that only those points with a creek channel nearby or that have a strong drop-off into deep water should be fished. These are always the best bets.

By looking at the drawing, you should have determined that Points #2 and #4 should be the best, because the creek channel moves right by them. That's why they are known as creek channel points. Our goal is to fish the most productive waters during the day, so, to save time, we will fish Point #2 and Point #4 only. Then we'll move on to another cove with creek channels and fish those points.

## 12. Cove points

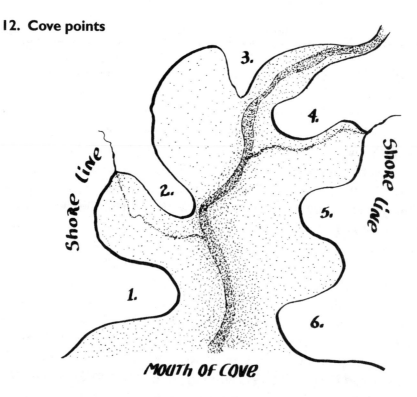

It has been our experience that we would be wasting valuable time to spend any longer in the cove unless we found some outstanding feature. This could be an underwater spring, a huge treetop, or possibly an old stump. In that case, it wouldn't hurt to give these objects a quick try. Let's say the treetop was on Point #5 and the stump on Point #3. If we made a few casts and didn't get a strike, we would pass up similar objects in the next cove and concentrate only on the creek cove points.

The reason we focus our attention on the points is simply that it is more productive to fish areas where a school of bass could be. Your chances of finding a school of largemouths on a point are a hundred times greater than finding them near a stump. A stump is usually good for only one or possibly two fish. Even during the times of year when bass aren't schooling, the creek bed points will still be the better spots and will consistently yield the larger bass.

Unless a cove is particularly large, with plenty of deep water, it will produce the greatest number of fish in the spring or fall months of the year. Coves are far more protected than the open lake; for that reason they will warm up much more quickly in the spring and cool off faster in the fall. These temperature differences between a typical cove and the main lake can be enough to attract baitfish. The bass will not only shadow the baitfish for food, but may also find the water temperatures more to their liking.

Glance at illustration 12 once more. There's a small pocket between

Points #3 and #4, where the creek enters the cove. This pocket will be the first choice for locating schooling bass when they are running baitfish in the back end of coves. Under certain conditions, largemouths will herd shad minnows into the shallow pockets to feed, and when they do it's usually the pocket from which the creek enters the cove.

You'll also find that this same pocket will be the best for spawning bass unless it is a *running* creek. Bass don't seem to prefer a pocket for spawning if there is a lot of fresh water pouring into it. The fresh water is characteristically muddy or dingy and it is often much cooler than the lake water. Both of these factors tend to interrupt or postpone spawning.

If the creek were running into the cove, we would probably take a hard look at the pocket between Points #1 and #2, especially if there were stickups along the bank. Our plan of attack would be to work the shoreline, going down the banks in search of spawning bass. And we would do the same thing at the back end of the cove to the left of Point #3.

Any pocket that has a creek that is not running along with stickups is a prime area for spawning bass. You may be fishing these areas at other times of the year, but when you find those conditions, take the time to jot it down in your notebook—and remember your notation the following spring when the bass invade the shallows.

Before you get the wrong idea, let us clarify our thinking on pockets with running creeks. Except when bass are spawning, these locations can be prime bass country. Running water brings oxygen and it can mean cooler temperatures at certain times of the year. Early in the season, however, the back ends of coves warm fastest because the water is shallower and there is less wave action from the main lake. At the same time, the pocket could cool off quickly from spring rains, particularly if a creek is bringing colder water into the pocket. About the time bass feel the urge to spawn, they don't have the patience to put up with rapidly fluctuating water temperatures and will probably move into a pocket where the water is more suitable.

On a sunny day in the winter or early spring, bass can suddenly appear in the back ends of coves to take advantage of the warmer water; underwater springs that blossom in a cove will be warmer in winter and cooler in summer. Except for a bass's dislike of running creeks during spawning, that same spot might be great in the late summer or early fall when the oxygen content in the middle of the lake might provide only a narrow tier for survival, while vegetation in certain coves produces more oxygen.

The most important aspect of cove fishing is to know each cove thoroughly and then apply this knowledge to the habits of bass. When you can do that, you'll have a fair idea of when you should be concentrating on coves and when you should be over other structure.

## CREEK SHOALS

Midland- and highland-type lakes are found in rolling to hilly country, and that in itself tells you that the passage of any moving water will create bluffs and shoals. Bluffs form where a creek channel swings into the bank, and shoals will form on the opposite shore. When a creek is flooded as part of an impoundment, the same type of terrain exists, except that the creek does not channel the water as it once did.

Coves with creek bluffs and shoals are great places to catch bass during the late fall, winter, and early spring. The creek, of course, enters the cove at the back end; in illustration 13 we have exaggerated the course of the creek to illustrate better how bluffs and shoals are formed. The bluff bank is normally rock, but it could very well be a high mud bank. The shoal side of the creek is always a much lower bank and is characterized by gravel, sand, or mud.

If you know that a creek enters a cove at the back end, you can almost trace the course of that creek on a midland or highland lake through the cove by looking at the banks. Where the bank is high, the creek channel moves in tight; where the bank is flat, you have a shoal, and the creek channel should be on the other side. A pass or two with a depthsounder will verify this for you.

The most productive places in this type of structure are the shoal edges, which we have marked with the letter X. This type of cove isn't the easiest to find, but when you do locate one, mark it well, because sooner or later you'll take fish on it.

Fish often will remain along the shoal edges for a considerable period of time, but just the opposite is true on the shoal points (marked Z). For some reason, bass are seldom found on the shoal points, and on the rare occasions when they are, they won't remain very long. It may be that they are on their way to another shoal edge or are ready to move back into the creek channel.

Sometimes you'll catch fish along the shoal edges and go back later only to find that the bass are gone. If you have worked the shoal edges thoroughly and even tried the shoal points without success, give the channel bed a good thrashing. It is entirely possible that the

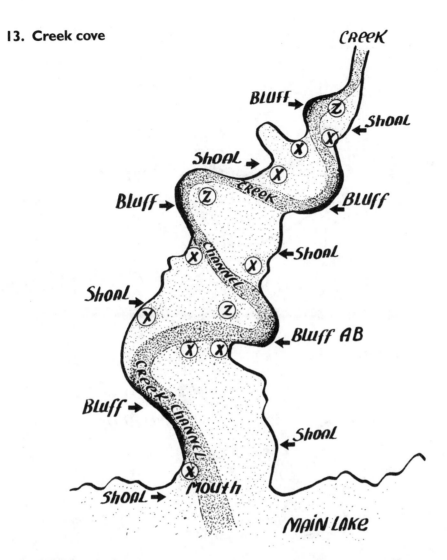

fish settled to the bottom of the creek channel at a depth that is suitable. This is especially true during the colder winter months.

It's a common mistake to think that bass won't bunch up in cold water. Not only do they bunch, but they can pack in so tightly that if you're not extremely careful, you might miss them completely. A large school of bass can occupy an area no larger than your boat.

## BLUFF POINTS

Anytime you can locate a bluff point with a ledge moving out into the cove along a creek channel, you've found a hot spot that should produce fish for you over the course of time (see illustration 13, Bluff AB). We have enlarged the bluff area (illustration 14) and added some imaginary depths to help you visualize a bluff point.

**14. Bluff point**

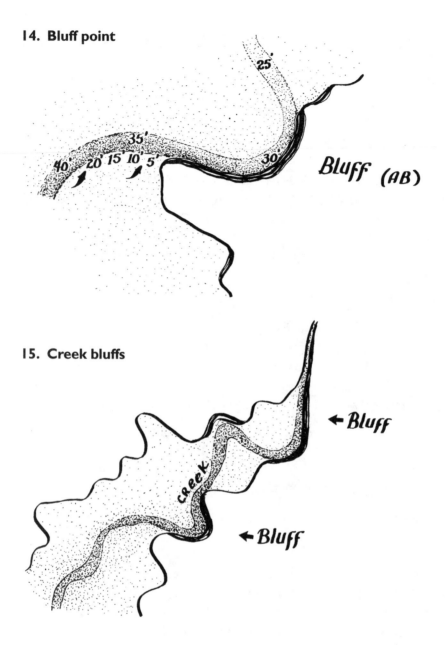

25'

35'

40' 20 15' 10' 5'

30'

*Bluff* (AB)

**15. Creek bluffs**

← *Bluff*

CREEK

← *Bluff*

When you find one, study the shoreline carefully and you'll get an idea of how it will look under water. The land contour above water doesn't normally change very much after it disappears beneath the surface—at least not for a reasonable distance. In our example, the bluff point forms a continuous ledge under water, moving deeper and deeper as it parallels the creek channel.

Notice how the creek gets deeper as it follows the bluff, giving you a variety of depths to fish in the immediate area. Refer to illustration 13 again and you'll see that there is another shoal area below the bluff point; this means that the bluff will slope and shoal to the left as you follow it out from the shoreline.

The bluff on the other side of the cove can also be very good if fished at the edge of the shoal, but the prime area in this cove is the bluff point. As we said earlier, we have shown a creek channel that moves from side to side for purposes of illustration. On the water, this is not always the case. There are many instances when a creek channel touches a bluff or two, forms a couple of shoals, and then moves out right through the middle of the cove (illustration 15). It would be fished the same way as we have described, only there will be fewer places to fish.

Finally, at certain periods of the year, the water level or the pool stage of a particular lake is at its low point or exceptionally low when compared to other years. This might not be a good time to fish, but you'll never have a better opportunity to explore. Get your boat as far back as you can in many of these coves and sketch the structure. Much of it could be exposed. You may even want to photograph it. When the lake fills up again, you'll have a firsthand idea of what the coves look like under water.

CHAPTER

# More on Structure

**F**ISHING STRUCTURE and establishing a pattern require concentration and observation. You have to think your way through the problem and come up with the answers. As you become oriented to structure fishing, you will start to recognize promising spots almost automatically—and because you believe the fish are over that particular structure, you'll fish it harder and probably do much better.

Remember at all times that the prime requisite of any type of structure is the presence of deep water close by. With deep water at hand, objects such as stumps, treetops, logs, stickups, and rocks take on new meaning. An isolated weed bed can be a hot spot, and bass may be around submerged humps. A deep hole in a shallow lake could be the best spot; or lily pads, weeds, grass, or reeds might hold bass. At one time or another, bass will be on any of this structure.

## CREEK OR RIVER CHANNELS

Locate a submerged creek and you know that somewhere along its length, you are going to find bass. In fact, bass will probably be at a number of locations. Remember that you should have an idea of the preferred depth for bass on that specific day, and then look for structure along the creek channel within the depth zone.

When compared to the main impoundment, the creek itself is structure, but there is also additional structure along the creek channel. It might take the form of a bend or saddle, and it would certainly be amplified by the presence of some type of cover such as weeds or brush.

Fish could be stretched along a straightaway in a creek channel, but you know that they will be concentrated along the bends, so that's the place to begin. You can locate these on a map and then pick them out easily with a depthsounder. Marker buoys will help you get the picture in a hurry.

Whether you select a U bend or S bend, the first thing to remember is that the fish will normally be on the outside bends. That's where the channel cut through, and this is part of a fish's behavior pattern if the channel weren't impounded (see illustrations 16 and 17 on page 272). If there is any cover, such as brush, on these outside bends, you can bet the fish will stay right there. If the banks are seemingly barren but there is cover a short distance away, the bass may trade back and forth from the cover to the channel.

The tighter the U bend or the S bend, the better the fishing should be. An oxbow can also be an effective place, but remember that the fish are seldom in the middle of the bend, but rather on either side of the middle. The more you know about a lake, the easier it is to find these places. If there is no cover nearby, the bass could be in the creek channel, using the submerged banks or bluffs as protection against the sun. These banks create the shadow for them, and the fish remain in the darker portion.

Another excellent place is a creek saddle, which is similar to a U bend except that the middle of the sides turn inward. They are really two outside bends that almost touch, and the fish should be between the two. Saddles are difficult to find, but they are extremely productive and worth the effort to locate. You should fish the area between the two channel segments thoroughly (see illustration 18).

When you are fortunate enough to find a saddle formed by two creeks running close together, you can start the victory celebration, because you've uncovered the greatest of all bass hangouts. When we look at a map for the first time, this is the object of our initial scanning. If the lake has two creeks that run parallel or seem to angle toward each other, we try to pinpoint this spot. It is productive nearly all the time and it is worth any effort involved to find it (see illustration 19).

You'll benefit from the flow of two separate bass populations—those that use one creek and those that use the other as a highway to move back and forth. From a fishing standpoint, you would work the area between the two creeks first; then, if for some reason that didn't produce, you might try the creek channels on the outside bends. When you find this type of structure, mark it well in your mind and notebook because you're going to want to come back to it time and time again.

Another place to find schooling bass is near the junction of two creeks (illustration 20). Usually the outside bends (marked A and B)

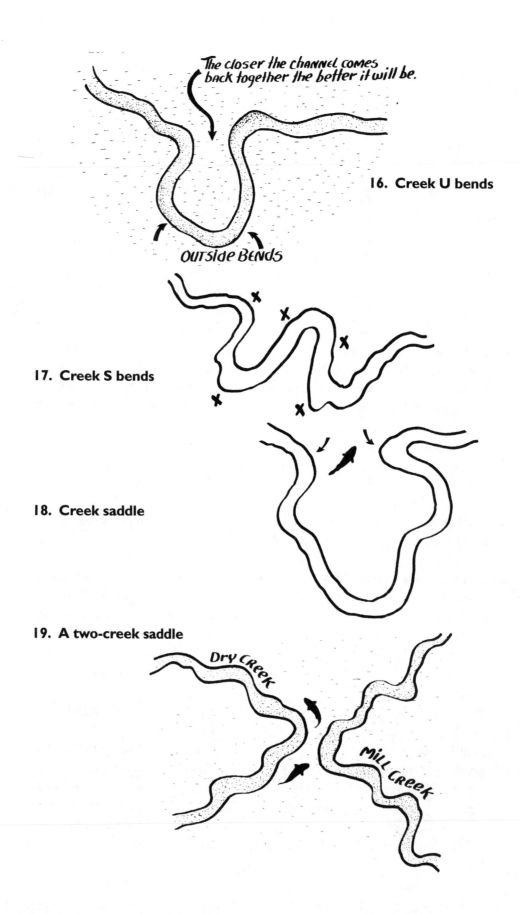

*The closer the channel comes back together the better it will be.*

OUTSIDE BENDS

16. Creek U bends

17. Creek S bends

18. Creek saddle

19. A two-creek saddle

Dry Creek

Mill Creek

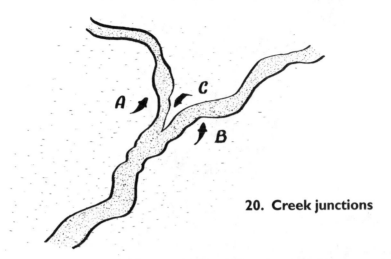

**20. Creek junctions**

are best. They will probably run along bluffs, while the shoal (marked C) is sometimes good if the depth is correct. In most cases, the shoal will be the deepest part and may hold fish if there is a drop-off on it or if the outside bends near the bluffs are too shallow or the temperature is not suitable.

Before the lake was impounded, the flow of current in the creek cut into the outside banks when the creek turned, forming a shoal opposite the bluff (see illustration 21). The bluff should have a sharper drop-off from the surface, but the bluff will also be shallower than the shoal.

When both banks of a creek channel are about the same and you don't have a bluff-and-shoal arrangement, the fish could be on either side. Your clue in this case is the amount of cover and secondary structure. Whichever side has more to offer the fish is the one the fish will be on—so study it carefully and you should come up with the answer.

If a slough, creek, or river channel runs through flat country such as under a lowland-type lake, long, flat points extending out will hold the fish (illustration 22).

We talked earlier about creek mouths and running springs, but it is worth alerting you again to their productivity, especially during certain times of the year. The key is to recognize that a flowing creek or spring will have a different water temperature from the water in the lake it enters. This means that the water near it will be warmer in winter and early spring, but cooler in late summer and early fall. Running water also produces oxygen, and this can sometimes draw fish into the area. Remember that running water indicates a temperature difference and an oxygen difference.

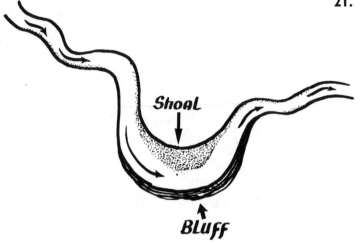

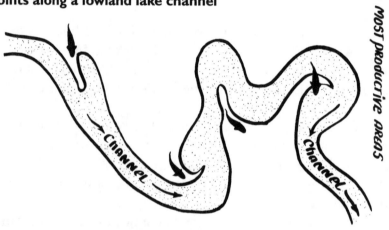

## STANDING TIMBER

Standing timber is inviting structure, and it can keep the average angler busy all day just casting at the base of every tree or between the trees. To fish it properly, however, and make the most of the time available, you should have some type of plan based on experience. The most productive areas of standing timber would be near a creek channel. This channel may be along the edge of the timber or right in the thick of it, but you know you've found a highway, and if bass are moving that's the route they are going to take—and that's probably the route they'll use to leave the timber, so you can bet they'll be close by.

Take a look at illustration 23 and refer to it as we point out some of our favorite spots when fishing timber. We would probably make our first stop right where the channel enters the timber (Spot A) if

## 23. Key spots in standing timber

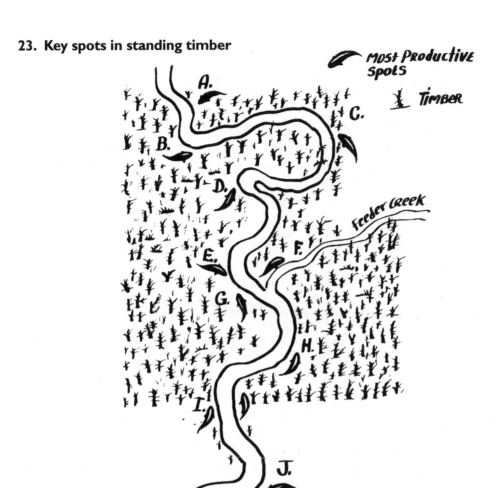

the depth is correct. Otherwise, we would pass it up and move down to the first bend inside the timber (Spot B). Spot B would be good if the bass were feeding along the timber edges. If the first bend is too far into the timber, you may want to pass it up.

Spot C is similar to Spot B, except that you have a U bend very close to the edge of the timber. Bass working this sector would most likely be right on the edge of the timber. If you don't find fish at Spot C, move on to Spot D, which is a very sharp U bend. We know from our experience with creek channels that a sharp U bend is usually a prime spot, and it would be worth checking out this part of the timber. Remember that bass would follow their normal pattern and probably stay on the outside of the U bend.

As we move down the creek channel, we find Spot E, which is an open U bend. Bass may use this as a holding place for a short time as they move back and forth between the creek junction at Spot F and the sharp U bend at Spot D. It's always worth a cast or two at the junction of two creeks, and Spot F would get that type of treatment before we moved down to Spot H. Spot G, of course, is the other side of the U bend that contains Spot E.

If you've followed us so far, you may want to make a stop at Spot H and fish the outside of that bend in the creek channel. This could be a holding point for bass, but it depends on depth and other factors. It won't take long to find out if the bass are using it.

Finally, the point where the channel comes out of the timber can also be excellent (Spot I), particularly if there is a good bend close by in open water (Spot J). Early in the morning and late in the afternoon the bass could be at Spot I, en route to the outside bend at Spot J, providing Spot J is only 50 or 100 yards away from the timber. We've seen bass follow this pattern time and time again.

Another very productive type of terrain in timber is the hump (see illustration 24). Bass will move in on top of it and take up stations on this rise above the lake floor. If the hump has a sharp drop-off, you can expect to find fish very close to that drop-off, but if it is just a high sloping area, the bass could be anywhere. Of course, they will seek the correct depth, and a good place to fish is near the heaviest cover on the hump.

The quickest way to find humps in the timber line is to look at the standing timber. If the growth is relatively the same age, simply look for trees that are standing higher than the others; chances are they appear higher because the lake bottom is higher—and that means a hump. It's not always true, but it can save a lot of time (see illustration 25).

In young timber, it may be hard to notice a difference in height among the trees, yet your map could show a high spot in that area. That means that you're going to have to check the area out with your depthsounder to find the hump. Don't forget to mark it with buoys at least the first time to give you an idea of the physical layout of the hump.

When you're fishing timber, you should be alert to the fact that bass often show a preference for one type of tree or bush over the others. We've seen it happen time and again. With all the different species of trees in a block, the bass will hang out at the base of cedars, pines, ironwoods, sycamores, fruit trees, or something else. We can only speculate that the tree type they select grows in certain soil or gives them some favorable type of cover. The important consideration, however, is to be aware that this happens and identify the tree the moment you catch a fish. If the next fish comes from the same species of tree, then concentrate on that species right away and pass up the other trees.

**24. Humps in timber**

**25. Higher treetops may indicate humps**

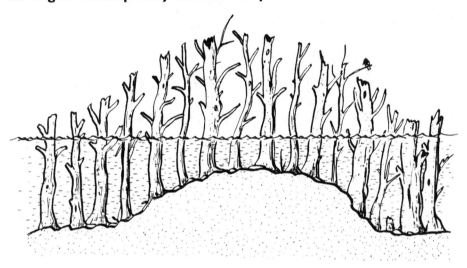

## Roads, Culverts, and Other Features

Anytime man has a hand in creating an impoundment or reservoir, it is generally in an area that was formerly inhabited. That means that there will be roads, foundations of houses, old cemeteries, and other forms of unusual structure. All these places can hold fish, and they are usually worth investigating.

Before the landscape was flooded, for example, the cemetery was moved to another location, but no one took the time to fill in the open graves. The cemetery might have been on a hillside and the open holes provide a sanctuary for bass, giving them plenty of cover and a lot of shade. Need we suggest more?

Roadbeds seem to fascinate bass and, for a reason that we can't truly explain, bass will move over the roadbed to feed. In fishing a roadbed, it is always best to look for an unusual feature: If there's a dip in the road, the bass might be right there; or they could be along

## 26. Submerged culvert

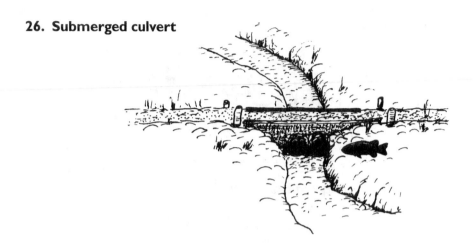

a curve. When the road crosses a creek channel, there's a culvert under the road, and this can be a key area. If the cover is the same on either side, you'll have to scout both sides for fish; but if there is a patch of brush on one side and nothing on the other (illustration 26), figure that the bass are in the cover and work that area first.

If the creek channel is wide enough, you know that the road would span it with a bridge rather than a culvert. The bridge may or may not be left standing, but the supports certainly will be there, and this is good structure to fish. Work the four corners where road and bridge supports meet (illustration 27), and check nearby bends in the creek channel both upstream and downstream. The fish could move into the bridge area at times and spend part of the day at the bends.

Drive along most country roads and you'll find a drainage ditch on at least one side—probably on both sides. These ditches can be great bass habitat, especially if they are filled with brush. The place to explore the roadbed and the ditches is wherever the road varies from its straight path. As we suggested a moment ago, look for dips or depressions or any spot where the road curves, and check that out first (illustration 28).

By this time, you should be well aware that you must search for the unusual aspects of structure. Stay alert to differences from the norm and then concentrate on these areas. It is impossible to outline every type of structure in detail, but we do hope that the examples we have provided will show you the things we look for when we are on the water. It won't be long before you start to develop your own patterns and theories. Just remember to record your spots and your ideas so that you have a constant source of reference for review.

**27. Submerged bridge and creek channel**

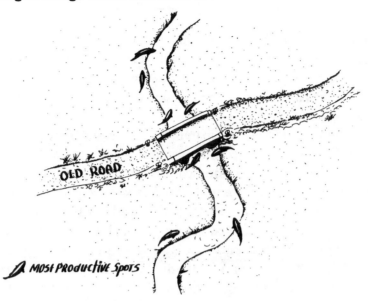

OLD ROAD

MOST PRODUCTIVE SPOTS

**28. Flooded roadbeds**

Road

Ditch

Road

Ditch

## WHEN DO FISH SCHOOL?

We have advanced the theory that it is far better to thoroughly cover those areas where there is a chance to find a school of bass than to spend the major portion of your time snaking out a fish or possibly two from an object. This, of course, is a personal matter, and you will have to decide for yourself which type of fishing you prefer over the long haul. You can catch single fish at any of the places we have suggested, but you also have the opportunity of running into a school.

Bass spend a good part of their lives schooled up with other members of the clan; they are not necessarily the loners that some anglers make them out to be. In our judgment, bass school during at least three-quarters of the year, and they probably remain in schools for 80 percent of the time during those months.

The exception, of course, is in the springtime, when they filter into the shallows to dig nests and spawn. That's when bass refuse to be gregarious and shun their neighbors. Remember, though, that not all bass spawn at the same time, and not all bass spawn when the water temperature is best. This works two ways. It tells you that there still might be schools of bass into the springtime, and it also indicates that the spawn can continue for several weeks instead of being limited to a short period.

As soon as the females spawn, they go right back into deep water, leaving the males to guard the nest and the young. When the fry swim up for the second time and scatter, the males also move back into deeper water, and for a period of a few weeks, you just can't seem to find the larger fish. The coves, points, and shoreline boast plenty of small bass, but the lunkers are gone—probably into very deep water.

By summer, however, schools of bass start to show up, and the husky fish will reappear. You might find these schools chasing shad minnows or over structure. The important aspect is that the fish are schooled up again, and they will remain in schools through the fall and winter.

Again, we should emphasize that not all bass are doing the same thing at the same time. Even though schools of bass are present in the lake, you may have established a pattern that is producing single fish. There's no reason that you shouldn't stick with it as long as you are catching fish. One of the basic rules of fishing is never to leave fish in order to find more fish. If you ply the piscatorial pursuits long enough, you'll realize the odds are against you when you leave the fish you have found.

## SUSPENDED BASS

Unless there is a current, it takes no more physical effort for a bass to sit a few inches off the bottom in 20 feet of water than it does for the same fish to suspend in treetops at the 20-foot level over perhaps 60 feet of water. Finding suspended bass is another matter. There's no other way to describe it except to note that it is an extremely difficult task.

In many cases, suspended bass are located by accident, and that is probably as good a way as any. However, there are some clues that can be gleaned, and we would like to direct your attention to them. We also reemphasize the need to hone your powers of observation and think through the problem. You must be alert to any eventuality in bass fishing and recognize it as soon as it happens.

If you've fished objects along the shoreline and structure in deeper water without catching any fish, you might suspect that some of the bass in that lake may be suspended at an intermediate level. If you're lucky, you may pick some fish up on your depthsounder, but don't count on it. When this happens, we may still fish those creek bed points, but we'll vary the technique somewhat to check for suspended bass. Instead of fishing at or near the bottom, we'll employ the countdown method and try different levels. We'll also try several lures that work in more places than just on the bottom.

Trollers can provide an excellent clue to suspended bass. If they start taking fish, you can surmise that the fish are out in the main part of the lake and that they are suspended. Work the creek bed points from both angles. Hold the boat off the point and cast in toward it, using fan casts to cover the area. Try to get the lure at various depths. Then try moving in close to shore and working out, fishing deeper and deeper. The mouths of coves are another good spot when you have an idea that bass are suspending. Don't forget to try baits that will sink, such as a tail spin, spinnerbait, spoon, and swimming bait. Count down on each cast so you know where the lure was if you should get a strike.

Bass love to suspend in timber, and show a marked preference for cedars and sometimes pines. Cedars and pines usually hold most of their limbs and provide more cover for fish than other species of trees. The bass can stay in the treetops and still enjoy the protective cover they seek (see illustration 29 on page 282).

Largemouths are particularly prone to suspend during the winter when the water is cold. They'll pack tightly in schools and will often go very, very deep in winter, but they can still be caught. As a rule, they will bunch together on the bottom and also suspend at the same depth (see illustration 30).

Bass are likely to suspend more in clear water than in murky or dingy water, and in some lakes may be in treetops at 45 or 50 feet during the chilly months. One cloudy day in the winter, we were fishing Toledo Bend, which has always been a good lake for suspended bass. The area we selected had a ledge or high spot in 25 feet of water, and we were catching bass in the 3- to 5-pound class using structure spoons and jig-and-eels. The drop-off was pronounced, and the depth plummeted sharply from 25 to 45 feet. Using our depthfinder as a guide, we hung over the drop-off, but very close to it. There were trees along this edge in 45 feet of water, and we finally started to ease up to a tree and drop either the structure spoon or the jig alongside the base of the tree.

When the lure hit bottom, we would jig it up a foot or two and

### 29. Suspended bass

### 30. School bass in winter

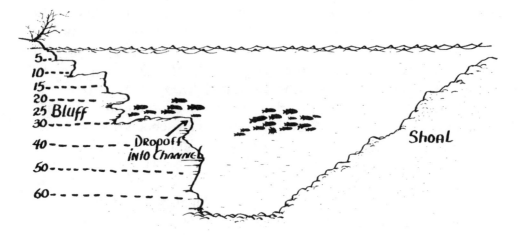

let it fall right back to the lake floor. Using this method, we happened on a good school of fish. Sometimes they would hit the lure on the first lift and other times on the fourth or fifth lift. Those fish had the trees surrounded at the bottom of the lake in 45 feet of water on a cloudy day.

You can bet we went right back there the next day and worked the base of each tree. Nothing happened. Maybe the bass were along the ledge, so we worked the entire length of that structure without a hit. Something was different today and we had to find the secret.

Then we remembered that bass will often move close to the surface in timber on a winter day when the sun is bright. They're seeking a little added warmth from the sunlight. The sun was shining brightly.

After turning the boat around and repositioning ourselves over the same spot, we quickly dropped the lure to the bottom and jigged it a few times. No fish. We then took five turns on the reel and jigged again. Still no fish. We continued doing a countdown in reverse by lifting the lure about 5 feet each time. Finally, when the lure was about 15 feet below the surface, the rod doubled over in that welcome and unmistakable arc. We had found the fish: They had moved up to take advantage of the warming rays of the sun. After that, we could use the countdown method to drop a lure to the 15-foot level where the fish would hit.

It has been our practice over the years to check for suspended fish by dropping a lure to the bottom and jigging it up in stages. This is very similar to the technique employed by fishermen who are trying to locate suspended schools of crappies. More important, before we leave an area for greener pastures, we'll usually steal a moment to try that type of retrieve once or twice. When it works, you've found the mother lode.

# Fishing the Shoreline

TRADITIONALLY, BASS FISHING has been a shoreline affair, and even the deep-water structure advocates make occasional sorties among the stumps, lily pads, fallen trees, and pockets in the banks. There's something exciting about working along the bank. Perhaps it's the constant anticipation that the dark little notch between the cypress tree and that stump next to it will produce a lunker bass. Maybe it's just the pleasure and solitude of being close to shore, listening to the many sounds, and quickening to the movement of birds and animals.

Pinpoint accuracy is especially important for this type of fishing. Being able to drop a lure exactly where you want it is part of the fun and excitement of fishing the banks—and it will produce more fish for you in the long run. Nothing is more frustrating to a shoreline fisherman than the constant need to ease into the bushes to release a lure that managed to impale itself on an overhanging limb.

## READING THE BANK

The new breed of shoreline fisherman wants to have the total picture at all times. He is vitally concerned with structure along the bank, and he knows the depth at which his lure is working. If, for example, a bass crashes a bait halfway between the shore and the boat, he immediately surmises that the fish are deeper and are coming topside to catch that bait. This type of alertness is crucial to successful shoreline fishing, and it goes well beyond varying the retrieve or changing lures.

The major concept of shoreline fishing is that the configuration of the visible bank and ground behind the bank does not stop at the water's edge. It really doesn't matter whether you are fishing a man-made impoundment or plying along on a natural lake; the lake floor should be a continuation of the surrounding area. As you cruise along the shoreline, look at it closely. If you see a ridge shoulder its way across a field and bow down toward the shoreline, you can assume that it continues under the surface of the water.

There might be a gully running between two sheepbacks, and there is every indication that the gully will continue. If the bank is rocky, the rocks should also be under water. Mud shorelines usually mean mud beneath the surface. Remember we suggested that you study fields and countryside as you drive along in your car; when you do this, select an imaginary water level and then try to picture how the land would appear below that level.

Reading the shoreline will give you a good idea of what you can expect right up to the bank, and it will provide the clues to the type of structure dropping off into the deeper portions of the lake. As you fish the shoreline, you must continue to search for irregular features. They may be the edge of a tree line, the beginning of a bluff, a place where a mud bank ends and gravel begins, or anything else where a change takes place. Bass like to hang out along marginal territory where the land is changing.

## THE BOTTOM

Lake bottoms are formed from a variety of materials that include mud, sand, clay, rock, gravel, grass, and even boulders. In most lakes, bottom materials change as you travel the shoreline, and they generally reflect the adjacent terrain. Look at the bank and you have a fair picture of the bottom structure. If the bank is sandy, the sand should extend into the water; and if there is small rock or gravel, the same material will be on the lake floor.

The majority of shorelines have transitional zones where mud might change to sand or gravel and rock might ease into a clay bottom. It's easy for anglers to let these changes pass unnoticed or to disregard them, but they can be prime fish habitat (illustration 31 on page 286). Bass love to lie along the transitional zone. They may feed on minnows, crawfish, and water lizards on a pebble bottom and then move just over the border to rest on a bottom formed from large rocks. When you work a shoreline, watch the bottom changes and try to relate them to a pattern. If you have a hit or hook a fish, check immediately to see if the bottom material changes; just glance at the bank and you'll have the answer.

**31. Changing shoreline**

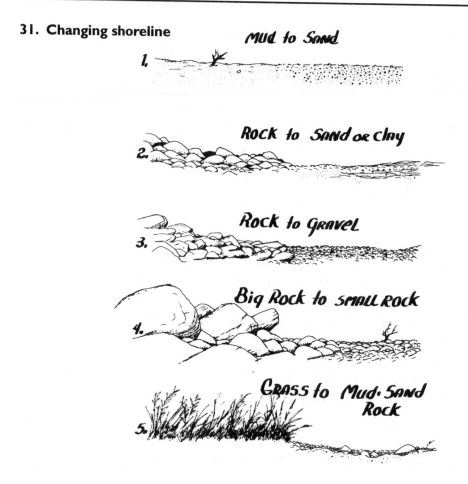

1. Mud to Sand
2. Rock to Sand or Clay
3. Rock to Gravel
4. Big Rock to small Rock
5. Grass to Mud·Sand Rock

If you do notice that the bottom changes where you hooked your fish, this might be the beginning of a pattern. Move down the shoreline until the same condition exists again. Let's say the bottom changed from sand to grass; you fish another changeover spot and catch a second fish. Don't waste any more time puttering down the shoreline. Move directly to the next area where sand changes to grass or grass changes back to sand and fish there.

## THE HOME RANGE TENDENCY

Anglers have disagreed on whether or not largemouth bass exhibit a home range tendency. That is, when the bass move into the shoreline, do they continue to occupy the same relative place repeatedly or do they pick new sections of shoreline at random, based on where they happen to be at the moment? Under the auspices of Southern Illinois

University, two scientists studied the bass population in a farm pond in Illinois and came to the conclusion that bass *do* have a home range.

The technique employed was to cover the shoreline in a boat and, using electrical shocking equipment, capture the bass on shoreline cover. The bass were then marked for identification and returned to the water. Over the course of several months, the procedure was repeated a number of times, and records kept of where each marked bass was found.

One of the more interesting facts to come from this study was that only 1.2 percent of the bass were on the shoreline at any one time, on the average. That meant that most of the bass population—over 98 percent of it—was in deep water the majority of the time. Recaptures indicated that 96 percent of the fish that did invade the shallows or shoreline were recaptured within 300 feet of the spot where they were first captured and marked for identification. With some fish, recapture took place three or four times, yet they were always within the same area. After wintering in deep water, the same bass returned to the same segment of shoreline.

## BLUFFS

A bluff is a high, steep, broad-faced bank or cliff constructed of mud, clay, or rock. Bluffs are predominantly found on midland or highland lakes and often result where a creek channel works into the bank. Some bluffs have timber on them, and there are those where the timber has been cleared but the stumps are still showing. When you find a timber bluff it could be a real hot spot, and you can anticipate that although the trees may have been cut for a distance under water, some will probably remain standing in deeper water.

The best places to fish on a bluff where the creek channel comes up against it are just before the channel brushes the bank and just after the channel starts to turn away. The better spot would be the downcurrent side where the channel has moved alongside the bluff and begins to turn away. We can't tell you why the down side is better, but it is (illustration 32).

Even though a bluff can be considered structure, stay alert to the presence of what we might term "substructure." Whenever you can find structure within structure, you know it is going to be a preferred spot. This is particularly true when you are fishing a bluff, and you should look for cuts, pockets, and points on the bluff, as well as ledges or other types of cover. Bluff banks can be great places for

**32. Bluff channel**

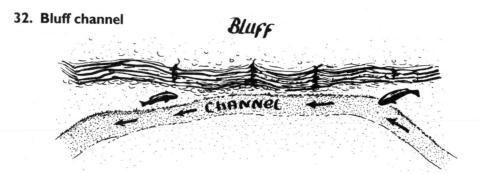

*Bluff*

*Channel*

**33. Features of a bluff bank**

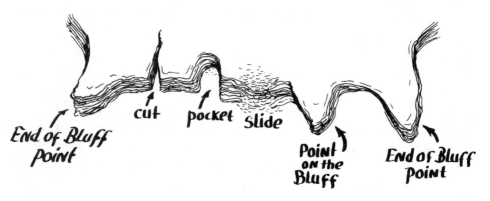

*cut*  *pocket*  *Slide*

*End of Bluff Point*

*Point on the Bluff*

*End of Bluff Point*

**34. Bluff ledges**

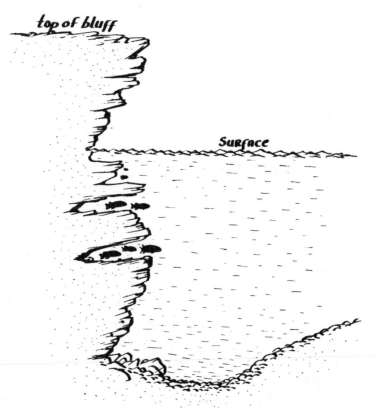

*top of bluff*

*Surface*

smallmouths, Kentucky bass, and largemouths, especially during the cold winter months (illustration 33).

Some of the most productive bluffs have ledges that extend under water. You'll see the effects of erosion above the waterline, and the strata of rock should tell you that there will be ledges under the surface. We refer to these ledges as *stair-stepped;* they are found only on rock bluffs (illustration 34). Which level the fish will occupy varies from day to day and is dictated by a combination of preferred depth and temperature; you're just going to have to experiment and work each one until you find the fish. Also keep in mind that there could be suspended fish off the ledges at approximately the same depth.

## FISHING BLUFFS AND LEDGES

There is no single method for fishing bluffs and ledges. Your approach must be varied simply because old Mr. Bucketmouth is so unpredictable at times. The best way to fish a bluff—at least on the initial pass—is to parallel it (illustration 35). With a series of fan casts and the boat in a parallel position, you can fish it more thoroughly and faster than by casting into it.

If the ledges extend way out into the lake, there are times when you might want to put the boat right under the bluff and cast outward toward open water. This, of course, will move the lure from deep to shallow. We have seen times when a creek channel shoulders up to a bluff, and you could sit beyond the creek channel casting toward the bluff without a strike. Reverse the boat and cast over the creek channel from under the bluff. The fish will hit anything you throw. We mention this because direction of retrieve can be important. You should be aware that if the retrieve doesn't produce fish from one direction, it could do the job from the opposite direction.

There are other instances when the only way you're going to catch fish on a bluff is to cast directly into it and work the lure from ledge to ledge (illustration 36). Walking a lure down the ledges takes a certain amount of practice and skill; if you lift your rod tip too much, the lure will probably move too far and miss a few ledges in between. The trick is to move the lure only a few inches and let it drop a foot or two to the next ledge. If you pulled the lure a couple of feet, it might fall 10 feet before striking a ledge and you would pass up all the water between the two.

It is somewhat easier to fish the ledges at a 45-degree angle or by keeping the boat parallel. Make a cast and allow enough line for the

**35. Paralleling a bluff**

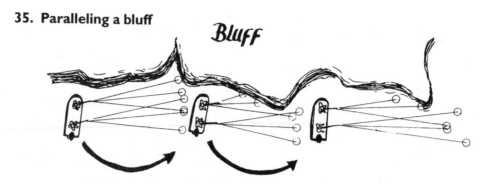

**36. Bouncing a lure down a ledge**

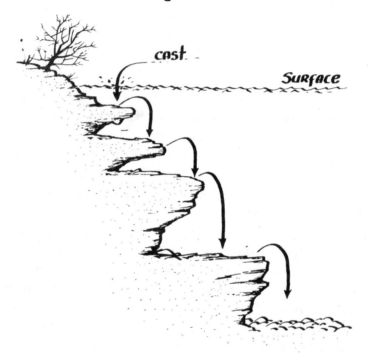

jig to fall on the ledge, but follow the free fall of the lure with your rod tip. Remember, there could be suspended bass right here, and unless you watch the line you may never realize a fish picked up the lure. When the lure hits the ledge, flick the rod tip slightly and drop the lure to the next ledge. Continue the same procedure as you walk the lure down the steps.

By keeping the boat parallel to the ledges, you can also cast down one ledge and retrieve, then work the next ledge, and so forth; or you can walk the lure down the ledges on a 45-degree angle. If you do fish directly into the ledges, as we indicate in illustration 36, you must be careful that you don't drag the lure back to the boat without letting it fall to each successive level. Bouncing a jig-and-eel from ledge to ledge is not the fastest fishing method ever devised, but it is an extremely effective one and a technique that could find bass for you at any level.

## SHADE

Almost every bass angler learns early in the game that bass are constantly seeking cover, and the best cover we can recommend is subdued light. For one thing, bright light seems to bother their eyes; for another, shade offers protection from predators and the advantage when feeding. A bass can hang in a shady area and gaze into a brightly lit area as if the fish were peering into a well-lit room on a dark night.

Most fishermen are visually oriented and are much more comfortable and far more confident when they can see their target. Shade offers this approach to fishing. We use the term *shade*, but we refer to *shadow* as well. Even on a cloudy day, there can be an almost imperceptible shadow coming from a bluff, tree, or rock on shore or in the water. As long as the spot you select for your next cast is a bit darker than the surrounding water, there could be fish in that spot. Make it a rule never to pass up shade. It's worth at least a couple of casts to satisfy your curiosity and perhaps that of the bass as well.

The clearer the lake, the more important shade and shadows can be. Naturally they will change as the sun swings around during the day. The fish will continue to reorient their position as the shadow line moves. Be alert to shadows, such as those from a tree or bluff, cast far out from the shoreline (illustration 37 on page 292). We have seen times when you could cast to the base of a cypress tree and hook a bass, then turn around and toss the lure into open water where the shade from that same tree offers cover. Another bass would be in the shaded patch almost 50 feet from shore.

## DOCKS AND PIERS

The most noticeable feature on any shoreline is a dock or pier. In fact, it is so obvious that most anglers either overlook it or pass it up. Docks offer shade and cover, and for that reason, you'll almost always find schools of baitfish patrolling the area, darting in and out among the supports or simply under the floating docks. No one need tell you that where you find food and cover, you find bass. If it is a big dock that is used constantly, the bass might move off during the daytime when there is a lot of traffic, but they could be on hand at daybreak before any commotion begins or late in the afternoon when the last boat is tied up for the night.

Bass can be on any side of a dock or pier, but they will be back in the shade. At times they might limit their activities to the shady side

## 37. Shoreline shadows

## 38. Dock and piers

Shadow side

SUN

(illustration 38), or they could be on the bright side but back under the dock. If your experience is similar to ours, you'll find these docks and piers best in the fall. We can't tell you why, but we know we catch more fish from this type of shoreline structure when the leaves start to turn.

If you don't limit your bass fishing simply to casting the shoreline, there's one other aspect of docks and piers that you should keep in mind. Study a contour map of the marina and dock sites. If there is a creek channel or a deep hole nearby, the bass might stay there during most of the day, moving into the dock area at dawn and again at dusk. It's worth a try to locate deep structure near a dock. Most anglers are too busy heading for the other end of the lake.

Launching ramps are another place frequently passed up. Bass will sometimes move right up on the concrete ramp, or they could stay right along the edges. Most ramps drop off into relatively deep water, so the escape routes are right there.

In fishing docks, piers, or ramps, you can use almost any type of lure that you would normally fish, and you'll soon learn that docks that have brush piled under them or nearby are better choices.

## DAMS AND RIPRAPS

The area around a dam is often a favorite haunt of the bait fisherman, but it can also be productive for the artificial-lure enthusiast. The key is to look at the dam as shoreline structure, taking maximum advantage of shadows, water flow (if there is any), channels, cuts, sloughs, and the edges where the dam meets the shoreline.

You can alternate your fishing from shallow to deep and deep to shallow. If the water channel cuts an edge along a shoal, you may want to parallel it and fan cast. When water is being pulled through the dam, baitfish are sometimes taken along for the ride, or at least they become disoriented in the flow of water. Bass could be on the prowl just out of the main current, picking off the hapless minnows as they struggle against the water flow. Moving water also carries more oxygen, and this could be an important consideration during the warm months, when oxygen content could become critical.

Ripraps are rock walls that help to hold back the water on the sides of a dam or where a bridge might cross the impoundment. They are designed to resist erosion. When these walls were constructed, the basic material came from the lake bottom. That means that there will be a trough or a drop-off nearby.

You can fish a riprap in any one of three ways. The most common approach is to hang over the deeper water and cast the lure into the riprap. If you prefer this method, try some casts at a 45-degree angle as well as straight in to the target. You may also want to parallel the riprap, casting up and down. Be particularly alert to the corners of the riprap, where it joins the normal shoreline. If all else fails, you could get out of the boat and walk along the riprap, casting on a 45-degree angle and straight out into the deeper water. Very often a riprap wall can be fished better from shore than from a boat.

When you fish this type of structure, be alert to other forms of substructure. Perhaps you find a break in the wall or a minor slide where some rocks fell into the water. Maybe it's a log or a stump or simply a large rock. Whatever the substructure, it's worth your time because, if fish are along the wall, they should be near the substructure.

## STUMPS

Of all the objects in the water, none seems to arouse the confidence of a bass fisherman more than an exciting-looking stump. For some reason, we all associate largemouths with stumps. On the other hand, some stumps can be more productive than others. As an example, a stump that sits on the edge of a drop-off will usually be better than a stump way back up in the shallows, if the depth is correct. When we say *usually* better, we mean on a consistent basis rather than a single experience (illustration 39).

Remember that the shady side of an object is normally better than the brighter side. Therefore, your first cast should always explore the shady side. At one time, bass fishermen always tried to drop a lure right on the object they were fishing. If the object was a stump, they would try to hit the stump on the cast and let the lure fall alongside. By doing this, they passed up a lot of productive water behind and alongside the object, and the sound of a lure falling over the head of a bass could spook the fish into deep water (illustration 40).

We prefer to make our first cast on the side and beyond the object. Sometimes a bass won't be right on the object, but near it. By casting in this manner, we can cover the back, side, and front with a single cast. Once the lure passes the object and is well on its way toward the boat, you might as well crank it in and cast again. Big bass will seldom follow a lure any distance. If they want your offering, they'll hit it as it comes by.

You can fish a variety of lures around stumps. Topwaters, spinnerbaits, worms, jig-and-eels, swimming lures, and diving lures can all be good choices. You're going to have to experiment to find out which ones are best for you. Keep in mind that you may have to vary the retrieve to catch fish. We have seen times when we can cast a spinnerbait past a stump and buzz it by quickly; a bass would nail it before it even reached the stump. The next day in the same area the bass wouldn't hit a spinnerbait unless we buzzed it up to the stump, stopped the lure dead, and let it fall. They would have it in their mouth before it dropped a foot.

The second cast around a stump should still be beyond it, but the lure should brush the object as it passes. There's no guarantee that a bass will hit your lure on the first or second cast, even if the fish is right there. You may have to cast six or eight times before you get a strike, and change lures in the process. That's bass fishing, and there is no shortcut to success.

**39. Stumps on a drop-off**　　　　　**40. Fishing a stump**

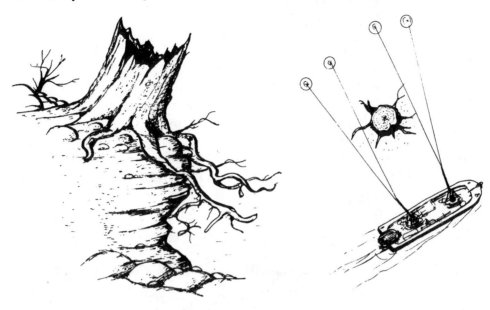

## TREES

Some old-timer once theorized that "if you ain't hangin', you ain't fishin'." When he uttered those immortal words, he must have been talking about treetops, because it is easy to hang up in this type of structure. If trees are left standing, the branches may protrude above the surface, or they could be just under the surface. The way we prefer to work a treetop is from the branches to the trunk (illustration 41).

Start with a spinnerbait and buzz it through the branches. You know, of course, that those trees with more branches and limbs offer better cover for bass and should be fished first. After you've tried the spinnerbait across the top, you could let it drop in the branches and work it carefully. Another choice would be to make a commotion with a topwater bait around the edges of the branches and then toss a worm into the middle of the limbs, letting it fall around the cover. Considerations include the time of year, clarity of the water, depth of the tree, preferred temperature, and similar factors. It's almost impossible to list all the variables, but you know from the previous chapter that, on a sunny day in winter, the bass could be right up near the top of the tree.

If the tree is under water, you might want to get the boat right over the top and use a structure spoon, if the time of the year is right. Or you could choose a fall bait and work it right down around the base of the tree. There's no single formula, but we hope these suggestions will trigger ideas of your own.

Shallow-water, light-tackle saltwater fishermen learned the value of

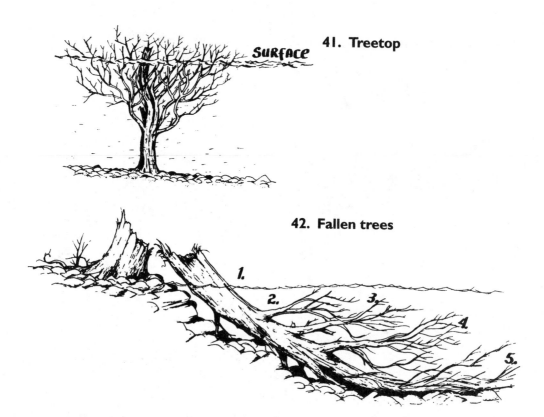

**41. Treetop**

SURFACE

**42. Fallen trees**

1.

2.

3.

4.

5.

polarized sunglasses a long time ago. They make quite a difference in looking through the surface of the water, and they can be invaluable in spotting objects below the surface. They are not miracle glasses, but rather a type of glass that eliminates surface glare, enabling you to see better.

Frequently, a tree blows down in a storm or rots out and comes crashing into the water. All that remains on the bank or in the shallows is a stump and a short end of the tree base (illustration 42). The spot looks perfect, and it probably is. Most fishermen will immediately begin to cast around the stump and the portion of the tree protruding above the surface, but for some reason, the average angler will totally ignore the fact that the rest of that tree is probably under the surface. The part of the tree extending above the surface can give you an idea of the underwater terrain. If it seems to stand almost straight up (upside down), you know that there is a major drop-off. If the log appears to lie flat, you'll probably see the branches at the other end and know that a drop-off isn't present.

It's not always easy to tell if there are limbs and branches left on the deep end of the tree, but it is certainly worth investigating. There are several different ways that this structure can be fished. If you are using a topwater bait, start a series of fan casts from the stump and stub of the tree across the area where the rest of the tree should lie.

## 43. Fishing a blowdown or fallen tree

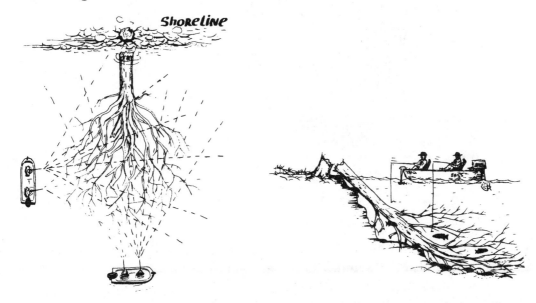

*Shoreline*

Then switch to a spinnerbait and follow the same series of casts, allowing the lure to fall deeper on each succeeding cast (from the shallow end to the deep end). You might also try a jig-and-eel or a worm and toss it back into the section of the tree that has branches.

Once you know that a particular blowdown has branches, a better way of fishing it is to position the boat out in deep water and fan cast along the length of the tree. The idea is to cast into the tree and retrieve in the direction the branches point. By doing this, you will minimize the chances of hanging up (illustration 43).

If the tree plummets almost straight down, you may want to electric-motor over it and use a structure spoon or jig-and-eel to probe the bottom branches. Each tree should be analyzed individually and fished according to time of year and the way it lies in the water.

### STICKUPS

Stickups don't provide very much cover for a bass, but they are significant structure in the spring when the bass move into the shallows to spawn. At that time, the fish are willing to sacrifice habit and ignore cover. One reason is that bass require sunlight in spawning, at least to keep the water warm so the eggs will hatch in the normal length of time. Rather than just stay out in the open, the bass will shoulder up to a stickup. Stickups on hard bottoms such as sand or gravel are usually the most productive.

A plastic worm or a spinnerbait is relatively hangproof and is an excellent choice for this type of fishing. The best way to cover a

## 44. Stickups

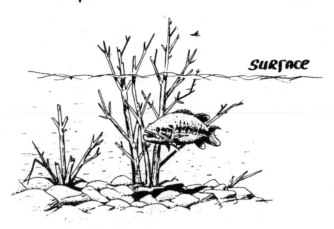

stickup is by casting to the left side, right side, and down the middle. If a bass is nearby, the lure will be seen (illustration 44).

Since stickups are in relatively shallow water, a quiet approach is necessary; any noise from a motor or noise that is transmitted through the hull will chase the fish into deeper water. However, since the fish are either spawning or guarding the nest when they are among the stickups, they are very aggressive and will come back quickly.

## TILTED LOGS

Anytime you see a log in open water with one end reaching above the surface, you can assume that the log is waterlogged on the larger end and has floated up against a ledge or drop-off. It's a good visual clue to structure and certainly worth investigating (illustration 45). The fish may be near the log, or other parts of the drop-off could be even more productive.

To fish a tilted log, apply about the same approach as you would use on a fallen tree. The log may or may not have limbs left on it, but

## 45. Tilted logs

you can determine this by working a lure through the deeper portion. If there are limbs, you'll feel a lure brush by. And you could also use a structure spoon in this type of situation.

## LILY PADS

The terms *bass* and *lily pads* are almost synonymous. From the time a youngster begins his fishing career, he learns that bass hang out around the lily pads waiting for a minnow, frog, or crawfish to happen by. Lily-pad fishing requires a lot of patience, because there are usually large areas of pads and it takes time to find the fish. Pads grow in the shallows, which makes the area somewhat sensitive and dictates a quiet approach.

Take a look at illustration 46 on page 300. We have created a typical lily-pad setup, and experience has shown that there are certain areas among the pads more prone to hold fish than are other areas. Concentrate your fishing on these key spots and then move on to the next set of pads. If you happen to establish a pattern in the pads, then you would naturally fish your pattern in every set of pads you could find.

You already know that anywhere there is a change in the shoreline or the bottom material changes, you could find bass. The same theory holds true when lily pads are present. There could be fish at Spots 1 and 10, where the pads start and where they stop. Try the corners and then move out to the first major point, indicated as Spot 2. Spot 8 would be the first point if you approached the pads from the other direction and could be equally good, regardless of whether you were fishing the shoreline from right to left or left to right.

When you find a small pocket reaching back among the pads, it can produce a fish or two and is worth a few casts. Spot 3 is typical of this type of structure among lily pads. One or two points that extend farther into the lake might also be good (Spot 4). Work either side of the point and back into those pads.

When you've found a pocket going back into the pads from the outer edge, give it a good working over. Spot 5 shows this type of pocket, and it should be fished at the points on either side as well as the mouth. Then you can move into the pocket and fish it. Any tiny offshoots such as Spot 6 warrant a cast or two.

Many assortments of lily pads have small circular openings completely surrounded by pads. It's tough to get a fish out of this type of real estate, but you can certainly get it to hit. Cast back and across these openings and work the lure through them.

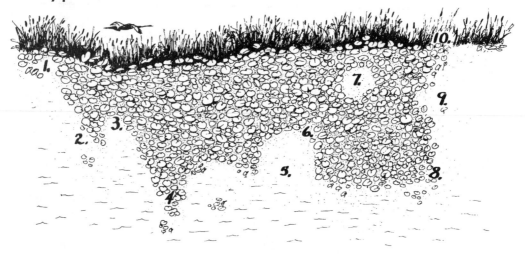

Finally, don't forget to consider the direction of the sun. Indentations on the shady side, such as Spot 9, could harbor a fish. You can easily spend most of the day around a set of pads, but the better approach is to concentrate on the highlights and high spots and then move on to different structure or another set of pads.

## LURES FOR LILY-PAD FISHING

The old standby for lily-pad fishing is a spoon, dressed with a pork rind or plastic skirt. These weedless spoons come with weedguards that enable you to drag the lure tantalizingly across the surface of the water, or you can let it sink and snake it through the pad stems. You have a choice of colors in both the spoons and the tails, and it is sometimes worth experimenting with a couple of different color combinations, such as a light spoon and then a dark one. When a bass hits this lure, come back on it hard and fast to set the hook; strike instantly.

Plastic worms are another good bait for lily-pad fishing, and they can be rigged with or without a slip sinker. You can crawl a worm from lily pad to lily pad, pausing to let it rest and then slither off a particular pad; or you can use a slip sinker and let it fall beneath the pads, fishing it like a weedless spoon. When a bass hits the worm in the pads, pause a second before setting the hook.

The weedless frog is an old-time lure that has taken its share of bass. It's basically topwater and should be fished around the pads as well as on top of them. You can pop it up on a pad and let it sit there for several seconds before moving it off. Do this two or three times and a bass might surprise you when it plasters the lure by blasting right up through the lily pad and eating pad and lure at the same time.

Of course spinnerbaits are a good bet in the lily pads, because they are basically weedless and can be worked in a variety of retrieves. You might want to buzz the spinner across the top of the pads or allow it to sink. Combine both retrieves by buzzing and stopping until you find the formula. When the extended wire on the spinnerbait comes back beyond the hook, it is much more weedless than spinnerbaits with shorter-span wires.

Unless a topwater lure is weedless, the angler who prefers this type of surface action will have to limit his activity to the edges of the pads and pockets or openings. Topwater fishing can also be used to explore the pad points. This gives the topwater devotee plenty of area to explore, and the commotion from such a lure could bring bass out from deeper in the pads.

Swimming and diving plugs suffer the same basic limitations as topwaters. They can be used to work the fringes of the pads, but toss one back into the thick of things and you'll have to motor over to get it out.

You've probably shared with us the experience of finding bass way back in the pads when the cover was just too heavy to drag a bass out. We've had our share of frustrations with this type of fishing, and on occasion we'll run the boat back into the pads, cutting them with the motor. That leaves an open pocket, but of course the bass have scattered. So we'll leave this honey hole for a while and come back several hours later to fish the new pocket we created. Not surprisingly, we'll catch bass.

**7**

# How to Fish
# an Unfamiliar Lake

A N UNFAMILIAR LAKE may be one that you have fished for a number of years and never really taken the time to learn, or it could be a body of water that is completely new to you and one that you are going to try for the first time. Some writers refer to this situation as "fishing a strange lake," but we believe that there is nothing strange about any lake that harbors largemouth and small-mouth bass.

It's all a matter of mental attitude. Even the finest bass masters sometimes experience difficulty on new waters, because they are over-whelmed by new and unfamiliar surroundings, thus failing to place the problem in its proper context. If you think for a moment, you'll realize that there will be many similarities between the new water and your favorite bass lakes. Equally important, you can expect the bass to follow the same habits and seek the same habitat it does anywhere else. Just because the physical layout of an impoundment changes doesn't mean that the characteristics of the species undergo a metamorphosis.

If you have analyzed the new lake carefully, you already know that bass will seek a preferred depth based on temperature and oxygen. Add to that the requirements for food and cover and it shouldn't be too diffi-cult to locate your quarry. All that is left to do is find the structure and features of the new water that are most likely to hold bass.

## START WITH A CHART

To fish an unfamiliar lake properly, you're going to need a chart or map to help you locate the type of structure that bass frequent. If your fishing is limited to shoreline casting, a detailed map or chart will still help you to find such areas of different soil consistencies as hills and creeks. As a general rule, always try to obtain a map with the smallest depth intervals. A 5-foot interval, for example, is always better than an interval of 10 or 20 feet. It might take several different maps to provide the information you need, including a navigational map, Corps of Engineers map, and Geological Survey map.

In addition to the maps, you will need a good temperature gauge that reads the water temperature at various depths electronically, and a depthsounder capable of displaying the bottom at realistic boat speeds.

Before you even depart for the new lake, study the maps carefully, trying to pick out features that could hold bass. Primarily, you are looking for structure, so concentrate on finding creeks, submerged channels, roadbeds, field flats, humps, high spots, old home foundations, and anything else you can find that is different from the surrounding area.

If you know a marina operator or a guide on the lake you're going to fish, a telephone call in advance can help you obtain information on the depth the fish are being taken at. Once you know the depth, spread your maps out in front of you and start to mark all the structure you can find that conforms to that depth. Perhaps you won't be able to pinpoint the depth exactly, but your own experience might tell you that most bass in that part of the country and at that time of year are taken in 12 to 20 feet of water. You can use that information to locate structure within the given range.

## Select a Small Area

There is a tendency among bass anglers with superfast boats (and even among some who own slower boats) to attempt to cover too much territory. They'll fish one spot, then crank up and run for another spot that might be 8 or 10 miles down the lake. Much of their fishing time is spent in running from spot to spot, with the result that they fail to cover any area thoroughly. The secret of finding fish in any lake is to maximize the time that your lure is in the water.

On an unfamiliar lake, study the chart until you have selected a few areas that seem to have the best potential. The lake may be 50 miles long or it could be 10 miles long, but that's still too much territory to try to cover. Instead, pick an area of possibly 4 miles that looks as if it has plenty of structure with creeks running through it. Mark every spot you can find in this limited zone on the chart, noting water depth. Three or four different-colored marking pens can help you establish a depth code. Red might mean 12 to 15 feet, blue could be 16 to 20 feet. That will help you pick out depths quickly.

Instead of running all over the lake to fish this place or that, our approach is to concentrate on the limited area we selected and fish it hard. If you don't have exact depth information, you can use your temperature gauge as an indicator, or you can fish a sloping point until you catch the first fish and then measure the depth.

## ESTABLISH A PATTERN QUICKLY

Most bass anglers fish an unfamiliar lake as part of a vacation trip or business excursion; often they won't be in the area very long, and if they are going to catch fish they must do so quickly. That means that the visiting angler must establish a pattern as soon as possible. Remember that there may be several patterns that will work at any one time, but you need only uncover one.

The more familiar you are with a lake, the easier it is to fish, so you must recognize this fact when you fish an unfamiliar lake and take extra measures to ensure you have found the right structure. Triangulation will help you pinpoint spots in midlake, and your depthsounder will confirm them. If you are going to fish a high spot or a creek channel or any other type of structure, don't skimp on putting out marker buoys. They'll help you to get oriented in the shortest time.

If, for example, you are going to fish a U bend in a creek channel, it may take 8 or 10 markers to delineate the bend, but it is worth the time crossing and crisscrossing the channel to drop the buoys. Then, when you look at it, you'll have a better idea where to fish. And if you do take fish in, say, 20 feet of water, pull out your map and see if there is another U bend in 20 feet of water. That's the next place you want to fish.

There's very little that is different when you fish an unfamiliar lake other than the physical features. If you can't catch fish using the techniques you know and the lures that you can work best, you probably won't have time to learn a new method.

## DEEP, CLEAR LAKES

Some of the best bass anglers in the country have had their share of problems with deep, clear lakes. Those fishermen who live near lakes of this type quickly tell you that the problem is strictly mental and results in a defeated frame of mind. An angler who can't miss on a shallow lake begins to think that he doesn't know anything about deep lakes. Mention that the water might be 200 feet deep in places and this veteran will go to pieces.

The truth of the matter is that you are only going to look for fish down to depths of possibly 35 feet or so. When you are fishing 35 feet of water, it is no different than fishing the bottom of a lake that is only 35 feet deep. All you have to do is ignore the deeper water and concentrate on the shallower sections. Once you do that, the deep, clear lake becomes like any other body of water you have fished.

Clear water, of course, means that the fish will probably be a shade deeper than they might be in dingy or murky water, so you would fish slightly deeper than you normally might, but that doesn't mean you have to fish depths of 50 or 60 feet. And you'll find that in clear water, lighter lines and smaller lures result in more fish.

## WORKING THE SHORELINE

You may not be the type of fisherman who enjoys fishing structure in deeper water, preferring to do your bass catching along the shoreline. The shoreline of an unfamiliar lake is basically the same as any other length of shoreline. It will have special features that will hold bass, and your job is to recognize these features.

Bass might hang out where gravel turns to mud, or where a bluff ends and a shoal starts. Fish might be along submerged timber, or at key points among the lily pads. The point to remember is that even though you are fishing the shoreline, you must remain alert to changes in terrain and try to establish a pattern.

The alternative is to waste a lot of time dropping a lure along every stump, every undercut bank, and anywhere else that looks as if it might harbor a bass. Points are always worth a few casts, and anyplace where running water enters a lake could prove productive. If you do uncover a pattern, stick with it and pass up places that don't fit that pattern. Otherwise, you could be spending too much time fishing unproductive waters.

## LAKES WITHOUT STRUCTURE

There are some lakes that simply cannot be structured. The underwater configuration of these lakes resembles a bowl or a frying pan. If you were to drain the water out of the lake, the bottom would be relatively smooth without much in the way of cover or drop-offs. However, unless you think your way through the problem, locating bass in water of this type could be like searching for the proverbial needle in the haystack.

A lake not too far from home fits the bowl-shaped description, and although it holds some husky bass, there is no way to locate these fish consistently except in the spring when they are spawning in the shallows. If we can locate a depression in the bottom one of these days, it should be filled with bass like a "hawg pen," but so far that lake bottom is completely level.

In a lake without visible structure, it is important to remain particularly observant. Subtle changes such as a sand-to-gravel bottom or a certain species of tree might hold the key to locating the bass. Every time a fish is taken, study the spot carefully and try to pinpoint the salient features. When the next fish is hooked, look for duplication of certain features; if you find some that occurred in the first spot, you may be on to a pattern.

Finally, keep in mind that in a lake without significant structure, even a minor change in the bottom can be enough to hold fish. So stay alert to a change of any type in a bowl-shaped or frying-pan-shaped lake.

## LOCATING TROPHY SMALLMOUTHS

Show most bass anglers a patch of rocky shoreline or a rocky point extending out into the lake and their first thoughts center on smallmouths. This may hold true for smaller specimens, but the husky smallmouths prefer a different type of terrain.

Spring and fall are the best times to fish for smallmouths. Dale Hollow Reservoir in Tennessee, for example, begins to turn over in late November when the water temperature ranges between 58° and 54° F. That's also the time when smallmouths move over the "flats" and begin to school in 18 to 35 feet of water, and they will remain at those depths until the water temperature dips below 45° F.

If you've been concentrating on rocky points for your smallmouth fishing, you've been looking for trophy fish in the wrong places. These fish are not in the fishy-looking spots, but over relatively clean bottom composed of clay, mud, or gravel. That's where the crawfish feed and that's where the smallmouths will be, since the crawfish is the mainstay of their diet. In fact, if a lake doesn't have a superb supply of crawfish, it probably won't hold trophy smallmouths, because smallmouths grow faster on crawfish than on any other food.

In deep lakes, most banks drop off sharply. You can tell this by studying the shoreline. Check the shore until you find a ridge or hump that tapers gradually to the water's edge. You'll probably see mud or clay at the water's edge. If this bank continues to extend gradually into the lake, it could be trophy smallmouth territory. Prime smallmouth country is a gradually tapering point that eases out into the lake with plenty of deep water all around it. Smallmouths require deep water nearby and, although they'll work the edges of the tapering points, they demand the safety of the depths.

Until you get to know a lake, you must rely on a depthsounder to help you find the gradually tapering points. The best method is to locate the muddy points that look flat on shore and then check them out with the depthsounder. If they drop into 35 feet of water or more, they are worth fishing. However, trophy-sized smallmouths can be difficult fish to approach, and they spook easily. If you have worked a point with a depthsounder or dropped buoys, you won't be able to fish it until the next day; the best approach is to spend your first day scouting the most likely-looking smallmouth spots and then return the next day to begin fishing.

## OBSERVATIONS ON SMALLMOUTHS

One reason largemouths are much easier to approach and fool than smallmouths is that smallmouths respond unfavorably to the presence of a boat or the glimpse of an angler. Don't for a moment delude yourself into thinking that fish can't see you, even in deep water!

In approaching a point that might have smallmouths, the trick is to move in as quietly as possible. Ease the throttle on your big motor some distance from the spot you want to fish, so that a heavy wake doesn't roll over the area. Then work in from the side you don't intend to fish and get the boat right up against the bank. You generally work from the shallow to the deep, so your lure will be pulled up the point from the deep to the shallow. Fish seem to hit it better in this direction, and it is much easier to keep the bait near the bottom.

With the boat near the bank, make a series of fan casts, retrieving the lure slowly so it is just off or bouncing along the bottom. When you have covered the sector, ease the boat into deeper water about half the length of a long cast and repeat the fanning. Move again and cast the new area. Most anglers don't work deep enough on these points, and it is good to remember that, although the fish might be a little shallow early in the morning or on an overcast day, they could just as well be in 30 feet of water.

When fishing over these flat points, always cast as far as you can. The bait should be allowed to sink to the bottom, and you must remain alert while the bait is falling (maintaining a tight line), because a smallmouth could inhale it on the way down. If a fish doesn't strike, the retrieve should be painstakingly slow, permitting the lure to skim the bottom. You can check the depth of retrieve by periodically dropping your rod tip. The lure should hit bottom within the count of two or three, or you're fishing it too fast and too high.

Smallmouths are creatures of habit, living in the same places year after year after year. Once you find good smallmouth territory, the schools will be there next year at the same time. They don't range very far during the entire year, moving deeper or shallower with the seasons.

During the middle of winter in lakes such as Dale Hollow, the smallmouths will be very deep. If you have a calm day, you may be able to fish them in 50 or 60 feet of water. However, with the first warm rains in March, the smallmouths can move shallower overnight and start to feed. During March, April, and early May (depending on the latitude), they'll move into the shallows in search of food, and they'll also spawn. Smallmouths usually spawn in slightly deeper water than largemouths, and how close they get to shore depends on the amount of cover available. If you have always wanted to catch a big smallmouth on a fly, this is the time of year to do it, but you must make long casts and approach the nests or the cover very quietly and carefully.

Finally, the clearer the lake, the lighter the line you should be using. You'll catch more fish in clear water on 6-pound test than you will on 10-pound test; and you'll discover that by eliminating terminal tackle, such as swivels, and using a small bait, you'll increase your chances of hooking a trophy smallmouth. Just remember that big smallmouths prefer small baits worked slowly along the bottom. They may occasionally hit a larger offering, but that's the exception.

# Weather, Water, and Seasons

ABOUT THE TIME you think you have carefully considered all the factors that motivate the behavior of bass and have cataloged them into a precise sequence, your quarry is going to begin playing the game with a whole new set of rules. Bass fishing is like that, and that is what makes it so great.

All of us know that weather affects fish behavior, and that this behavior can be amplified by the season of the year and the type of water. The problem is that fish aren't always affected the same way. And we might as well tell you that there are no rigid rules. Certain lakes, for example, have their own peculiarities, while latitude will introduce another variable.

The key to capitalizing on the changes in weather, water, and seasons is a degree of alertness on your part and the willingness to continue to observe and record your findings in the lakes that you fish most often. Very frequently, bass on another lake will react the same way to atmospheric changes, and your experiences in one area will pay dividends in another.

Recognize that there are differences between muddy, dingy, and clear water. The windy side of a lake might not be the same as the lee shore; a high barometer has a different effect on bass than a fast-falling barometer; cloudy days can cause bass to modify their behavior pattern from what it was on a sunny day. Fish may not be in the same "lunker holes" in spring, even though you found them there last fall. These examples serve to illustrate the complexity of the problem and the infinite number of variables that guard the solution to where a bass will be and when. We'll give you some of our general observations as a starting point, and we hope you'll pursue the subject on your own favorite bass waters.

## WEATHER AND WATER

During a fishing tournament, we had a school of bass pinpointed in 15 feet of water. The sun was shining, and we'd hook a bass with every third or fourth cast using a blue plastic worm. Suddenly, the activity stopped. Our first reaction was to analyze what we were doing and what could have happened. Before we got halfway through this approach, we began to catch fish again. Then the fish stopped a second time.

Searching for an answer, we noticed that the sky had begun to cloud over with big, puffy, white clouds. Taking this one step farther, we then discovered that when the sun was covered by a cloud, the fish stopped hitting. In clear water on bright days, blue worms have been a favorite of ours, but on cloudy days we prefer black. So without hesitating, we switched to a black worm and started to catch fish when the sun was blotted out. As soon as the cloud passed, the black worm became a futile effort, so we switched back to blue.

To satisfy our own curiosity (and we're sure yours, too), we then rigged two rods—one with a blue worm and the other with a black one—and conducted an experiment. As unbelievable as it might sound, when the sun was out, we could cast a black worm and never get a hit. Toss the blue worm in the same spot and a bass would take it. The reverse held true when the sun wasn't shining.

You might think that this is an isolated instance, and it well might be, but it does point up the importance of being observant and of modifying your techniques to gain harmony with the weather. As a general rule, most bass fishermen prefer overcast days to those when the sun is shining brightly. For one thing, the fish might be a little shallower when the sun isn't out, and for another, they are easier to approach. We believe fish are more active on cloudy days, yet the best time to fish is when you are there, and that includes sunny days.

On a bright day in a clear lake, our preference would be for dingy water rather than the windowpane-clear water, and we'll take the time to search for colored water. That doesn't mean that the water will be muddy, but it will be somewhere in the transitional zone where fish will respond better.

Of course, we have continually pointed out that bass are sensitive to bright light; on a sunny day, the odds are in your favor if you concentrate your fishing on the shady side of an obstacle or along a shady bank. If you are fishing a creek channel, work the submerged bank that is on the shady side.

The barometer must also be considered seriously. If we were given a choice, a slowly rising barometer seems to provide the best fishing for us; and we have done well on a fast-falling barometer at times. That follows the theory that fish bite well just before a storm. On the other hand, an extremely high barometer has produced poor fishing for us more times than not, and a slowly falling glass also creates problems. This doesn't mean that you can't catch fish under those conditions, but they just don't seem to be as good as other times.

Let's delve into water clarity once more so that you'll have it firmly implanted in your mind. The rule is that the muddier the water, the shallower the fish will be. In a very muddy lake, you probably won't find bass deeper than perhaps 15 feet. At the same time, you must tailor your selection of lure colors to those that will be visible, and that's the place to concentrate on vibrating baits. In a clear lake, you'll do better with lighter lines and smaller lures, and the fish will be relatively deeper than they would be in dingy or muddy water.

Although wind can be enough of a nuisance to make fishing uncomfortable, it can also be an ally and help you find fish. The windy side of a lake is often better because the breeze creates more oxygen, and it also pushes baitfish against that shore. The ripple it creates also gives bass a slightly stronger sense of security, and they may be a bit shallower than they would be if the lake were slick calm; and wind masks the surface of the water, permitting you to approach closer to your target without being detected. This is always important, but even more so in a clear lake where you can consider wind to create additional cover.

Fishing is often better along the ripraps that border a dam when they are on the windy shore; the same seems to hold true with bluff walls. If the wind isn't too strong, our preference is to concentrate on the windy side of the lake, but if the zephyrs approach a tropical disturbance, we'll seek the shelter of the lee shoreline.

You already know that oxygen is much more important to a fish than temperature and the natural comfort zone of 68° to 72° F. Wind adds oxygen to the water, and on very hot days during the summer, when water temperatures are above the 80° F mark, you'll often find bass in shallow water on the windy side, trying to glean the extra oxygen.

Speaking of water temperatures, we should make it clear that the comfort zone is merely a guideline, and that bass will leave their preferred temperature range for a variety of reasons. However, to find a pattern it is necessary to have a starting point, and the comfort zone provides a place to begin. Experience and judgment (plus a gut feeling, at times) will help you to modify your thinking and probe outside the comfort zone when conditions warrant.

If you are fishing a lake in the middle of summer or winter, when oxygen levels in the lake would normally be low, do most of your fishing around milfoil, if it's present. Bass will swarm around it because of the oxygen it produces. Many a veteran fisherman will tell you to look for coontail moss during periods of low oxygen; when you find it, you'll find the bass.

## WINTER FISHING

It wasn't too many years ago that most bass fishermen would pull their boats out of the water and hang up their tackle for another season just about the time that the weather was getting chilly. In fact, there are still some northern states with bass seasons that legally end in the fall and don't open again until late spring or early summer. However, in other northern waters, bass are taken through the ice during the middle of winter, and anglers across the nation are beginning to recognize the potential of winter bass fishing.

Latitude plays an important part in winter fishing. For purposes of our discussion, we will eliminate those waters that lie far enough south so that the water temperatures never really drop far below the comfort zone of the bass; instead, our thoughts will center on those areas where water temperatures might drop into the 50s and might even get down to 40° F.

A number of bass fishermen erroneously believe that bass disappear during winter, but obviously this is not true. Since all fish are cold-blooded creatures, their metabolic rates are directly affected by surrounding water temperatures. Body functions are at the norm when bass reside within their comfort zone, but as water temperatures fall, the fish become sluggish. They don't need as much food to sustain themselves, and their digestive rates are correspondingly slower.

Significantly, bass will not chase a lure very far in cold water, and they are more prone to pick up smaller tidbits than to attempt to gorge themselves on larger prey. A fisherman's understanding of this is the key to winter fishing in many areas of the country. When you are fishing cold water, *think slow.* The idea is to fish a lure as slowly as you can, and even then, you're still probably fishing it too fast. Old Mr. Largemouth isn't about to work for food, and a bass that is ravenous in the summer can probably, in 40° F water, get by on about one-tenth its usual food intake.

To be successful when water temperatures are low, you must either drop a falling lure right in front of a bass or inch a lure along the bottom so that it tantalizingly passes directly in front of your quarry. If you insist on buzzing a spinnerbait in cold water, your chances of success are virtually nil.

During the winter bass often school, and schooling usually takes place according to the size of the fish. Fish in the 1- to 3-pound class will be together, and larger fish, in the 4- to 8-pound range, will school separately; they can really bunch up tightly, with an armada of fish taking up little room in the water. On new lakes, schooling by size doesn't always hold true, although we can't tell you why. However, on a young lake you may find 2-pounders mixed in with 6-pounders.

Depth is also a problem in the winter. Fish can be anywhere from 2 to 70 feet or deeper; it all depends on the weather and the specific lake. Normally, however, fish will be deeper in the winter; and they will be deeper in a highland lake than they will be in a midland or lowland lake. The deeper they go, the more difficult they are to locate and catch. It is certainly tough to fish a light lure very deep and still maintain the necessary control and feel.

Although bass do go deeper in highland lakes, they'll move up closer to the surface on calm, bright days in the winter. They'll still be over deeper water rather than the shallows, but they'll suspend in the tops of submerged trees, or you'll find them in the flooded timber areas. Our fishing preference during the cold weather is a midland lake such as Tennessee's Pickwick. The waters are clear, with rock bluffs and gravel bars, and the fish don't seem to stay as deep in this type of lake.

Regardless of the type of tackle you prefer during the rest of the year, winter fishing dictates ultralight spinning gear with lines testing 4, 6, and sometimes 8 pounds. Obviously, if you are fishing lowland lakes such as Toledo Bend or Sam Rayburn, you'll need heavier lines in the timber areas, but the light mono works well for schooling fish over open water.

Spinning has many advantages at this time of year. It allows you to cast the very light lures that are necessary, and there is more "give" to spinning than bait casting, so you won't break a light line as easily. Our choice is a rather stiff rod that measures 5 or 5½ feet in length.

Not only does this type of rod have plenty of backbone to handle bigger fish, but the stiff tip is much more sensitive than a soft one, and it allows you to feel the lure.

There's no question that you'll get more hits on light lines and small lures. Among the better winter baits are structure spoons, jig-and-eels, jigs, single spins, and twin spins. Jigs should be ⅛ or ¼ ounce at the most, made of bucktail, polar bear hair, or marabou with a 4-inch split-tail eel trailing from the hook. The best colors are a white jig with a white tail, yellow jig with a yellow tail or a white tail, black jig with a black tail, brown with a black tail, or yellow with a black tail. Take your pick, but our favorites are a white jig with white tail or a yellow jig with a white tail. These same color combinations work well on smallmouths and Kentuckys.

Cast the lure into a bluff, along a point, over a drop-off, around an object, or wherever there is structure. As the lure hits the water, close your bail and take up the slack line. Remember that you must fish the lure as a fall bait, and that bass will frequently hit it on the way down. If you can keep the boat in one position during the cast, it's easier to feel the lure.

Again, you must walk a tightrope, allowing the lure to fall freely, but keeping the line tight so you can feel a fish take it. This is important. Watch the line closely, because you will usually *see* the strike (a slight pull on the line) before you feel it. You must try to fish the bait as smoothly as possible, and this, of course, depends on how deep you must probe. Hold the rod tip steady slightly above a 45-degree angle and really concentrate on what you are doing.

Sometimes we'll twitch the wrist slightly, giving the bait a little action. At other times we'll let it fall, twitch or swim it just a hair, and then let it fall again. If the lure hits a ledge, ease it off and let it fall again. If you keep score, you'll discover that 99.9 percent of the time the bass will hit the lure on the fall. The less you do to the lure and the less action you impart, the more fish you will catch. Keep the rod and line as motionless as possible and watch for the unmistakable "flick" in the line when a bass picks it up.

Bass anglers sometimes look down on those who use spinning tackle, but in the winter, light spinning is the best method on midland and highland lakes. The terrain might be rugged and you may have to go a little heavier, but when you can get away with 4- or 6-pound-test line, use it. It will produce a lot more fish than winch outfits with 20-pound-test, and you'll have more fun in the process.

# NIGHT FISHING

If you are fishing a relatively clear lake during late spring, summer, or early fall, and if you're not catching fish during the day, try the lake at night. Big bass are sometimes deep and tough to locate during daylight hours. At night the lake comes alive, and these same fish may move into 3 to 10 feet of water to feed. Darkness gives them cover, and it also makes it easier for them to expend less energy in attacking their prey.

The strange world of night fishing is a thrill that most fishermen never know. Beautiful scenery is replaced by solitude, night sounds are amplified, and this is the time when a sensitive rod tip and a good pair of hands make all the difference. Nights are peaceful on the water, and the hustle and bustle of boats, water-skiers, and swimmers is replaced with the haunting sounds of hoot owls and feeding fish.

There is little doubt that on very clear lakes you'll catch more fish at night and bigger fish than at any other time. Night fishing begins to get good when the water temperature rises into the upper 50s, but it is best when the thermometer reads well above 60° F. Any lake that contains a healthy population of crawfish or spring lizards (salamanders) is usually a good night lake. If the lake is rocky or has gravel, these are the areas that would hold crawfish and are therefore prime bass locations. Crawfish move around a lot more at night than they do in the daytime, especially after a rain or when the wind is blowing against the bank. Off-colored water on the windward side is excellent, and you'll also do well where there is a drain or runoff; and don't pass up mud or gravel banks with deep water nearby.

The jig-and-eel and the spinnerbait are good night lures on most lakes during the spring and fall of the year. During the summer, a plastic worm or a spinnerbait will take more fish. Crawl these baits right along the bottom, because bass will be searching the lake floor for crawfish or salamanders. At night on a lowland or midland lake that does not stratify, bass will often move into 3, 4, or 5 feet of water to feed. Lakes that do stratify through the summer—mountain or highland lakes—are also good at night, but the fish will feed deeper than they will in lowland or midland lakes. Surface plugs also often provide exciting action at night.

If you are going to fish a lake at night, it's important to know it well so that you can locate bass hangouts—and also for safety reasons. The best procedure is to study the lake for a day or two during the daytime to learn your way around and to know where dangerous navigational obstacles lie. A lake with a lot of trees and stumps can be tricky at night; as you scout it in the daytime, select those routes from spot to spot that will be easiest to travel at night.

Since there won't be many fishermen on a lake after dark, you must be even more safety conscious than you are in the daytime, and prepare for any emergency. Besides extra spark plugs for your motor and a full complement of spare parts, your boat should be rigged with navigational lights, and you should carry emergency-type lights and flares. Water-safety devices and life jackets are a must.

In our experience, it doesn't really make a difference whether you fish on a bright night or on one when the moon isn't shining. Bass seem to feed as well on a moonlit night as they do during the new moon. However, you can certainly see better when the moon is out, and navigation is a little easier then. If the moon is bright, treat it just as you would the sun and concentrate your fishing on the shady side of objects or along a shady shoreline.

Once your eyes become oriented to the darkness, make certain that you don't look at bright lights or even a cigarette lighter. This will temporarily destroy your night vision and it could be several minutes before it returns. Fish are also sensitive to light at night, because their eyes are geared to darkness. If you shine a light across the water, and especially along the area you want to fish, you'll probably succeed in chasing every bass out of the area. Scientists call it light shock; the fish panics when suddenly confronted by bright light. It's similar to the way you feel when you walk out of a dark theater into bright sunlight.

In planning a night trip, you should concentrate on organizing your tackle and your boat so that you can find anything easily and without the use of lights. If you own a number of outfits, rig up four to six of them with various lures you might want to try. That way, you can change lures by merely picking up another rod; you won't have to use a light to tie on a new bait. At the same time, your tacklebox should be arranged so that you can get to anything blindfolded (or in the dark). This little bit of preparation can make night fishing much easier and more enjoyable.

Finally, you should understand a little bit about the moon. On the night of a full moon, the moon will rise exactly at sunset and stay visible in the sky throughout the day and the night. In the middle latitudes, on the day after the full moon, the moon will rise about 40 minutes after sunset. The second night after the full moon, moonrise will be 1 hour and 20 minutes after sunset. Each night, the moon rises approximately 40 minutes later and it gets smaller in size until there is no moon at all.

At new moon, you won't see any moon at all. The next night there will be a tiny sliver of moon at sunset, and it will stay up for about 40 minutes; on each succeeding night, the moon will stay up 40 minutes longer, until full moon.

## Spring and Spawning

The coming of spring not only pumps adrenaline through the veins of every bass master, but their quarry also becomes more active. Warming waters send bass into the shallows to feed and to spawn, making it the perfect time of year for fast fishing action.

Perhaps the most important piece of equipment you can own in the springtime is a temperature gauge. Things happen fast as the sun moves north of the equator; temperature is the tip-off. For one thing, shallow water warms faster than the deeper portions of a lake, and bass will prowl the shallows to feed. Way back in creek coves is a perfect spot to look for bass, especially if there are plenty of stickups along the channel. Keep in mind that bass are cold-blooded and, as the water warms, their metabolism quickens its pace. Digestion rates increase, and the need for more food correspondingly rises. There will be more food in the shallows at that time of year, so that's where your quarry is going to be.

In some lakes, the transition can be so sudden that fishermen are often taken by surprise. One or two warm rains after a rugged winter can bring fish up overnight, and they'll herd into the shallows like charging rhinos.

Determining spawning time is not difficult as long as you are willing to take water temperatures. About the time that the thermometer reads in the high 50s or low 60s (this, of course, depends on the latitude), bass will be over the nests. Largemouths spawn in relatively shallow water, smallmouths just a bit deeper. How shallow they are depends on the clarity of the lake and the amount of cover. In a clear lake without much cover, spawning will take place deeper than it would in a dingy lake with plenty of places to hide.

For best results, working the shallows requires a stealthy approach. When bass are over a nest, you can flush them and they'll return, but it is far better to approach silently and make a good presentation the first time. Since water temperatures are on the rise and fish are more active, you can move the bait much faster than you normally would in cold water.

Throughout most of the South, plastic-worm fishing doesn't really prove effective until after the water temperature reaches 60° F, but in some northern areas, worms have taken bass when temperatures were below 50° F. Spinnerbaits are a good choice over the beds and whenever bass move into the shallows.

## FALL FRENZY

Some say it's the shorter photo period (length of daylight), others point out that the sun has moved south and the rays are no longer directly overhead, even at noon, while still others tell you it's the dropping water temperatures. Whatever the reason, bass seem to move into the shallows for one last feeding binge before winter grips the landscape; it is a great time for capitalizing on largemouth movements.

Bass will occupy a variety of habitats during the tail end of the year, but one excellent place to look is in coves, especially those with creeks emptying into them. Cooler temperatures allow the fish to be comfortable in shallow water, and they know they have to take on plenty of food to add weight before their metabolism slows.

The exact dates, of course, depend on latitude, and things are going to happen earlier in the North than they will in the South, but that's merely timing. In lakes with large populations of shad, the bait will be tightly schooled and bass will be lurking nearby, often feeding on the surface.

You'll find jig-and-eel combinations along with spinnerbaits and tail spins to be good lures for this time of year, and you can also do well on topwaters. The point to remember is that your quarry is going to be on the move; your first task is to locate the fish. Be particularly alert to changing water temperature during this period and, as the mercury plummets (in the water), begin to switch to smaller baits and slower retrieves.

Just like spring, fall is a transitional period, and you must constantly modify your techniques to take maximum advantage of the weather. There will be warm, bluebird days, and there will be times when cold fronts plunge through the region.

# FIELD& STREAM

# The Complete Fisherman

## Book Five

## Fly Fishing

Leonard M. Wright

CHAPTER

# 1

# Setting Out and Setting Up

*"Ther ben twelve manere of ympedymentes
whyche cause a man to take noo fysshe . . .
the fyrst is yf your harnays be not mete
nor fetly made."*

—Dame Juliana Berners

OST FINANCIAL columnists I read complain that we Americans are compulsive consumers. We save less and run up more personal debt than the citizens of any other industrialized nation in the world, they say.

I'm now going to do my part in trying to reverse that trend. If you're about to take up fly fishing, do not—repeat, do not—rush to your nearest tackle store and pig out. Resist the temptation until you've acquired more knowledge and some sort of casting style of your own.

Instead, try to borrow a decent outfit from a friend who's an experienced fly caster. Don't be afraid to ask. After all, you're not begging for the loan of his wife or toothbrush. Just a reasonable fly fishing outfit. The chances are he already possesses more of these than he'll admit to around the house, including some he hasn't used in years.

If he seems reluctant, go straight to gambit II. Suggest that he take you fishing so that he can personally supervise and safeguard his property. This is where you should end up anyway—free equipment plus free lessons. Only the most flint hearted of fisherpersons can resist such wheedling and cajoling. Fly fishers are born proselytizers, all too willing to spread the faith.

# RODS

The best or easiest rod to learn with is one that's relatively long and has a slow and forgiving action. I couldn't recommend one under 8 feet, and one of 9 or more might be better if you have a choice. All things being equal, a longer rod bends more, making it easier for you to feel how it's working during the cast. A flabby rod is a disaster, but one with a "slow" action—meaning that it bends throughout most of its length instead of mainly in the tip section—will help you feel the cast better, too.

# LINES

The fly line must be matched carefully to the action of the rod. This is so important that rods are usually described by the line weight they take as well as their length. The line scale runs from the lightest, 1, up through the heaviest, 15. The code refers to the weight of the front 30 feet of that particular line. The lightest you're likely to encounter fall into the 3- to 4-weight class. Many prefer these for casting tiny flies on glassy limestone or spring creeks. Most rough-stream anglers choose slightly stouter outfits in the 5- to 6-weight range. Those who cast bulky streamer flies and bass bugs on still waters seem to prefer 7- or 8-weights. Saltwater fly casters usually choose rods that handle 8- to 10-weight lines and some, like those who cast for giant tarpon, swear by 12-weights.

All good fly lines are tapered. The double taper starts out relatively fine, increases diameter gradually for 6 to 10 feet, then runs fat and level for most of its length before dropping down into a short taper again. This type of line is ideal for gently placing small flies on tranquil water, to spooky fish. If one end of a double-taper line gets cracked or worn, you can reverse it on the reel and fish with an identical, unused section.

Weight-forward, bug, or saltwater tapers are one-ended, though. They taper more quickly up to a fat, belly portion that, after about 25 feet, tapers down into a thin running line for the rest of their length, which shoots more easily through the rod guides. Despite some disadvantages, this type of taper helps you get casting line out quicker, gives you slightly more distance, and makes casting bulky lures easier.

## REELS

Most fly reels are relatively simple affairs: They serve mainly to store the line you're not casting or holding in your left hand. A single-action model (one turn of the handle equals one turn of the spool) with a minimum drag will suffice for nearly all freshwater fishing. For salmon, steelhead, and large saltwater species, you may need a reel with a strong, adjustable drag, though in some cases a multiplier (a reel in which one complete turn of the handle results in more than one turn of the spool) can come in handy.

## LEADERS

Your leader should continue the taper in the front end of your fly line down to a thin section nearest the fly. You can buy ready-made leaders at most tackle stores. They come in many diameters and several lengths—9 feet being the most common. Some taper down to as fine as 1-pound test while stouter ones, for saltwater use, may end up at 12-pound test or even stronger. The size of the fly you're going to cast and the fish you expect to catch will dictate the size you put on that day. You'll also need some spools of monofilament in several weight categories to vary the thickness of your tippet (the very end of the leader) or to renew it.

## KNOTS

There are dozens of fishing knots, but for fly fishing only three knots are essential. The Improved Turle is best for up- and down-eyed hooks, while the improved clinch is superior for straight-eyed models. For tying two pieces of monofilament together, use the blood knot.

## FLIES

We have now, finally, reached the business end of your tackle. The fly, after all, is the only part of your inventory that any fish should ever see. Flies come in all sizes, shapes, and colors, but they can be grouped into five basic styles that are easy to recognize.

Dry flies are tied on light-wire hooks; they have upright wings and a bushy collar of stiff hackle (rooster neck feather) to help them float on the surface. Wet flies are usually tied on heavier hooks with wings and sparse, soft hackle sloping back toward the bend of the hook, and are designed to sink quickly under the surface. So are nymphs, which are imitations of the larval stages of aquatic insects. These look much like wet flies without wings. Streamers (and bucktails) are large, long, and slim and represent various types of minnows. Last, bass bugs (and poppers) are big, bulky, and made out of deer hair, cork, balsa wood, hollow plastic, or various combinations of these so that they will float on the surface.

## WADERS AND ACCESSORIES

Equipment for fly fishing rarely ends with just the basic tackle, however. Since you're going to be on, or in, the water, you'll need help in keeping dry.

In some cases, this calls for a boat. A canoe may be your best choice for small lakes or ponds. At the top end of the scale are bluewater sportfishing boats that can cost up to a million dollars fully equipped. It all depends on where you fish, how elegant you wish to be, and what you can afford.

More often, you'll need only hip boots or chest waders to separate you from the chilly water. Boots are fine for brooks and small streams. Larger streams, rivers, lake margins, and surf usually call for waders. Whichever you end up with, get ones with felt on their bottoms where they come in contact with slippery rocks. They can spare you uncomfortable, sometimes dangerous, dunkings when you're negotiating slimy rocks. There are a few notoriously treacherous streams where metal cleats or chains are a virtual necessity. There are also some with sandy or gravelly bottoms where regular rubber bottoms are satisfactory, but for all-around work, I'd put my money on felts.

You should have a pair of glasses for eye protection, and polarized sunglasses, which cut the glare and let you see beneath the surface, are usually the best choice.

Fly fishers seem to have a special weakness for accessories and

Dry fly.

Wet fly.

Nymph.

Streamer fly.

Popping bass bug, with heavy piece of monofilament positioned as a weedguard.

gadgets. (Perhaps those hand-wringing economists are right, after all.) You decide how much you want to lug around.

## RIGGING

Before you actually start fishing, you have to rig up your tackle and, even here, there are Dos and Don'ts. There are several ways to knot or splice your leader to your fly line and this to the backing line that fills up your reel spool. All will slip through your rod guides easily, but there's a better way to make these connections.

Since nearly all leaders come with loops on their heavy ends, you can change them much more easily if there's a loop in the end of your fly line, too. Simply insert one loop through the other and pull the rest of the leader on through and you have a firm, neat attachment. The same system works for your line-to-backing linkage. The illustration on the next page shows you how to whip on these loops. I'd recommend a loop of 20-pound-test monofilament for the leader end of your fly line. A small length of backing—that lighter, limper bait-casting line you use to fill up the reel spool underneath your fly line—makes a neater connection on the other end. Just double the backing line back on itself and fasten it into a loop by the same method. Make sure this is large enough—6 to 8 inches should do—to pass over the reel.

When stringing the line through the guides, double back the first few inches of fly line and poke this highly visible part through each guide in turn. You're much more likely to skip a guide if you try doing this with the nearly invisible monofilament leader. And before you knot on your chosen fly, make a final inspection to make sure you haven't missed a guide or spiraled the line around the rod someplace. It is surprisingly easy to foul up this simple process if you're trying to rig up when fish are rising all around you!

Now hook your fly in the first, or stripping, guide of your rod, run the leader around the rim of the reel, and then reel in the slack until the line is tight. Don't put the fly in that small keeper ring many rod makers place just in front of the grip. It's far more likely to hook one of your fingers there, and it will also mash the hackles of a good dry fly.

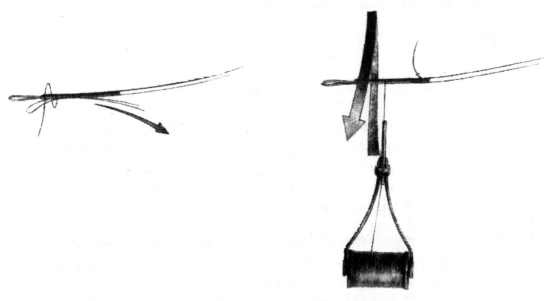

Wind several wraps of thread back over thread end, then trim end. Wind several turns over thread loop, insert thread end through loop, then pull loop and thread through windings. Clip flush and varnish well.

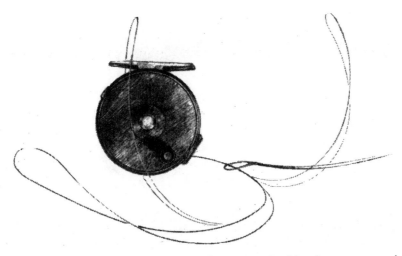

Insert backing loop through smaller line loop, pass backing loop over reel, then pull tight.

A rigged-up rod, ready for along-stream travel.

Now that you're finally rigged up and headed for the river, here's a last tip. Carry your rod pointed forward: It's by far the easiest way during daylight hours. Tip pointed rearward may be safer for the rod when you're feeling your way back to your car after dark, but be forewarned, you'll hang up on far more twigs and branches that way. When you must carry the rod butt-first, make sure the line is still rigged through the guides and the hook is firmly attached. Otherwise, when your rod gets hung up in the bushes, the tip section may get pulled loose. Then it's lost and gone forever.

CHAPTER

# Casting

*"The faults one naturally looks for in
a learner are taking the rod too far back
and not waiting until the instant when the line
is extended."*

—Eric Taverner

CASTING WITH A fly rod, when done properly and automatically, is one of the great joys of fly fishing. Its motion is fluid, graceful, gratifying, and, like virtue, is a reward to itself. However, it takes a lot of concentration and practice to become an expert caster, and it's not really easy to become even a good one.

For the complete novice, learning to cast well takes determination. Despite the fact that there are entire books devoted to this art and that most start out with the assumption that the reader has never cast a line before, I frankly don't believe that fly casting can be taught from scratch by printed words and pictures. Get an experienced friend or a fishing school to help you through the early stages. This will spare you hours of agony and frustration.

If this is, indeed, to be your very first try, string up the fly rod, attach a leader of about 9 feet, tie on a fly (preferably one with the point and bend snapped off), and pull 20 feet or so of line out beyond the rod tip. Now have your instructor/friend make several casts and explain carefully what he's doing. This will give you some inkling of what you're going to try to duplicate.

After a few of the basics have sunk in, take the rod in your own hand and grip it properly, thumb up, as pictured on page 330. Grasp it

329

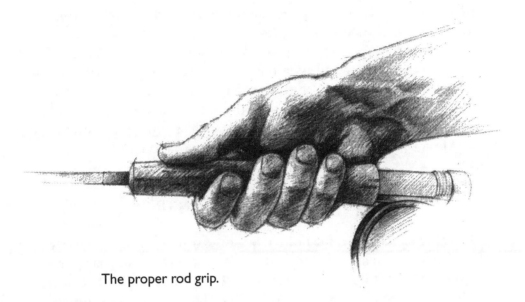

The proper rod grip.

firmly, as you would a hammer. There's no need to clutch it like grim death: It's not likely to get away.

Now take a comfortable stance with your feet about a foot and a half apart and face 45 degrees to the right of the direction you intend to cast. You're now in position to execute the simple overhead cast, which is the one you'll use most of the time.

## THE OVERHEAD CAST

Don't try to cast solo yet, though. Instead, have your experienced friend stand directly behind you and wrap his hand around yours. Relax your hand and arm while he does the casting for a while. You'll quickly get the feel of how much force he's using, how far he's moving the rod tip, how long he waits for the line to extend to the rear before starting the forward cast.

Gradually start participating in the casts by taking over part of the efforts of the coaching hand. Keep increasing your percentage of the power while your friend decreases his. At some point soon, a cast will probably fail—either slapping the ground or water behind you or falling in a heap in front of you. At that point, you should relinquish control to the instructing hand and try the sequence all over again. Twenty minutes to half an hour of this, with a running commentary from your coach, is about all you can absorb in one session. Only when you've made several good casts in a row while the instructing hand is passive should you start trying to cast on your own.

If you practice at regular intervals—just casting, no fishing— you'll improve rapidly and won't acquire some of the bad habits that are so hard to correct once they get ingrained. But that's probably asking too much. Once you get near the water, the temptation to fish is overpowering. If, however, you keep a clear mental picture of how and why a fly rod works, you may avoid the worst pitfalls.

## THE HOW AND WHY OF CASTING

Fly casting is actually a misnomer, because you're not casting a fly at all. What you're really casting is the center of gravity of that portion of your line that's beyond your rod tip. If a fly line weren't relatively fat and heavy, you couldn't cast it 10 feet. Fly casting works the way a bullwhip does, with the energy carried along a traveling loop that delivers the fly as a by-product. What keeps the line in the air and keeps it unrolling is the speed or energy you give it. A rod helps you increase this line speed in two ways.

A fly rod is, in one sense, just a lever that lengthens your arm. Since the average forearm measures only about 1½ feet, if you held the line in your bare hand—without any rod at all—your hand would travel only about 1½ feet during the classic casting motion. Now add to this 8½ feet of rod, and the line can be activated through 10 feet of travel. If the hand cast and the rod cast are accomplished in the same amount of time, the rod cast will create more than six times as much line speed. (I once knew an expert who could cast 30 yards with his bare hand, but don't even *think* of trying it.)

The rod is also a simple leaf spring that can store energy and release it with a quick snap. This imparts extra speed to the line in much the way a bent-back, plastic ruler can zip a spitball across the classroom.

If you keep these two essential functions of a fly rod in mind while you're casting, it may help you avoid the most common and crippling mistakes. Since your aim is to propel the line out in front of you (and, alternately, straight behind you), the rod, as both lever and spring, will be most efficient when it is positioned at a right angle to the line's direction of travel. In other words, your rod and your power stroke are most effective when the rod is vertical or nearly so. The most common cause of a bungled or sloppy cast is the powering of your cast when the rod has traveled back too near the horizontal position.

There's another excellent reason why power should be applied quickly and crisply when the rod is in the near-vertical position and not through a long, lazy arc. You want the unrolling loop in your fly line to be small. The tight loop formed by a high rod tip is far more efficient. It will cut through the wind resistance more easily, giving you either a longer cast or one the same length but with less effort.

## TIMING THE CAST

The second deadly sin in casting is starting to power your cast too quickly, before the line has straightened out behind or in front of you. For example, if the line loop has only halfway unrolled behind you, only half of the weight of your line can act to bend your rod backward, building up energy for the forward cast. You'll be using only half the rod's potential as a spring and you will get some other nasty side effects, as well.

How long, then, in terms of seconds or fractions thereof, should you pause for line straightening? I'm afraid that's one of those questions in a class with "How long should a man's legs be?" You'll have to acquire that split-second, intuitive sense of timing through experience and practice.

Obviously, the longer the line you're casting, the longer you'll have to wait for it to straighten out. Unfortunately, you can't wait until you feel the rod being bent backward because, by then, it's too late to start the forward cast. Human reflexes just aren't quick enough for that. You'll have to start your forward power stroke a mini second before you feel that tug.

The best way to time your cast is by watching. Since your stance is opened up 45 degrees to the right of your line of casting, it's easy to turn your body and swivel your head to observe your fly line as it travels behind you. I find that, with my casting style and reflex time, I have to start my forward stroke just before the highly visible fly line (you can't see your leader, usually) straightens out completely. You may find your best timing point occurs either slightly earlier or later. One thing is certain, though. When your timing has been perfect, you can feel the sweetness of it right down to your heels—just as you can when you hit a tennis ball in the dead center of the racquet.

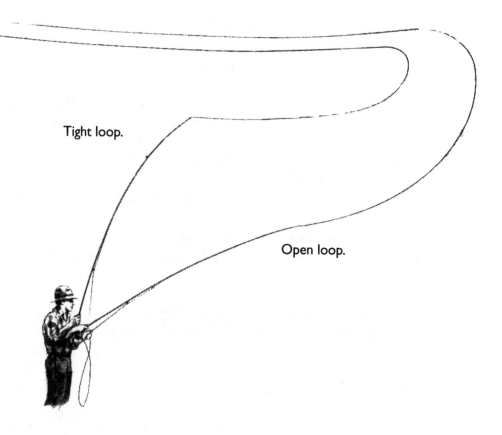

Tight loop.

Open loop.

Of course, even tournament casters don't time every cast absolutely perfectly. If you're only a tiny fraction early or late and you've done everything else properly, you'll still get a good, fishable cast. There's that much forgiveness in the system.

To increase the amount of line you're casting, pull more off the reel, hold this excess in your left hand, and then feed it out through the rod guides at the proper moment. In this way, several feet of line can be added on each stroke, forward or backward, while you keep the line aerialized, never touching the water. This is called false casting and is, by the way, an excellent practice exercise.

The only trick here is to know exactly when to let the extra line go. If you release a loop too soon, it can rob the traveling line of velocity, making the cast collapse. A good rule of thumb is to let line go only after the line loop is at least halfway unrolled. This will ensure that there's enough weight of line traveling beyond the rod tip to pull the new line handily through the guides.

This feeding in of extra line can be done in quite large increments as long as extra power is added, too. If the line is coiled neatly and sufficient power applied, it's easy to "shoot" an extra 15, 20, or even more feet of line on the final, forward cast.

## CASTING POWER

There are two distinct schools of thought on how you should power your cast. The old, or classic, school maintained that you should use the wrist almost exclusively. Pupils were made to practice while standing on cobblestones with a small, glass flask of whiskey pressed between elbow and side. They kept their arm motion to a minimum or they went thirsty.

Some modern theorists claim you shouldn't use your wrist at all. They insist that your forearm, upper arm, and shoulder should do all the work.

I'm not going to take sides because, as in most such cases, there's some merit to both theories. Tournament casters, striving for maximum distance, use not only their whole arms, but their backs and legs as well, and some throw a fly an incredible distance that way. On the other hand, there's seldom any need to strain all those muscles, because probably 90 percent of all trout are caught on casts of 35 feet or less.

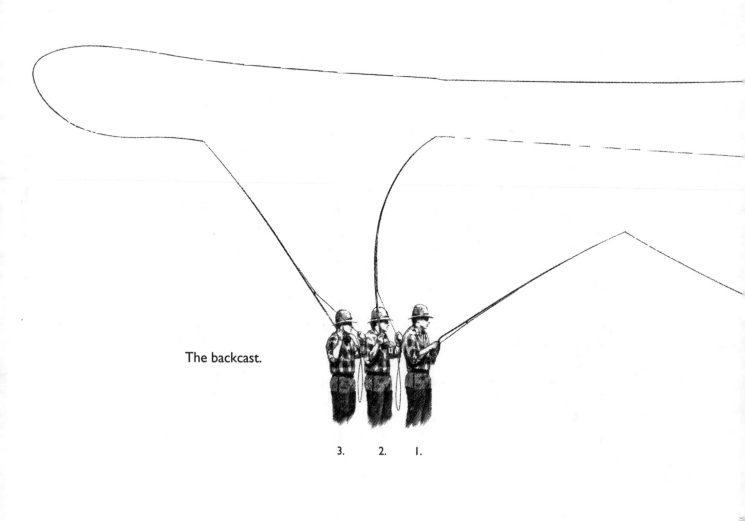

The backcast.

3.  2.  1.

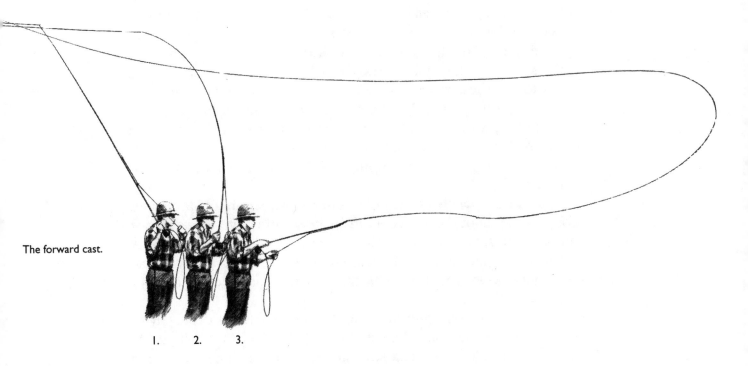

The forward cast.

1.    2.    3.

If arm and rod extend 10 feet in front of you and the leader is 9 feet long, only 16 feet of fly line needs to be aerialized to reach out 35 feet. You can do that easily with a flick of the wrist. I find wrist casting gives me a more delicate touch in presenting a fly at short range. It also tends to make rod motions shorter and crisper, keeping the rod near vertical during the entire cast. When I go for more distance, my arm and then my shoulder come into play readily enough.

## THE ROLL CAST

The only other cast you'll need to master is the roll cast, and this is far easier than the overhead one. You won't have to use this cast while fishing lakes, ponds, or the ocean from a boat, but it's a godsend when trees, bushes, or steep banks leave you no room for a backcast.

In making the roll cast, you rip the line off the water rather violently and send it out again in a rolling loop. Point your rod straight down the line then raise it smoothly at medium speed until it has reached the one o'clock position or slightly beyond the vertical. Wait a split second until the line bellying in toward you slows and starts to sag, then instantly make a strong forward power stroke. Your hand will try to slam the rod all the way down to the water surface to create more rod-tip travel, but you must resist this impulse. You have to stop the rod tip in a fairly high position to create a small, tight loop on the forward cast. In a few tries, you'll find out how long a line you can snatch off the water and aerialize with the outfit you're using.

Handy though it may be, the roll cast has some shortcomings. If you're casting with a sinking line, you'll find the roll cast somewhere between difficult and impossible to execute except for very short distances. You can snap a rod by trying to jerk too much sunken line out of the water.

A forward-taper floater is little better. It will come off the water surface easily enough, but you can make an effective forward cast only with the short, fat belly of the line. The thin running line in back of that won't transmit enough energy to power out the forward cast. That's one reason why the double-taper floater is the best choice for most stream fishing.

The roll cast won't present your fly on the water as delicately or as accurately as the conventional one will. This is no great hardship when you're slamming out a streamer fly, but it can be frustrating

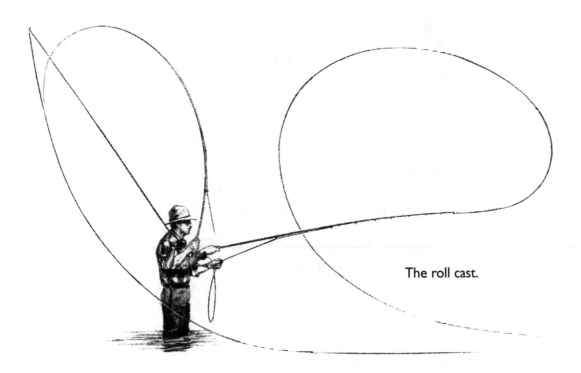

The roll cast.

when you're trying to present a dry fly properly. You can't get as much distance out of a roll cast as you can with the overhead cast, either. But when you have a wall of willows at your back and large fish rolling 40 to 50 feet in front of you, the roll cast will give you at least a fighting chance.

## TROUBLESHOOTING

In one way, casting is like golf: No matter how expert you become, errors will creep into your stroke. Even the most famous golfers have to engage another professional from time to time to tell them why they're driving so many balls into the rough. When you find you're botching too many of your casts, have a companion (preferably one who's more expert than you) watch you cast and pick out the flaws. If you're not yet very experienced, it's a good idea to get a regular checkup, anyway. Sometimes you can even do the troubleshooting on your own. Some symptoms help you diagnose the disease.

All too often, your backcast will run out of steam halfway through the unrolling process and drop dead on the cobbles or slap the water behind you. This kills any chance for a decent forward cast. You may never in your lifetime catch a fish that's behind you, yet your backcast deserves every bit as much attention and rod power as your forward one does. If you make a flabby power stroke through a wide arc and allow the rod to drift too far back from the vertical, you're asking for a wimpy backcast.

There is one other possible cause of a failed backcast, though. If there's too much slack in the line on the water in front of you, you'll have difficulty in loading up the rod to snap your line up and to the rear. This is seldom a problem when you've cast in a downstream direction, because the current keeps tightening the line. But when you're fishing a dry fly or nymph upstream, the current is constantly building in slack. The best way to foil this cast spoiler, I've found, is to use a false roll cast on the pickup.

This sounds fancy, but it isn't. As the line travels downcurrent toward you, raise your rod straight and high to form a line belly, then execute the previously described roll cast. The only new wrinkle is that this time, as the line straightens out, but *while it is still in the air,* start your standard, overhead backcast.

If you hear a loud crack during your backcast, stop fishing and reel in. You have just snapped off your favorite fly. How could you possibly have done such a thing? By not waiting nearly long enough for the line to straighten out behind you before starting the forward cast. Remember, this is fly casting, not crack-the-whip.

When your leader won't straighten out and deliver the fly properly, your hands won't smell very fishy at the end of the day. Occasionally, too light a fly line or an improperly tapered leader can be at fault. But even with balanced tackle, it's all too easy to deposit your fly on the water amid slack coils of leader. Check for either of these two mistakes—or both: (1) a dying backcast or (2) applying your forward power stroke too late and too low, creating an enormous line loop that runs out of energy before it can straighten the leader.

Sometimes your line will roll out over the water like a giant hoop, the belly of it landing on the surface several seconds before your fly does. This isn't a serious problem when you're fishing lakes and ponds where there are no currents, but it can be self-defeating on streams and rivers. If you're casting at right angles to the flow, that portion of your line nearest the rod tip will start moving downstream well before your fly hits the water. This will mean that, instead of lying on the water in a straight line, your fly line will have a huge, downstream curve in it that will whip the fly through the water at trout-frightening speed. And even in upstream casting, that part of the line nearest you will hit the water prematurely, start hurrying downstream, and pull your late-arriving fly downcurrent at an unnaturally rapid pace.

This "hoop" syndrome can indicate that your cast has been only half wrong, which means that you're already showing improvement. Your backcast may well have been high, tight looped, and properly timed. You went wrong in continuing your forward power stroke too long and right down to the water surface. This can create a line loop 10 feet in diameter, and that portion of your fly line near the rod tip will hit the surface almost instantly.

While you're learning, it's a wise idea to examine your fly and leader every few minutes. If you've broken the point off your hook on the backcast, the sooner you find out, the better. Even more frequently, you'll discover that some sorcerer has tied small knots in your leader. These so-called wind knots—usually simple overhand knots—should be dealt with immediately. They reduce your leader's strength by about 50 percent. Pick them out with a needle or hook point if you can. If you can't, tie on a new strand of tippet material. Neglect these knots and the biggest fish you'll see all year is sure to choose that moment to take your fly—and snap your half-strength leader.

These knots are thrown in because there was a "closed" or "tailing" loop in your fly line. And what causes this malformed loop? Again, starting the power stroke of the forward cast too early—before the line has straightened out behind you. When you can fish an entire day without picking up a single leader knot, you're getting very proficient, indeed.

## #@*! Wind!

Wind is the fly caster's mortal enemy. It has caused more blasphemy than lost flies, broken rods, and pratfalls into ice water combined. And yet it is so frequent and ubiquitous it has to be dealt with somehow.

A wind coming straight at you sounds like the worst-case scenario, but it's not. It will keep your backcast up and straighten it sooner, reducing errors in that troublesome area. Then, if the wind is not too strong, you can make a good forward cast merely by adding power to your stroke.

There's another tactic that can help you cheat a headwind. Try the sidearm cast. I won't describe this in detail because it is made exactly the way the overhead one is and with all the same Dos and Don'ts. The only difference is that it's executed in a horizontal plane instead of a vertical one. The advantage here is that, due to friction with the earth's surface, wind velocity 2 feet off the water is usually only half what it will be 10 feet up.

When the wind is coming from your left, you shouldn't have too much trouble, either. It will blow your line to the right, away from your head and body. You can still create a tight loop in your line on the forward cast if you angle the rod diagonally to the right on the forward stroke.

Wind blowing from your right is far more annoying. As the line passes overhead on the backcast, it will tend to hang up on the rod or on your head and shoulders. If this happens, bring the rod back over your left shoulder when you pick the line off the water for the backcast, pause, then make your forward cast in the normal manner, in line with your right shoulder. Line, leader, and fly will then pass you safely on the leeward side. This may create a wider, less efficient line loop, but it beats getting hooked in the ear. (By the way, always wear a hat and some sort of glasses when fly casting. A hook in the scalp can be painful, one in the eye a tragedy.)

The nastiest wind of all is the one that blows from behind you. It beats down your backcast, makes it slow to straighten out, and multiplies the chances of your making the greatest mistakes. There are three countermeasures against this ill wind, but they are only partial ones. First, try a sidearm backcast to keep the line below the worst of the wind. Second, backcast a much shorter length of line. You can make up some of the lost distance by shooting extra line downwind. And third, add extra power—but *not* extra rod-tip travel—to your backward stroke. If you use all three tactics, you still won't achieve the range or delicacy you'd expect in a dead calm, but you'll be able to hang in there.

All very well, but what do you do when the wind at your back is gusting up to near gale force? I'm afraid your only resort then is the roll cast. (And what heroic roll casts you can make downwind!) But perhaps it's wiser to reel in and quit. Fish seldom feed, or take flies, well when the wind is blowing that hard. You'll see why in the very next chapter.

# CHAPTER 3

## Where to Fish— and When

*"It's ill work fishing when the fish'll no' take:
and it's worse when they're no' there."*
—Quoted by
Lord Grey of Fallodon

NOW THAT you've learned *how* to cast, the next step is to figure out *where*. Izaak Walton himself couldn't catch one undersized chub if he were casting where there weren't any fish. On the other hand, if he knew the hot spots, the village idiot could fill his creel. There's a strong hunting element in fly fishing.

Sometimes fish give themselves away, as when they, or the swirls they make while feeding, can be seen in shallow water. All too often, though, your quarry is not that obliging and, when you peer out over the water surface, you feel like you're looking for a needle in a whole field of haystacks.

Fortunately, fish are self-serving creatures controlled by three basic drives: food, comfort, and safety. Knowing this is a fine head start, but it doesn't answer all the specifics. Which species of fish are out there? What kind of food do they eat? Where does their food hang out? What water temperature does this gamefish prefer? And where does it feel safe—under a rock, in a weed bed, or in deep water? You'll need answers to whittle down the odds against you. I warned you that fly fishing was a thinking man's game.

You are probably already familiar with the types of gamefish that inhabit nearby waters. When visiting new territory, you can readily

343

**Brown trout sheltered under a log.**

pick up this information from the local tackle store or baitshop. And the arrivals of seasonal, migratory, saltwater species are usually announced in the outdoor columns of the daily newspaper.

Information on food, temperature, and habitat preferences is harder to come by. You should study up on any species that's of special interest to you.

## Reading Running Water

Streams and rivers are the most important resource because they're shallow-water habitats and have the heaviest concentrations of the aquatic insects that make up the foundation of fly fishing. Many types of gamefish inhabit running waters, but by far the most important are the several species of trout: brook, brown, rainbow, and cutthroat. All these have basically the same habits and requirements. Shad, salmon, and sea-running trout migrate up coastal rivers, but their distribution is so limited that I won't go into them here. Smallmouth bass are, however, fairly common stream-dwelling fish, even though they take a backseat to the trout.

In a stream environment, trout behavior is strongly territorial. This means that once a fish has found a suitable lie in the river, it'll stay there, repelling smaller challengers, for most of the season. This characteristic ensures that trout will be fairly evenly distributed throughout the fishable length of a stream. You won't find a large school in one pool, then nothing for the next mile, for example.

When you take a good fish from a certain lie, mark the place carefully. Another fish is almost certain to move into that choice spot within a day or two, and you'll know exactly where to cast.

Early in the season, when water temperatures are still below 50° F, and again in the fall when water cools down, trout will huddle in slow, deep pools. On opening day and for a few weeks thereafter, it pays to concentrate on the slowest, deepest water you can find. Trout rarely feed actively until the water hits 45° F, and they turn off again when it heats up to over 70°. Smallmouth feeding range is about 5° warmer. It's wise to carry a stream thermometer with you. It can save you a lot of wasted time and effort.

Once the readings get up to approximately 55°, many trout will

Rainbow trout.

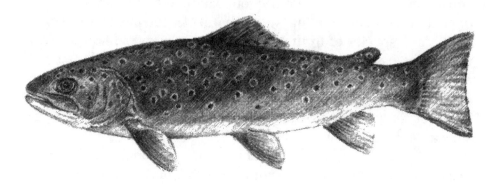

Brown trout.

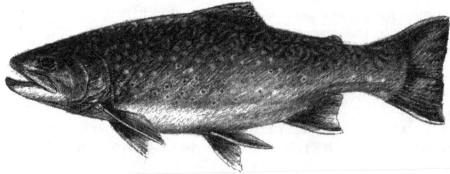

Brook trout.

leave the pools for faster water—runs, riffles, and pockets where they will remain until autumn's chill sends them back to the wintering holes. The warming waters of spring make for classic fly fishing because, during this period before full summer sets in, the hatches of aquatic insects are the heaviest of the year.

In late spring and summer, trout feed in predictable places, where they'll wait passively for the endless belt of the current flow to bring them their food. That's why they'll position themselves in the tongue of a current where the most food is funneled to them.

Trout, at least decent-sized ones, have one other criterion for selecting a lie. In all but the largest, deepest rivers, they need a sanctuary—a safe house to hide in when threatened. In addition to anglers who stumble through their waters, trout are harrassed by ospreys, herons, and kingfishers from above and by mink, mergansers, and larger relatives from below. Their refuge may be a root tangle, undercut bank, or rock they can squeeze under. Where you find a concentration of such places, you should find excellent fishing. When a trout's in a mood to feed, it will drift out of its hiding hole and take up a station in the thread of a nearby current.

Some typical, preferred lies are pictured on the next page. Outsides of bends make ideal trout territory because most of the current, and therefore most of the drift food, will be concentrated there. The digging force of floodwaters strikes hardest here, too, so this outside rim will provide deeper, safer water.

Trout also have a fondness for "pockets"—those mini pools that are dug out behind large boulders during high water. Here they can find shelter under the overhanging sides of the rounded boulder and dart upward to grab any morsel that drifts by.

One of the choicest places for both trout and fishermen is near the head of a pool where the inrushing water slows and deepens. Insects carried down from the food-rich riffle above are easy targets here, and the deeper water gives fish a sense of security.

Deep runs can be productive, especially during hot weather. Whitewater chutes may be too fast for trout comfort, but deep glides with standing humps on their surfaces can hold fine trout—especially rainbows. Those big bumps in the current flow indicate there's a sizable rock under the surface that checks the water speed near the bottom, where the trout will hold while the main current races by overhead.

Eddies or small whirlpools are formed where water enters a pool faster than it can empty out at the bottom, or downstream, end. In

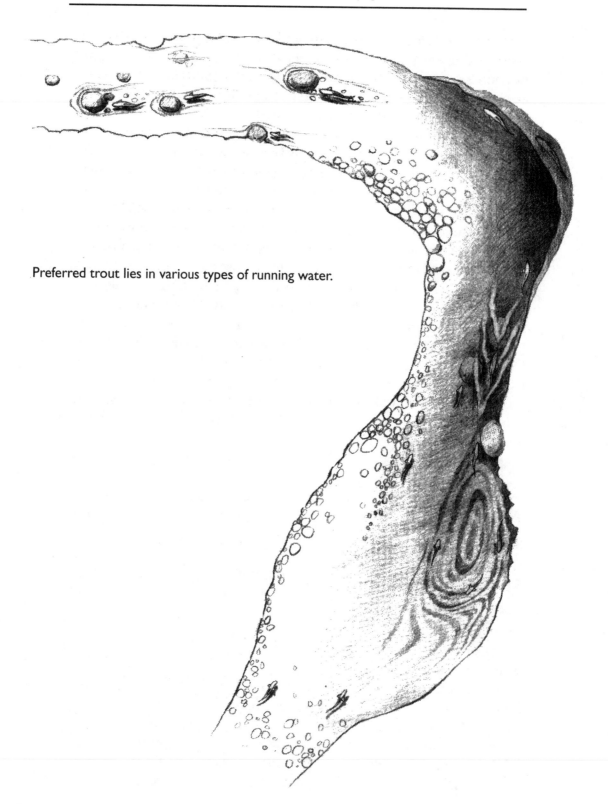

Preferred trout lies in various types of running water.

such cases, the current along one or both banks will flow, for a distance, in the "wrong" or upstream direction. Trout may or may not be lazy, but they certainly prefer to dine with a minimum expenditure of energy. A slow countercurrent acts like a lazy Susan, serving the fish and often bringing the same morsel around several times before it can exit the pool. Given reasonable depth or cover, eddies often contain more feeding fish than the main downstream current.

There's one last location I should point out because, at first glance, it seems an unlikely one, and many anglers pass it by. I'm referring to shallow tails of pools. Fish do avoid such exposed lies during daylight hours, but from dusk until pitch dark, the best fish in the pool may feed here. On summer evenings, flies that have mated and laid their eggs float downpool, dead or dying on the water surface. Trout, once the light has faded enough to give them courage, often drift down to the slow shallows to gorge on these easy pickings.

Of course, these are only a few of the most typical places where you'll find good trout. There are too many minor variations and combinations to describe them all in detail. But if you keep on the lookout for food-concentrating currents, reasonable depths, and nearby cover, you should find enough trout to keep you busy.

## READING LAKES AND PONDS

Still waters are harder to "read" than flowing ones. There are no obvious currents crinkling the surface to show you where the food is gathered. Lake fish don't get the "room service" river fish enjoy. They have to cruise around to find their meals, and moving targets are notoriously elusive.

Still waters also, as they say, run deep—making it hard for the angler to see what's below. Only occasionally is it possible to make out the weed beds, boulders, or bottom structure you're casting over.

The most common fly rod gamefish in this environment are largemouth and smallmouth bass, pike, pickerel, sunfish, perch, and, of course in cooler waters, trout. It's usually wisest to pursue one species at a time. With the possible exception of the small-bass-and-panfish combination, each type of fish will occupy slightly different territory and prefer a special type of food.

**Likely lies of lake and pond fish.**

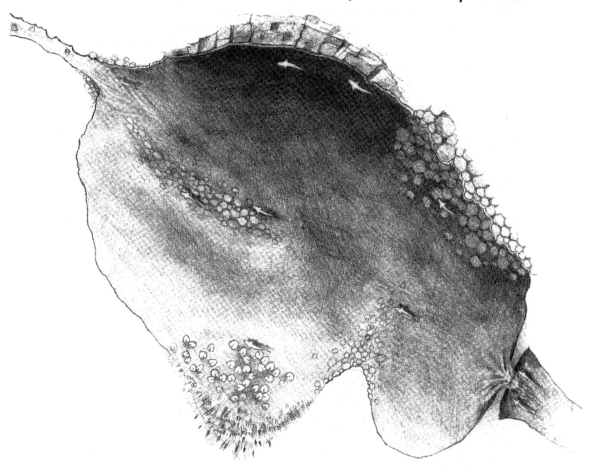

Admittedly, some fish will be out of the fly rodder's reach some of the time. In midsummer, trout may stay in the depths, and even small-mouth bass can be too deep in some weather. You may be able to reach down a way with a fast-sinking line, but dredging more than 10 feet deep with a fly outfit can be arduous work for marginal results. I never promised you fly fishing could catch all of the fish all of the time.

Clues to what lies under a lake or pond surface are seldom provided by the water itself. More often, the tip-off comes from the terrain that surrounds it.

Where a steep hillside plunges into a lake, this contour should continue under water, so expect considerable depth near shore. If there's a cliff on the shoreline, you should, again, find deep water below it plus the rocky or rubble bottom that smallmouths prefer. In fact, rocky or rock-strewn shorelines of whatever pitch tell you to expect underwater rocks or boulders.

Where the land slopes gradually into the water, look for shallows to extend well offshore. If there are reeds, arrowheads, or lily pads close to shore, you may have found prime pickerel territory. Farther out, in 5 to 10 feet of water, there could also be underwater weed beds that attract northern pike, but you'll have to use your polarized glasses to locate them.

Points of land jutting out into a lake should get special attention. Fish cruising along the shoreline at varying depths have to pass through a relatively small area off the tip of a peninsula. Such a funnel for moving fish increases the odds in your favor.

Coves, which offer shoreline protection from most wind and waves, are favored by frogs and the young of many types of fish. Largemouth bass, attracted by this food supply, are especially fond of such places. If there are also weed beds and depths of 5 feet or more, expect pike to hang out here, too.

Underwater reefs and islands are prime spots and easy to find when they're marked by buoys to warn off motorboats. If they're deep enough not to need marking, you'll have to search them out when there's good light and an unruffled surface.

Wherever a brook, stream, or river enters still water, not only is extra food brought in, but the current itself also seems to attract some fish. Soon after ice-out, large schools of gamefish-attracting smelt will hang out near the mouth, waiting to push up into the current for

Smallmouth bass.

Largemouth bass.

nighttime spawning. And in the fall, trout and landlocked salmon will concentrate here prior to their own spawning run.

## READING SALT WATER

Saltwater gamefish are usually the most difficult of all to locate, simply because the territories you have to prospect are so vast. In northern waters, your quarry will usually be an essentially schooling species—striped bass, bluefish, or mackerel. When you find a school feeding near the surface, fishing can be spectacular. On the other hand, be advised that there will also be enormous fishless vacuums between such concentrations of fish.

Wheeling, diving seabirds are a sure sign that a school of baitfish has been driven to the surface by larger fish just below. This is the ideal fly fishing situation. Approach cautiously and quietly if you're in a boat so you won't alarm the gamefish and drive them away or down into deep water.

In some locations, you can depend on currents to help you pinpoint likely places. Tides, lacking in freshwater situations, are the ocean angler's ally.

Where a tidal pool empties back into the ocean marks a choice location. Such ponds are nurseries for all types of marine life. On a falling tide—especially the last half, when currents are strongest—shrimp, crabs, sand eels, and minnows will pour out with the flow, creating a popular "free lunch" for waiting gamefish.

A similar situation is created by a tidal river or creek. Here you have the additional factor of fresh- or brackish-water influence, which is especially attractive to striped bass in the north and to tarpon, snook, and other species in the far south.

Wherever there are tides of at least several feet and there are flats or islands obstructing water flows, you'll find strong currents at certain tidal stages that concentrate opportunistic gamefish. If a stream of shrimp, swimming crabs, or bait minnows pours through a narrow cut on a making or falling tide, predators will have discovered the place long before you stumbled onto it. Any condition that creates a food funnel is money in the sea angler's bank.

Another way to increase your percentages is to use the fly rod as a backup rather than a primary technique. Many anglers troll or surf cast

Striped bass.

to locate feeding schools, holding their fly rod in reserve until they hit pay dirt. A fly rod is easily stowed in boat or beach buggy. When fish start slashing on the surface nearby, a quick switch of weaponry can be made. Unfortunately, when you're blind prospecting over large areas, a fly rod provides the least-efficient method of water coverage.

## FLATS

The long rod comes into its own, though, when fishing southern or tropical flats. These large areas of thin water covering sand or turtle grass are hunting grounds for bonefish, permit, small barracudas, redfish, and sometimes mutton snappers. Here you cast only to seen fish or their swirls and the fly rod, delivering the likeliest, quiet-entry imitations, can be the most telling instrument.

As a general rule, fish move up onto the flats on a rising tide and fan out, looking for crabs, shrimp, and other morsels. There are variations, though. Each flat seems to be governed by a slightly different set of rules. Until you learn the patterns of peculiarities of your nearby flats, you're better off with a local guide to show you the ropes.

## WHEN TO FISH

When you fish—on which day and at what hours—can be as crucial as where you cast. Disappointingly, fish don't feed well every day or

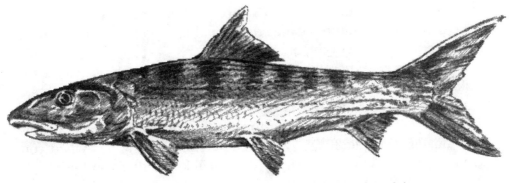

Bonefish.

all day. Unless you're rich, retired, enormously patient, or have the arm of a blacksmith (or possibly all four), you'll want to focus your efforts on prime times.

One of the oldest and most widespread bits of misinformation holds that dark, drizzly days are best for fishing. Nothing could be farther from the truth. Bright, crisp, blue-sky days when the barometer is high or rising are head, shoulders, and pectorals above windy, rainy, cloudy ones. You know you feel friskier on such days and so, for some reason, do the fish. If the weekend weather forecast calls for wind and rain on Saturday, but clearing on Sunday, do the long-promised household chores on Saturday and play hooky on Sunday.

Even the most beautiful, bluebird day, however, is like the proverbial curate's egg: Only "parts of it are very good." In midsummer, it may grow light at five o'clock and not get dark until after nine. Which of these 16 long hours will be the most productive?

Much depends on the time of year, of course. Early or late in the season, when temperatures may be on the low side for the species you're after, it's wisest to fish during the heat of the day—say from noon until four o'clock. Sun is the main warmer of water, moving or still, fresh or salt. A sunny day, early or late in the season, means fish metabolism, and appetite, will peak when temperatures do.

Running water heats up, or cools off, more rapidly than larger, deeper ponds, lakes, or bays. This is because streams, being shallow, moving ribbons of water, pick up heat from the sun-warmed stones on the bottom quite quickly during daylight and are cooled by the night air striking their high surface-to-volume ratio after nightfall. I have seen good-sized streams heat up, or cool off, by at least 18° in one day—a temperature change that could take weeks in the body of a lake or the bosom of the ocean.

This is why a thermometer is so valuable to stream fishers. If we take the biologists' word that 63° F is the optimum temperature for trout feeding and that 68° is best for smallmouth bass, temperature readings can help you find the top feeding hours. Let's take a trout stream, for example. If the water temperature is only 57° when you arrive at nine o'clock on a sunny day, you'll know that good fishing is just ahead of you, about an hour or two away, when the temperature has pushed upward near 63°. Similarly, if, on that same day, you get a reading of 68° at five in the afternoon, you'll know that the next good fishing period will occur in the evening, when the sun goes off the water and it starts cooling down again toward that magic 63° figure.

Lakes and ponds won't show such a wide swing in daily water temperatures, even though their smaller changes may also influence fish feeding times. Perhaps more important to the shallow-water fly fisher are time of day and light intensity. Smallmouth bass, for example, may stay relatively deep during midday in summer to avoid the bright, overhead light. However, since most of the food is produced in the relatively shallow lake margins, they'll cruise in within fly rod reach during the evening and should still be there in the early-morning hours. Trout in lakes show much the same pattern in late spring or fall, but may not make this journey at all during July and August if the shallows get past 70°. Pike, pickerel, and most panfish, which seem anchored to their favored habitat, may be more obliging and remain in reachable, shallow water all summer long.

Salt water has several sets of rules. Fish often stay out of the littoral zone, where they could be vulnerable to fly rodding, during the sunny hours. This may be due to the increasing number of swimmers and boaters using the shoreline. Reports indicate that there were more gamefish foraging in the shallows during the day back in the '20s and '30s than there were by even the '80s.

Because of this trend, which seems more pronounced in the north, your chances with the fly rod are best at dusk and again at dawn. Even if you're offshore in a boat, these are still your prime times. When the light is dim, fish find it easier to see their prey above them, against the lighter sky. At this hour, they'll often drive schools of baitfish up to the surface, where they'll slash at them from below. Here, they're easy to spot and they're perfect targets for your fly rod.

Of course, they're also likely to stay within your reach all night long, but I really can't recommend fly fishing when it's pitch dark.

Some southern waters—especially the flats—can give you just the opposite situation. Blind casting here is out of the question. When you're poling or wading over these shallows, you have to see your quarry, or at least its shadow or swirl. You need good light for this and the higher the sun, the better. From about nine o'clock in the morning until four in the afternoon are your best hours. Even so, if it clouds over or the wind kicks up, your chances are greatly reduced.

Fish that feed up on the flats give you one last opportunity in case you haven't had enough during the bright hours. Often they'll move into even shallower water, just a few inches deep, in the hour before darkness. Here you can see their tails as they nose down for food; sometimes the water is so shallow that you can see their backs as they cruise along. They're extremely spooky when they're in such shallow water. The spin fisherman, with his heavier, splashier lure or bait, doesn't stand a chance here. But the fly rodder is at the top of his game.

# The Approach

*"Getting there is half the fun."*
—Cunard Line

THE FLY FISHER should try to get as close to a fish as he can, without, of course, running the risk of alarming it. Close range should make your cast more accurate, your presentation better controlled, and setting the hook far easier. You may be able to get within 15 feet of a trout upstream of you in choppy water, and you should do so if you can. On the other hand, you may not dare to get any closer than 50 feet to a bonefish in shallow water. Fish stalking is an exciting part of fly rodding, and you'll soon learn what you can, and can't, get away with under various conditions.

In all cases, when you're approaching a seen or suspected fish, try to be stealthy. Gamefish sense they are more vulnerable when they're in the shallows or near the surface. It doesn't take much of a ripple, noise, or motion from a nearby angler to send them bolting out of reach. Whether you're wading or fishing from a boat, there are several things you can do to make your presence less detectable.

## RUNNING WATER

When fishing streams and brooks—especially small, clear ones—a clumsy entry into a pool can render any subsequent casting a sheer waste of time. On these intimate waters, if you startle a small fish out of the shallows, it can spread the alarm, Paul Revere style, to all the

358

**Sneaking up to a small pond.**

other residents when it charges up the pool. Always look, plan, and scheme before you step into a stream.

Fish in larger rivers are usually less spooky, but it still pays to stalk them with respect. They can't hear your above-water voice, no matter how loudly you shout, but they can hear a pin drop under water. Don't scuff your feet, and stay off teetering rocks that could send a warning noise ahead of you.

Fish have a blind spot directly to their rear. Since stream-dwelling fish always head into the current, this allows you to get quite close to fish upstream of you. Crinkled water obscures a fish's above-water vision and lets you get even closer. However, when you're fishing a sunken fly across and downstream toward fish facing in your direction, it's wise to cast a fairly long line.

A slow, quiet pool calls for extra caution. Glide into position slowly and gracefully. If you send out rings of telltale ripples, fish will be alerted. They may not dive under a rock or race upstream, but they probably won't look at a fly, either, for 15 to 20 minutes after becoming suspicious.

It's always wise to stay as low as possible, even if you have to crouch. Never allow yourself to be silhouetted against the skyline. There's little advantage in wearing camouflage, but do avoid light-colored or bright clothing. A white hat is the worst thing you can put on your head. Avoid any unnecessary motions—especially abrupt ones—and try to advance directly toward a fish. This will make your approaching form appear nearly motionless. And don't be too proud to kneel while casting.

You may think the act of wading is as simple as merely walking through water, but it's not. Most underwater stones are slippery, and big, flat ones are notoriously so. Avoid them wherever possible. Try to plant your feet on the fine gravel that collects between larger rocks. And resist the temptation to wade out deeper by using the tops of underwater boulders as stepping-stones. That's risky business. If you must try it, be sure you have a change of clothing nearby.

Strong currents can make wading difficult, but there are ways to reduce their force. Stand sideways to the flow. Your legs and body offer less water resistance in this position. (That's also a good point for ocean waders to remember when they see an especially large wave bearing down on them.) Move one foot at a time; only when that one is securely planted should you move the other one. Move the upstream foot first, then bring the other up next to, but never ahead of, it. A wading staff, or one improvised from a stout stick, can be a big help in high, fast water. The best wading advice of all, though, is "When in doubt—don't."

## BOAT FISHING

Most lake and saltwater anglers usually operate out of some sort of boat, and I'll have to assume you're proficient at handling your chosen craft. It's not within the scope of this book to teach you how to paddle your canoe or dock your 48-foot Hatteras.

There are, however, several specialized Dos and Don'ts that the boater-turned-fisher should keep in mind. First of all, make a point of being quiet. Ship your oars or put down your paddle noiselessly when you're approaching fish. Lower your anchor softly, too. Any splash or thump will put nearby fish on the qui vive. I once spooked a school of bonefish that were more than 100 feet away by clumsily dropping my Zippo onto the bottom of a flats boat.

If you're using a motor, turn it off well before you reach the intended fishing area, then coast or scull your way in. A few species of fish may seem undisturbed by engine or propeller noises, but most of them know better.

In choppy water, waves slapping against the side of your boat can alert nearby fish. You can sometimes cut down this annoyance by pointing your boat bow-first into the waves. And, of course, in a flat calm avoid sending out advance-warning ripples.

In the shallows or on the flats, the boat angler has an advantage over the wader. He has a higher viewing point and can pick out fish at a greater distance. On the other hand, fish can spot him from farther away, too. Even here, it sometimes pays to cast from a crouch or a kneeling position. And don't try to get as close to a fish as you might when you're wading.

CHAPTER

# Presentation

*"Be still, moving your flies upon the water."*
—Izaak Walton

E VEN THOUGH you have dropped your fly onto the water at precisely the right time and place, you still have to convince the fish that your offering is, indeed, lean red meat and not just a fraudulent bunch of fur and feathers. Exactly what you now do or, rather, make your fly do will depend on what sort of food you're trying to imitate and what species of fish you're trying to fool.

## Dry Fly on Running Water

The dry, or floating, fly is one of the most effective lures for stream fishing, because heavy concentrations of insects hatch out on, or fall onto, the water surface and are eaten by trout. It is also the most visually exciting method of fly fishing. A take on the surface means that you'll see not only a swirl or a ring on the water, but probably also the fish itself.

The best practice is to select an artificial fly that matches, as closely as possible, the size, color, and shape of the natural insects you see, or expect to see, on the water. All dry flies should be anointed with some type of floatant—paste, liquid, or spray—so that they will float as high and as long as possible. And before you start fishing in earnest, check that particular fly's stance on the water. Cast it a short way upcurrent and look it over carefully as it floats down past you. An occasional fly that looked great in your box will fail to sit well on

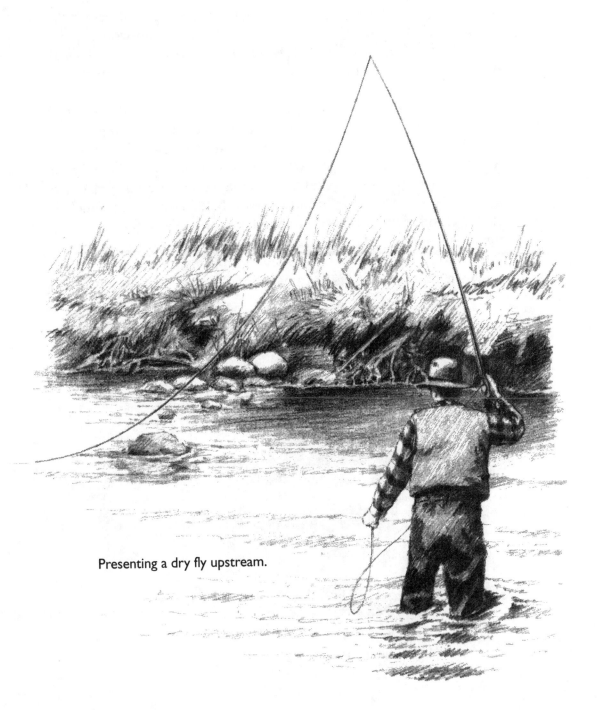

Presenting a dry fly upstream.

the water. Some flop over, unappetizingly, on their sides. Worse still, a few may insist on floating on a vertical, rather than a horizontal, plane with tail and body submerged. Now—before you've wasted a half hour casting it—is the time to discard that rogue fly and tie on another.

The conventional method of presenting a dry fly calls for a cast in an upstream or up-and-across-stream direction, landing the fly about 2 feet directly upcurrent from where you saw either a fish or its riseform. This should allow the imitation to float back downstream like a natural insect. If it skitters or drags across the current unlike the real flies on the water, trout will usually let it pass by, untouched. However, there are a few, but only a few, occasions where it pays to break this rule.

There are some choice places that simply can't be covered from a downstream position. Lies just upstream of major snags or large trees

Capture a live insect, then try to match it from your fly box.

that have been toppled out into the stream flow can only be reached from upcurrent. Stand nearly directly upstream from the fish and let the fly coast down to it on a slack line. Of course, you run the risk of alarming the trout when you pull the fly back at the last moment so that it won't get caught in the branches. However, this trick works often enough to be a valuable tactic, and some of the best fish in any stream occupy these hard-to-reach places.

On other occasions, you may have floated your fly several times over a fish that continues to rise, but ignores your artificial. This usually calls for a change to a better imitation, yet even this doesn't always bring the desired result. As a last resort, give your fly a tiny twitch—only enough to make it twinkle on the surface—just before it passes over the fish. This often convinces a trout that, even though your fly looks a bit different from the ones it's dining on, it is, at least, alive and good to eat, too.

## DRY FLY ON STILL WATER

There's little reward in fishing a dry fly on lakes and ponds unless you see fish actively surface-feeding. There's just too much blank territory to prospect with an almost stationary fly. But when fish are rising—and this is quite common on calm evenings—it's the most enjoyable way to catch trout, bass, or panfish.

The traditional method is to cast your fly as close to a riseform as possible and let it sit for 10 or 20 seconds. If it goes untouched, make it jiggle on the water surface, then pause again after this small advertisement. You can usually repeat this procedure several times before the fly becomes drowned. At that point, pick it up and dry it out with a few false casts; then send it out to another likely spot for a repeat performance.

## BASS BUGS AND POPPERS

Although these lures are fished on the surface, I can't really call them dry flies—even those that are tied up out of deer hair and then clipped to shape. In fact, only a few of the smaller "bass bugs" imitate any kind of bug. Most of them are supposed to look and act like frogs or injured minnows dying on the surface.

You do present bugs much as you would dry flies, though. You cast them out, let them sit for half a minute, jiggle them a bit, and wait again. You follow the same procedure with a cup-faced popper, only you give this a sharp tug each time to create extra surface disturbance and the loud "pop" that attracts fish from quite a distance. Frog imitations are fished differently and a bit faster. Catch a medium-sized frog and toss it out 30 feet from shore. It'll teach you far better than I can how to make your retrieve.

When fishing for bass and panfish, slow and seductive does it. Most anglers fish these floaters too rapidly. That agonizingly long pause between twitches or tugs really pays off.

On the other hand, when you expect pike or pickerel, speed things up. For some reason, a frog or minnow imitation that appears frightened and eager to leave the vicinity in a hurry seems to excite the killer instinct in these slim, toothy predators.

## WET FLY AND NYMPH ON STREAMS

The nymph is designed to imitate the underwater, or larval, forms of several aquatic insects, mainly mayflies, caddisflies, and stoneflies. Wet flies, especially the soft-hackled, no-wing models, are probably mistaken for nymphs, too, though some of the gaudier, winged patterns may suggest tiny fish or fry.

Both of these small, underwater flies are usually fished in essentially the same manner. The standard, and easiest, method is to cast them across and slightly downstream and let them swing with the current through a wide arc on a tight line until they hang in the current straight below you. If you take a step or two downstream after each cast and repeat this process, you can cover virtually all the likely water in a run or pool on a fair-sized stream in a surprisingly short time. This classic, "chuck-and-chance-it" approach may call for minimum finesse, but it is enormously productive—perhaps because the fly passes over so many fish.

There are, of course, infinite variations on this basic theme. The best wet-fly fisherman I know casts his fly slightly upstream, letting it sink and drift for 15 or 20 feet freely with the current; then, as the line tightens, he starts twitching the sunken fly with short pulls on the line until it hangs dead in the water below him. He feels that the free-drifting-and-sinking, first part of this presentation imitates a nymph that has lost its footing and is being swept downstream. The second, or dragging, part of this delivery attempts to convince the trout that the fly, now rising and swinging up overhead, is a nymph swimming toward the surface to hatch out into an air-breathing, adult insect.

An even more sophisticated way to fish these flies is in an upstream manner, drag-free, the way you would fish a dry fly. This is probably the most advanced, difficult form of fly fishing. It is also the most productive. An expert in this discipline can catch trout when all other fly fishers are drawing blanks.

An upstream nymph can fish quite deeply, especially if slightly weighted, because the longer it drifts on a slack line, the farther down it sinks. A trout—even one with little desire to feed—will open its mouth and take a nymph that threatens to bang it on the nose. When water and weather conditions are utterly abominable, this is often the only method (short of live-bait fishing) to catch a few fish.

You can't cover much water fishing this way, so you'll also have to be an expect at reading currents. Concentrate on the known choicest lies where you can pinpoint fish. Learning how quickly or slowly to recover line during each drift, to stay in touch with your fly, takes a lot of judgment and experience. So does detecting the slight pause in the downstream travel of your line, indicating that a fish might have taken your nymph. Such fishing demands the skill and concentration of a brain surgeon, and very few anglers have the patience to master it.

## WET FLY AND NYMPH ON LAKES

This is the bread-and-butter method of catching trout in lakes and ponds and, fortunately, not a very demanding one. You cast your fly out over likely territory, or where you've caught fish before, and retrieve it with fairly slow twitches of several inches at a time. Outside of discovering where the trout are on that day, there are only two variations in this rather methodical technique that are left to your discretion.

One decision you have to make is at what depth your fly should travel. Some days (most likely, evenings), fish will take just under the surface, where you can see the swirl of the strike. Other times, you may have to pause for several seconds and let your fly settle a few feet before starting your retrieve. When fishing is especially dour, you may have to resort to a leaded fly and a sinking line to fish near the bottom for a few, apathetic fish that weren't eager enough to swim up a few feet for a free meal. Generally speaking, if fish are feeding well, they'll take near the surface.

The speed of your retrieve is the other variable you'll have to consider. Sometimes tantalizingly slow is best, while on other occasions fish will prefer a fly that's stripped in quite briskly. You never know in advance. Experiment.

The only other lake fish with a fondness for sunken, insect-imitating flies are small bass and most panfish. The methods described above work well for them, too.

## STREAMER FLY ON RUNNING WATER

Not only do trout love minnows, but the bigger the fish, the higher the proportion of its smaller relatives that make up its diet. That's why so many of those huge trout that stare down at you, glassy eyed, from the wall were caught on bucktails or streamers. These flies imitate minnows, and they're the trophy fisher's (and the taxidermist's) best friend.

Streamers are usually fished in much the same way as wet flies, only with a bit more vigor. They are cast across and downcurrent at about a 45-degree angle to the flow and twitched or pumped in the current to act like a bait minnow in distress. There's something about an injured or dying minnow that brings out the bully in both trout and bass.

There are two major points to keep in mind when fishing streamers. The first is that they're most effective in fast water—deep runs or heads of pools on modest flows. They're also strong medicine during the torrents of spring or when water levels are up after a summer rain. They're deadliest when they force the fish into making a snap decision.

The other thing to remember about streamers and bucktails is that a poorly timed cast can render them useless. The feathers or hair that make up their "wings" are typically twice as long as the hook shank, and if these get snagged in the bend of the hook, fish won't touch the now off-kilter imitation. (You might think this would make the fly look and act even more like a crippled minnow, but somehow

A self-snapped (and useless) streamer fly.

it doesn't.) On windy or gusty days, I always check my streamer after every few casts, and it can't hurt to take a look every few minutes even on calm days. You can feel pretty stupid when you discover you've been casting for a half hour with a fly that was completely out of commission.

## STREAMER ON STILL WATER

Bucktails and streamers are probably the most productive flies for lake-dwelling trout, bass, and pike. Two-inch flies are the usual choice for trout, 3- to 4-inchers for bass; and for pike, go for the biggest and brightest you can buy.

Again, fish them much as you would a wet fly on these waters, only a bit faster and with more pronounced twitches. Sometimes bass, which are inordinately fond of crawfish, will respond to a brownish fly, like the Muddler Minnow, fished slowly and just off the bottom on a sinking line. Pike, on the other hand, show a decided preference for a fast-moving fly.

## SALTWATER STREAMER

Since most saltwater gamefish live on baitfish, streamers and bucktails are the mainstays of the seagoing fly rodder. Big, pike-sized flies are almost always best, but they won't last long in the briny unless they're tied on stainless-steel hooks.

Most saltwater baitfish travel a lot faster than freshwater ones, so your retrieve should usually be brisk. This may mean that you'll have to cast out more often, but it will also mean more strikes.

In a few cases, you'll be hard pressed to move your fly rapidly enough. If fish keep following your fly, then turning away, try a more frenzied retrieve. Some barracuda specialists cast out, jam their rod handle between their legs, and retrieve line hand over hand (yes, with both hands) like madmen. This takes some practice, but the barracudas eat it up.

## FLY FISHING THE FLATS

The flats are a world of their own. The fish that feed in this thin water and their food are different from most oceanic types. The bonefish, permit, and redfish that cruise the shallows aren't looking for minnows, but for shrimp and crabs. This sort of food is not swift, but it manages to survive by concealment in the grass or by burrowing in the sand or mud when threatened.

Here, your fly should imitate not only the appearance of crabs or shrimp, but also their scuttling, secretive behavior. Such flies should be tied upside down—that is, with most of the hair or feathers on the underside, instead of on top, of the hook shank—so that the fly will ride hook-point up. A conventionally tied fly will hang up on the bottom or pick up weeds too frequently to be useful here. It's best to cast your fly 10 to 15 feet ahead of a cruising fish, which will minimize your chances of alarming it in such shallow water. Give your fly a couple of good tugs to catch the fish's attention and to make it appear that it is trying to escape. Then let your fly drop quickly to the bottom.

The fish, at this point, should swing over to investigate, but even if it doesn't, you have one last resort. Give your fly another sharp tug, which should kick up sand or a puff of mud from the bottom. That should do it. Now, as the fish approaches, resist the temptation to overdo it and strip the fly again. The fish knows where the fly is, all right. Your job now is to make your imitation act as if it were trying to burrow out of sight.

Try to just jiggle the fly on the bottom. If the fish starts to turn away, twitch a little harder, but don't strip. Stay with your game plan. The fish may, indeed, refuse your fly. Flats fish—especially permit, but also heavily pounded bonefish—can be very picky. But scooting your fly rapidly along the bottom is, at this point, only going to look unrealistic and may, perhaps, alarm the fish. Most anglers manipulate their flats flies far too much.

If the fish is a stationary tailer, your tactics should be slightly different. Cast as close to it as you dare or within, say, a foot or two, and in front of the fish. Let it sink and then twitch it ever so slightly, so that it acts like an animal that's been dislodged by the fish's rooting and is trying to dig down and hide again.

I can't promise you that you'll take every fish you cast to by following these instructions. You'll spook a lot no matter how careful you are. And some days the fish won't take anything. But you'll take your share of them, and a far higher percentage of fish you cast to, than the compulsive stripper will.

# Hooking, Playing, and Landing

*"...my bended hook shall pierce
Their slimy jaws ..."*
—William Shakespeare,
*Antony and Cleopatra*

ONGRATULATIONS! You've done everything right so far, and you've inveigled a fish into taking your fly. Now what?

## SETTING THE HOOK

Artificial flies don't taste like natural food and most don't even have a similar texture, so they're usually ejected by the fish shortly after they've been taken. However, some species of fish will mouth a fly longer, or take it in a different manner from others, so the art of hooking fish is one with several subtle variations.

### Running Water

Let's take the easiest case first. When you're fishing any type of underwater fly—nymph, wet fly, or streamer—across and downstream in flowing water, your line is tight and you should strike the instant you

feel a fish touch your fly. By this, I don't mean you should try to yank
its head off. More than 90 percent of all trout broken off are lost
through heavy-handed striking. A quick, but gentle, twitch of the wrist
is enough to ensure that the hook is pulled in over the barb. In fact,
the fish will often hook itself before you have time to react, and nothing could be simpler than that.

However, when anglers fish wets and streamers in this standard
manner, too many fish are missed. You feel a thump and they're gone
before you have time to strike. This, unfortunately, is one of the draw-
backs of this technique, but there is something you can do to hook a
higher percentage of fish. Try to cast an absolutely straight line onto
the water and to keep it straight, without bellying, during the swing.
It's surprising how many more fish you'll hook firmly when you're in
direct contact with your fly at all times.

Striking a fish that takes a dry fly is quite different. Here, you
should hook a much higher percentage of takers because, since
you're casting upstream, you're pulling the fly back into the fish's
mouth. (In downstream fishing, you're actually yanking the fly away
from the fish.) And since the fish isn't instantaneously pricked by the
hook, you can afford a slight pause before striking.

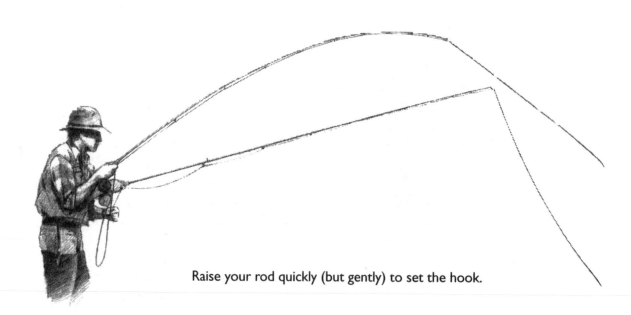

Raise your rod quickly (but gently) to set the hook.

Probably a fish that has risen up to the surface—a zone of jeopardy—wants to get back down to its lie before sorting out what it has managed to grab. Whatever the reason, trout will hold a dry fly in their mouths for as much as several seconds before spitting it out. British chalk-stream anglers maintain that, when a trout takes a floater, you should wait until after you've intoned "God save the queen" before striking.

I'll have to confess that at such moments I'm seldom preoccupied with the salvation of the queen, but I do wait about a second before making contact. If you think of this act as more of a quick tightening than a true strike, you'll save a lot of flies and tippet material. The majority of anglers hit a rising fish both too quickly and too heftily.

You should be even more deliberate and tentative when fishing tiny flies (size 18 or smaller) or the spent-wing imitations of dead mayflies at dusk. Both types of artificials are virtually impossible to see on the water, so it's a mistake to rear back when you see a dimple or ring appear in the vicinity of your fly. If the trout has taken a nearby natural instead, ripping your fly across the water may put the fish down. If, on the other hand, the fish has taken, a hearty strike will all too often snap the leader. And if this happens in late evening, it's usually too dark to tie on another one. The best procedure here is to wait a second, raise your rod slowly, and feel for contact with the fish. Slight rod tension is usually enough to set these small hooks securely.

## Still Waters

Wet- and streamer-fly fishing on lakes calls for a different hook-setting technique. Twitch-retrieve with your left hand pulling the line. Don't try to add action by twitching the rod tip. Your rod should stay motionless, pointing directly down the path of the line. After each draw, pinch the line under the forefinger of your right, or rod, hand (see illustration) so that it's always under tension. When you do feel a fish tighten, do *not* raise your rod tip for a conventional strike. Just keep retrieving at the same pace until the rod bucks and the fish takes off. Then raise your rod.

Why this is more effective than striking as you would in running water, I don't know. I have never been submerged with mask and snorkel nearby when a fish took a streamer in still water. But any Maine guide will promise you that this is the surest way to hook

Hand and line positions for wet-fly or streamer retrieve.

trout, bass, or landlocked salmon on wets and streamers, and he's absolutely right.

Bass bugs and poppers, on the other hand, call for instant retaliation. The moment you see the swirl or splash of the fish, strike—and this time I really mean it. Most bugs are tied on big, heavy-wire hooks, and it takes a healthy yank to pull this over the barb into a bass's tough mouth. A flabby strike will usually mean that your popper will be tossed free on the first, head-shaking jump.

While retrieving or manipulating your bug, point your rod straight down the line, exactly as you would when retrieving a streamer. Only this time, you should make the strike by both hauling back on the line with your left hand and raising your rod sharply. You can afford this strong, two-fisted strike because a bug leader is usually plenty strong.

It's almost impossible to strike too quickly, and it's easy to strike too late. Only on those rare occasions when you see the fish swimming up under your bug could you snatch it away prematurely. Under usual sighting conditions, though, and with the relatively long line you're casting, the fish will have your bug firmly in its mouth and will already be headed for the bottom by the time your strike energy reaches him.

## Salt Water

Fishing streamers in salt water calls for much the same tactics you'd use on lakes, except everything is a bit more heroic and vigorous. You should be using a relatively strong leader in this game, so there should be no worry about breakage. Once you feel the fish has fastened, rear back hard. Big, stainless-steel hooks don't penetrate easily, so hitting a fish hard and even doing it twice is good insurance.

## Flats

Again, fish on the saltwater flats behave differently than other saltwater species. Usually, the only sign that a fish is taking your fly is a tilting of its head toward the bottom. You seldom feel the strike. But if the surface isn't too ruffled, you can see the fish nose down quite clearly. Wait a second or even two, then draw in a foot or so of line slowly and feel for the fish. If it's still only looking, all is not lost (as would be so with a full-fledged strike). With this tentative move, your fly will only scoot along the bottom for a foot or so, and you're still in the ballgame.

If, however, you feel solid contact, strike hard and with both hands at the same time. Quickly do it again. Hit three times if you can. Bonefish have leathery mouths. But hit them only during that short truce bonefish usually agree to before they realize they're in trouble. Once they start their dash, don't try to set the hook again. That would be risking a break-off—even with a stout 10- or 12-pound-test tippet.

## PLAYING A FISH

When it comes to playing and landing fish, the fly rod really shines. Being the most delicate and sensitive of rods, it magnifies the fight and transmits every throb and move of the fish intimately to the hand of the angler. A 2-pound fish is more fun on the long rod than a 4-pounder is on bait-casting or spinning tackle.

The fly rod is also the deadliest instrument. A long, supple rod cushions the shocks so that even a lightly hooked fish can usually be landed. And its greater leverage helps you guide the fish in the direction you want.

When stream or river fishing, try to conduct the fight from a position directly crosscurrent from the fish. This will tire it faster and tend to keep the hook firmly lodged. Keep your rod tip high and well bent at all times. If a sizable fish makes a determined run, relax pressure and let the fish go, pulling line off the reel. The minute the fish stops or turns, put the pressure back on again. Don't try to pull a fish back upcurrent, but follow rapidly until you're abreast of it again. Then keep it working.

Always play a fish relatively hard. You'll be doing yourself and the fish a favor. By "hard" I don't mean ham-fisted horsing. But tire the fish out quickly (then either kill or release it) by applying steady pressure up near the limit of what your tippet and hook size can withstand. The longer you play a fish, the greater the chance of losing it and the poorer the odds of the fish recovering from the fight if released.

If a large fish tries to sulk in slack water, get it moving again as soon as possible. Get below it and try to pull it off balance. Pluck the tight line to annoy it. Don't give it a breather or it'll get a second wind and prolong the fight.

Try to keep the fish working in a fairly strong current. Here it'll have to fight both the rod and the flow. When it's in close, hold your rod to the side, parallel to the water, but keep the same bend in it. It's this side pressure that makes swimming difficult and tiring. Pulling upward on a fish won't fatigue it nearly as much.

On ponds and lakes or in the ocean, currents can't help you tire a fish, but your general tactics should be the same. Try to maintain steady, even pressure at all times except during determined runs. Keep the fish on the move without any rest periods.

You can usually tell when a fish is playing out. First, its runs will get shorter and shorter until they're reduced to small surges. Then the fish will start rolling over on its side, an obvious sign of fatigue. Very soon now, you should be able to land it.

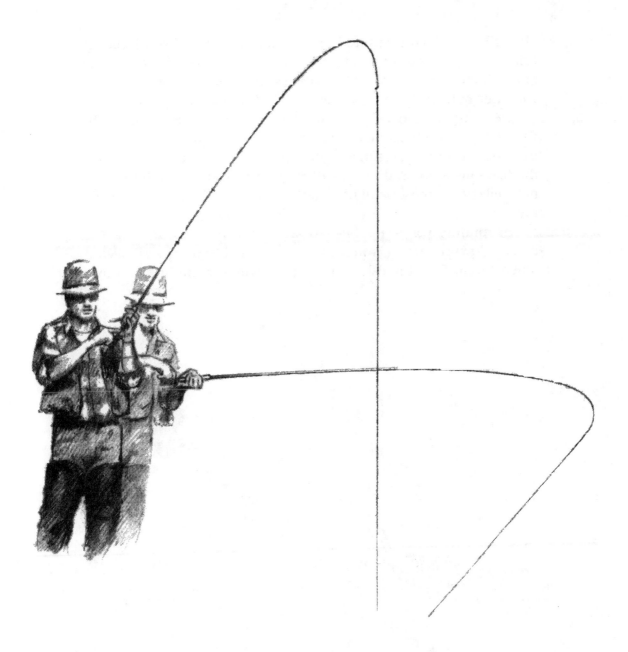

Hold the rod tip high when playing a fish, but lower it to horizontal when the fish is near you.

### LANDING

Most fish are finally captured in a landing net, but if you forget to bring one or it's out of reach, you can beach fish—even quite large ones—if the terrain is suitable. Gaffing and tailing are now such rare, and often outlawed, methods that I won't describe them here.

Never try to land a fish by sweeping the net toward it. Make the fish swim into it, headfirst, while you hold it stationary. Submerge the rim just under the surface, tilted at a 30- to 45-degree angle, get the fish's head up on the surface, and slowly lead or pull it over the net. Only when most or all of its body is over the bag should you lift the net.

In running water, it's best to face upcurrent, so the bag will extend downstream. This may mean that you'll have to step slightly downcurrent from the fish for this final maneuver and bring it down

A tired trout being netted properly.

to the net. Again, the fish's head should be on, or slightly above, the surface. Fish also seem more docile, or less likely to see the net, if they're lying flat on their sides, too.

Bass, and perhaps a few larger panfish, can be landed by an easy method involving no extra equipment. As a played-out fish comes within reach, put your thumb in its mouth, bend the lower jaw down, and pull the fish out of the water. This lower-jaw grip seems to paralyze, or at least tranquilize, bass. Never attempt this with toothy species such as pike and barracudas, for obvious reasons.

Beaching is a tricky, last-resort business that is only possible on accommodating terrain. You'll need a gently sloping beach or cobble shallows and at least 20 feet of room behind you. When the fish is on its side in the shallows, point the rod toward the fish with only a slight bend in it and start backing up.

If the fish panics and heads for deeper water, as it often will, let it go. Then bring it slowly back to the original position, its head directly

A captured—and pacified—bass.

toward you, and start backing steadily up the beach. Once the fish's body hits the sand or gravel, it will usually start flopping. Now, if you keep applying firm, steady pressure by backing up more rapidly, the fish will keep "swimming" on dry land until it's a safe distance above the waterline. Admittedly, this game takes a little practice, but it comes in handy and sometimes it's the only game in town.

# FIELD& STREAM

## The Complete Fisherman

## Book Six

### Tackle Care and Repair

C. Boyd Pfeiffer

CHAPTER

# 1

---

# The Care of
# Fishing Tackle

TACKLE CARE begins when tackle is bought. If you buy a spool of line and place it on the rear shelf of your car where it will be in the sun for a long time, you are setting the stage for that line to fail when you take it out of the clear container to use it. When you buy a reel, mount it on a rod then, and throw it into a car trunk where it will rattle around with jacks and tire chains, don't be surprised if that rod or reel is damaged when you take it out to fish.

Each type of tackle—rods, reels, lines, and various types of lures and accessories—must be cared for differently if it is to retain its usefulness. Some of the basics for this follow.

## RODS

Rods are particularly susceptible to breakage, primarily in car and home doors. At home, rods should be stored in special racks or rod cases (more on home storage tips later) and kept away from heat, humidity, and out of home traffic patterns where they might be damaged. When taken out for fishing, two- or multipiece rods should be broken down to prevent breakage. One-piece rods or rods that you do not want to break down should only be taken outside after a screen or storm door is locked open or when someone holds the door for you. Many rod tips are broken when they get caught by an inadvertently slammed door.

### Rod Cases and Bags

The best place to keep any rod is in a bag or tube, which either comes with the rod or is available separately. The most protection is provided by using a fitted bag and a plastic or aluminum case or tube. The soft bag protects the rod guides and blank from scratches and nicks. The hard case protects the rod from major blows. Bags should have compartments for each section of the rod so that the sections will not scratch each other. Some rods, primarily expensive fly rods, will come with a bag and aluminum case. Other rods only come with a cloth or vinyl bag or plastic case. These are less effective than a bag and case, but better than no case at all.

Rod in bag in small PVC tube.

Rods without cases or bags can still be protected. It is easy to make a bag from mill-run ends and flannel remnants, which are soft, inexpensive, and readily available from fabric shops. Flannel is easy to sew on a sewing machine, but be sure to allow for the largest guide or the trigger of a casting-rod handle so the rod will easily fit the case. It is not necessary to add special ties. Just make the bag several inches longer than the longest rod section so that the end can be folded over and held in place with a rubber band.

Travel cases that hold several or more rods are also available. Rods should be separated by either placing them in cloth bags or rolling them up in a flannel sheeting so that the sections are not touching. Most travel cases range from 3 to 4½ inches in diameter and in lengths (some telescoping) up to 8 feet. Rod cases such as these are available from companies such as Rod Caddy (Bead Chain), Plano, Fenwick, Flambeau, Wright & McGill, and other manufacturers.

## Home Storage of Rods

Rod storage at home is important, because that is where many breaks and tackle accidents occur. Some storage possibilities are:

**Vertical Storage** This type of storage is great because it keeps the rods up, usually along a wall or in a special rod rack, and prevents a set or bend from developing that could damage the rod. There are two ways to keep them vertical. One is to hang the rod by its tiptop or upper guide; the second is by fitting it into a commercial rod holder or rack. The problem with hanging any except light rods is that in time, the rod's weight can be too heavy for the tiptop joint. This joint has the tube of the rod tip glued to the rod blank. In time, the weight of the rod could pull the rod free of the tip.

Hanging the rod by the first guide on an L hanger (available by that name from any hardware store, and in several sizes) solves this problem. A heavy rod with a light tip, such as a West Coast live-lining or albacore rod, could still exert a

Some anglers use right-angle cup hooks to hold and hang rods by the tips. If doing this, do *not* keep reels on the rods, since the weight will make for too much strain on the rod's tip joint.

bend on the rod, since the hanging point is not in line with the rod blank, but at an angle from the blank at the rim of the guide ring. Too heavy a rod might also, in time, weaken the guide or guide wrap.

An additional problem with any storage system like this is that for the angler with many rods, they do take up space—usually wall space. The obvious advantage is that the rod is ready to grab on a moment's notice. One solution to the space problem is to make racks—like the fold-up racks used to sell posters—mounted with L brackets to hold the rods.

This method can also be used another way, in which the rod rests on a base support or socket and is held in place at the upper end of the rod. Foam, spring-lock mechanisms, brush-type holders, and rubber grippers are available in standard rod racks from fishing-tackle manufacturers. You can build vertical racks of any length for any number of rods by making sockets for the butt cap of the rod and using a clasp to hold the upper part of the rod blank. Butt-cap sockets can be made with a hole saw or Forstner bit (a special woodworker's blind-bottoming drill bit) in a 2 × 4, using 2-inch PVC pipe-end caps, or plastic caps from household spray cans. Upper rod clamps can be made of foam, spring locks, broom spring holders (cover the metal fingers with tape or tubing, though), and similar holding devices available at hardware stores.

**Horizontal Storage** Horizontal storage is fine, provided that the rods are supported properly, either on a flat surface or at several support points. Rods can also be stored flat in their cases, but take the end cap off to prevent moisture from accumulating, which can bubble the finish on the rod. (This also occurs when a wet rod is cased.)

Other systems that work well are a high rafter shelf in a basement, on which rods can be placed flat, or a system of hooks, or hooks and loops, to hang rods at the handle and at a balance point farther up the rod.

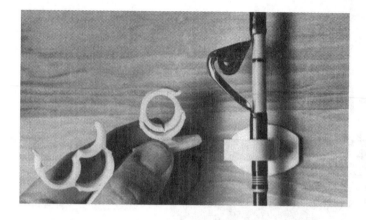

Snap-open holders like these are ideal to hold the upper end of rods. They hold a rod securely yet won't mar it.

A perforated board with hooks can provide similar horizontal support along a wall. In any of these arrangements, be sure the rod is supported to prevent severe bends. This often means that the spacing between the two support points will vary according to the type of rod. A long surf rod, for example, might have a 6- to 8-foot separation. An ultralight panfish rod might need less than 3 feet of space between supports. Flat storage in a garage or carport is also good, particularly for long rods (such as those used for surf or jetty fishing), if they are protected from theft and rodents.

Author with his overhead basement storage of rods. The hook-and-loop system works well to hold a number of rods horizontally.

Some fishing-tackle companies make horizontal rod racks. These consist of two foam racks into which the rod sections are secured.

I use the loop-and-hook arrangement, storing rods on the rafters in my basement. The loops are heavy nylon cord, stapled into a board. Each loop is 3 inches deep. I use 6 inches of cord, with a 2-inch space between loops. The other end of the rod is held by 1¼-inch cup hooks, also spaced 2 inches apart. For easiest construction, make up the brackets on separate lathing strips in the length you need and tack the bracket into the rafters.

## Car Storage of Rods

The best place for a rod in any vehicle is in a case. I've seen enough uncased rods break in closing car windows and cluttered trunks to last me a lifetime.

Lacking cases, rods are best stored out of the way—broken down into two or more sections across the back window shelf, along one side of the car (be careful of windows and doors, though), or stretched through the center of the car in hatchback models. On wagons or vans, a horizontal racking system along the roof line is great, because it provides enough space for any but the longest rods, holds them generally out of sight, and keeps them where they cannot be damaged. Berkley and Rod Saver have such systems. These have a snap-down end to hold the handle and a ring or strap-down end to hold the rod's other end. The ring idea is the best choice, although you must take care when removing a rod so the guides won't catch on the ring. A similar homemade arrangement uses rope or aluminum straps at the handle and PVC pipe or golf tubes to hold the tip end. Up to 10 rods can be held in most vehicles this way.

## Boat Storage of Rods

Rod breakage in boats usually results from too few rod holders or racks to secure the rods when they aren't being used. Rods in boats must be kept so that they are out of the way, yet instantly available. The best storage spots on small boats are

Large rods are best protected for car travel by storing them on outside rod racks (as shown) rather than trying to cram them into small cars.

Rods and reels are best protected on boats by using some sort of rod holder, as shown on this small center-console fishing boat. These rod holders are under the wide gunwale to protect the tackle. This allows you to carry ready-rigged rods and reels and still protect them.

along the gunwales. On bass boats there is often little space here; Velcro straps, attached to the front deck to hold rods down, are the best solution. On larger boats (usually 16 feet and longer) the best spots for rods are underneath the wide gunwales that these boats often have. These areas can hold horizontally racked rods in ring-and-clip, clip and PVC pipe, or similar systems. The best storage solution is to place the rod tip into a sleeve or tube and hold the handle or butt with a spring clip or elastic cord. That way, the rod is completely protected but is readily available. The arrangement is similar to pulling a sword from a sheath.

Another solution, used primarily on center-console boats for obvious reasons, is vertical rod racks. These use butt sockets and foam or spring clips to hold the rod blank upright. Vertical racks are best for rigged rods, but use them only if there is enough space around the rod rack for easy passage. For under-gunwale rod mounts, a wide gunwale is necessary to prevent a hook from snagging pant legs.

## Travel with Rods

Travel with rods requires large-diameter rod cases. Use a cloth bag for each rod, then put them in the case. I use a large sheet of flannel and roll up the rods in it. The flannel must be several feet longer on each end than the longest rod. Lay the flannel out on the floor, lay the rods out in the middle of the cloth, fold the ends over the rods, and roll up, making sure that a layer of flannel protects each rod section. Use straps or ties to hold the bundle together and place it in the large travel case. Label the case, both inside and out, with your name and address.

## REELS

Reels are compact and sturdy for their intended purpose, but they must also have adequate care if they are to last a long time. And they can last a long time.

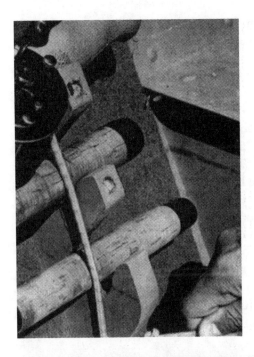

The rack end of rod holders usually consists of homemade wood racks to hold and support the rod handle. The bungee (elastic) cord shown holds the rods down while running the boat.

When traveling, rods must be protected by using a large-diameter travel rod tube. For best results, wrap up the rods in a large flannel cloth before storing in the rod tube.

A friend recently brought me a bait-casting reel that he had been actively using for more than 20 years. The reel needed a new pinion gear, and we added a new main gear and spool for insurance. It should now last another 20 years. But this friend takes care of his tackle, regularly checking, cleaning, and lubricating it.

When stored or not used, all reels should have the drags backed off until the drag is loose. Drags are made up of alternating soft (usually fiber or leather) and hard (metal) washers, with the metal washers keyed alternately to the spool and the reel shaft. The pressure on the drag screw creates resistance in the layers of washers to turning, thus creating the drag on the spool. Leaving a drag tight deforms the soft washers and can make a drag less effective, erratic, and jumpy.

Poor drag performance is the main reason for lost fish and broken lines when playing a fish. Similarly, casting reels should also have the cast control slightly loosened to reduce pressure on the bearings and spool axle.

## Reel Bags and Cases

Most reels break when they are dropped or when something bangs into them. The simple solution here is to keep a reel as protected as possible. Reels should be washed after use (more about this in chapter 3, Reel Maintenance), dried, and stored in a tackle- or reel box or protective bag. Leather bags are not good, particularly for saltwater reels, because they hold moisture and salt that can corrode the reel. The best bags are made of cloth or nylon and have a drawstring top.

An alternative to a bag is to store the reels in a clean, dry tacklebox when not in use. Some tackle companies make hard- or soft-sided containers specifically for carrying reels.

On many spinning reels, the bail and/or handle folds down to make the reel more compact for easy storage. This should be done whenever and wherever a reel is to be stored, since these parts are also the most susceptible to damage.

## Reel Storage: Home, Cars, and Boats

Keep reels at home in boxes, bags, tackle bags, on shelves (protected from dust), or hanging from perforated board hooks for ready availability and display. Back off the drag as outlined above. (Cleaning, maintenance, and line spooling are covered in chapter 5, Accessory Maintenance.)

The best storage in cars is in a *dry* tacklebox or similar hard container, preferably with the reel in a bag. Bag protection is particularly important if there are several reels kept in the same compartment, or if the reel is stored with other accessories that might scratch or damage it.

In boats, keep reels in tackleboxes or boat storage compartments. Better still, mount reels on a rod and store them in rod racks.

## Travel with Reels

Reels can be easily packed for travel. They are best stored with the bails, handles, and any other parts folded down, protected in reel bags, and stored in a hard case or tacklebox. For air travel, pack reels in a regular hard-sided suitcase or in the center of a duffel bag where they are protected by layers of clothing.

## LINES

Line *must* be replaced regularly. Some tournament fishermen replace line after each hard fight or trophy fish. Bass pros often change it after each day of tournament fishing or after each tournament. Most of us need not go to that extreme, but line should be changed each year. If you don't, the line will eventually twist, become brittle, or break from abrasion—all of which can result in lost fish. And lost fish are not the only casualty from inadequate line care. In a poll of a number of manufacturers, most reported that many reel problems are caused by poor, old, or insufficient line on the reel. Insufficient line makes casting difficult and distance impossible. Twisted line can get caught around the rotor shaft of spinning and spincast reels, or under the spool of some casting and offshore models. That not only ruins the line, but can ruin reel parts. The original problem, of course, is not the reel, but the line.

Line care is simple. For monofilament lines, simply keep them out of the sun, away from moisture, and in a cool, dry, dark place. If you buy reel-fill spools and use them immediately, all these precautions are unnecessary. Storage of bulk line spools, however, is important.

Experts, such as those from Stren and Berkley, major fishing-line manufacturers, agree that most things that come in contact with monofilament will not harm it. Greases, oils, other lubricants, suntan and aftershave lotions, perfume, deodorants, demoisturizing sprays (WD-40, CRC), gasoline, and so on, will not damage monofilament. Battery acid, though, will ruin all line.

Fly lines are different because most of them consist of a PVC coating over a braided core. This coating can be damaged by many of the above, especially suntan lotions and gasoline, and also insect repellent. In short, any strong organic solvent or chlorinated hydrocarbon can harm the PVC coating. All such substances should naturally be kept away from line where and when possible—even mono—because they could be absorbed by the line and impart a smell that might repel fish. There are some exceptions, although any contact with line by such products is best avoided.

## LURES

That lures last as long as they do and look as good as they do after being repeatedly thrown into water, and bounced off rocks, logs, and barnacles, is nothing short of a miracle.

Store lures in tackleboxes. Ideally, each lure should be in a separate compartment to prevent scratches from the hooks of other lures. But for most of us, this is impossible. Most anglers organize their tackleboxes with adjustable compartment dividers so that several or more lures fit into each slot. Sort lures by type, though, if for no other reason than to keep hard-plastic and wood crankbaits (plugs), soft-plastic lures, worms, and spinnerbaits with their skirts separated.

The reasoning for this is simple. Soft-plastic lures release a solvent (the plasticizer used to make them soft) that will attack hard plastics such as those used in crankbaits. Soft plastics will even attack the paint on wood plugs. They will also damage any tackleboxes that are not labeled "wormproof," although most boxes today are not affected by worms.

In addition, soft plastics should be kept isolated by color and type because

Boots—short hip boots and waders—can be either stored in a plastic bag and in a box or hung up as shown. Proper hanging will reduce the wrinkles, which are a main cause of rubber breakdown and ozone damage.

direct contact of differently colored soft plastics will result in the colors "bleeding" from one lure to another.

The rubber, plastic, and vinyl skirts used in spinnerbaits can become gummy and harm hard lures. Soft plastics also attack spinnerbait skirts and the paint on the leadhead. Jigs with similar skirts will also react and be affected the same way.

## ACCESSORIES

Accessories such as nets, gaffs, creels, boots, tackleboxes, and other fishing equipment also need care. This usually involves commonsense storage and handling. Hang up nets in a clean, dry area. Left in the bottom of a boat or on a damp garage floor, the bag might need replacement before fishing next spring.

Protect rubber and hip boots and waders from ozone. Many boot manufacturers recommend storing them in a sealed plastic bag that has had as much of the air as possible removed. Many anglers hang their boots up; the main caution here is guarding against folds or wrinkles that might stress the rubber and provide a place for ozone to attack the material.

Keep gaffs clean and stored where they are out of the way and can't get damaged or hurt anyone.

More and more fishing accessories run on batteries. These include portable depthsounders, line strippers, flashlights, pH meters, thermometers, GPS, and so on. Batteries can leak when not used, so remove them from such equipment when they won't be used for a long period.

CHAPTER

# Rod Maintenance

GOOD ROD MAINTENANCE can be as simple as visually checking the rod, or as complicated as occasionally recoating the rod wraps on the guides or even refinishing the whole rod. More extensive work involves replacing guides, handles, and tiptops, fixing loose reel seats, and the like (all this is covered in chapter 6, Rod Repair).

Admittedly, just where maintenance leaves off and repair work begins is subject to interpretation. A new coating on a guide wrap might be maintenance for some and repair for others. I've taken the position that anything that maintains a rod in its original working condition is maintenance. Anything that requires actual removal, replacement, or fixing of the rod or rod parts is repair and will be covered under that chapter.

Rods have no working or moving parts other than the hood on the reel seat and the rollers on roller guides on offshore rods. They are simple to check and maintain. Problems with rods and reels arrive when the reels are left on rods, particularly after saltwater fishing. This allows salt to build up in the crevices around the reel seat/reel foot, and will usually corrode these parts. If the reel seat is not cleaned regularly, it can weaken the seat and movable hood, corrode the threads in the barrel and hood, and lock up the seat and make reel removal impossible. The argument could be made that this won't happen on rod/reel combinations in which the reel is all graphite and the seat is graphite or stainless steel. Reel seats of graphite fill and stainless steel are on many modern factory rods and even on custom rods in which the Fuji FPS style of reel seat or a similar design is used.

In other seats, corrosion can begin where metal reel seats come in contact with metal reel feet. The dissimilar metals set up a galvanic action, which produces an electrical current that will corrode both metals. The best answer is to remove the reel from the rod so that both can be washed independently.

Ideally, rods should be washed off after each fishing trip. This, however, depends upon fishing conditions. When fishing in clear, clean fresh water such regular care is unnecessary. If the fresh water is murky or filled with algae or weeds, such cleaning is a must. Algae or silt from the murky water will be picked up on the fishing line and deposited on the guides, around the guide feet, and on the rod blank. When fishing in salt water, salt spray will coat the rod, so washing with fresh water is a must to keep the rod functional.

How you wash the rod depends upon how dirty and salt caked it is. For light

395

cleaning, a simple spray with a garden hose is ideal. Even in saltwater areas, most cleaning tables or boat docks have a freshwater hose for this purpose. For very dirty rods, scrub with a light brush or rag and give particular attention to the areas around the guides, guide rings, guide feet, and reel seat. To keep the reel seat working, it is best to screw the movable hood all the way to one end of the barrel, scrub the threads on the barrel with a rag or washcloth, screw the movable hood to the other end, and repeat the cleaning. It takes only a few minutes and will clean away any salt or scum. Roller guides such as those by AFTCO also require special cleaning around the rollers to keep them free of salt and to keep them rolling. This is easy to do with an old toothbrush, working with soapy water around these fittings.

One method that I use is to take all my rods into the shower with me at the end of each day. It is easy to clean me and the fishing rods at the same time. Use a washcloth around the reel seat and guides; use the old toothbrush on the rollers and reel seats. After washing, I rinse the rods completely, stand them in the shower stall until dry, then store them in the basement.

## Checking Rods

How often you check a rod, and how thoroughly you check it, depends upon many things, including how rough you are on tackle, how rough a particular fishing trip was, and whether you were fishing in salt water or around murky or algafilled water. A check after each trip might be good. In other situations, an annual check is enough.

A careful check of any rod is suggested under the following conditions:

1. After any trip in which the rod has been abused, knocked around, possibly damaged.

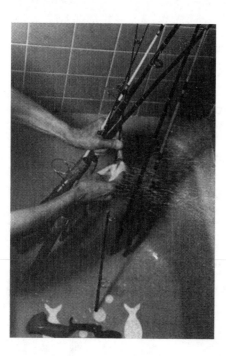

Rinse all rods after each trip, especially if used in salt water. These rods are being rinsed in the shower, using a wash rag to give particular attention to the guides and reel seats.

2. When fishing extensively with light tackle for big fish, because such conditions can severely strain tackle.

3. Anytime you have a problem casting, fighting fish, pumping a fish, holding the reel on the reel seat, and so on. Such conditions indicate a problem with the rod or reel.

4. Anytime you see something wrong with the rod, such as a loose thread on a guide wrap, wobbly guide, gouged cork handle, and so on.

5. When you have been fishing in scummy, alga- or weed-filled water, such conditions will coat the rod with scum that can cause line wear in time.

6. After fishing extensively in salt water, especially if using roller guides, because rollers can become nonfunctional and clogged with salt spray.

7. Anytime you fall down with, or on, a rod, because the blank can fracture or guides can bend or break.

Things to check on a rod, and possible corrections, include:

**Butt Cap** Check for damage or looseness. If it is a metal cap, check for any signs of corrosion or pitting, especially if fishing in salt water. Butt caps often come loose. An easy solution is to remove the butt cap, use a knife or file to scrape out any loose glue, and reglue it. It is best to abrade the cap's inside to provide more tooth for the glue, and to use a good glue such as a 24-hour epoxy. Epoxy rod finish is also excellent to use for rubber or soft-plastic butt caps, because it is more flexible and will give with the rod butt.

**Handles and Grips** Handles and grips can become dirty and require nothing more than a cleaning, or can become damaged, requiring repair. Cleaning a handle or grip requires more than the simple scrubdown for rods described in chapter 1, although a regular washing will do a lot to keep grips clean and usable.

Cork grips and handles in time become discolored from repeated handling. To restore a cork grip to the original, light-buff appearance, sand with a fine sandpaper. Use only fine or extra-fine grades because coarser paper will roughen the finish and remove cork. Take care to avoid scratching any other parts of the rod such as butt caps, reel seats, and rod blanks. The simple solution here is to wrap these parts with masking tape and remove it when you are finished sanding.

Some synthetic grips (Hypalon, Foamlite, and similar names are used for this pliable spongy material) become shiny and slick in time and lose their holding surface. To restore the grips to their original finish, sand them with a medium or coarse sandpaper. Again, protect other parts of the rod with several layers of masking tape.

Wood handles on some boat and jetty rods generally require little more than a good scrubbing to keep them in good order. Most of these handles have a protective finish of varnish or epoxy, and this might become worn or flaky. Scrubbing with a hard nylon brush or nylon scrubbing pad will loosen and remove any flaking, but a true restoration is really in the repair department and involves removing the old finish and refinishing.

Aluminum handles such as those on offshore and boat rods can only be scrubbed clean, because abrasive materials will scratch and may remove the anodizing that protects the aluminum finish.

Factory handles, such as those molded for casting rods, can only be cleaned. For these use a scrub rag, nylon scrub pad, or other nonabrasive cleaner.

When you are cleaning and checking handles and grips, also look thoroughly for damage that might require repairs. Cork grips are subject to gouging, crushing, cracking, and splitting. Most of this is a result of blows to the handle that damage the cork. You can repair gouges, replace cork rings, fill holes, and so on (see chapter 6, Rod Repair).

Hypalon can't really be repaired, but seldom suffers damage the way cork does. Check for cuts, cracks, and dents, which can occur when trolling rods are placed in boat rod holders where rod pressure dents the grip. Wood handles can also become splintered or dented, but they are generally easy to repair with standard woodworking practices.

**Reel Seats** It is particularly important to clean reel seats thoroughly after each use, especially after fishing in salt or muddy water. Reel seats are made of aluminum, chrome-plated brass, and graphite or graphite-filled plastics. If they are cleaned regularly, a check can consist of nothing more than a simple examination of the reel seat for corrosion, scratches, loosening, split hoods, worn barrel threads, and the like. Most of these problems are prevented by careful cleaning. Corrosion usually starts with a scratch or break in the finish that allows water to penetrate and the metal to oxidize. If this occurs, the only maintenance is constant cleaning and checking.

When working with a bare metal, such as chrome over brass, metal polishes are best for removing corrosion and keeping the reel seat attractive. If working with an anodized reel seat, carefully rub away any corrosion and clean regularly to prevent heavy oxidation from returning. Using metal polishes cavalierly will wear the anodizing, and the seat will lose the color and protection provided by the coating.

To avoid scratches, keep the rod protected in bags and/or cases and in holders at home or in boats. Avoid allowing the rod to come in contact with the ground, sand, and equipment or tools that might scratch the seat. Loose reel seats are a result of poor gluing and are a repair problem.

Split hoods can result from flimsy manufacture, but they are often caused by too much pressure on the hood. The split is almost always on slip-over reel seats with swaged hoods. (Swaged hoods are those made by taking a round collar and using dies to force it into a shape in which a recess is formed to hold the end of the reel foot.) The split often occurs along an area of maximum stress, such as the edge of the recess for the reel foot. This is impossible to repair; the only solution is to replace the hood or, more likely, the entire reel seat.

**Rod Blank** The rod blank is the "pole" that makes up the basis of the rod. Maintenance involves nothing more than keeping the rod clean, keeping it protected, and avoiding blows that will damage the hollow blank construction of any glass, graphite, boron, or composite rod. (A few rods are solid or have solid tips or sections. Any solid rod or part is less subject to damage, but a hard or crushing blow will still ruin it.)

Use a soft cloth to wash the rod regularly so the factory finish will be preserved. In time, some finishes have been known to flake and look like a bad case of peeling sunburn. There is no maintenance program to prevent this, and the poor appearance will not affect performance or action. The only solution is to remove the old finish with fine steel wool and refinish the rod with a brush-on or spray epoxy. Be warned, however, that no home refinish can equal the oven-baked factory coating.

**Guides** Guides are difficult to clean properly, what with the frames, added supports, small-sized rings, and light-wire construction, but some tips will make it easier. First, guides should be cleaned often with a rag or washcloth as outlined in chapter 1 on general care. Periodically, depending upon usage and need, it helps to clean the guides with an old toothbrush or similar small brush. Use these to work around and clean the junction of the frame with the wrapped guide foot, the frame's junction with the wire ring, and the guide ring itself. Use the same methods to clean roller guides, then wash, rinse, and liberally oil the roller and the bushings and pins that hold it. It is easy to remove the small screws holding the roller and bushing in place for a more through cleaning.

Small bends in the guide frame are usually easy to see, and can be straightened with small wide-jaw pliers. Guide rings are more difficult to check. Guides that have an inner wire ring (stainless steel/hard chrome is most commonly used) will develop grooves in time from fishing line passing over the same spot on the guide. Initial grooving is difficult to detect, although the deeper grooves that come with time are readily apparent. Guides with inner rings of ceramic, aluminum oxide, silicon carbide, Hardloy, and similar materials will not groove, but a blow to the guide can crack them. The nylon shock ring holding the inner ring in place keeps the crack from showing or the guide ring from falling out, but the crack can rapidly damage line.

The best way to check for cracks is to pull a fine material through the guide and see if it catches. Nylon stockings, cotton balls, or tissue paper will all work. Grooved guides in chrome rings must be replaced, because the line running in the groove will constantly be abraded. Cracked aluminum, silicon carbide, or Hardloy rings should be replaced, but if the single crack is in a position that will not catch the line on retrieve (close to the rod in a spinning rod and far from the rod in a casting rod), you can probably live with it for some time without damaging the line.

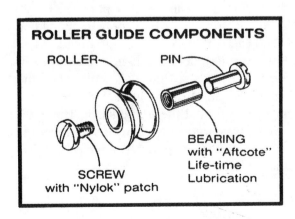

Parts of roller guides can be taken apart and cleaned, then reassembled. *Courtesy of AFTCO* .

**Tiptops** Tiptops are special guides that fit on the end of a rod. The checks and minor adjustments possible with guides also apply here. The wire support frames can be bent into shape if deformed, and the rings should be checked for grooves or cracks.

**Ferrules** The self-ferrules of glass-to-glass or graphite-to-graphite used in most modern rods require little care or maintenance. To keep them working properly, periodically coat the male portion of the ferrule with candle wax. The wax—usually a mixture of paraffin and beeswax—seats the ferrules without slippage and also keeps them from binding together. When waxing ferrules make sure that they are first free of grime or dirt.

Metal ferrules or rod joints are seldom seen today because of the influx of self-ferrules, glass-to-glass or graphite-to-graphite. Older metal ferrules sometimes become stuck because dirt and grime can make them difficult to seat properly or remove once seated. To correct this, wash them carefully with a soapy solution to cut any grease or grime. If they are still sticking, and not deformed in any way, consider lightly polishing them with very fine steel wool. Buff sparingly, and clean and check the ferrule after every few strokes. The only thing worse than a too-tight ferrule is one too loose.

Ferrules can lose their shape. The best solution is to replace them (see chapter 6, Rod Repair), but a simple Band-Aid-type repair can be done by inserting a ferrule into a large drill chuck and, using the key for the chuck, re-forming the ferrule back into an almost-round shape. Because there are three jaws in drill chucks and they are often slightly concave, this method works well as a temporary solution to a bent ferrule.

Another maintenance problem that can develop with self-spigot-type ferrules is when the edge of the female ferrule seats against the lower lip of the male portion because of excessive wear. When this happens, the ferrule will begin to loosen because the friction that holds the two in place is lost. To fix this, use a file or emery board to file down the end of the male ferrule. Be careful, because you only need about a $1/8$- to $3/16$-inch clearance, and excessive filing will cut into the thread wrap necessary to maintain hoop strength.

**Rod Wraps** There are two types of rod wraps: functional and decorative. Functional wraps are threads that hold the guide feet on the rod or wrap ferrules. Decorative wraps adorn the rod handle, at the tiptop, and at any other spot on the rod.

Guides are not glued to the rod, so the thread wraps are the only thing holding them in place and in line with the reel and each other. Ferrule wraps are necessary to give the rod blank hoop strength. Hoop strength helps maintain the hollow rod blank in a round configuration and prevents the blank from collapsing when the rod is bent, such as when casting or fighting a fish. This strength is built into a rod with transverse fibers in the rod blank that help hold the round shape. The ends, however, where rods join at built-in ferrules are particularly vulnerable to breakage (especially when they are glass-to-glass or graphite-to-graphite). The wrap here prevents the ends from splintering and other damage.

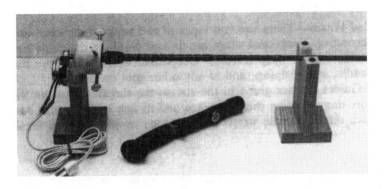

A professional-type rod-wrapping device will hold any type of rod for slow turning and curing of epoxy.

Replacing these wraps is a repair job (see chapter 6, Rod Repair). Often, however, this repair can be avoided by carefully checking and maintaining the protective coating on the wraps. At one time these coatings were varnish but today they are usually thicker, harder, and more durable epoxies. Wear often comes when a rod rests with too much pressure in a rod holder, against boat seats or gunwales, and so on at the point where these wraps are located. After the finish is worn through, the wraps begin to fray. To avoid this, refinish any or all wraps with an epoxy when they become slightly worn or show signs of wear. Areas around the wrap's edge are particularly vulnerable because fraying begins at this point.

Refinish only the thread wrap, because the rest of the rod, whether custom-made from a rod blank or a factory model, has a baked-on finish that is far better than anything that can be done at home.

A new finish can go over any old finish. Old finishes can be varnish, spar varnish, epoxy, manufacturer UV-activated finishes, one-part air-dry urethanes, two-part air-dry urethanes, and similar coatings. Varnish, epoxy, and some urethane finishes available to the hobbyist will all work. Varnish is seldom used anymore, except by fishermen who like to build and maintain rods that boast traditional construction and appointments. Many rod manufacturers use UV-activated urethanes. Some experts feel that these look great initially, but break down and get cloudy in time and require replacement or refinishing. These coatings are not available to fisher-

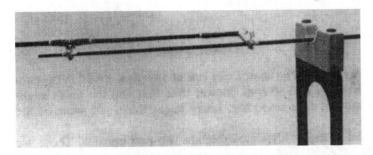

In some cases it is necessary to refinish an entire rod using spray epoxy. In this case, the rod cannot rest on the rod support as in refinishing individual wraps. To solve this, run a short rod blank or dowel through the guides, tape them, and let the dowel or rod run on the support as shown. This way, the entire rod can be sprayed.

men, because they are highly toxic and their application requires special machinery to emit UV rays for curing.

No special tools or machinery are needed to refinish rod wraps, but if you have a rod-wrapping motor (low-rpm motor) or a rotisserie motor for your barbecue grill, it will help. The first slowly turns rods while the wrap finish cures, the second can be jury-rigged with a butt cap to hold the rod in the blind square hole in the rotisserie motor. In most cases, the rod must be supported above the midpoint with an additional bracket. You can support the rod on a small cardboard box with a V cut into it (on the same plane or level as the rod motor), or cut a strip from a plastic milk carton as a bed on which the rod can ride to prevent scratches. The motor can run at any slow speed between a range of 1 and 60 rpm. Slower than that and the finish might sag and not cure smoothly; faster might throw off some of the finish.

Most of the finishes available are two-part epoxies. These are also the best coatings available to the home hobbyist because they can be used with one coat. To assure a good new finish on top of the old, clean the wrap finish carefully with soap and water to remove dirt. Allow it to dry overnight, because a thorough cleaning often leaves water around the junction of the guide frame with the guide foot wrap. For proper adhesion, buff the remaining rod finish with fine steel wool. To prevent scratching the rod blank, cover it immediately adjacent to the wrap with a layer or two of masking tape. (Any misses with the steel wool will hit the tape, not the rod finish.) Once buffed, remove the tape, clean the area thoroughly, and apply the epoxy finish.

Epoxy finishes are two part and they set up rapidly so they must be mixed and used carefully, according to Roger Seiders, president of Flex Coat, a Texas manufacturer of rod finishes and accessories for rod building, maintenance, and repair.

Seiders feels that epoxies mix best when they are at 80° to 90° F. He uses the heat from a lightbulb to gently warm the separate bottles before mixing.

"If you heat it," noted Seiders, "it will mix better, draw up into the thread better, form less bubbles, and be stronger."

Some mixes, such as Seiders's Flex Coat, come with syringes, although separate syringes or small mixing cups are available for mixing other epoxies. The small pharmaceutical or 1-ounce disposable medicine cups are ideal for this,

An alternative is to use ball-bearing swivels and attach the rod tip to a support via several swivels. This also allows spraying the entire rod, since the swivels will allow the rod to turn.

because the two parts can be easily measured. Do *not* use medical syringes, because these are usually lubricated with a silicon coating. Silicon causes extensive problems when using epoxies.

When mixing the two parts, stir them thoroughly. Seiders used to recommend two minutes of stirring, but has revised that to a visual check of the solution as you mix it. He explained that during the mixing process, Flex Coat will first become cloudy and then clear as it becomes mixed. With good light this is visible. Other finishes may not have this characteristic, in which case a thorough, timed mix is best. It also is best to use a round mixing stick because flat sticks pick up tiny air bubbles and incorporate them into the mix. If possible, fold the two parts of epoxy together to minimize bubbles. Don't beat it to a froth; that will create and increase bubbles.

Once mixed, any two-part epoxy will heat up, hastening the catalytic reaction that will cause the mixture to cure. To slow this and prolong "pot life" so that you can get the mix carefully on the rod wrap, pour the mixture onto something flat. This will get it "out of mass," help eliminate any residual bubbles, and control the curing time. Seiders suggested using aluminum foil because it is cheap, disposable, and helps dissipate the mix's heat buildup, further prolonging the working life.

Another way to dissipate the bubbles is to blow or breathe on the surface. Experts are unsure why this works, but it does. Their theories include a change in vapor pressure, the carbon dioxide in our breath, and the unsettling of the surface tension.

When the mix is ready, spread the finish with a fine brush. Disposable brushes are best, because they are cheap and perform well. Working in good light, cover the end of the wrap, making sure that the epoxy touches the rod all the way around the blank so water cannot reach the threads. Similarly, work the finish under the guide frame and around the junction of the guide frame with the wrap. Make sure that the entire wrap is finished. When you use a good strong light, you will be able to see the sheen of the finish as you turn the rod and apply the finish to any missed spots. If working on a long rod, or on one with many guides, begin at the butt end, because it will be easier to apply any curing and thickening finish to the smaller wraps on the rod's tip end.

Once all the finish is applied, place the rod in the motorized turner and allow it to turn for several hours. Make one last check to make sure that no spots are missed and fill in any gaps. If you don't have a motor, you can still finish a rod. Apply a thin coat of finish and turn the rod 90° every 5 to 10 minutes. (Television specials are great for this, because they have enough interruptions to permit you to make each turn and last long enough for most rods to set up.) Curing will take about 24 hours, although temperature and humidity might affect this.

High humidity will cause a dull finish, or what is sometimes called a polyamine blush. The finish, however, will hold and work just as well as if it had a high-gloss, glassy shine.

CHAPTER **3**

# Reel Maintenance

REEL CARE begins with how you use the reel. Use a reel properly, carefully, protect it from excessive exposure to water (especially salt water) and dirt and sand, and the reel will reward you with a long life and lots of fish.

"Protect it from excessive exposure to water" is not as silly as it first sounds. Many fishermen leave rigged rods in rod holders to and from the fishing grounds. This is typical on any larger boat that has a vertical, gunwale-mounted rod holder. Rough seas, however, can create constant spray that constantly soaks reels and rods.

Rods won't be hurt—they can be washed off—but this water could get inside a reel through the seams in side plates and fittings. Salt water is particularly damaging because the internal reel parts will start to corrode almost immediately. The salt water will also begin to break down any grease. This will start with exposed areas such as the levelwind worm gearing on casting and popping rods. Unfortunately, you won't see or feel this until the reel begins to go bad, so keep it inside a cabin or, if mounted on a rod, in protected racks during long runs.

Whenever you clean or check a reel, take it off the rod. It's not only easier to handle the reel this way, but the contact between the reel foot and the seat is eliminated. Corrosion and galvanic action can occur at this spot, and both will ruin the reel and the reel seat.

## Storage

One of the common causes of reel damage, according to manufacturers, is improper storage. Broken bails and handles on spinning reels, broken levelwinds and handles on casting reels, and bent frames or spools on fly reels unfortunately

Reels that are not cared for can quickly become corroded, as shown by these two reel spools.

are not uncommon. Follow the tips in chapter 1 on general care for suggestions on proper reel storage.

## Trip Checks

For want of a better term, I call these trip checks—done after each trip to be sure that everything is working properly. In essence they are nothing more than a quick look, a turn of the reel handle, an on/off check of the antireverse (spinning reels) or thumb bar/push button (casting reels), and spin of the drag before packing the reel for a trip or mounting it on a rod for fishing near my home. But you can check a lot in this, as follows:

1. Turn the handle a few times to check if the reel is working properly or if there are any binding, damaged or corroded ball-bearing drives, bent spools, broken levelwinds, and so on.
2. When turning the handle, flip the antireverse of spinning reels on and off a few times to make sure that it works properly and easily. When it is on, turn the reel handle backward to ensure the internal cog is grabbing the gear and preventing the reel handle from backturning.
3. Tighten the drag knob a turn or two and turn the spool on a spinning reel, or pull line from the reel on a fly, trolling, or casting reel. This will give you a rough, but immediate, indication of the drag performance and any binding, jerkiness, or erratic action.
4. Check the amount and condition of the line on the reel. The reel should be full and the line should be in good condition.
5. Push the push button or thumb bar of casting reels and pull lightly on the line to be certain the line release is working. Try the same thing after switching the flipping lever on those reels with this feature. This should place the reel in free spool when the thumb bar is depressed, and on drag when released. (In the casting mode, though, it will stay in free spool when released, and until the handle is turned.) Check other features of the reel now, too, because some casting and conventional reels have on/off clicks, antireverse switches, and so on.
6. Open and close the bail on spinning reels to make sure that this often-damaged part is freely working. Turn the handle at least once with the bail open to make sure that the trip mechanism closes the bail sharply.

It might seem as if this check and the regular check and cleaning listed below are the same, but they are not. This check can take less than a minute and requires no reel cleaning. In addition, this check prevents you from using a broken or nonfunctioning reel.

Two examples: On a recent airline trip I took four casting reels, which I packed in my luggage. At my destination, I used only two of the reels. When I returned home, I did not check or clean the reels that I had not used. Later, preparing for another trip and running through a trip check with those two unused reels, on one of them, I found that the shaft on which the levelwind runs had broken, making it inoperative. This probably occurred on the return airline trip, but I didn't notice it at the time.

After another trip I washed and cleaned a reel and stored it away, checking it at the same time. The next time I took it out and ran through the trip check, I immediately found that the main ball-bearing drive was frozen and corroded from salt water and that the reel handle would not even turn. That's the only time that this has occurred—probably because of hasty or improper cleaning, and the ball bearing corroded between the time of the washing/cleaning and the next trip.

**Regular Checking and Cleaning** Be very careful when choosing and using solvents. Many modern reels have plastic parts that can be damaged by organic solvents and cleaners. These include gasoline, acetone, carbon tetrachloride, kerosene, mineral spirits, and other canned or aerosol grease-cutting solutions.

I learned this lesson years ago when I dismantled a reel and dumped the entire contents into a small container of organic solvent. A few minutes later when I pulled the handle pad and the drag knob out, they were completely deformed. Many reels have slide plates, gears, levers, ratchets, drag knobs, and so on that can be ruined by the wrong solvent. Don't be fooled by appearance; many reel parts are plastics that have been plated or finished to look like metal.

To be safe, clean with a strong soapy solution, not a plastic-reacting solvent. When you want to determine if a part is metal or plastic, dip a cotton swab into the solvent and touch the part. If it then sticks, mattes the finish, softens the part, or does anything other than wipe on and off, do not use it. Even if it appears safe in this test, though, it may react during prolonged contact.

Another good cleaning method is to use Reel Scrubber. This 16-ounce aerosol solvent by Birchwood Casey Laboratories uses both high-powered propellent force and a strong solvent to remove dirt and grime without removing reel parts. Their tests so far show no problem with plastic parts of any reel, although it still pays to be careful and test a small area if unsure. It works well, although removal of strongly caked grease can be hastened with an old toothbrush working in conjunction with Reel Scrubber.

Use of Reel Scrubber, a pressurized reel solvent that will not harm reels, makes it easy to clean up a reel like this. On cases like this with old, built-up grease, a small brush in combination with Reel Scrubber works best and also reduces wasting of the solvent.

A good alternative to this is one of the computer and electronics micromolecular cleaners, such as Electro-Wash, which are used for cleaning circuit boards and other electronics. These products evaporate completely and clean thoroughly, but are best for light cleaning of reels and tackle parts.

Another solution is to use air pressure alone, such as the compressed air (like Dust-Off) available at most camera shops.

A Zebco spokesman suggests using a very diluted solution of nondetergent, organic soapy cleanser (such as Amway) to quickly break down the mineral deposits on the reels for a complete cleaning.

Reels will get dirty and require internal and external cleaning. Generally, internal cleaning and checking can be done annually. All reels have external parts, however, that can affect reel performance if they are not regularly cleaned. These include the line rollers on spinning-reel bails, the bail-pivoting mechanism that opens and closes the bail, the many parts on automatic one-hand-opening bails (in which a lever that raises as the line is picked up also opens the bail for instant casting), the front of the rear drag-control knob, handle parts, levelwind pawls, tracks on casting reels, various switches, levers, clicks, and other controls.

It is best to check and clean a reel after each fishing trip. Everybody seems to have different ideas on cleaning reels. Some like to use a garden hose, but most reel manufacturers specifically warn against this, probably because a hard spray could inject water into the reel. The high pressure caused by a nozzle can, theoretically, force water, dirt, and grime through the reel opening and side-plate flanges into the reel gearing, causing more problems than not cleaning.

If the reel was fished in salt water, the salt intrusion from such a hard spray could completely destroy the reel. In addition, a simple rinse or quick dip in fresh water will not remove the salt, only slightly dilute it for a moment.

The cleaning method that has worked well for me in both fresh and salt water includes the following:

1. Immediately after fishing, reduce the pressure on all drags. This will preserve the soft drag washers so that the drag will be functional the next time out.
2. Once home, remove the spools of those reels that allow easy removal. This includes spinning and most fly reels, and might even include some casting reels.
3. Fill a tub, dishpan, or sink with lukewarm water. Put the reels and spools into the water *briefly*—only enough to wet them.
4. Use a small scrub brush (an old toothbrush is ideal) to lightly scrub the reels, paying particular attention to small cracks and crevices, controls on the side plates, and so on. Do not allow the reels to soak a long time, because too much water can get into the reel. (Some water will get in, but this can occur to a slight degree when fishing also.)
5. Rinse the reels with clean fresh water, shake to throw off as much water as possible, dry as much as possible with a terrycloth towel. Place in an open area to air-dry, or use a hair dryer to dry the reels more rapidly.

This is really a two-part program, with the second procedure undertaken after the reels have completely air-dried. This includes lightly lubing and oiling external parts, as well as other protections. The best steps for this include:

1. After ensuring that the reel is completely dry, check all its working parts to be sure that it is properly functioning.

2. Referring to the reel's manual, lightly oil or grease each part indicated. This usually includes:

   A. Casting reels: Pawl or line-guide pin, worm or levelwind gear, left and right ball bearings, handle knob(s) and shaft, spool shaft ends, star drag control or levers. Dismantle the reel every few cleanings and grease the main, pinion, and cog gears. Take care with the leaf-spring-operated antireverse controls, because lubrication is seldom needed here—they are used so seldom—and excessive lubing can make them slip.

   B. Spinning reels: On the sides or under the rotating line roller, any rotating or lever bail arms or fittings, drag-knob nut and spring (front-drag reels), spool drag washers (but *only* if called for by the manufacturer because many reels' drags should be kept free of oil, grease, and water), antireverse lever or switch, handle nut, handle knob and shaft, and main shaft (underneath the removable spool).

   C. Spincast reels: Rotary pin (pickup pin) and spring (underneath the nose cone, which must be removed), handle knob and shaft, drag adjustment dial or star drag, antireverse lever, and main shaft (under spool).

   D. Single-action fly reels: Main shaft (remove spool) handle, drag lever or knob, internal drag controls, and spool-locking catch—if present.

3. If desired, and especially if fishing in salt water, consider spraying the reel lightly with a demoisturizing agent such as LPS #1, WD-40, CRC, or a similar solution. You might wish to cover the line or remove the spool so you won't spray the line. It won't hurt the line, according to line manufacturers, but might leave an odor. (This could be good or bad—some anglers use WD-40 on their lures as a scent to attract fish.)

Also check parts for wear. Wear is usually heavy on parts such as the levelwind pawl of casting reels and the roller on spinning reels. To check for easy rolling, run a piece of heavy line, string, or cord under the roller and slide it back and forth to check how freely it rolls.

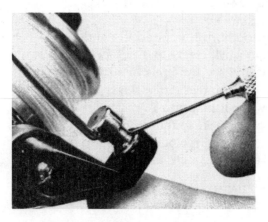

Using a needle-nose oiler to oil the roller on a spinning reel.

Chart of lube and oiling instructions for a variety of reels. These are Daiwa reels, but the basics would be the same for any reel. *Courtesy Daiwa.*

**Baitcast Reels**

1 Line guide pin
2 Worm shaft
3 Left and right ball bearing
4 Handle knob and shaft
5 Cog wheel
6 Both ends of spool shaft
7 Drive gear shaft (remove handle nut, plate screw and plate)
8 Pinion gear and spool shaft

**Spincast Reels**

1 Rotor pin and spring
2 Handle knob and shaft
3 Drag adjustment dial or star drag
4 Anti-reverse lever
5 Main shaft

**Spinning Reels**

1 Under Rotating line rollers
2 Arm lever and screw
3 Inside drag knob, nut and spring
4 Ball balance holder plate
5 Inside spool washers
6 Anti-reverse lever
7 Handle nut
8 Handle knob and shaft
9 Main shaft

Lube all screw threads and free them from corrosion

**Baitcast Reels**

1 Both ends of spool shaft
2 Left and right ball bearing
3 Drive gear — all surfaces
4 Drag washer — all surfaces
5 Pinion gear — all surfaces
6 Clutch lever and clutch stopper plate — on moving surface
7 Drive gear shaft
8 Star drag — on moving surface
9 Worm shaft — all surfaces
10 Line guide pin
11 Cog wheel shaft
12 Handle — knob and shaft

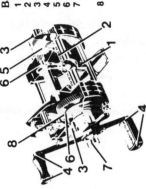

**Spincast Reels**

1 Drive gear — all surfaces and teeth
2 Pinion gear — spring and teeth
3 Drive gear shaft
4 Drag adjustment dial
5 Rotor pin and spring
6 Spool washer
7 Spool metal — all surfaces
8 Handle — knob and shaft
9 Anti-reverse cam

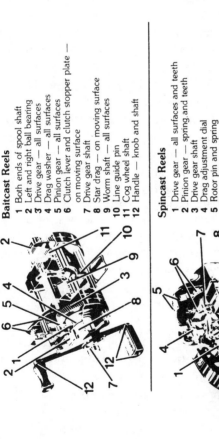

**Spinning Reels**

1 Inside drag knob, nut and spring
2 Inside spool washer — all surfaces
3 Mainshaft
4 Ball balance holder plate
5 Under rotating line rollers
6 Arm lever and screw — moving surfaces
7 Bail spring — all surfaces
8 Spool washer
9 Main shaft — all moving surfaces
10 Ratchet and screw
11 Ball bearing or bearing metal — all surfaces
12 Pinion gear — all surfaces
13 Oscillating gear and oscillating pinions — all surfaces
14 Drive gear teeth and shaft — all surfaces
15 Oscillating slider
16 Anti-reverse camshaft
17 Handle — knob and shaft

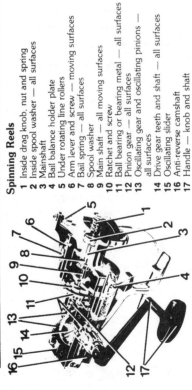

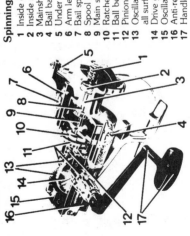

The levelwind pawls on casting reels are easily removed from a small cap on the underside of the levelwind housing. Remove the cap, pull out the pawl, clean off old grease, and check for wear. The working end of the pawl should have a small concave edge. If it is too thin from side to side, or reduced to a pinlike projection, it may cause binding, loosen the levelwind mechanism, or wear on the levelwind worm gear. Replace if necessary. (Most reels come with a small kit with spare levelwind pawls.)

Usually this regular check is enough to protect reels between annual checkups and lubes. The above might seem excessive, but it really does not take much time. The soak and quick scrub take no more than a few minutes for an average assortment of tackle, say four to six reels. The oiling takes a little longer once the reels are dry. How long will depend on whether you apply only external oil or internal oil, too. Oiling should not take more than a minute or two for each reel, and it will protect them. Make sure that when you are through, you back off the drag to protect the soft drag washers.

## ANNUAL CHECKS

Every extensively used reel should have an annual check, preferably at the end of the old season, not at the beginning of the new. You want to have time for repairs, which you won't if you wait until a day or two before you go fishing.

The annual check should be done after the washing outlined above. (You can skip oiling the reels, though, because it is part of the annual check.)

During an annual check you will strip the reel down to its basic parts, though not necessarily dismantling every single piece.

Basic tips for this annual check are:

1. Use a compartmented box such as a biscuit tin, egg carton, or plastic utility box to hold the parts. You will be partially disassembling the reel, so you need to keep the parts in order for easy reassembly. A handy tip here is to always work in one direction—left to right. That way the last item you took off will be in the box's farthest right-hand side, and will also be the first part that you put back on. You will never get mixed up.

2. Have all necessary tools ready. These include the reel tool that came with the reel, a set of small screwdrivers, and small wrenches. (For more details see chapter 10, on tools and equipment.)

3. Gather other cleaning materials. These can include old toothbrushes, pipe cleaners, small scrub brushes, old rags, cotton-tipped swabs, and so on that are used on large surfaces, in cracks, and around controls.

4. Make sure that you have the appropriate oil, grease, and demoisturizing agents. If possible, use the oil and grease recommended by the reel manufacturer. Do *not* use oil on gear parts or other reel areas where grease or a thick lubricant is suggested. A light oil here will run off and not protect. Do *not* use petroleum jelly, since it has poor adhesion and will not protect the gears as well as specifically recommended greases.

Some sort of compartmented box is best for dismantling reels, so that each part in turn can be placed in order in one of the compartments. This egg carton is ideal for this.

5. Keep a small pan of solvent nearby to clean parts when the reel is disassembled. *Do not* use organic solvents such as gasoline, carbon tetrachloride, acetone, or other highly flammable, dangerous, or unhealthy products. Gasoline is just plain dangerous to use, and carbon tet gives off toxic fumes. See note on cleaning and checking reels for details on solvents. Use soapy water or grease-cutting household cleaner to cut the grease, following directions on the bottle. Rinse thoroughly after cleaning each part. (Gasoline and organic degreasers, aside from the health and hazard dangers, will also leave a film on reel parts, which prevents proper molecular adhesion of any grease or oil.)

6. Dry the reel parts thoroughly after cleaning and rinsing, and before adding any oil or grease or reassembling. Air-drying is okay, but a hot-air hair dryer also works well. Make sure, though, that the forced air does not blow away any small or lightweight parts.

7. Work only on one reel at a time to avoid mixing parts.

Annual cleaning of reels follows the same procedure regardless of the type of reel, although the instructions for disassembly of each reel are different. The steps of cleaning and lubing should be as follows for all reels.

1. Disassemble the main parts of each reel. Work on only one reel at a time. How much disassembly is required will vary with the reel, how heavily you use it, and how comfortable you feel taking it apart (and putting it back together).

2. Once the major reel parts are disassembled, wash, clean, and examine them for wear or breakage. To clean the parts, take each in turn and scrub it carefully in the soapy, grease-cutting solution. Use an old rag or small scrub brush for the major parts, such a side plates and reel housings, and use a pipe cleaner or old toothbrush to clean around controls, levers, fittings, and other crevices that will harbor dirt and grime. If scrubbing a unit that holds smaller parts, do so with care to avoid dislodging any small loose parts. Or remove these small parts first, scrub thoroughly, and replace.

Most spinning reels have simple gearing that allows conversion of the rotary handle motion into the rotary bail movement (at right angles to the handle movement), along with an in-out reciprocating spool motion to help lay down the line. This reel has both a side plate and an end cap that must be removed.

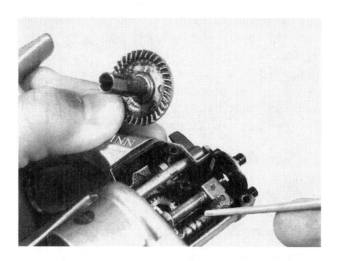

Removal of the main gear shows the gearing. The pointer shows a worm gear that gives the spool the reciprocating action.

Once all the grease and dirt are removed, rinse the parts several times and place on an absorbent terry towel or under a hair dryer to completely dry them.

3. Examine each part carefully. If a part is damaged or worn, you will have to repair or replace it (see chapter 7). If you are satisfied that the parts are clean and not worn, reassemble the reel, lubricating each part as you replace it.

Use only recommended grease on gears. These include pinion, main, cog wheels (gear), worm (levelwind gear on casting reels), spiral (on main shaft of spinning reels) and ratchet gears, levelwind pawl, and ends of spool shaft. Follow directions to lightly oil, if required, the drag washers, handle shafts, screws (to ease removal and reduce corrosion), spinning-bail rollers, star drag, spinning-reel main shafts, any controls, ratchets, springs, levers, and so on.

In most cases, fishermen add too much grease and oil. Apply *only* enough to cover the parts and coat the gears. There are two dangers in using too much grease or oil: Excessive grease or oil will hold dirt or grime into the reel, which will wear out the moving parts; and oil or grease will flow or migrate during warm weather and travel to other parts of the reel, where it may slow casting or interfere with a drag system.

Zebco tackle experts suggest applying oil with a dental pick or toothpick, which will ensure you use the right amount of lubrication and get it in the right spot. They also suggest applying grease with a toothpick to every two or three gear teeth on the main and pinion gears, so that it is properly distributed around the teeth. Some manuals suggest that you place a blob in only one spot so that the meshing of the gears will spread the grease. This does not always work as it should. Instead the grease is pushed to the outside flat area of the gear, where it does no good. A safer bet is to use Zebco's method.

Disassembling each type of reel is different, and each brand of reel will vary from other manufacturers' models. The following is a *general* guide. It should work well if you do not have your reel manual. If you do have your manual, follow it for detailed instructions.

**Casting Reels** Remove the right or handle side plate. In most reels this will remove a casing that holds all the gears in a side-plate housing. With the side plate removed, take out the spool. In older reels take care to not misplace the small brake blocks (centrifugal casting-control blocks) found on tiny shafts on the main spool shaft. To check the internal gears, you must remove the handle. To remove

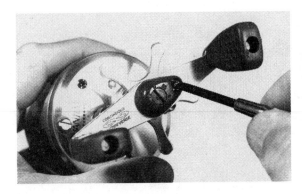

Checking a casting reel—step one—removal of the cap that covers the nut holding the handle in place.

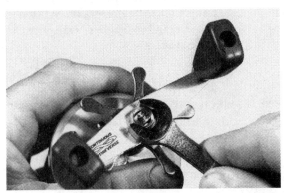

Checking a casting reel—step two—removal of the handle retaining nut.

Checking a casting reel—step three—removal of handle and handle washer.

Checking a casting reel—step four—removal of star drag (threaded—must be backed off).

Loosening screws (usually thumbscrews) removes the handle side plate from the reel body.

Centrifugal brake blocks on spindles on the reel spool (shown by pointer).

Removing screws that hold the external side plate to the base plate that holds the gearing and drag.

Side plate of the reel removed, showing the gearing and drag. The drag washers are on the handle shaft.

the handle, loosen and remove the handle nut. Most reels will have a small screw underneath this nut, which also must be taken out before the handle can be removed. To check the drag, back off the star drag to remove it and expose the flat and soft washers underneath that control drag pressure.

Additional screws in the side plate can be removed to expose the pinion (small) and main gears in the reel by which the handle turns the spool. Inspect it

The soft drag washer (left) rides in a recess on the main gear with the hard washer (raised).

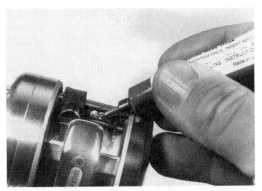

Because they are open and in constant use when fishing, levelwinds on casting reels must be lubed frequently, usually daily. A long-nose tube of grease is needed to reach the worm gear.

On some casting reels, removing the screws will remove the cover on the left side plate.

Magnetic cast-control reels do not have centrifugal brake blocks, but instead use small magnets to create a magnetic field to control spool rotation.

all carefully. Loosen the screws on the left side plate to expose any gears and the spool shaft socket. Follow manual directions to remove the levelwind pawl (now more frequently called the line guide pin) and check for wear.

At this point, wash all parts as previously outlined, dry, oil, and grease as called for in the reel manual and reassemble.

**Spinning Reels** Remove the spool from the reel. Do not misplace any of the small, thin washers that are often on the shaft directly underneath (in back of) the spool. Take off the reel handle. Many spinning reels have both right- and left-hand drive, and the handles are removed in one of two ways. Hold the spool or engage the antireverse and turn the handle backward to loosen the screw shaft holding the reel, or remove the small screw on the opposite side of the shaft holding the reel body (the screw holds the shaft in place). When the screw is undone, slide out and remove the handle.

Remove the side plate. On most reels the left side plate is held on with several

Most reels today have convertible handles (convertible from right to left). The one on the left uses two different-sized threads to screw into the side of the reel shaft. Backing up the handle removes the handle. The center and right have straight-through shafts that are fastened in place with a cap on the side opposite the handle.

Parts of a simple spinning reel. Shown are the main reel body, handle, side plate, end cap, side-plate screws, gearing, and ball-bearing race.

(usually three) screws. Beneath the side plate you will see the reel's internal gearing, along with any rear drags, line slippage systems for bait fishing (these override the drag to allow line to pull from the spool with only light pressure), main shaft, antireverse systems and levers, and so on. In most cases, the main gear and drive (called pinion or planetary gear) are the only parts that will need attention.

If the grease on these parts is dirty, remove the pinion gear and wash it. Use a cleaning-solution-soaked toothbrush to clean the spiral gearing on the main shaft. Be careful not to dislodge any small parts that might be loose. If there are loose parts, remove them first, carefully noting their position and the settings on the reel. Occasionally, parts will not go back properly if a setting, such as an antireverse, is changed.

If the reel has a rear drag, drop some light oil on the drag washers, and turn it by turning the reel spool. Make sure that the drag is completely backed off to allow for maximum penetration of the lubricant. Also lube the handle, bail, handle shaft, and so on as previously outlined.

**Fly Reels** Single-action fly reels, which are used most widely and uniformly in both fresh- and saltwater fishing, are simple spool-and-frame devices. Even the

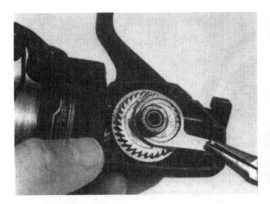

Removing the pin on a reel. This pin holds the cam lever into the reel spool shaft, causing the reciprocating action of the spool while turning the handle. Often removal of some part like this is necessary to get the gears out and exposed, although all reels are slightly different.

Gearing of the above reel, with pin in place to show position; cam lever removed.

Gears in all reels *must* be lubricated by depositing a drop of oil or grease on each gear tooth. You cannot deposit the grease or oil in one spot and count on the turning gears to distribute the lubrication.

Gearing and controls in some reels are more complicated than in others. This reel has all the typical gearing, with a rear bait-release drag system (in addition to the standard front spool drag).

most expensive and exotic fly reels, such as the Fin-Nor, are made of only a few simple parts that are easily disassembled and maintained.

First remove the reel's spool. On many reels a small button or spring lever releases the spool from a catch on the main shaft. Once the spool is removed, check the clicks and drag mechanism on the inside of the frame. Drags will vary with fly reels, ranging from the larger brake disc, such as on the Fin-Nor and other specialty saltwater models, to smaller lever-tension devices found on smaller reels.

Cleaning and lubing are easy because these reels are open and simple. Just removing the spool usually makes it possible to scrub and clean the inner reel frame and the spool. Light lubing on all moving parts is also easy and all that is required for most fly reels.

**Spincast Reels** Spincast reels are generally easy to clean and lube. On many of

Fly reel with the spool removed, showing the simple pawls and drag systems used on most of these reels.

them, removing the nose cone releases the inner gearing and spool for cleaning, examination, and lubing. Other spincast reels have a removable side plate or side-plate screws that release the inner gearing and controls. Once these are exposed, examine them carefully.

Since spincast reels are enclosed in a protective one-piece housing only opened through the removal of the overlapping nose cone, they generally stay clean. The exception can come from poor handling when sand and dirt enter through the push-button control or drag setting. Clean and lube as above, using grease on the gears. Greasing properly here is equally as important as on spinning reels, so use the proper grease and the toothpick application method mentioned above for general cleaning and lubing. Replace the gears in the main housing, and reassemble by replacing the nose cone.

Removal of cone from spincast reel often allows opening of the reel cavity and simple gearing. This makes lubrication and repairs simple.

A good trick to make gearing on new reels smoother is to apply toothpaste. This should be done *only* if the reel is new (use will have smoothed the gears out already) and if the gearing is high-quality brass or stainless steel. If the reel has cast- or pot-metal parts or nylon gears, this procedure may ruin the gearing. The toothpaste is packed in the gear housing of the reel (casting or spinning) and the reel handle turned to "lap" the gearing. The toothpaste must be removed with water and the reel regreased before use.

# CHAPTER 4

# Lure Maintenance

WHERE YOU DRAW the line between lure maintenance and lure repair is imprecise and somewhat subjective. Check chapter 8, Lure Repair, for additional help and suggestions.

Lures might not seem to require maintenance or special care, but they do. While lures don't require lubing like reels, or guide checks to prevent line damage, they can and do become damaged if not handled properly. Lures can also damage other lures or tackle. A prime example is keeping soft-plastic lures with hard lures in the same tacklebox tray over a winter, only to find a sticky, gooey mess come spring.

As with the chapter on lure repair, each type of maintenance procedure will be covered.

## Sharpening Hooks

This is listed first because of its prime importance. A lure lacking an absolutely sharp hook is not as effective as it should be for fishing. With the possible exception of chemically sharpened hooks, no hook is as sharp out of the box as it should be. This applies especially to lure hooks.

Banging around in a tacklebox, scraping against a boat, hitting a snag, knocking against a rock, scraping a barnacle or oyster bed, hooking into a duck-blind piling, in short, anything that a hook comes in contact with will dull it. This includes hooked fish, especially those species with hard, bony mouths.

How to properly sharpen a hook is based on its style.

1. To properly sharpen a curve-point hook (like the Eagle Claw–style), use a curved hook hone to work on the curve's inside and a flat hone or stone on its outside. Work in a curved motion, following the hook's shape, and move from the barb to the end of the point. Use lighter pressure at the point end to avoid rounding and dulling it.

2. For straight points, use a hone to triangulate the point, again working from the barb to the point. To triangulate the point, work with a file, hone, or stone at an angle on the hook's inside, working first on one side and then the other, so that you form a slight knife or wedge edge on the inside from the point to the barb. This is easy to follow because most hooks have a

dark finish (japanned, bronze, or black), and the sharpened point will become shiny as the coating is removed. To complete the triangle, concentrate on the flat outside of the point, working across it to make one flat side and two more wedge edges.

The result is a point that has three flat sides and three flat edges that form a cutting-edge triangle in cross section. When sharpening the point this way, do not weaken the point by removing too much metal. This method is ideal for any hook point—no matter what the size.

3. Hooks can also be triangulated with the flat surface in the *inside* of the hook point and the two angled cutting edges on its *outside*. Just reverse the sharpening methods mentioned above. I feel that on some hooks this removes a little more metal in the point area, which may weaken the hook somewhat. It is far easier to work angle cuts on the outside of the hook point, however, rather than on the inside, where the file or hone must run between the shank and the point. This is a good method for flies, bugs, and grubs that could be damaged if hit with the file.

4. Another method for sharpening straight-point hooks is to use a diamond shaping. The only difference here is that the hook point is finished by making two more angular sharpening motions on the outside of the hook point in the point and barb area.

The result from the two cuts on the hook's inside and two on the outside is a point that will have a diamond-shaped cross section instead of a triangle form. The only danger in using this method is on small hooks, because it might remove too much metal and weaken the hook point and barb area. For larger hooks it is ideal, since it provides four cutting edges and four flat sides that offer good cutting and hook penetration.

The problem with sharpening is that as soon as the hooks are honed, they can quickly become dulled by rattling around in a tacklebox. Yet there is a real advantage to sharpening hooks at home or during the off season, since you don't want to spend all your fishing time sharpening hooks. One way to do this, yet still protect the hooks, is to sharpen them at home (there are several electric or battery-operated hook sharpeners available to make this easy), and then add hook guards.

There are several ways to maintain sharp hook points. One is to lay hooks in a row between two strips of masking tape, but this can get messy. If the tape gets old, it is also difficult to remove. Another method is to save old torn-up plastic worms to use as a protective sheath on the hooks. Once all your hooks are sharpened, use a low heat to melt down the old worms (color won't matter) and, when liquid, dip each hook into the molten plastisol to cover it with a protective soft-plastic coating. When fishing, it takes only a second to rub off this protective coating.

Sharpeners must be chosen according to hook size and style. There are a number of hook sharpeners on the market, ranging from small rectangular, triangular, and rounded stones; diamond hook hones; and electric hook hones, such as the battery-operated Berkley Line Stripper (which has a hone on its end), and the

Pocket Hook Sharpener and Power Stone (both battery operated), by JWA. I like a small half-round cross section, D-shaped hook hone (the Ocean Pointer) by Diamond Machining Technology for field and boat use. Other diamond hook hones such as the small pen-type hone from Gaines and the several grits (fine, medium, and coarse, depending upon the size of the hook) from Eze-Lap are also excellent.

Larger hooks, such as those used for offshore fishing, often require a file. Good files include those made by Red Devil and Nicholson Rotary Mower Files, and the smaller files from Luhr Jensen, the West Coast tackle company. Any file will rust rapidly. To prevent this, make a sheath for the file and keep it well soaked with WD-40. A sheath can be made from a fancy leather or nothing more than a stiff plastic bag, folded and taped to hold the file.

## Lure Storage

Proper lure storage is probably the second most important concern in lure maintenance, because as previously mentioned, mixing lures of different materials can ruin lures. The main problem is mixing soft and hard lures. Soft plastics are made of a plastisol that will attack harder plastics. At one time this was a problem with tackleboxes, because the then-new plastic worms would soften, melt, and erode the box trays. Manufacturers have since wormproofed boxes by using materials such as polypropylene that resist attack by most lures. Avoid using other boxes for lure storage, such as lightweight plastic utility boxes, or old tackleboxes, because they may erode. If you have an old pre-wormproof box, you can still use it, but keep all the worms in plastic bags.

When soft-plastic worms and other lures come in contact with each other, the worms melt and the lures' finish is damaged. This chemical reaction will affect molded-plastic lures, painted finishes, plastic and rubber skirts, such as those on spinner- and buzzbaits, and enameled jig heads. They won't attack metal-plated lures, though softened plastic will stick to and ruin metal spoons and spinners.

Contact between soft-plastic lures and spinnerbaits, and buzzbaits and similar skirts and rubber tails, be they plastic or vinyl, are equally damaging, causing these parts of both lures to react and melt.

The degree of reaction and damage depends upon the type of soft plastic. All soft-plastic lures are made of a plasticizer, or softener, which makes the lure soft, and a plastisol, a hardener. The degree of softness or hardness of a lure is based strictly on the ratio of the softener to the hardener. Color dye or pigments are also added, along with (occasionally) scents, salt, and other chemicals.

Harder baits, such as those used in salt water for grubs, plastic trolling lures, trolling eels, and so on are harder and less reactive. The soft-plastic lures, however, have more plasticizer in them, which makes them more slippery, and they are more likely to release this liquid when in contact with another lure or when heated to high temperatures. Some manufacturers take pains to prevent this interaction.

Some lures have a hard body into which a soft-plastic tail is inserted. This is done in order to make the soft-plastic tail replaceable. The hooking arrangement is in the hard-bait body—not in the soft-plastic tail. In most cases, a special type of paint is used so that the soft-plastic tail and hard-plastic body don't chemically react with each other.

Other companies have similar protection for their lures. Most of these are more durable, soft lure-resistant finishes, according to several lure manufacturers, which are epoxy instead of the urethane and lacquer finishes normally used. The epoxies are two-part paints, making them harder to mix and requiring longer drying times than the urethanes, all of which makes production time slower. Most companies at the present do not seem to like epoxies and do not generally use them.

Vinyl lures are less likely to react with hard baits. These lures and teasers consist of hard plastic heads with vinyl skirts. They are seldom carried in tackleboxes with other lures because of their size, and are more typically stored separately in a rolled-up lure bag.

Soft lures will generally not attack each other, but avoid mixing different brands that might use different plastics. When different colors of soft lures are mixed together, the colors may bleed. The darker color usually bleeds into the lighter or translucent lures. This won't be a noticeable problem if you keep black, grape, and blue plastic worms together; it will be a problem if you mix black with translucent yellow. Fluorescent colors will also bleed into each other.

Bleeding, reacting with other lures, and melting are all exacerbated with heat. Some soft-plastic lure companies have tested lures in closed tackleboxes with temperatures of over 200°F. This caused the softener of the soft-plastic lures (the plasticizer) to leak out of the lure. Even if the plasticizer does not attack another lure's finish, it will leave a gummy coating. To prevent this, keep tackleboxes out of the heat or cover with a wet towel when fishing.

Ironically, in some tests by outdoor writer Lefty Kreh, heat buildup does not seem to be affected by a tacklebox's color. Lefty drilled a hole in several boxes so he could glue in dial thermometers to check temperatures in brown and white tackleboxes left in the sun during August. There was no appreciable temperature difference, so be sure to keep your boxes out of the heat.

All rubber skirts eventually break down in time and will mat with and attack the finish of hard lures. This is more frequent with natural rubber skirts than with vinyl or plastic skirts. It is also more prevalent when the lures are exposed to sun, which happens with any of the clear- or translucent-top satchel-type tackleboxes, because UV rays penetrate the box. To prevent this, keep the skirts in a separate box, keep the tacklebox out of the sun, or cover it with a towel. Keep all skirted lures apart from other lures.

In addition to separate storage, there are ways to keep rubber skirts so that their action is still what it should be when the lure is fished. Several experts and lure manufacturers suggest storing skirts in a bottle of pork rind, which keeps the rubber flexible and prevents matting. You can use a freshwater-filled old pork-rind jar, baby food jar, or plastic screw-lid food jar for the same purpose. ArmorAll will help to clean and free stuck skirts.

Another possibility is to remove skirts and store them in cornmeal, cornstarch, or talcum powder. All will keep skirts from sticking and matting. Also, carefully examine lures periodically and replace skirts where necessary.

The best solution of all is to be aware of the potential problems and avoid mixing lures. Some suggestions include:

1. Store different lures in separate compartments. Especially important is keeping hard lures, spinnerbaits, buzzbaits, jigs, spoons, and soft-plastic lures separated.
2. To prevent soft-plastic lure colors from bleeding into other soft lures, store different colors in separate tacklebox compartments or use lightweight sandwich bags to hold different brands and colors of soft plastics.
3. To keep spinnerbaits and buzzbaits from melting, store them in the spinnerbait compartments in some tackleboxes, in a bottle of water (or pork rind), or in cornmeal or cornstarch.

Rusted hooks and lures become a problem when they are poorly stored. Hooks in particular are damaged by excessive moisture trapped in a closed tacklebox. Plated spoons, metal lips, and bills on crankbaits, spinners, spinnerbaits, and buzzbaits are less subject to damage because of the nickel or chrome plating. Avoiding rust problems begins when you're fishing. Shake lures to remove any excess water before putting them back in a tacklebox, and do not leave a tacklebox open during a rain drizzle or where or when it could be hit by boat spray.

One easy solution to this when boat fishing is to mount lure holders on the boat. At the beginning of each trip, pick out the lures you think you might use and place them in the lure rack. (Even if you use more lures during the day, this gives you a head start.) Keep the lures in the rack until the end of the day, or even after you trailer the boat home, when you can properly dry them before replacing them in the tacklebox. Often just the air-drying on a trailer trip is enough to remove most of the moisture. If lures are not thoroughly dry when you put them back in the tacklebox, leave the tacklebox open to allow the moisture to escape and the box to breathe.

Saltwater lures present problems. These are primarily caused by the leaders used with offshore trolling lures and by the size of many lures. Large lures should be kept in large-compartment tackleboxes that are expressly made for their storage. Satchel-type boxes come with compartment dividers, but the dividers do not have to be used. Instead, individually fit large lures in the compartments. Saltwater trolling lures used for billfish, wahoo, dolphinfish, and so on are large, have vinyl skirts and are usually built on leaders ranging from 6 to 20 feet long. These won't fit in a tacklebox but should be stored. You can use one of the popular soft lure caddies that feature clear vinyl pockets (the better to see and select lures) in an apron that can be fastened on a boat with hook-and-loop fasteners, Velcro, grommets, or snaps. The large pockets make it possible to roll up the leader with the lure for storage, while the apron can be taken down and rolled.

Other large-lure storage methods include built-in-the-boat lockers and large-diameter lure tubes, which are similar in principle to 35mm film canisters.

### Washing Lures

Lures can become dirty, especially when you've been fishing in dirty, stained, muddy, alga-filled, or polluted water. To protect lures and restore their finish, wash them off at home. To do this, soak them in warm water, and scrub with a small stiff-bristle brush. An old toothbrush is ideal for this. A little liquid soap helps, particularly if the lures are coated with algae, slime, or dirt.

Once clean, rinse the lure thoroughly, set it on a draining board or hang on a lure rack, and allow it to dry before replacing it in the tacklebox.

Saltwater lures, in particular, should be washed, because the corrosive effects of salt water on hooks and metal are far more damaging than fresh water. Again, the solution is to soak, wash, and rinse in fresh water.

One word of advice on washing lures. Do not boil them or place in any hot liquid. According to a major manufacturer, an angler tried this with about 40 dirty lures. The result was—and will be—lures that were deformed, split, and swollen, just like the adverse reaction that can occur from excessive heat in a tacklebox.

Another word of advice. Consider removing hooks if you are scrubbing them very hard or you are working with many lures. Otherwise use extreme care in washing them to avoid injury.

### Tuning Lures

Whether tuning is repair or maintenance is anyone's guess, but I consider it more maintenance because it involves adjustment.

Some simple tuning methods for various lures are as follows:

**Crankbaits** If crankbaits lack a line tie—split or jump ring, line connector, Duo-Lock snap, and so on—add one. This is particularly important for maximum action of the lure, and especially when heavy-pound-test line, which limits lure action when tied directly to a lure, is used.

Lures can become bent or damaged so that they will not run true. There are two ways to correct this. One is to bend the line-tie eye to rebalance the lure. Hold the lure with the eye facing you and use pliers to just slightly bend the eye in the direction opposite to which it runs. (If the lure runs to your right on retrieve, hold the lure with the eye toward you and bend the eye slightly to the left.) Check the retrieve and rebend until the lure runs straight.

You can also shave the side of the lip on plastic-lip lures. Again hold the lure with the eye toward you and shave the side opposite that of which the lure runs. Check the retrieve and repeat until satisfied with a straight retrieve.

**Spinnerbaits** Make sure that the wires are straight, the blades free, and the skirt unmatted. If the right-angle wiring bends when landing a fish, re-form it to the original position for proper action.

**Buzzbaits** Buzzbaits must also have straight wires, although some are designed so that they will work better if the wire is slightly bent down so that the lure and

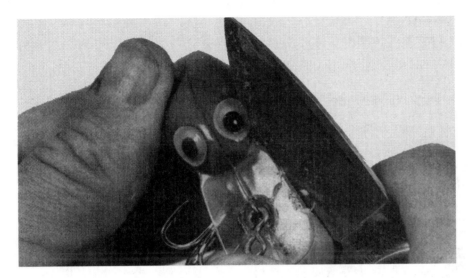

One way to tune a lure to make it run straight is to scrape the side of the plastic lip as shown. To make the lure run true, always scrape the side opposite the way the lure runs. Thus, with this lure running to the left of you on retrieve, scrape the right side as you hold the lure with the head facing you (as in this photo).

hook ride lower in the water. For maximum action and noise, bend the upper arm down slightly so that the propeller blade will just tick against the lower arm as the blade turns.

**Worms** Make sure that the worm is rigged on a straight hook for maximum natural action in the water. If not, remove the hook and start over. (An exception is bending or twisting the worm to make a "swimming worm.")

**Spoons** Use an eye ring or snap for maximum action and to prevent the line from cutting off with the stamped ring on most spoons.

## Removing Lure Dressings

Lure scents are tremendously popular today, with dozens of companies offering various aromas for almost every fish. Included are scents for largemouth bass, smallmouth bass, crappies, trout, salmon, catfish, carp, walleyes, saltwater species, and so on.

Some lures are even designed to hold scents with flocked surfaces (spinnerbait heads, jig heads, bullet worm weights), flocked materials (jig collars, flocked beads and bubbles), and special spongelike scent holders that fit into scent compartments. In many cases, however, and particularly with soft lures such as worms, scents will harm the lure if they are allowed to remain. For example, when scents first appeared, many bass pros soaked their worms in them for days before a fishing trip or tournament. The result was often ruined, gummy, or melted lures.

To avoid this, yet to still take advantage of the scents, soak lures only for a day and soak only those lures you know you will be using. Scents can be washed off lures after a trip to prevent damage. Scents are water or oil based, but soapy water will clean either.

## Component Attachment

Many plugs or crankbaits come with wobbling plates, lips and bills, hook hangers, and so on, which are attached with screw eyes and small screws. In time, these can loosen, and you can lose hooks and fish. To prevent this, check lures annually to see if eyes and screws are secure.

Use a small screwdriver, like the one in your rod/reel repair kit (see chapter 9 on tools and equipment), to refasten screws, and use small needle-nose pliers to turn screw eyes farther into the lure. If screws and screw eyes seem excessively loose, remove them, apply a small amount of epoxy or instant glue into the hole, and quickly reinsert the screw or screw eye. A straight pin or straightened paper clip works well to get the glue into the hole.

It's also worth gluing eyes and screws into lures when fishing for larger-than-normal fish, because the eye or hanger is more secure. Another safety device consists of running a short length of wire or monofilament leader from the tail hook eye, through the belly hook eye, then fastening it to the lure's split-ring line tie or forward screw eye. Crimping sleeves work well to hold these in place with minimum interference with the lure. The result holds large toothy fish when a lure might break during the fight or be splintered on the strike. It is not necessary on saltwater plugs that feature through-wire construction for hanging hooks or use a plate insert as hook hangers.

For information on hook and part replacement and repainting, rubber coating, dyeing, polishing, re-forming, remelting, gluing, refinishing, and rerigging lures, see chapter 8, Lure Repair.

# Accessory Maintenance

ACCESSORIES REQUIRE CARE and maintenance. Failure to do so can result in the greater expense incurred replacing them, the real chance of lost fish when nets and gaffs fail, and the frustration of having pliers that won't work and knives that won't cut when you need them.

## Spooling Line

Line must be spooled properly on reels to prevent twist, tangles, and other problems. Most line problems are caused by improper line spooling, using lures without adequate swivels so line twists, or turning the reel handle without retrieving line (as when snagged, fighting a fish resisting drag, taking out line, and so on).

Monofilament line has a characteristic called memory, which means that it will "set" in the position that it has when spooled on a service spool or spool filled for resale. For best line performance, fill the spool so that the line goes on the reel in the same way that it comes off the spool. There are several ways to do this, as follows:

1. On any revolving-spool reel (such as a casting, conventional surf, boat, or offshore trolling reel), run the line end through the levelwind (on casting reels) or line guard (fly reels) and tie with a simple overhand knot around the reel spool arbor. Maintain tension and spool the line on the reel with the spool turning in the same direction as the reel spool.

2. For spinning reels, there are two schools of thought. Traditionally, it was thought that spinning line should be spooled on a reel off the end of the spool, again going in the same direction. In doing this, the line comes off the side of the spool. Spool diameters vary widely (a 100-yard spool might measure 4 or 5 inches), so it is often necessary to turn the spool over during the spooling to prevent twisting.

   To check for twisting when spooling the line, periodically relax the tension on the line between the reel and manufacturer's spool. If it twists, turn the spool over and continue, checking again after about 15 to 20 turns of the reel handle. This may have to be done several times when spooling large reels, especially if using large-diameter service spools.

A standard method for spooling line is to spool spinning line off the end of the spool and casting line off the side of the spool. This prevents twist problems.

The second method of spooling line comes from research done by Berkley when they introduced a new line and spool packaging. They found that spool position or alignment makes no difference in line spooling. Their packaging is made so that the line spool can be hung on the rod in front of the butt guide and spooled directly onto the reel. They discovered that even though the line is coming off a revolving spool and being spiraled onto the end of a spool, it seemed to make no difference in fishing performance.

Proper tension is a must when spooling line. Too much tension will pack line on too tightly; no or too little tension might leave loops or looseness in the line. The best way to spool line is to mount the reel on the rod, run the line through the butt guide of the rod, and use a fishing towel or old rag to maintain tension as the line is spooled on. Turn the reel handle with your reel hand while using the other hand to control the line tension.

## Line Care

Line care is simple but differs depending on the type of line. Fishing lines include monofilament typically used for all spinning and much casting, surf, and offshore fishing; braided Dacron and the new gel-spun fiber lines, used for some casting and offshore trolling; wire used for deep inshore trolling, lead-core line, also used for deep inshore trolling; and fly lines. Each of these will be covered in turn.

**Monofilament** Line manufacturers report that nothing short of battery acid will hurt monofilaments. Insect repellents, suntan lotions, sunblocks, perfume, deodorants, aftershave lotions, oil, grease, demoisturizers, gasoline, cologne, fly-line cleaners and dressings, leader sinks, baits, scent lotions and gels, chum, and so on will not harm monofilaments. They might impart a smell that could repel fish, but neither the tensile and knot strength nor any other critical property of the line will be damaged. Oil or grease will not harm line, but they will pick up dust and dirt that will abrade the line and the rod guides in time.

Basic monofilament care involves keeping the line twist-free and clean. To keep twist out, spool line properly on the reel and fish with care. Lures that turn in one direction, such as spinners, will impart twist to any line. When fishing these lures, use a keel, several good ball-bearing swivels, or change lures periodically to reduce twist. Twist can be taken out by removing the lure from the end of the line and trailing it in a current or behind a moving boat for several minutes.

Twist can also occur by cranking the reel handle on spinning reels when the drag slips. If the drag slips, it means that the line is not coming in and that each turn of the spinning-reel spool is putting one turn of twist into the line.

Abrasion will damage and weaken line. Line fished around obstructions should be checked and cut back a few feet at a time throughout the day to prevent breakoffs.

**Braided Dacron** Braided Dacron is ideal for revolving-spool reels when fishing in open water or when the least amount of stretch is desired. Care in using Dacron involves splicing the line (see instructions that come with the line for loop and line-to-line instructions) or using specific knots to prevent breakage. It does not have good knot strength when using the same knots that are popular for monofilament.

Gel-spun fiber lines and their related thermal-treated lines are ideal for casting and spinning (thermal). They are very thin in diameter when compared to monofilament of equal strength and have even less stretch than Dacron. Thus, they are ideal for bait and supersensitive fishing. They do require special knots.

**Wire** Single-strand wire is used inshore in salt water and in freshwater lakes for deep-water trolling, often for trout or cold-water species that travel open water in or near thermocline levels. You must prevent wire from kinking or bending. Kinks must be either replaced or repaired with a line-twisted splice of the two broken ends (almost like a haywire twist) and finished with a tight wrap. To avoid kinks and bends, it is necessary to control the line—never free-spool it without control over the spool. Lack of control when setting out lines results in overruns and kinks.

**Lead-Core Trolling Line** This is more forgiving than single-strand wire, because a break in the lead does not mean that the line will break. This line is made of a lead core covered with braided nylon. This covering is usually about 40-pound test. It still requires care, however, to avoid sharp bends and breaks.

**Fly Lines** Fly lines come in a variety of styles, sizes, and types, including floating and sinking (several sink-rate lines); level, double-taper, and weight-forward; shooting and running lines, specialty intermediate floating, sinking-tip lines, and so on. Most of these, however, are made of a PVC coating over a braided nylon core, and require different care than the lines previously covered.

Fly lines can be harmed by chlorinated solvents, which include products such as gasoline, insect repellents, and suntan lotions. Avoid them and either apply products, such as suntan lotion or insect repellents, with the back of your hand, or wash your hands after application to prevent damaging your fly line.

## Pliers and Crimping Tools

Pliers, along with related tools like crimpers, seem almost indestructible, but they do require care. For example, pliers can rust and the joint can bind up from rust or saltwater corrosion. To prevent problems, regularly clean pliers in soapy water, dry completely, and spray liberally with a demoisturizing agent such as WD-40. Do not keep them in a holster after a trip (especially salt water), because this will prevent the pliers from drying out. If used in salt water, rinse with fresh water, then spray with WD-40.

If pliers do get tight or bound up, there are several remedies. One is to open and close them several times while sprinkling them with a powdered kitchen cleanser. The cleanser will act as a mild abrasive to polish the joint and make it work freely again. Rinse between each time. Then dry and spray as above.

Another solution is to spray pliers liberally with WD-40 or Liquid Wrench and let them soak overnight. This will usually release rusted or corroded pliers.

## Line Clippers

Line clippers are not wire clippers. Use them for monofilament and nothing else and they will last a long time. Cutting wire or anything else will damage cutting jaws, rendering them useless for cutting line. Keep them clean, and rinse with WD-40 between trips.

## Fillet, Bait, and Other Knives

Keep knives sheathed when not in use and keep them sharp at all times. To sharpen any knife, use a good sharpening stone, coat liberally with oil, and run the knife across it as if trying to "cut" the stone while holding the blade at about a 10° to 15° angle. Use the shallower angle for fillet and sharp slicing blades; the wider angle for blades used for bait cutting, chopping, and coarse knife work.

## Rules and Bumping Boards

Keep rules and bumping boards clean and where they will not get scratched or the numbers defaced. Most anglers keep the engraved or stamped aluminum or plastic bumping board in the live well of the boat, where it is ready to use and protected from damage.

## Sharpening Stones and Hook Sharpeners

Keep sharpening stones for hooks and knives separate because the hooks will often groove a stone in time, and a grooved stone will not effectively sharpen a knife. To keep stones from filling with steel filings from the sharpening process, float them with oil before using them.

## Nets

In this age of nylon-net bags there is no longer the problem with mildew and rot that there was with bags of other materials. Bags should be washed regularly and dried, however, before storing.

## Gaffs

Gaffs should be kept sharp, using the same methods of triangulating the hook as a fishhook (see chapter 4, Lure Maintenance). To keep gaffs either from being damaged or damaging other things (including anglers), store them properly in gaff holders or racks under the gunwale of the boat.

## Rod Cases and Bags and Reel Cases

To keep the threads on better aluminum rod cases working smoothly, touch them occasionally with candle wax or spray them lightly with WD-40.

Keep rod bags dry and clean. If they get dirty, wash and dry them before using. Do not store wet rods in rod bags, particularly if the bagged rod is going into a case. If you must put a wet rod in a bag, leave it out to dry completely before storing it in a case.

Use the same care with reel cases as outlined with rod bags.

## Ice-Fishing Tools

Spray with a demoisturizer, such as WD-40, after the season to keep all metal tools—ice spuds, ice skimmers, and so on—in good condition.

## Waders and Hip Boots

There are two schools of thought on caring for waders and hip boots. First, most anglers agree that the major problem comes from rubber or rubberized canvas/nylon, not neoprene. Rubber can break down in time, primarily from stress (wrinkles, folds, stretching, and so on) and from ozone, an oxygen radical ($O_3$) that will destroy rubber. Ozone is formed naturally in the air, but is also actively discharged by electric motors. For starters, don't store any boots or waders near any electric motors.

Of the two schools of thought, one suggests folding hip boots and waders, storing them in a sealed plastic bag, and, if possible, removing air from the bag with a vacuum cleaner. Then store the bag in a box and store in a cool, dry, dark area.

A cool, dry, and dark area is also suggested for the second storage method, which is nothing more than hanging the boots or waders upside down from boot hangers. The best hangers for this purpose seem to be those that grip the boots right above the heel and hold them securely without gripping or touching the upper, more flexible, and thinner part of the boot.

Boots *must* be completely dry before storage. You can allow them to air out after a trip by folding them inside out (or inside out as far as possible for boot-foot waders). Special air-dryers such as electric boot heaters, and even a hair dryer stuck down a boot, will hasten this. Don't assume that the boots are dry just because you did not fall in the water. Perspiration also moistens the inside of boots and will lead to early dry rot and fabric breakdown if not removed.

## Tackleboxes

Tacklebox problems result from abuse. A Plano spokesman notes that tackleboxes are typically overfilled by fishermen, who try to stuff 10 pounds of lures into a box designed to hold 5 pounds. This results in stressed and broken hinges, cracked lids (especially on satchel-type boxes), and damaged or broken latches. The commonsense solution is to buy another box for the other 5 pounds of gear.

Tackleboxes loose in a boat can cause problems for both the boxes and other tackle. Three of my satchel boxes weigh between 9½ and 10½ pounds each, and they would be heavier if I carried metal spoons or jigs. Tackleboxes will bang around the deck of a boat in rough water and, regardless of the manufacturer or construction, they just can't take that abuse. Lids will crack, as will boxes. Common sense dictates using a special hook-and-loop (such as Velcro) fastener or elastic (bungee) cord to hold boxes in place when running.

A third problem involves too much heat, a point also emphasized by lure manufacturers. Too much heat can result from a hot day or from storing a box in a closed car. The result can be temperatures in the box that, according to some reports, approach 300° F. At that temperature, soft lures will leak their elasticizer into puddles in the box, and hard lures can deform, split, and even blow up.

Damage is caused by the excessive heat, which is close to the temperature of the plastic when it is made by injection molding, along with a gas that develops from soft-plastic lures and expanded air or gas in the hard lures. This is not the fault of the tacklebox, because this will occur at the same temperatures and conditions whether the tackle is in or out of the box. The result is messy plastic puddles in lure compartments, puddles of plasticizer on hard plugs if they leak from one compartment to another, and UV penetration through the box's clear lids, which damages soft-plastic lures and rubber skirts. The gas that can build up can cause a slight warpage of the box, lids, and compartment sides according to tacklebox manufacturers.

The solution when fishing in the heat is to use a box with an opaque lid (which prevents UV rays from penetrating the box) or to cover the box with a light-colored towel. When it is very hot, wet the towel so that evaporation will help cool the box. You can also open the box slightly to prevent buildup of pressure or damaging gas.

Another problem, according to some, is the potential for different chemical interactions by lures stored in the boxes. "Chemicals have been added to this sport," one tackle rep notes. The combinations of worm hardeners and softeners; colors, salts, and scents added to soft-plastic lures and worms; the varying contents of worms from overseas; and the homebrews made by do-it-yourselfers can result in effects that are impossible to predict. Again, the commonsense solution is to keep worms in sealed plastic bags within the tacklebox.

## Depthfinders

Depthfinders are beyond the scope of this book, but help is available from several manufacturers. If you own a Humminbird depthfinder, write for the specific owner's manual of your unit, c/o Techsonic Industries, No. 3 Humminbird Lane, Eufala, AL 36027 (800-633-1468). Lowrance Electronics provides similar information in the back of the owner's manual supplied with each unit. Information can also be obtained by calling their customer service department (800-324-1356) or writing to Lowrance Electronics, Inc., 12,000 East Skelly Drive, Tulsa, OK 74128. Similar help from Eagle is available by calling 800-324-1354 or by writing to Eagle Electronics, Inc., Box 669, Catoosa, OK 74015.

CHAPTER

# Rod Repair

RODS CAN EASILY be repaired by most anglers because the principles are simple, the work is easy, and the tools and materials required are minimal. Rod repair can include anything from replacing a guide, to fixing a loose reel seat, to rebuilding a damaged cork grip, to even repairing a broken rod section.

Whether rods are factory or custom-made, they are assembled from parts, with the butt cap, grips, and reel seat all mounted and glued in place on the rod blank; the guides wrapped in place with thread.

Each part will be discussed in turn with the repair problems encountered and their solution or solutions.

## Butt Caps

Butt caps are made of rubber or plastic and are usually found on any rod with straight-through construction. This rod is built with the rod blank extending through the handle instead of ending at a ferrule or adapter as on some bait-casting rods and on some boat and offshore rods, which use detachable butts.

Considering the low cost of any butt cap, the simplest solution for any cracking, breaking, and so on is to replace it. If a similar type of butt cap is not available through a tackle shop or specialty supply business, then a rubber crutch tip will also work. Crutch tips are available in two lengths and four or five sizes. Similar to these are the firm plastic slip-over chair tips that also come in sizes suitable for fishing rods. The main disadvantage is that these are slippery, which makes it more difficult to prevent sliding and damage when propping a rod against a gunwale or on a hardwood floor. Their hard material makes gluing more difficult, too.

When replacing butt caps, first remove the old cap (you can take it along when you buy a new one, or get its measurements). If the cap is loose, it should easily slide off. If it is damaged but not loose, you should be able to cut it off carefully with a sharp knife or chisel.

Once the old cap is off, you are ready to put on the new one. First file or rasp any old glue off the end of the rod. Then use a rasp or small roll of sandpaper to rough up the inside of the butt cap for a better grip by the glue. Use a 24-hour epoxy glue or rod-finish epoxy, and slide the butt cap on tightly. The epoxy rod finish (such as Flex Coat) is excellent because it is flexible, as are the flexible butt caps.

Some glue will probably ooze from the junction of the butt cap with the rod handle, and it should be wiped up immediately. If the rod has a foam handle, wrap the end of the rod handle with several layers of masking tape, wrap the butt cap the same way, slide the parts together, wipe up any glue, then remove the tape to uncover a clean surface. Once the butt cap is in place, place the rod upright with the butt on the floor to prevent the butt cap from loosening or sliding off.

If your rod has a swaged aluminum butt cap, and it is only damaged but not loose, you may have to heat the cap to loosen the glue. Wrap the handle up to the butt cap with a damp rag to protect the grip and use repeated quick passes with a propane torch until the butt cap loosens. Use another rag or heavy gloves to avoid burning yourself, and remove the butt cap. If you don't care about the butt cap, gently applied pliers will also work. If the butt cap is an aluminum sleeve with a rubber end and will not come off, use a knife to cut away the rubber end and then use the propane torch to remove the aluminum.

You can also use a cutting tool to remove a metal or aluminum butt cap. These include a grinder, a small cut-off wheel as a grinder, or hand tool such as the Dremel Moto-Tool. With these, it is possible to grind or cut through the butt cap at several points, then pry it loose with a chisel or screwdriver. When doing this, be sure to wrap the handle with heavy layers of masking tape to prevent damage to the grip.

With a damaged grip or splintered wood handle on a boat rod, you may wish to save the aluminum butt cap or aluminum gimbel knock (a slotted butt cap for use on boat rods, which fits the rod into a holder or belt for fighting fish) for a new handle. Use care in applying heat and use only a rag or heavy gloves to remove the butt cap. Clean it up and reapply as outlined above.

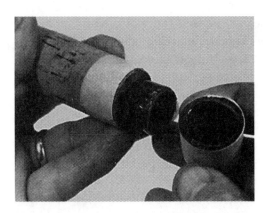

Flexible butt caps are best glued in place with an epoxy rod finish, since the rod finish will stay more flexible than most glues. For this step, wrap both parts (butt cap and end of rod grip) with masking tape to make cleanup easier.

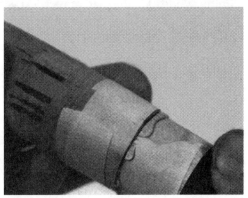

Fitting the butt cap in place. Note that the glue that oozes out can be easily cleaned up, and the tape removed, leaving the parts completely clean.

Some lightweight spinning rods have a small aluminum plate that serves as a butt cap. These will have a small metal extension that goes into the rod blank and helps to glue the plate in place. The best way to remove this is to slide a thin-bladed knife or razor blade around the edge to loosen the plate.

## Grips

Grips or handles are made of many materials. Cork, foam (Hypalon, Foamlite, and other synthetics); wood, often varnished as on boat rod handles; and aluminum, used on offshore rods, such as the UniButt system on trolling game rods, are all used.

**Aluminum Handles** These can't really be repaired, unless repair means replacing a part, such as a sliding hood, knurled ring, ferrule collet nut, or something similar that can be easily slipped off and replaced.

**Wood Handles** These are on the rear of many saltwater boat rods. They are seldom severely damaged, but do suffer severe wear. If the damage is severe, such as a bad crack, it is best to replace the wood handle. Remove the reel seat and butt cap and replace the wood part. Some wood handles separate from the rest of the rod and attach with a ferrule or adapter that fits into the forward end of the reel seat and usually is held down with a collet nut. These are easy to replace, because they require only removal of the reel seat and knock, then regluing these on a new handle.

Use the methods listed above to remove the butt cap (often an aluminum or chrome-plated brass gimbel knock) and the reel seat. These are usually metal (few plastic or graphite-fill reel seats are available), so the best removal is with a propane torch, heating slowly and evenly to melt and break down the glue so that the reel seat and knock can be removed. Do *not* use a torch or heat on anything other than metal reel seats and gimbels. Be sure to use only heavy gloves or a damp rag to grasp these parts, because pliers will mar the finish. Once removed, clean out the reel seat and knock and use 24-hour epoxy glue to remount them on a new wood handle.

Some saltwater rods with wood handles are built on long, straight-through blanks, with the wood handle drilled and glued to the blank. Heat won't work here. Instead, place the handle in a vise and use only firm pressure so the handle and the blank it contains will not be crushed. Then use a chisel to carefully plane away the wood until you reach the blank. Repeat this on several sides until the blank is exposed or you can pry off the remaining wood. An alternative method is to use a carpenter's plane to remove the wood. Clamp the handle horizontally in a vise so that the side of the handle is above the surface of the vise. This will prevent the vise from nicking the plane blade.

In most cases, wood handles are designed for specific brands and sizes of reel seats, making regluing easy. If this is not the case, you may have to build up the recess for the reel seat, if the reel seat is loose on the handle, or thin the recess, if the wood is too thick for the existing reel seat. The best way to build up a seat is to use heavy thread or light cord as a shim to fill the gap. Don't use a circular wrap, which may be pushed out of position as the reel seat is slid on, but run strands of thread over the end of the handle and down the other side to make cord strips that are parallel with the reel seat.

Depending on how much shim you need, you can have four, six, eight, or more spines of cord along the reel seat recess. Keep the cord or thread in place with masking tape or wraps at the middle of the handle. The shims will keep the reel seat parallel to the handle, and the cord cannot be pushed out of position as you glue the reel seat on the handle. Once close to the final position, cut the cord, then push the reel seat down the last ½ inch so that no cord will show. The same method will work for positioning gimbel knocks, although too much space here will leave a gap between the handle and the gimbel. If this occurs, it might be better to cut the end of the handle back ¼ inch at a time until you get a proper fit. This only works on handles that taper to a thinner diameter at the gimbel knock.

The best way to cut down a handle to fit a reel seat or gimbel knock is to decrease the size on a lathe, using inside/outside calipers to check for the proper diameter, or removing the handle to fit the reel seat and/or knock. Lacking a lathe, use a wood rasp, working with equal strokes every 90° around the reel seat recess so that you remove equal amounts of wood on all sides. Once close to the right size, remove the corners to make the cross section into a rough octagon, then round off the wood with a rasp to bring it to the final size. A fine finish is not required, because it will be glued into the reel seat.

If working with a rod requiring a straight-through handle, you will have to get a drilled-through handle, then add the reel seat and gimbel knock as described. Use a straightened coat hanger to run 24-hour epoxy glue into the hole, smear some on the lower part of the blank, and insert the blank slowly into the handle. To prevent glue from getting on the blank or reel seat, wrap both these parts (at the point where they will fit) with several layers of masking tape. Once in place, wipe up any glue and remove the masking tape.

Wood handles with peeling, worn, or damaged finishes can be easily refinished. Wrap layers of masking tape around the reel seat and gimbel knock or butt cap. This will protect their metal finishes as you remove the handle finish. To remove the old finish, use a paint-and-finish stripper and follow the directions on the can, or sand the handle down to bare wood. When the wood is clean and bare, add a new finish of waterproof urethane, epoxy, spray epoxy, or spar varnish. Unless using a thick epoxy, add several coats for maximum protection.

**Cork Grips** These are subject to gouges, chipping, and even blows that can ruin several of the rings that are used to make up grips like this. Several repair possibilities are possible, depending upon the extent of the damage. For slight chips and gouges, clean and refill the mar.

To do this, clean out any loose or cracked areas in the gouge. Do not sand it smooth or try to make it completely concave or dishlike. This will make it harder for the glue to grip the cork and increase the likelihood of the repair falling out.

Once the gouged area is clean and prepared, use a rasp to make some cork filings, preferably from high-quality cork. Wine corks, bass bug bodies, or cork craft

Small dents and dings in cork handles can be repaired with a mixture of cork dust and glue. Force the glue/cork mixture into any holes or gouges. Allow to cure overnight and file and sand to shape.

items will work for this. Remove any large chunks so that only cork "sawdust" is left. Mix this with a thick glue. I like to use waterproof or water-repellent carpenter's glue such as Elmer's Aliphatic Carpenter's Glue, which is thick, cork colored, water resistant, and easy to work with. Epoxy glues are also good, if you carefully limit the amount you use. Epoxy glues are harder and more difficult to work if you do not get the right cork-to-glue mix.

Mix the glue thoroughly with the cork, using only enough glue to hold the cork together. Spread glue on the gouge, force in the cork mix, and build it up into a slight mound above the grip. When cured completely, use a rasp to rough the repaired area down toward the grip. Use successively finer grades of sandpaper to finish this, smoothing the cork until it matches the surface and shape of the grip. At this point, you may wish to protectively tape the butt cap, reel seat, rod, or any other parts and use the finest sandpaper to smooth and clean the rest of the cork grip to match the lighter color of the repair area.

Deeper gouges, those that remove a section of the grip, can be repaired in one of two similar ways. First, if the damaged portion is only on one side of the grip, you can remove it and replace that section of cork with cork ring pieces that can be sanded to shape, finish, and size. Missing cork rings, or damage all around a grip section, can be repaired by removing the rings in that area and replacing them with new ones. In both cases you will need some cork rod-building rings. These are available in ½-inch thickness, various hole sizes, and 1⅛-, 1¼-, 1½-, and 2-inch outer diameters. The hole size does not much matter, but if you have a choice get the smallest hole available. Holes can be enlarged easier than they can be filled up. Such rings may be available at your local tackle shop or through mail-order rod-building supply houses.

When damage is on one side of the grip, use a rasp to file down the area, taking out a section that will not cut into the rod blank, but will be squared off. The section must be in ½-inch length increments. This is necessary because the cork rings you will use for repair are all ½ inch thick. Next, cut the cork ring in half through the hole. Use a rasp to lightly roughen the cut surface. Check to make sure that the cork rings fit snugly into the space provided and make any adjust-

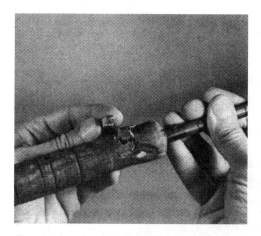

Damaged corks in cork handles can be repaired without removing and replacing the entire handle. Damage to several rings in the cork handle is shown here.

The damaged portion must be removed in increments of ½ inch. Here, the cork is being removed with a file. Take care not to damage the rod blank.

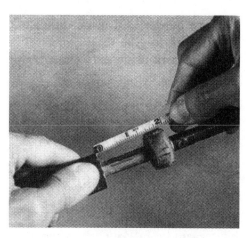

Opening gap is measured to be sure that it is in increments of ½ inch, so that the cork rings will fit properly.

Replacement cork rings are cut in half as shown to be fitted into place.

ments necessary. The cork rings will be thicker than the grip but will be sanded down after the glue cures.

Spread carpenter's or epoxy glue onto the grip's damaged area, on the cut, and on the facing surfaces of each cork ring. Put each cork ring in place. Wipe up any excess glue, especially if using epoxy because epoxy is more difficult to work with, sand to shape and size when cured. Use rubber bands or masking tape to secure the cork rings in place as the glue cures. If using rubber bands, place a cushion of cardboard on the side of the grip opposite the repair, to prevent the rubber bands from cutting into the grip. Once cured, remove the tape or bands, and use a rasp, file, and fine sandpaper to shape and finish the cork repair.

Repairing more extensive damage is done similarly, except that an entire section of cork grip must be removed and replaced. To do this, use a rasp to remove

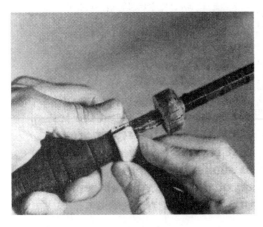

Replacement cork ring halves being fitted into place.

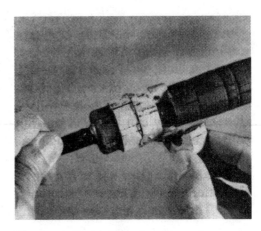

The last cork ring being fitted into place.

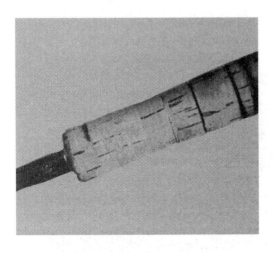

After filing and sanding, the replacement cork rings fit perfectly into the old grip.

the old damaged cork. The section removed must again be in ½-inch increments. Use cork rings that are larger than the diameter of the handle so that they can be sanded to fit. In most cases, 1⅛-inch-diameter rings are fine for fly grips, 1¼-inch are fine for spinning- and popping-rod grips, and 1½-inch are fine for saltwater and surf-rod grips.

When the rod blank is exposed, make sure that the facing corks in the remaining grip are parallel and squared off. Cut the replacement rings in half and at a slight angle for maximum gluing surface. Be sure to keep each of the two halves together or keyed in some way.

Spread glue on all the adjoining surfaces—the rings, rod blank, half holes in the cork, cut portions of the cork rings, facing corks in the grip. Add half rings on one side because this will wedge them into place. Add the other half rings, making sure that they join with their mate to prevent mismatching. Then rotate the rings so that no joint is in line with another. This will create a stronger bond. Wrap with tape or rubber bands and allow to cure overnight. After curing, remove any tape or bands and rasp, file, and sand to shape. This method allows cork rings to be added to any fore or rear grip, without having to remove the remainder of the grip or removing guides to rebuild the handle from scratch.

New handles for rods can be made from cork rings. These cork rings are reamed out to fit on a rod blank.

Cork rings are glued in place using a waterproof glue and gluing to both the back and also the cork-to-cork surfaces. Guides must be removed from the blank or from the butt section of the rod to slide the cork rings in place.

To complete the handle, the cork is filed first on four sides, then eight. After this step, it is easy to round off the edges and smooth the cork for a handle.

Shaping the rod handle with a rasp.

Finished cork handle. This will be removed from the dowel and then glued onto a rod.

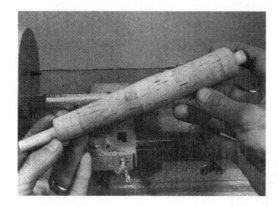

**Hypalon or Synthetic Grips** These can't really be repaired as can cork, but they can be replaced on rear grips. With a damaged rear grip, remove the butt cap and cut off the old grip. Often the best way to do this is to use a sharp razor blade to cut down the full length of the grip to the rod blank, peeling the grip off as you do the shell from a steamed shrimp.

Once the old grip is off, you can add a new one from the rear, instead of from the tip end as the rod was built. This does present difficulties, because all grips like this are best made using a grip with a smaller-diameter hole than that of the blank to assure a tight fit. In building rods, this is no problem because of the taper; grips are seated from the tip end of all blanks. During this repair job, you must get a new grip up over the thicker butt end. There are several ways to do this. One is to use a grip with a diameter close to that of the blank, and use epoxy glue to hold the grip in place without slipping. The second is to make a double-tapered dowel (one taper to roughly fit the blank, the other end to lead the grip on) so that the grip will slide on.

You must use a lubricant to slide the grip in place. Glue usually is best used for this. Spread it inside the hole of the grip and on the dowel and blank. Wrap several protective layers of masking tape around the end of the reel seat and the end of the grip. Push the grip in place. Often a good way to do this is to use a board with a center hole just larger than the blank diameter. Place this board into a vise. Then, using a dowel as long as the grip, place the dowel into this hole and push the rod to move the grip up on the blank. Do not push too hard, because the blank might split. Once the grip is in place, remove the dowel, "milk" the grip into the shape that you wish, and wipe up any glue that has oozed between the grip and reel seat. Remove the tape, glue the butt cap back on (use tape to prevent glue stains on the cap or grip), and allow to cure overnight.

There is no way to replace synthetic foregrips other than removing any guides that might be on the butt section. If the rod does not have any guides on this section, such as on some popping off-center ferruled rods or short-section pack rods, then the grip can be cut off and the new grip can be slid down the blank to a previously glue-coated section.

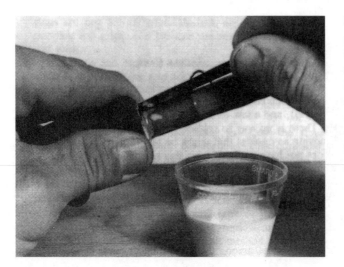

Sometimes foam handles and grips can become loose. There is no easy solution to this short of a difficult replacement, but one possible solution is to open up the gap between the rod blank and the foam and force glue into this opening. Water-based glue is best, since cleanup will be easier.

## Reel Seats

Reel seats are among the most difficult parts to repair. If the reel seat is completely damaged and unusable, then it can only be replaced. Take off the grip, heat the reel seat to remove it if metal or saw it off if it's graphite or plastic, replace with a new reel seat, and remount the grip following the above directions.

A new reel seat may or may not be the same diameter as the one removed. If it has a smaller inside diameter, you may have to remove some or all of the bushing material from the rod blank. If you remove it all, you will have to build up a new one. This is done by lightly coating the rod blank with epoxy glue, and wrapping cord tightly and repeatedly around the blank to build the cord up to the correct diameter. With each layer or two of the cord, add more glue. This should be a spiraling wrap that will leave open areas. Finish the cord by tying off with several half hitches. Add more epoxy glue, wrap the ends of the reel seat and the butting grip with tape to ease cleaning, and slide the reel seat in place.

Do the same thing to build up an existing bushing. In these cases, though, one or two layers of cord are often enough. Avoid using too large a reel seat, because it will not match the ends of the grips.

It is also possible to build up or add to bushings with adhesive paper tape or masking tape. Be particularly careful with masking tape because it is flexible and spongy and will break down in time. When using tape as a bushing ring, be sure to use enough glue to bond the reel seat directly to the rod blank. This is done by making several shims of tape rings at each end of the reel seat area, partly sliding the reel seat on, pouring glue into the open reel seat, sliding it on the rest of the way, then placing the rod vertical so that the glue will cure around the rod blank and out to the reel seat.

A vexing problem with a reel seat is when it works but is loose. There are, unfortunately, no simple solutions. You can remove the grip and reel seat, replace the reel seat (and bushing if needed—poorly glued or tape-type bushings are a principal cause of loose reel seats). Lacking this somewhat complex repair, other solutions include drilling several or more holes in the reel seat and bushing area and using a small syringe to inject epoxy glue into the area that's slipping.

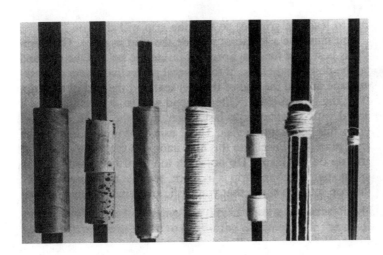

Types of bushings that can be used for replacing reel seats. Left to right: fiber bushing, cork bushing, wrapped paper tape bushing, wrapped cord bushing, masking tape bushing, cord axis bushing, and thread axis bushing.

You can also use a hacksaw to cut out the center barrel portion, remove its bushing, slide the ends (fixed hood and threaded barrel/sliding hood) to the center, reglue them in their original positions, then build up a cork insert section in the reel seat using the half cork rings as previously described. This gives a custom, professional result, although it does take work. Make sure that both hoods are lined up with the guides when gluing them in place.

## Guides

Guides can seldom be repaired, but they can be easily replaced. Guide repairs include only the following:

1. Frame repairs: Bent, not broken, frames can be returned to the original shape with flat-nose pliers. Work slowly and carefully to avoid breaking any bends.
2. Grooved wire-ring guides: Slight grooves in wire-ring guides can be temporarily repaired by using crocus or fine emery cloth to polish out the grooving and restore the ring's smooth surface. This is only a temporary solution, however; ultimately the guides will have to be replaced. Grooving in metal rings is caused by the line running in one place and wearing through the guide. Even after polishing, friction in this spot will continue. Polishing is only a stopgap measure.
3. Roller guides: Guides such as those by AFTCO can be repaired by replacing the parts of the guide. These parts include the roller, pin, bushing, and screw of the guide. These can be replaced without affecting the frame or guide wrap.

Guide replacement is easy, because it requires only cutting through the old thread to remove the guide, wrapping a new guide in place, and covering the thread with a rod-wrap finish.

Use a sharp razor blade to cut off the old wrap. Use the blade as if it was a carpenter's plane to shave through the full length of the thread wrap. If you cut straight down, you can go through the gel-coat finish of the rod and into the fibers that make up the rod. Shaving allows you to take off successive layers of threading

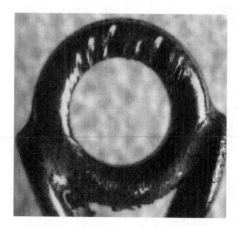

Grooved tiptops like this require immediate replacement to prevent line damage and lost fish.

In replacing guides, old wraps must be cut off. The best way to do this is to use a razor blade like a small carpenter's plane, slicing through the wrap but not the blank.

until the blank is barely exposed. Then, if color preserver was used on the wrap, just peel the wrap off.

If color preserver was not used, the epoxy penetrates the wrap so you must continue shaving the finish and wrap, taking care not to damage the rod blank. After removal, you might find a few threads at each end fastened to the rod, but these are easily removed. You will be replacing the guide in the same spot, so lightly sand any remaining finish at the ends of the wrap with a manicure emery board. Take care not to cut into the blank, or to scar the finish of the bare rod.

Use the same ring size and style for replacement as the guide removed. With companies rapidly changing in the component parts field, you may not get an exact match, but should be able to come close. Guides close in style are important, however. An ultralight rod refitted with a double-foot guide might feel sluggish or slow. The same could happen when changing a five-guide rod to six guides, or using a large-sized guide ring. If you suspect this problem may develop, tape the guides on and cast or fish with the rod briefly to see if the guide harms the rod's action or power.

Once a guide is selected, file the end of the guide to a knifelike edge. This is necessary for a smooth and even transition of the thread from the blank to the guide foot; otherwise there will be a gap in the thread at the end of the guide foot. Also, lightly rub the bottom of the guide foot to remove any burrs that might have resulted from filing both feet.

Thread comes in different sizes and colors. Be sure to use only rod-wrapping thread, which is a special nylon, because other threads (cotton or synthetics for sewing) lack the necessary strength and sleekness, resulting in a poor wrap. Use size A thread for fly rods, ultralight spinning rods, light spincast rods, and light casting rods. Use size D for heavy saltwater fly rods, medium-action casting rods, medium to heavy spinning rods, and most freshwater and light saltwater tackle, such as light boat rods, surf rods, and boat spinning rods. Use E thread for heavy surf rods, 50- to 80-pound-test class trolling rods, heavy jigging and boat rods, and similar tackle. EE thread is made for the heaviest rods such as offshore shark rods and International Game Fish Association 130-pound-class or heavier trolling tackle.

Pick the same thread color as that used by the rod maker. This may be difficult

# SELECTING THE PROPER PERFECTION GUIDES AND TOP

## Choosing the correct size guide

Determine the Perfection guide size for your rod building requirement by referring to the chart below. When sizing a guide needing replacement, simply use the chart to match its outside ring diameter to the corresponding Perfection size.

Lay your rod on this page as shown. Look straight down on the guide ring from above and match it with the Perfection guide closest in size.

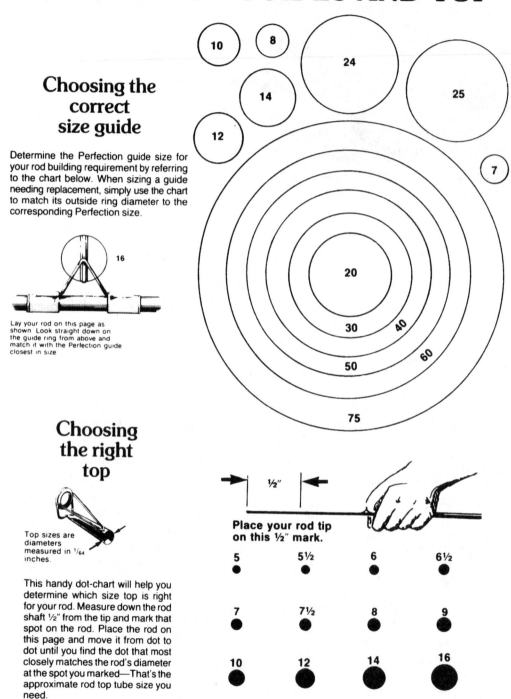

## Choosing the right top

Top sizes are diameters measured in 1/64 inches.

This handy dot-chart will help you determine which size top is right for your rod. Measure down the rod shaft 1/2" from the tip and mark that spot on the rod. Place the rod on this page and move it from dot to dot until you find the dot that most closely matches the rod's diameter at the spot you marked—That's the approximate rod top tube size you need.

1/2"

Place your rod tip on this 1/2" mark.

| 5 | 5½ | 6 | 6½ |
| 7 | 7½ | 8 | 9 |
| 10 | 12 | 14 | 16 |

Tiptop and guide gauge for choosing the correct size of guide. *Courtesy of Perfection Tip.*

All guide feet of all guides must be filed to a knife edge before being wrapped in place. This prevents gaps in the wrapping.

on factory rods because some manufacturers use colors that are not available commercially, so pick the closest color possible. It is often best to choose a slightly lighter color, and then use no color preserver, which will cause the thread color to darken when epoxy is applied. (Lighter thread colors will get lighter if no preserver is used.)

If you are concerned about the match, do a test wrap on a scrap piece of rod or dowel to check the final color after coating with a finish. One important point here is that the lack of color preserver will also make the thread slightly transparent. A guide with a bright frame might be visible through the thread wrap, and a black guide with a filed (bright) end foot might also show through.

When you have assembled all your materials, file and tape the guide in place with masking tape. Suitably thin ⅛- inch masking tape is available from some rod supply houses or from auto shops that specialize in body work (the tape is used for pin-striping). Otherwise, take regular masking tape and cut thin strips, each several inches long. Tape the guide so that the foot's end is exposed so that you can begin wrapping the thread on the guide before removing the tape. Tape the guide in place, centering it so that there will be equal-length wraps on each guide foot and so that the guide is lined up with the tiptop, and reel hoods.

Rod builders have special tools for wrapping rods and maintaining thread tension. If you have these, great, if not, you can easily get by with a teacup, telephone book, and two sheets of typing paper. Place the thread in the teacup (to keep it from rolling off the table or around the floor), run the thread through the two sheets of unused typing paper (to keep the thread clean) in the center of the phone book. The weight of the phone book creates the thread tension, which can be adjusted by the thread's position in the pages. For more tension, just add books on top. Hold the rod in your hands or put the rod on a cardboard box that has the front removed and notches cut in the front top sides to create Vs to support the rod.

Roger Seiders of Flex Coat likes a different method. He places the cup holding the thread behind a chair, runs the thread over the chair seat, and sits on the chair to maintain tension. He rolls the rod on his lap away from him and so he can watch the wraps as they are laid down.

Begin the wrap in the same spot as the original wrap, making several turns

Begin a wrap on a rod by taping the guides down and also taping the borders of the wraps. Note that the guides wrapped down leave the end of the guide foot exposed so that the thread wrap can be begun before the tape is removed.

around the blank and over the thread to secure the thread end. Make sure the threads are parallel and have no gaps between them. After six to eight turns, cut off excess thread from the end. Continue wrapping, rotating the rod and maintaining thread tension. Watch for gaps or overlapping of threads. The best way to do this is to keep the thread at a slight angle to the previous wrap so that each wrap is laid down tightly against the previous one. Use care at the beginning of the guide foot, and wrap up on the guide foot.

Remove the tape, continue wrapping until you are six to eight turns from the edge of the guide frame. At this point, wrap down a doubled loop of thread with the loop end pointing toward the center of the guide. Continue wrapping to the guide frame. Holding the thread, cut it, and insert the end through the loop. Pull the loop through the wraps, at the same time pulling the end of the thread to secure it. Cut the excess thread, using a razor blade to cut straight down between the wraps and cut the end. Use your thumbnail or a smooth pen as a burnisher to close up this gap and any other spaces that might have developed during the wrapping.

Turn the rod around and repeat this on the other guide foot. This type of

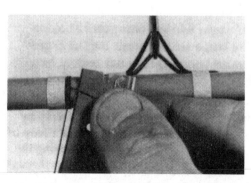

Start the wrap by wrapping over the thread about four to six turns and then cutting any excess thread as shown.

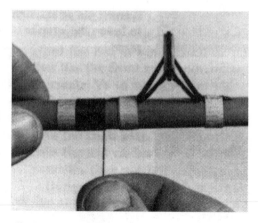

Continuing the wrap.

The wrap as it begins to go up over the end of the guide foot.

wrap is similar to other rod wraps that might have to be replaced, such as the simple decorative wrap about the handle, wraps at the ferrules, and the short wrap at the tiptop.

Heavy rods may have a wrap underneath the guide wrap and this should also be replaced. Remove all wraps, make the underwrap on the rod, then add the guides as outlined. Underwraps are aesthetically pleasing and provide a good cushion between the rod blank and the metal guide foot on big-game rods.

After the wraps are completed, they must be protected with a finish. To prevent the thread color from changing, you must use a color preserver. Color preservers come in two bases: solvent and acrylic. Solvents are usually clear and have a distinct lacquer smell. The acrylics have a different smell and often look white and milky. Both preservers should cover the wrap, soaking it, with any excess blotted up. Use a small disposable brush to apply the color preserver, beginning with the wraps at the tip end and working down to the butt end of the rod. Then return to the tip end to blot any residue with a paper towel or napkin. A second layer can be added within minutes after the first coat, but then wait 24 to 36 hours before adding the rod fin-

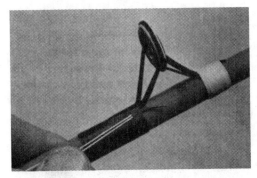

Finish the wrap by wrapping over a loop of thread and tucking the end of the wrap through the loop. Here the loop is being pulled through to fasten the wrap in place.

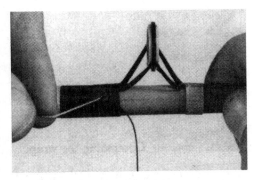

Continue to pull the thread through with the loop of extra thread.

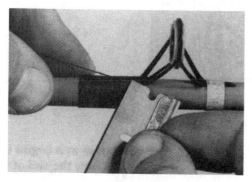

Finished wrap, burnished to smooth the wraps in place.

Once the thread is pulled through, cut the end with a razor blade, as shown. Another way of doing this is to open up a gap in the wrap, and cut straight down with the razor blade.

Finished wraps must be protected with a coat of color preserver. For best results, apply liberally and then blot any excess.

ish. A good way to check if enough time has elapsed is to closely smell the wrap. If you still smell the color preserver, wait until you can't. It is also important to use the right preserver. For example, Flex Coat recommends only their color preserver because other lacquer-base color preservers might cause the epoxy finish to color in time. Following color preserver, rod finish (epoxy or other type) must be added to protect the wrap. The color preserver will *not* protect the wrap — only preserve the thread color. See instructions in chapter 2.

**Tiptops** These guides differ from others on the rod because they are attached by a tube that fits on the end of the rod blank, instead of a frame connected to one or two feet that are wrapped in place on the rod. Tiptops can become loose and require retightening. If a tiptop is loose, the easy solution is to slide it gently off the rod. Use a toothpick or paper clip to clean old glue out of the tube and with a pocketknife or razor blade, scrape any glue off the end of the rod blank. When scraping glue off the blank, take care not to damage the thread wrap. The wrap

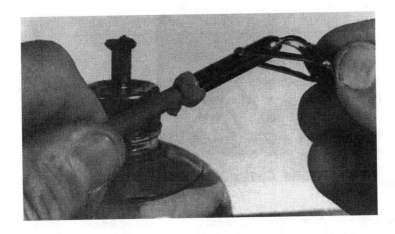

Cementing new tiptop on rod. Use of heat-set cement is most popular as shown here, but regular glues can be used.

here is strictly decorative and does not hold the tiptop in place so it does not have to be removed to reglue or replace the tiptop.

When the old glue is removed from the tube and the blank, thoroughly mix the epoxy, insert some into the tube with a paper clip, smear a little on the rod blank, and slide the tiptop back in place. Use clean rags or paper towels to wipe any cement that flows out of the tube onto the thread wrap. Also carefully check the end of the tiptop, because some tiptops have a small hole in the end of the tube through which glue can flow. If this occurs, wipe the glue away with a tooth-pick and clean up this area.

Glue is very runny right after being mixed, so you may find it difficult to adjust the rod so that the tiptop is precisely aligned with the rod guides. One method is to lay the rod flat between two supports so that the guides hang straight down. Then the tiptop can be adjusted so it also hangs down by the weight of the guide ring, and automatically lines up. It also helps to make a last-minute alignment check as the glue begins to set. For 5-minute epoxy, check this after 2 to 3 minutes; with standard epoxy, wait about 30 minutes, then make any adjustments when the tip-top is still movable but before the glue completely sets.

## Rod Finish

Older rods will sometimes experience peeling or flaking of the factory finish. It might seem simple to refinish the rod, but the longevity of the results often leaves something to be desired. Brush-on and spray epoxies or urethane finishes can be applied to the rod. The result will be beautiful for several years or so, but it will not be nearly as durable as the higher-quality, factory finish.

In cases of severe peeling or wear, though, a new finish might be the only solution. Other cases where refinishing is required include rods that are rebuilt with the guides repositioned. (Guides may be repositioned because a broken tip required rebuilding, the rod's function changed, or the number of the guides or the length of the grip/handle was changed.) In these cases, refinishing is almost a must, because the original position of the wraps will show ridges where the thread has grooved the surface of the blank.

As a result of color changes and sun on the exposed blank, you can never hope to refinish a rod so that the previous guide positions do not show.

To refinish a rod you can remove the guides and refinish the blank, then rewrap the guides, or you can refinish the rod with the guides still in place. If the guides are damaged, threads are frayed, and so on, pick the first choice; if the guides and wraps are fine, pick the latter.

To refinish a rod in either case, you cannot allow the rod to ride on a central support as you do when finishing wraps, because this would mar the new finish. Several solutions are possible. If the guides are on the rod, run a thin dowel or old rod blank through the tiptop and first two to three guides, then rest the dowel on a support to hold the rod as a motor turns the butt end. If finishing a stout rod blank, with the tiptop removed, you can run a dowel or rod blank into the hollow end of the blank and rest this extension on the support. For completed rods, you can also tie a loop of cord to the tiptop, attach a ball-bearing swivel, tie in another loop, and fasten this loop to a support just beyond the end of the tiptop. This way, the rod can be turned to cure the finish and the swivel will prevent tangles.

Finishes can be brushed on, as outlined for wrapping guides, or sprayed on with long, even strokes. In most cases, the thinner coat of spray finishes does not require turning the rod. You should check the spray coating carefully as you work and immediately thereafter to ensure that it is even.

## Broken Rods

Repairing a broken rod is not difficult in most cases, but it is time consuming and requires the right materials, such as a scrap blank that can be used for reinforcing the broken area.

Rod tips will frequently break just a few inches down from the end. The best repair is not to try to reinforce and replace the broken section, but to remove the broken section and add a new tiptop to the broken end. If the break is a split, splintered break, or break where the fiber peels off, this may not be possible. Fortunately, this is seldom the case. If the rod is splintered, you may not be able to repair it. If the splintering is slight, you can cut the rod blank back to a point below the splintered fibers and adjust (rewrap) the position of the remaining guides as desired.

With surf, some spinning, steelhead, offshore, boat, and similarly large rods that have guides far apart, you can usually sand down a clean break and remount a tiptop, using a larger size to fit the new, larger diameter of the rod tip.

For casting or fly rods, in which the guides are close together, the best solution is often to remove the top guide, cut the rod back to this point, and replace the guide with a new tiptop. A new tiptop is necessary because the taper of the rod blank will be too wide for the original tiptop. Use a fine-blade hacksaw (32 teeth per inch) or fine triangular file to score the rod blank where you want to cut it. When the outer skin is scored, file or saw through the blank slowly and evenly. Replace the tiptop and wraps following the previous directions.

For breaks farther down on the rod, repairs are often possible but *only* if the break is a clean one and not splintered or damaged over a large area. If a one-piece rod breaks at, or below, its halfway point, consider adding a ferrule. Pick a ferrule

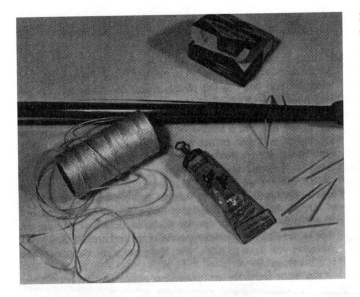

Split-bamboo rods can sometimes be repaired. *If the damage is to a fine bamboo rod, first check with a reliable repairman or rod appraiser for value of the rod. Home repairs like this are best only with inexpensive bamboo rods of little value.* In this splintered damage, toothpicks are used to hold apart the strips of the rod for gluing. The cord is used for wrapping the rod while the glue cures.

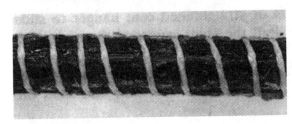

After the glue is applied, wrap the rod firmly with cord. This cord serves to clamp the parts together and will be removed once the glue is cured.

that will snugly fit on the rod or, if mail-ordering a ferrule, measure the rod carefully about 1 inch below the break.

Cut or file both ends of the break smooth, then roughen them with fine sandpaper or emery cloth. Check the ferrules for a good fit. If the fit is too tight, you may have to sand the rod blank slightly. If it is too loose, shim the rod blank with thread, bringing the thread up over the ends of the break and down the sides of the rod blank so that the shim threads are parallel to the blank. Coat the blank with good waterproof epoxy glue, smear some on the inside of each ferrule part, and slide the ferrules in place. Wipe away excess glue, cut any threads if required (if thread was used for a shim), and allow to cure overnight before testing and using.

To repair a break without adding a new ferrule the break must be clean, and you need to closely match the broken ends. You also need a scrap piece of fiberglass or graphite the same size and roughly the same taper as the broken rod. Remove the butt cap of the rod, cut a section of the scrap blank to fit the break area, slide and glue it into place, and glue the broken tip end onto this splice. Follow with a long wrap of fine thread to reinforce the rod and give it hoop strength in this area.

This will not work if this is a powerful graphite rod and broken in the tip end, because the thin-spliced section probably will not be strong enough to hold up under the stresses on the rod. There is no simple rule for the diameter or action limiting this type of repair, but the more powerful the rod and the less inside diameter you have to work with, the greater the danger of later rod breakage.

The basic steps for this operation once you have the proper materials are as follows:

1. Remove the butt cap of the rod if the break is in the butt section or if the rod is one piece.
2. Slide the scrap piece of blank into the rod at the broken end to determine the junction of the fit. Mark this spot on the scrap rod.
3. Cut the scrap rod 3 inches above and below this mark. Extend the cut shim (splicing) section into the rod, using a second blank section or straightened coat hanger to slide the blank in place. Pull the shim snug and then wiggle it slightly sideways to determine the degree of play or looseness in the blank. If it's loose, determine which end of the shim blank is loose, remove the shim, and sand the required area.
4. Replace the shim and check for proper fit. Repeat until the shim fits.
5. Repeat the above with the shim in place, checking for a proper fit of the broken tip end over the shim.
6. Coat the thicker half of the splicing-blank section with epoxy glue and slide it in place. Once it extends from the end of the blank, pull it into place and remove excess glue from the blank. Coat the protruding end of the shim with glue. Carefully slide the tip section onto the shim, making sure that the shim does not loosen. (You may wish to wait until the glue cures in the butt before replacing the tip section. This prevents pushing the splice or shim back down into the rod.)

    Once in place, match up the sections, and remove any excess glue. If there is a gap between the two broken sections (as will occur in a slight crushing break), allow some glue to remain in the gap to fill the space to the level of the blanks for wrapping. Allow to cure overnight.
7. Use thread the color of the blank to wrap the break. Begin 2 inches below the break and wrap 2 inches above it. Coat with epoxy finish as you would with a guide wrap.

Some tips for working with stout rods include using scrap pieces of graphite or glass blank to build up a shim section of two or three layers for added strength. The best way to check to see if this is needed is to flex the rod near the break and compare the strength and flex with the scrap blank/shim material. To do this, make up layers by gluing smaller sections into larger ones until you add enough wall thickness to the shim to be used in the repair.

## Ferrules, Collets, and Butt Adapters

Metal ferrules are rarely used on modern rods, but you can still find them on older models. A method of restoring bent ferrules was mentioned in chapter 2. The only real repair for metal ferrules, however, is replacement. The difficulty is finding parts, because the major manufacturers of these ferrules are out of business. Good ferrules—read expensive—of nickel silver are still available for custom, usually bamboo, fly-rod construction and repairs.

To replace a metal ferrule, first remove the old ferrule. If it is already loose, gently pull it off. If it is not loose, protect the rod with several layers of masking tape, then use a cigarette lighter or alcohol lamp to heat the metal while turning the rod to distribute the heat evenly. Pull the heated and loosened ferrule straight off the rod with pliers. Most repairs require new male and female pieces, so also do this with the other ferrule.

Clean the blank to remove old glue and, if necessary, rough the blank lightly with steel wool to give the blank some "tooth" for a better gluing bond. Test the new ferrule set on the blank for fit. If the fit is too tight, sand the blank to reduce its diameter. Do this with care, because sanding reduces the strength of the blank in that area. Thin-walled blanks allow almost no sanding.

You can fix a fit that is too loose by cutting back the butt section of the blank slightly, in ¼-inch increments. This will allow fitting on a slightly thicker area of the blank because of its taper. You can't cut back the other side, because the increasing taper of the tip will make any fit looser. The disadvantage of cutting the rod is that if too much is removed, the rod's two sections will be slightly uneven.

A better method is to use shims of rod-wrapping thread as spacers between the blank and the ferrule. The secret is to run the shims of thread parallel to the axis of the rod. To do this, use masking tape to secure a thread several inches from the rod end. Run the thread parallel to the blank and up over the end, down the other side; secure with masking tape. Do this several times evenly around the blank, to build up two, four, six, or eight shims. How many depends on the blank diameter and the amount of shimming needed. Shim thickness can also be controlled by the size of the thread. Use A thread for light shimming, D for heavier shimming, and E for extra-heavy shimming. The advantage of parallel thread and shim placement over circular thread wrap is that the latter can be pushed out of place when the ferrule is mounted, whereas the parallel shims will retain their original position.

Once the shims are taped in place, mark the rod for the final position of the end of the ferrule. Be careful when measuring open-end female ferrules, because there is no separation between the part glued to the rod and the part fitting the male ferrule. When measuring the male ferrule, add ⅛ inch for glue and shim spacing.

Once the rod is marked, spread glue inside the ferrule and over the rod. For

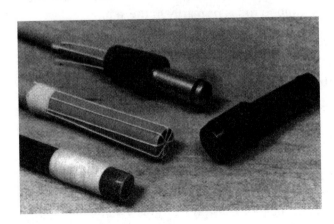

Shims for seating replacement ferrules and butt adapters on rods are easily made from cord, by wrapping around the blank (foreground) or stringing the cord along the axis of the blank (middle). Background shows butt adapter in place, before the cord is cut off.

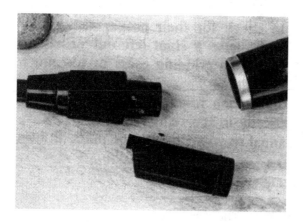

Damage to a rod from breakage of a butt adapter. The fault is not with the butt adapter—the rod blank was not inserted completely into the butt adapter when the rod was built by a custom rod builder. Replacement is easy by splitting off the adapter and adding a new one.

best results use a 24-hour epoxy glue. Slide the ferrule in place, wipe excess glue from the blank or ferrule, and use a razor blade to trim excess shim threads.

Repeat with the male ferrule, seating it all the way on the rod blank. When the glue is cured, finish it off with a thread wrap that begins on the blank and runs slightly onto the ferrule. Use the same color of thread as used on the guide wraps, and coat with an epoxy finish.

Collets for offshore rods and butt adapters or ferrules for detachable-handle casting and popping rods can be shimmed and repaired the same way. The difference is that you will be dealing with the male fitting that will go into a reel seat or rod handle.

Bamboo rods can be repaired this way, too, but there are some additional factors. Some older bamboo rods have a small pin driven through the ferrule and the rod. The ferrule cannot be taken off unless this pin is removed. To remove it, use a small punch or drift (a small nail set works well) to drive it out.

The hexagonal shape of split-bamboo rods also does not conform to the round shape of ferrules. You can use a larger ferrule and slip it over the rod blank, slightly crimping its end to match the flat surfaces of the hexagonal rod blank.

A second method is to use a key-tightened three-jaw chuck in two different positions to form the fitted section of the ferrule into the hexagonal shape of the rod. Both of these methods preserve rod strength because no bamboo skin is cut or removed. The strength of any bamboo rod is primarily in the skin.

Another method involves trimming the corners of the hexagonal rod in the area of the ferrule so that the round ferrule will exactly, or more closely, fit the rod blank. This also keeps the ferrule from looking too bulky, and is easier to trim-wrap with thread. It does weaken the rod slightly, though, because some of the bamboo skin is removed.

CHAPTER

# 7

# Reel Repair

**R**EEL REPAIRS can be simple or extensive, depending upon the degree of wear or damage. Repairs should only be done if you feel confident of your ability to dismantle and reassemble the parts necessary for the repair required. Some tackle manufacturers, warranty centers, and reel repair service centers caution against fishermen repairing reels. This is self-serving to a degree, but it does point out the necessity of care in any reel repairs. This does not mean, however, that reel repairs are difficult.

Some reel repairs are nothing more than a quick replacement of a part, and might almost constitute part of a maintenance program instead of reel repair. Such might be the case with replacing rollers on spinning-reel bails, bail springs, pawls on casting reels, and click drags on fly reels. However, they are replaced because they are worn or damaged, and technically constitute repairs.

If there are any rules when repairing reels they are these:

1. Work on one reel at a time.
2. Make sure the reel is clean and free of grease or grime so you can see what you are doing and how the parts fit and mesh.
3. Have a good work area and a compartmented box to hold parts as you remove them.
4. Pay particular attention to shims, small washers, small springs, and so on to check for their proper reassembly order. This is critical because a shim left out or in the wrong position may result in grinding gears or too much play in part of a reel.
5. Work from left to right when removing parts so that replacement is automatically in the right order.
6. Consult the reel's manual so you can examine parts, fittings of parts, and the part number if you need to order an item.
7. Have the necessary tools and replacement parts before you start. An exception here might be when you know the reel is damaged, but you do not know which parts you need to fix it. Make sure that you can leave the reel disassembled, with the removed parts in order, while you buy or mail-order the required replacements, or that you reassemble the reel after determining what will be required.

It is very important to remove most of the grease from reel housings and gear-

The need for proper care is evidenced in these reels, now completely ruined. The left and center reel have corrosion built up under the side-plate frame and the line guide. A properly cared-for reel is shown on the right.

ings. Failure to do so will prevent you from seeing the small parts and how they fit. And since every reel is a little different, it is important to proceed slowly and to examine the reel parts carefully as you remove them so that you can see how they all fit together.

Before beginning on some basic replacements and repairs, it should be noted there are probably exceptions to the information on fittings, screw positions, gearings, and access to parts. The following, however, should apply to most reels.

## Spinning Reels

**Roller Replacement** The rollers on a spinning-reel bail prevent the line wear that would occur if running over a nonmoving part. The line makes a right-angle bend at this point, turning at right angles as the bail lays the line on the spool. Roller replacement does not require removing the bail. All rollers are held in place by a screw at the end of the bail arm, where the bail wire attaches to the bail arm support.

Loosen this screw and remove it, holding the bail at the same time so no small parts will be lost. Assembly might be as simple as a screw holding the roller in place on the end of the bail wire arm, or might include a bushing under the roller, lock washer under the screw, and bail collar.

Once the screw is off, remove the roller and bushing and replace. If replacement is not required, clean and oil as described in chapter 3, Reel Maintenance.

**Bail Assembly** Bail assemblies are high on the list of broken parts of spinning reels, according to a poll taken of spinning-reel manufacturers. This is not a design or manufacturing fault. These arms are vulnerable because they are exposed. Dropping a reel can break or bend a bail arm. Bail terminology will vary with each manufacturer, but the bail assembly includes a bail arm attached to one side of the reel rotor (the rotating framework immediately behind the spool that holds the bail and moves it around the spool), with the other end holding the roller and attached to an arm or arm lever assembly. Both of these are held in place with screws.

The screw attachment can go directly through the end of the bail arm into the rotor housing, or be on a separate plate attached to the rotor housing. The lever arm holding the roller end of the bail is held in place with a screw, but a plate arm hides the springs and levers that hold the cocked (open) bail in place until the bail release closes the bail.

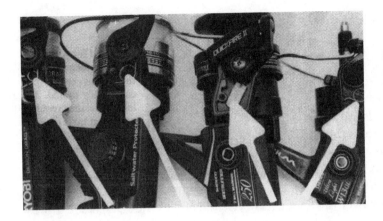

Bail springs most commonly require replacement and repair in spinning reels. These can vary from compression springs to lever springs. Springs are shown on these four spinning reels (arrows pointing to springs).

If the bail is bent, remove the bail arm by unscrewing it at the rotor attachment and at the roller. Remove the bail, and carefully bend it into its original shape. Check the shape to make sure that it will fit back into place without more bending, twisting, or stressing. Reattach and open and close the bail to ensure it works properly.

If a bail spring is broken, the first job is finding it on the reel. Most are directly under the plate covering the arm lever. On older reels that do not feature skirted spools, these were often positioned inside the rotating cup. Once you locate the spring, remove it carefully. The spring is under tension, so you must hold it with small needle-nose pliers or tweezers to prevent it from flying off. If this is impossible, hold your thumb or finger over the spring and pry out one end to release the tension. Then carefully lift the spring out.

If the spring is broken you won't have this problem. Just lift it out and put in a new spring. Use the same cautions for seating the new spring, because the spring must go in under tension. Hold your thumb or finger over the spring and lever or pry one end into place. If a tension spring, such as found on older reels, hook one end in place, hold that end, and lever the other end of the hook into position.

Once the spring is in place, replace the cover and reassemble the arm lever and bail.

**Handle** Handles also break when reels are dropped or handled roughly. Most spinning-reel handles are easy to replace because they are detachable. Handles are made in two ways. In one, the handle is on a square or hex shaft, which slides through a fitted socket and is held in place with a screw fitting and cap on the opposite side of the reel. The other handle uses two sets of threads on the reel shaft. The handle is backed up to unscrew the shaft from the side housing, and replaced on the opposite side. A small screw-on cap covers the open side to prevent water or dirt intrusion.

**Gears** Most gears are easy to replace once you open the reel's side plate. The side plate is removed by first taking off the handle. Then loosen the small screws around the perimeter of the housing and lift them off. In most cases these small screws (two or four of them) are the same size and length. If not, note the position of each screw for proper reassembly.

Once you remove the side plate, the gears are fully exposed. If the gears are

459

binding, rough, or grinding, they will have to be replaced. (Be sure, however, that this is not the result of rough, corroded, or damaged bushings or ball bearings.) In most cases, the drive gear is easily taken out for replacement. If the drive shaft containing the pinion gear is damaged, it is necessary to remove the main drive shaft by removing the spool from the reel, loosening the main nut surrounding the shaft, and removing the rotor. This will usually make it possible to slide out the main shaft. Most reels have additional gearing in the main housing to allow for the reciprocal (back-and-forth) motion of the main shaft. This allows the roller on the bail to lay the line down evenly over the spool. If this is attached to the main shaft, it must be removed so this shaft and pinion gearing can be replaced.

On most reels, the shaft is separate from the pinion gear. Removing the spool rotor and the shaft exposes the cover that holds the pinion gear in place. This cover must be taken off to remove and replace the pinion gear.

Whether this is necessary or not will depend upon the reel's care, usage, and construction. Inexpensive reels with zinc or low-quality gearings will require replacement in time. Those with high-quality, cut stainless-steel or brass gearing will last a long time and, with care, maybe a lifetime. Reels not cared for or lubed regularly and properly can also wear, regardless of the gear construction. In most cases, this extensive a dismantling of the reel will not be necessary except under extreme circumstances.

Once the parts are removed, grease and oil them as per the manufacturer's instructions and replace in exact reverse order in which they were removed.

**Drags** Drags on spinning reels are in either the spool or rear housing (as in rear-drag reels). All reels that are fished heavily for big fish will ultimately require drag replacement. Spinning-reel drags in the spool are easy to replace. First remove the spool. Most reel drags have a small spring-retaining ring to hold the drag washers in place. Use pliers or a small screwdriver to pry the spring out, holding your thumb over the spring to prevent loss. Once this is removed, the drag washers slide out.

These are alternately hard and soft washers, with the hard metal washers alternately keyed to the spool and the shaft. This is how the drag works. Pressure on the drag through the drag-adjustment knob creates friction in the drag. The hard washers keyed to the shaft stay stationary while those keyed to the spool rotate. The soft washers between them keep the drag running smoothly while the pressure on the drag controls the degree of breaking power used in the drag.

Multidisc drags, as these are often called, will have, in order: a hard washer keyed to the spool, a soft washer, a hard washer keyed to the shaft, a soft washer, a hard washer keyed to the spool, and so on. Some drags also have a spring at the bottom to help control the pressure and provide more drag control.

In these drag systems, as in any such system, only the soft or fiber washers are changed or replaced. Hard metal washers normally never need replacing. Metal washers can be washed and polished, but do not use steel wool or sandpaper because they will abrade the surface and make the drag rough acting.

When replacing a drag system, check with the manufacturer or reel manual for oiling instructions. Some drags use a light oil, while others should never be oiled. Ignoring this can be critical in how and how well the drag works.

Other types of spool drags are being developed. Some manufacturers are eliminating small multidisc drag systems and going to large single-disc drag features. These can be on top of the spool, or under the spool, as in some Fin-Nor spinning reels. These are no more difficult to reach, only different. A small retainer ring usually holds these drag systems in place. Removing the retaining ring exposes the drag washer or washers. The main difference is that there is usually only one hard and one soft washer. This does not mean that these drags are inferior because they lack parts—some of the finest reels in the world use similar systems. The larger washer spreads the breaking over a bigger area to better dissipate the heat buildup caused by friction. These are usually far smoother reel drags.

Drags in the rear of the reel housing (rear drags) are more difficult to reach, and often vary more widely in construction with reel manufacturers. To expose and replace these soft washers, remove the handle and the side plate as above. To remove the washers you must fully extend the shaft. This is easy to do before removing the handle or after removing the side plate by inserting and turning the handle in the reel socket. You will have to remove the rear drag control. In some reels this is held in place with a U-shaped retaining ring, which prevents removing the drag knob. Remove this, and the drag knob can be completely unscrewed. An alternative method uses a screw to hold the drag knob on from the rear. Remove this and the knob comes off. Once the knob is off, the washers can be exposed and removed. Some can be lifted out of the side of the reel, while others come off the back, after removing a retaining ring that holds them in place like the spool-drag washers.

Replace the soft washers, oil if called for, replace the drag assembly in the reel, and reassemble in order.

Some reels have a front spool-operated drag system in combination with a light-pressure rear system. This is used to control line taken by a fish when bait fishing. Two examples are Shimano's Baitrunner system and Silstar's Baitfeeder. In both cases, the rear drag exerts only very light pressure on the line when a fish takes bait. These operate as a drag on the spool shaft with the main drag working with the shaft stationary and against the spool drag. These rear controls are just like any rear drag in construction and replacement of washers.

**Other Parts** Most other reel parts are readily accessible. The only other part of spinning reels is the antireverse click. This might be as simple as a lever with a leaf spring, or as complicated as a silent antireverse system. Rarely do these need replacement, and all are easily reached and repaired, either in the reel housing or underneath the spool rotor.

## Spincast Reels

Spincast-reel gearing is similar to that on spinning reels, though simpler.

**Handles** Handles break in falls just as they do on spinning reels. Replacement is simple, because most handles are held on the shaft with a screw or nut. Unscrew to remove the broken handle and replace with a new one.

**Gears** Gears are reached in one of two ways. On some reels the reel's entire working mechanism comes out of the housing when you remove the nose cone. Remove the nose cone by turning it counterclockwise to remove screw attachments, turn counterclockwise for about ½ inch to remove those with a lock-on bayonet mount. Pull out the gearing/handle parts. The gearing will be visible from the rear, where it can be lubricated or checked for wear and replacement. Other reels feature access through the side plate, just as with spinning reels. As with spinning reels, you must first remove the handle, then the star drag (turn counterclockwise). Remove the screws in the side plate to lift it off and expose the gearing.

Some shafts holding the main drive gear are free and can be slipped off for replacement, though others require removing other parts or brackets to get the gear loose. A bracket usually holds the central shaft and pinion gear in place; removal of the bracket or other parts will allow replacement of the shaft and gear.

**Spool** To take off the spool, first remove the nose cone. Remove the winding cup—the protective cone under the nose cone that holds the pickup pin, which retrieves line—by turning it counterclockwise.

Once the winding cup is removed, the spool is exposed and can usually be slipped off, though others require removing other brackets and retaining features before removing and checking.

**Pickup Pin** It is also possible to check the pickup pin on the underside of the winding cup when you look at the spool. Pins operate on a cam or spring system and are easy to check or replace if worn.

**Snubber or Line Brake** The snubber or line brake, which holds the line when casting or slowing at the end of the cast, is on the outside (front) of the winding cup. It may be hard rubber or plastic. It can sometimes separate from the winding cup and cause problems. To repair this, use a good flexible rubber cement or epoxy to recement the snubber. If the snubber is worn or brittle and cracked, pry it off and replace with a new one.

**Drag** The drag on spincast reels works and looks like those on casting reels. The star drag on some spincast reels is under the handle and consists of pressure plates that compress soft or fiber washers to create the friction on line pulled from the reel. (Metal pressure plates alternating with soft washers are basic to any drag system, however.)

To check or replace the washer, remove the star drag wheel by turning it counterclockwise. Then remove, in turn and with close attention to their position, each of the successive washers, shims, plates, springs, and other mechanisms. Replace the soft or fiber washers if required and reassemble.

## Fly Reels

Most fly reels are simple, with some consisting of no more than a half-dozen main parts and a few screws. Most damage to fly reels results when they've been

The rim overlapping feature makes rim-control fly reels far more susceptible to damage. Sometimes they can be bent back into shape. Here a small pair of pliers is being used to bend out a rim-control spool. The strip of cardboard protects the reel from damage.

dropped and the frame or spool has been bent. The frame or spool may be bent back into shape, but this may crack the part, because these reels are often hard-tempered aluminum alloys. If they are plastic or cast metal, they usually can't be rebent to their original shape and will crack.

To rebend a bent spool or frame (you have nothing to lose, since with a bent part the reel can't be used anyway), use pliers with the jaws wrapped with several layers of masking tape to avoid marring the reel. Bend gently and slowly, and check periodically for clearance. Do not bend more than is absolutely necessary for clearance, because this might crack the reel.

**Handles** Dropping reels can bend the handles. Some handles are riveted on the spool so replacement is impossible. Try to bend the handle back in place. If the handle can be removed, replace it with a new one.

**Line Guards** Line guards are those small, hard brackets that are designed to protect the line from wear when it is pulled off the reel when casting. These are usually easily replaced. You may have to dismantle the reel on models in which this part slides into place under a framing plate.

**Clicks and Drags** Most fly reels have simple clicks and drag mechanisms. On most reels, these are under the spool, on the inside of the frame. They vary widely in design. Some have large pressure-plate drags, a fine example of which would be the Fin-Nor fly reel. Others have small cam-control click drags or combination click and pressure drags. The better pressure-plate drag systems are on large saltwater and salmon-sized fly reels (which need them), while most other reels have small click drags.

## Casting Reels

Before removing the left side plate on magnetic casting reels, it is *very important* to check your reel manual. Some of the controls are geared and spring loaded. Failure to place the setting to that indicated by the reel manual may result in the magnetic control not setting correctly when reassembled, and not working properly!

Old pawl has been removed and a new one is ready to be inserted into the reel.

This usually means setting the controls on 10 or the maximum setting, because this is the position at which the north/south magnets in two concentric rings will automatically position themselves. But check the reel manual!

**Pawl** These are small toothlike pins that control the back-and-forth movement of the levelwind. They are easy to replace. Use a screwdriver or reel tool to remove the cap on the underside of the levelwind mechanism. Pull out the pawl and replace. These are usually supplied in a small bottle of parts that comes with the reel. Pawls should be regularly checked.

**Worm Gear** The worm gear is the crisscross gearing in which the pawl rides. It makes it possible for the pawl carrying the levelwind to move back and forth and evenly place line on the spool. Worm gears also wear and, in time, require replacement. Removing and replacing them is possible from either the right or left side of the plate, which varies with the reel manufacturer.

Some levelwind worm gears slide out after the pawl has been removed, when the right or left side plate is removed. Others have a small retaining ring holding the worm gear in place, while still others are held by small locking brackets that must be slipped off before removing the worm gear.

**Handle** Handles can break or bend during falls and knocks. They are easy to replace. Most are fastened with a nut that, in turn, is held in place with a locking washer (handle nut-locking plate) and screw. Remove this, then loosen and remove the nut. Some handles have an additional screw in the end of the shaft under the nut. This also must be removed before taking off the handle.

Once the handle is removed, the drag can also be adjusted, cleaned, or replaced.

**Drag** Remove the handle as above. Then unscrew the star drag control counterclockwise. Remove the screws that hold the side plate onto the base plate (on which the gears, antireverse, and free-spool mechanisms are secured) and remove the side plate. Lift out the bearing spacer, drag-spring washers, drag washers, spacers, pressure plates, and other parts. These must be removed in order and kept in order for proper reassembly. Replace the soft drag washers if required and reassemble.

Casting reel with, left to right, main gear, drag washer, antireverse plate, spacers, and pinion gear.

Spinning-reel drags on front-drag systems are almost always found in the spool. These typical drags are examples from three reels. Note that the soft and hard (metal) washers alternate and that spring clips hold all of them in place. The hard washers alternately have "ears" to engage the spool and a square hole to engage the shaft of the reel. The pressure between these two parts creates the braking or slipping action of the drag.

**Pinion and Main Gears** These are on the handle side of the reel. The main gear is attached to the handle shaft and turns the pinion gear. The size and number of teeth in each gear determine the gear ratio, for example, 4:1, 6.1:1, and so on. The teeth can be checked and replaced when the handle and side plate are removed (see above). In most cases the drive gear (along with the drag system previously mentioned) is on one main shaft and can be lifted out and examined or replaced.

**Other Parts** Make sure all other parts are in place during reassembly. These include click alarms, antireverse pawls, flipping controls, and so on. Many of these operate on a spring or lever mechanism to change the on/off controls in these systems. As casting reels become more complicated, more attention must be given to these parts. Check the reel manual for specific details on proper positioning of parts.

## Conventional Offshore and Boat Reels

These are nothing more than large rotary-spool reels and resemble sturdy, simple casting reels. They usually contain click alarms, but lack the levelwind, flipping

New gearing in place on casting reel. The main gear also hides the drag washer. Spacers are on the shaft that the handle fastens to and the pinion gear is also shown.

feature, magnetic cast control, free-spool cast control, and similar appointments that are on small freshwater casting models.

Some simple repair suggestions follow, but casting-reel instructions should also be consulted.

**Handle** These are usually locked in place with a handle lock plate, which must be removed. Handles are easily replaced on big-game reels.

**Pinion and Main Gears** These are under the handle (right) side plate. Remove the handle and the star drag wheel. Remove all the screws around the perimeter of the reel. Keep these in order, because some screws might be different lengths. Remove the side plate. Undo the smaller screws in the side plate that will allow removal and exposure of the main and pinion gears. Most of these gearing systems are simple and easy to replace, especially when compared to smaller casting reels. Pay careful attention when removing screws to prevent parts from falling out, which will make replacement positions difficult to determine. Check, replace needed parts, and reassemble.

**Drag** The drag is similar, although heavier, than that of a casting reel. It is directly under the star drag wheel. All screws must usually be removed to expose the drag so soft washers may be replaced. Replace the washers and reassemble.

After you have repaired and reassembled any reel, check it out thoroughly to be sure it works properly. This is just like the trip check listed in chapter 3 to ensure that the reel is completely functional. If something is not right or if reassembly was incorrect, you want to know it now, not when you are out on the water.

Exposed gearing on a casting reel.

CHAPTER

# Lure Repair

L URES ARE SELDOM thought of as fishing tackle that is repaired. As their cost has gone up, however, so has the interest in keeping them serviceable and repairing them when possible. Many repair basics apply to many lures, so generic repairs will be covered first, followed by a short section on repairs for each type of lure.

## Hook Replacement

Hooks can be replaced on most lures. In many lures, such as crankbaits, plugs, top-water lures, structure spoons, spinners, trolling lures, in-line spinnerbaits, or weight-forward spinners, the single, double, or treble hooks are free swinging. If hooks are attached by split rings, repair is simple. Open the split ring, preferably with split-ring pliers, and remove the damaged, broken, or rusted hook. Once you begin to remove the hook, and have the split ring spread, you can slide the new hook on with the same motion.

If the hook is attached to the lure with a wire ring, as on a spinner, or with a molded-in hook hanger, as on some plugs, cut the hook eye (*not* the hook hanger) and remove it, replacing it with hooks on split rings. One problem that sometimes develops with plugs is that the split ring adds length to the hook so that the several hooks on a plug can catch together.

If this occurs, there are two solutions. One is to buy short-shank hooks (they are made in single and treble hooks); the other is to buy an open-eye hook, such as an open-eye Siwash salmon single hook or open-eye treble. When closed with pliers, the hooks are sufficiently strong.

Trolling spoons often have single fixed hooks that are fastened to the spoon blade by a pop-type rivet or bolt and nut. They are easy to replace, but generally you must use the same style and size of hook as the original, to conform to the bend and shape of the lure.

Hooks on standard spinnerbaits, jigs, buzzbaits, and trolling or weed spoons with welded hooks cannot be easily removed and replaced. If you are adept with soldering and welding equipment, you may consider removing hooks from fixed-hook trolling and weedless spoons and resoldering new ones in their place.

## Repainting, Recoating, and Polishing Lure Bodies

Almost all lures can be repainted. This is easier than ever, particularly because some companies have introduced paints just for lures. Both hobby paint companies and tackle companies have introduced such paints. These paints can be used on all lures. They are hard, quick-drying, high-gloss, waterproof paints. They can be used either in the home workshop for detailed refurbishing, or for quick color changes of lures when fishing.

When making quick color changes with these paints, make sure the lure is dry, and repaint it in the shade. If finishing in the bright sun, turn so your body shades the lure. The shade lengthens the curing time, which is important because these paints set up in seconds. The best technique is to first design a pattern or pick a color and use the applicator brush fastened to the cap to rapidly apply the paint. Avoid going over the paint repeatedly.

There are some portable spray systems, which are different from the brush systems above. These systems use a sprayer nozzle that connects with tubing to a master aerosol air propellent. This propellent sprays the paint on the lure, where it instantly dries. It will not wash off with water. Simple kits that operate from aerosol cans are available from art and hobby shops.

There are several techniques for repainting lures at home under more controlled conditions. The brush-applicator/quick-dry paints work well and provide bright colors. They are best used when painting a lure one color or when repainting lures with several contrasting blocks or bands of color. (Many fishing-lure manufacturers believe that hard contrasting colors make the best-attracting lures.)

Methods of painting lures include:

1. Brushing: Best for quick-drying acrylic paints. Some paints, like those from Testor's, have a built-in felt tip for painting lures. In both cases, apply sparingly, evenly, and rapidly; avoid repeating brush strokes over the same area. Slower-drying paints should be applied the same way, although some overlapping is possible.

2. Dipping: Dipping works best with thin paints. Apply repeated coats and dip slowly to prevent runs, sags, and drips from curing on the lure. Use a long trough for the paint and line up the lures in holders. Dip all the lures and hang them over the paint so that the lure bottom barely touches the paint. This allows rapid runoff of excess paint, after which the rack of lures can be hung to dry. It is important to keep the level of the paint in the trough constant to allow runoff to occur, and to use the same-sized lures.

   In cases where this is too slow, hang the lure rack, then later blot the bottom of each lure to remove excess paint. Dipping is most effective on jig, spinnerbait, and buzzbait heads before the tails are attached.

3. Spraying: This is only possible with aerosol enamels or lacquers. It's not widely used because it is messy and wastes paint. It can produce good results, though. One possibility is to spray a light color, such as white, cream, or yellow, on a crankbait belly with one pass of color; follow with a streak of side color (green, red, blue, tan, silver are popular); and finish with a strip along the back in black, dark brown, or dark blue/green. The result is

a natural-looking, professionally finished plug with a color pattern similar to that of a live baitfish or minnow.

For an added touch, wrapping the sides in scale netting before painting will produce a scale finish. Each spray of paint must be allowed to dry or cure before the next is applied. Painting many lures with the same color scheme maximizes efficiency and minimizes paint waste.

When spray painting, it helps to use a special painting box to contain the airborne paint. You can use an open cardboard box, with the open end on the side, and line the box with cloth scraps, cotton batting, or sponges. These will capture and hold the spray.

Most spoons are polished, and those that have lost their gleam can be painted to give them new life. For this, scrub the spoon with steel wool to remove any dirt, rust, or corrosion. Then mask the hook, line tie, weedguard, and so on that you do not want to paint with tape. Dip or spray with an anti-rust primer, allow to dry, then finish with two coats of enamel or other lure paint. If using light colors, first apply a white base coat. Many primers are dark, and light-colored paints will not adequately cover dark colors.

You can repaint lures when you are afield. Hold them carefully or grip them with finishing pliers and use the paintbrush cap to completely coat any lure. If you like to paint each lure individually, use disposable plastic gloves to keep your hands clean.

When repainting and refinishing lures at the end of the season, set up an assembly-line system. Use a rack to cure many freshly sprayed or dipped lures. Depending upon the lure type, one possibility is a wide U-shaped wooden rack with a hanger across the top. Use hangers of bead chain, standard small-link chain, or pipe strap (a flexible strap with holes every few inches, from which lure hooks can be hung), which will prevent lures from sliding and touching.

Repainting can include applying special patterns. Two of these are scale netting and stencils.

Scale netting comes in several sizes and patterns from lure part companies. Veiling or tulle, found in any fabric store, can be a good substitute. Try to find a coarse material with spacing suitable to the scale pattern you want to create.

There are two ways to use netting. One is to hold the lure, with the scale net-

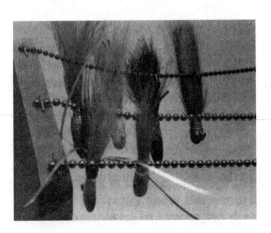

All painted lures must be hung up to dry after painting. Use special racks of bead chain (as shown), strap iron (which has holes to separate the lures), or regular chain. These keep the lures separated. Plain cord or wire will sag and the lures will all slide together.

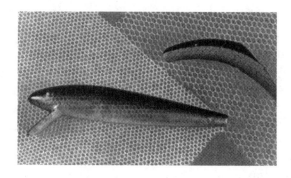

Old lures can be made to look as good as new ones by spray painting them through scale nettings (tulle, available at fabric stores, also works well). Examples of scale netting and painted lures.

ting wrapped securely around it, and spray the side of the lure. When working this way, paint a number of lures by spraying one side, letting the paint cure, then spraying the other side.

A second way to do this is to mount the scale netting loosely in an open frame. Press the lure against the netting, spray it, then turn it over to spray the other side. To prevent damage to the still-wet finish on the first side, mount the lure body on a nail held by a pair of pliers or, if working with a spinnerbait head or jig head, hold the hook with pliers. Another possibility is to lay the lure body on a foam pad, push the frame with the loose netting on top of it, and spray straight down. Lift the frame, carefully remove the lure so the fresh paint won't be damaged, and replace with another lure body. Do one side of a number of lures, allow them to cure, and repeat on the second side.

An embroidery hoop, designed to hold fabric tightly, is ideal for holding scale netting. They come in sizes ranging from about 3 to 24 inches in diameter. If you are really serious about this method of repainting, check silkscreen and printing supply houses and needlework mail-order firms for special hinges that fasten hoop and rectangular frames to a worktable for productionlike work. Lacking this, other hinges could be fastened permanently to a net scale frame.

Stencils are cutout patterns that protect the areas you don't want painted. (We all used stencils in school to outline letters for projects.) Stencils with wavy patterns, spots and dots, scalelike cutouts, and other designs are available from art supply stores.

You can also make stencils by cutting a pattern from sheeting with fine scissors. Paper or cardboard can be used for such templates, but I prefer clear, stiff plas-

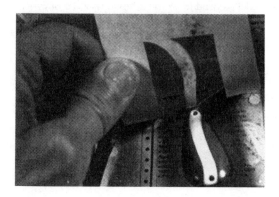

Old lures can be painted using templates to add stripes or spots. Templates can be easily cut from cardboard or lightweight plastic.

tic—the kind used for term paper covers. It is easy to cut, and the clear sheeting allows for proper placement over the lure (until the stencil is covered with paint). Cleaning off the paint after each session keeps these stencils clear enough for long-term use. Stencils can be used in two ways. If you want a hard line of sprayed color, keep the stencil in contact with the lure. For a diffused line, keep the stencil about ¼ to ½ inch away. Experiment for the best results.

Heavily rusted lures can also be painted, first removing any roughness and sealing with a primer coat before painting.

**Rubber Coating** Rubber or plastic-dip coatings are ideal for refinishing and repairing some lures. These coatings are solvent based so that they are water-proof, and are really designed for coating tool handles such as pliers, hammers, wire cutters, and so on. They can be bought from specialty hardware supply houses such as Brookstone, in some better hardware stores, and through industrial tool distributors. You won't find a variety of hues, but you should have no problem locating basic colors such as red, green, yellow, white, black, blue, and orange. The stuff is expensive, because it comes in about 8-ounce cans that cost $6 to $8 each. The coatings are designed for slow dipping, and are ideal for lures such as jigs and stripped spinnerbait or buzzbait heads. A spray-type coating is also available, but would be wasteful because the lures are so small.

**Dyeing** Lures can also be dyed. Sometimes this finish looks almost like a new paint job. In most cases, though, it results in a translucent overlay of color through which a base color can be seen. Dyes available include everything from those used in permanent felt-tip markers, shoe dyes, clothes dyes such as Rit and Tintex, and those specifically made for lures, available from several companies. Technically, a dye colors an object by saturating it with a coloring solution. Dyes are also described as coloring with a hue or tint of a color, which would apply to the uses described above. The main difference between paint and dye is the visible coating left on products by the former.

Soft and hard lures can be colored with dye. Soft lures such as fur, feather, synthetic products, rubber, and vinyl plastics absorb the coloring. Hard lures such as jig heads, spoons, plastic crankbaits, and painted wood lures take on a hue or tint of color when the dye solvent evaporates. Dyes usually dry more slowly than the quick-dry paints, but far faster than standard paints.

Hard lures, such as jig heads, spinnerbaits, spoons, spinners, and so on are best when dyed a light color. White is the only base color that will take a true dye color. Dyes are best applied by dipping.

**Polishing** Metal lures can easily and quickly become tarnished and dull, which will deter their ability to catch fish. To correct for this, polish the lures to restore them back or close to their original luster. Methods of polishing include:

1. Metal polishes: Polishes for silver, brass, and copper will all work well. Brands such as Flitz, Brasso, Twinkle, Oneida, and so on are all good. On high-sheen lures, which might be scratched by these cleaners, use fiberglass

polish or Chrome Foam, used by photographers for cleaning and polishing ferrotype plates. In most cases, however, standard metal finishes are okay.

2. Colas: Colas (that's right—the kind you drink) are often used to remove corrosion from metal lures. If there is heavy finish damage, soak the lure overnight. Often this will be enough, but be sure to wash the lure after soaking.

3. Abrasives: Dirt or fine sand is an abrasive you can use afield, though it might scratch the finish. Obviously, scratches are less important than catching fish, so this is a minor disadvantage.

Cigarette and cigar ashes are also finely abrasive. When wet and rubbed on a lure, they also provide a quick field fix.

A small piece of emery cloth carried in a tacklebox or field repair kit (see chapter 9) helps to polish any metal lure. Unlike sandpaper, which is on a paper base that will be damaged by moisture, emery cloth is on a fabric base. It can be used for a long time without losing its abrasiveness.

Spoons that cannot be restored by polishing can be repainted.

## Re-Forming Lures

Metal lures can bend during fishing. Strong fish, casts into rocks, snags, and stuffing lures into tacklebox compartments all can cause bending and damage. Most damage involves light-wire lures such as spinners, spinnerbaits, and buzzbaits, but spoons, jigs, metal plates, and props on crankbaits and topwater lures are not immune to abuse. Wires, plates, and props are often easily bent back into shape with pliers. Spring wire is often used on these lures, so you usually will have to bend the wire past the point desired, and allow it to spring back to the original position.

Light, thin, metal spoons can also get bent and be rebent into their original position with pliers. Lure hooks can be bent out of shape from fish and snags. Hooks are tempered wire, so take care when bending them back into shape. Hold the lure carefully, grip the hook point with parallel-action fishing pliers or vise-grip pliers for added strength, and, taking care not to bend the barb, slowly and evenly bend the hook back into position.

## Remelting Lures

Soft-plastic lures can be remelted or heat-treated to repair minor tears and abrasion. Save old worms and soft lures instead of throwing them away so that they can be reused. This involves not so much repairing old lures as making new ones out of the old.

Some possibilities include:

1. Take a worm with a damaged or torn head, cut off the damaged portion, and heat it with a flame to round off the head into a new, shorter lure.

2. Remove the damaged tail from one worm and the damaged head from another. Join the salvageable parts by heating the ends in a flame.

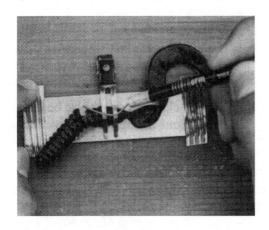

This tool was made specifically for rewelding plastic worms. The clamps hold the worm in place, the heating tool plugs into a 12-volt cigarette lighter and heats the worm to weld it. The same thing can be done at home using an AC welder or macramé cord-cutting tool.

3. Remove salvageable curly tails from damaged worms and join them side by side with a flame to make double spinnerbait, buzzbait, spoon, or jig tails.
4. Remove salvageable tails from worms and use heat to adhere them to the sides of worms to make lizards and salamanders.
5. Use heat to add curly worm tails to soft minnows and fish to make eels.
6. Do all of the above in contrasting color parts to make different lures than those commercially available.

Using a flame is not difficult, but you must take care because molten plastic can burn (soft lure plastic usually melts at about 375°F). For best results, use a disposable lighter, which burns cleaner than other flames. Any flame will work, but unclean flames or too high a heat will burn and dirty the plastic.

Have a fishing buddy hold the lighter as you use both hands to hold the parts close to the flame. This way both parts are heated at the same time and a stronger joint will be formed when they are joined. Cooling is almost immediate, so that you can fish with the new lures seconds after making them. If you don't have a friend to hold the lighter, consider buying a standard lighter that will stay on unattended when lit. That way you can sit the lighter on a boat seat or picnic bench and hold the plastic parts in the flame.

For cleanest results, hold the parts to be joined to the side of the flame, not directly over it. The result is more evenly controlled heat and less danger of burning and discoloring.

## Gluing

Many plugs, crankbaits, and topwater lures are made of hollow plastic. As a result, these lures can open along a seam line or crack when they hit rocks or are struck by a toothy fish. Cracks often can be repaired with an instant glue or five-minute epoxy. First make sure the lure is completely dry. If it has been recently fished, you may have to open the crack with a toothpick to drain the water.

When it is dry, leave the toothpick in place and use a second toothpick to spread glue on the joining edges of the crack. Remove the toothpick, hold the lure firmly to squeeze these parts together, and use a paper towel to remove excess glue.

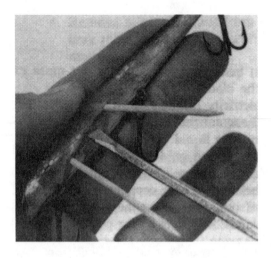

Split or cracked crankbaits (hollow injection-molded plastic lures) can be repaired by regluing them. The crack on this hollow lure is held open with toothpicks. The screwdriver blade helps to get the toothpicks into the crack. The toothpicks should be at the end of the split to hold it open for gluing.

Hold the lure together until the glue is dry, which will take only seconds with an instant glue and no more than a few minutes for a five-minute epoxy. If using a long-curing glue, hold the lure under constant pressure with a carpenter's spring clamp.

You might have to glue metal wobbling plates into a crankbait or topwater plug when they become loose. Remove the plate, which is usually held in place with tiny screws, add glue to the holes (looseness often results from enlarged holes that are too big to hold the screws), add glue to any other necessary contact parts, replace the plates, and screw them in place.

If the damage is extensive, you may have to replace the screws with longer ones (available from tackle supply houses), but be careful so you do not penetrate a lure's hollow body. If this is a possibility, force more glue into the hole so that the combination of screw and glue will seal any opening.

**Refinishing Metal Parts** Metal lure parts such as spoons, spinner blades, buzzbait blades, metal wobbling plates, spinner bodies, and so on can be repaired with metal refinishing or replating kits available at craft and hobby shops. While this is fun, it's not often economically wise, because the kits can be far more expensive than replacing the blades.

Most kits work on electricity (battery or AC). Metal is replated by running a small current through the part when coating or soaking it with a refinishing liquid. Available finishes include nickel, copper, brass, silver, and gold. In most cases, nickel, copper, and brass finishes can be used on any metal. Gold and silver finishes can only be applied over copper or brass plating.

The main advantage of replating is that the blades on rigged lures, such as spinner blades on a long-leader cowbell rig, can be refinished without removing them from the rig.

## Retying Tails

Many lures have tied-in tails of feathers, fur, or synthetic fur. These include spoons, topwater lures, and crankbaits, with tails on the tail hook; jigs, spinnerbaits, and buzzbaits, with tails on the hook shank or collar; and saltwater hose lures and spinners, which have tails tied on the hook.

To repair these, use a razor blade or sharp knife to cut off all the old fur or feathers and the thread holding it in place. Clamp the hook or lure in a vise. A fly-tying vise is preferable, but lacking that vise grips will do if they are mounted on a workbench or held in a workbench vise. Larger lures can be held directly in a workbench vise.

Use fly-tying or rod-building thread (size 2/0 or A for smaller lures, size D on larger ones) to wrap the hook shank or lure part. Be extremely careful to prevent cutting the thread with the hook points. One way to prevent the hook points from cutting the thread is to cover the points with masking tape, tie the lure, then remove the tape when finished. Make several wraps with the thread and trim the tag end. Maintaining tension, wrap in the new fur or feathers.

To wrap in feathers, determine the length of the feather you wish to use and strip off all the hackle, hurl, or feather fibers forward of this point. To tie in fur, clip the fur close to the skin, or fabric base if using fake fur, and hold the fur by the ends. Use a small comb to strip out any underfur that would add bulk (making it difficult to tie) but no action or length to the fur. Cut the skin end of the fur to the length desired.

Lay the fur or feathers over the spot where they will be tied down and wrap them with the thread. For best results, get an even distribution of the fur or feathers around the hook or lure. There are several ways to do this. With treble hooks it is usually best to divide the material into three equal bundles and tie each in place between the two points of the treble hook. Another method, which is ideal for jigs, is to tie in the entire bundle. Loosely wrap the thread three or four times around the body and material. Then pull tight, working the fur or feathers around the body of the lure for even distribution. On larger lures, you may wish to do this in two or more bundles to get a large tail in place.

Once the new tail is secured, clip off excess material forward of the wrap. Then continue wrapping until the cut ends are completely covered. At this point, finish off the wrap using three or four half hitches, binding each of them down into the wrap.

Cut the excess thread and protect the wrap with a coating of paint (this can be done at the same time a lure is dipped to paint the head), epoxy finish (such as that used in rod building), or varnish. For a quick protective coating, several coats of nylon-based clear nail polish work well.

## Rebuilding Lures

Some lures can be completely rebuilt. A prime example is a spinner, because all its parts can be removed and used as replacements in other damaged lures, or it can be rebuilt after cleaning, polishing, or repainting. To do this, cut the eye of the spinner shaft at either the line-tie or hook end. (Do this with care, because the cut end will fly off forcefully. Aim this end at a waste container.)

Once this is done, remove the parts and save them. The usual assembly procedure for rebuilding a standard spinnerbait involves working with an eyed shaft. If you do not have access to these, they can be made with round or needle-nose pli-

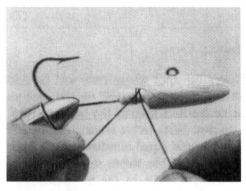

Old jigs can be cut down, repainted with a base coat of white, and retied, as with this lure. Here, thread is being tied in place.

Tail material is being tied down.

Tail material clipped for wrapping collar.

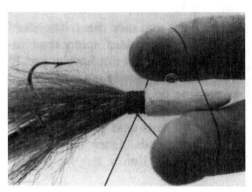

After the collar is wrapped, the tying is finished by wrapping off with half hitches.

ers and .030 wire. Using this eye as the line tie, put the clevis on the spinner blade and then thread the clevis onto the shaft, making sure that the concave side of the blade is next to the shaft.

Continue by adding the body or beads. Once these are in place, form the final eye with the pliers. Before the eye is complete, add the hook, then wrap the eye around the spinner shaft. The eye must be aligned with the spinner shaft and not cocked to one side.

Similar lure rebuilding can be done on spinnerbaits and buzzbaits. Remove the skirts and blades and rebuild them to your own design, or replace damaged or corroded parts.

## Rerigging

Some lures are built onto wire or monofilament leaders. The leader is an essential part of the lure, because otherwise the lure cannot be tied to the line. Examples are offshore trolling lures, cowbells or long spinner blades for deep lake trolling, and tandem lures that are connected with monofilament or wire.

When these rigs are damaged, the simple solution is to rerig the lure. The leader on offshore lures can kink badly when fighting a large fish, which makes the leader weak and unsafe to use. On the same lures, the constant skipping on the surface can abrade the leader where it comes through a hole in the lure head. Corrosion, toothy fish, poor storage (which twists or bends leaders), and fighting fish can also damage leaders.

Leaders can't really be repaired or restored, so they must be replaced. Cut off the old leader, taking note of how the leader and lure were originally rigged. Replace the leader with identical material. Leaders have loops for tying on the line or terminal hooks that are tied in knots, made with a haywire twist or formed with leader sleeves and a crimping tool.

To retie, use a perfection loop or figure-eight knot or similar loop that will be aligned with the main leader strand. Practice making haywire twists so they will be done correctly. To make these, loosely twist both wire strands together, finish with a tight wrap around the main strand of wire, then break the excess wire to form a tight loop with no protecting wire end. To do this, form the wire into a small handle, then bend the wire against the completed wire turns to break it by metal fatigue.

To make loops with leader sleeves, use the correct sleeve for the size and type of leader. You only need a simple loop for most leaders, but for offshore leaders, make a compound loop in which the loop is doubled and twisted before the loop end is run back through the sleeve. This creates extra strength in the loop for the heavy strain of this fishing.

Possible repairs for various types of lures include:

1. Topwater lures: Hook replacement, repaint lure body when discolored or damaged, reglue if cracked, refasten and cement wobbling plates or lips.
2. Crankbaits (medium- and deep-diving plugs): Hook replacement, repaint lure body when discolored or damaged, reglue if cracked, refasten and cement wobbling plates or lips.
3. Worms and soft-plastic lures: Smooth damaged worms and soft lures with heat or a flame, make new lures from old ones by joining parts together with heat or flame.
4. Spinners: Polish, refinish, or replace blades, replace hooks, replace tags and skirts, paint bodies, rebuild spinners.
5. Spinnerbaits: Repaint bodies, rubber-coat bodies, straighten wires, replace skirts, refinish blades, polish, re-form, or repaint spinner blades, replace stinger hooks, rebuild spinnerbaits.
6. Buzzbaits: Repaint or rubber-coat bodies, straighten wires, replace skirts, polish, refinish, straighten, or repaint blades, replace stinger hooks, rebuild buzzbaits.
7. Weedless spoons: Rebend spoon blades, straighten or replace hooks (where possible), repaint, refinish, or polish blades.
8. Structure or jigging spoons: Replace hooks, polish, repaint, refinish, or rebend blades.
9. Jigs: Repaint, replace weedguards and skirts, retie tails.
10. Offshore trolling lures: Repaint, replace hooks, rerig, rewrap skirts.

# The Fisherman's Tool Kit

THE TOOLS THAT YOU NEED to maintain and repair tackle are minimal. What you use will vary with the tackle being repaired. Most of these tools you will have or can obtain easily at low cost. If you get into tackle repair extensively, you will need more and better tools to cope with the range of tackle.

The following is a complete list of repair tools. Not all of these are required for simple or onetime repairs. When repairing a rod, for example, you will need only razor blades, brushes, a rasp, file, sandpaper, and a burnisher. With those tools you can rewrap any rod guide and repair any handle, grip, or reel seat. For most reel repairs, you will need only a set of small screwdrivers, a small wrench, and the repair tool that came with the reel.

## Rod Repair Tools

Rod repair tools are similar to those used for rod building. What you need depends upon the extent of repairs you wish to do. The tools needed are simple and include:

**Brushes** For adding epoxy and color preserver when recoating or finishing rod wraps. Best brushes are inexpensive and disposable. I like those from Flex Coat because the bristles are bound into the tip end so that they cannot come out and mar a finish.

**Razor Blades** Razor blades are a must for removing old wraps and finish from a blank and trimming excess thread when completing a new wrap. Best and cheapest are the boxes of industrial single-edge blades.

**Heat Source** A heat source, or sources, is needed for several tasks including removing a tiptop, metal butt caps, reel seats, and metal ferrules. When removing a tiptop, it's hard to beat a disposable butane lighter. For larger tasks, a laboratory-type alcohol lamp has a clean flame and works well. A propane torch may be needed for tasks such as removing metal ferrules on offshore rods and metal reel seats.

**Emery Board** Ideal for removing the last vestiges of old epoxy on guide wraps.

**Round File** Useful for roughing up the inside of reel seats and butt caps for better glue adhesion, and for enlarging the hole in cork rings when replacing grips.

**Tiptop Gauge** This isn't necessary to repair a rod, but it is a handy tool to have for repairing and building rods. The tiptop gauge is a flat plastic rule with molded pegs to fit tiptops from $\frac{4}{64}$ to $\frac{32}{64}$ inch in size. The gauge makes it possible to easily check tiptops when you want to buy another in the same size. A gauge also measures the tip diameter of a rod when the last few inches break off. Gauges are available through most of the do-it-yourself tackle catalogs.

Internal calipers can also measure a removed tiptop; external calipers can measure the tip of the rod blank.

**Guide Gauges** As with tiptop gauges, these are not necessary but are helpful. Simple gauges are just a chart that shows the diameter of guide rings in millimeters and inches. A second type of gauge measures the ring diameter of a removed guide.

**Rasps** These are rougher than files and come in many shapes. Flat rasps are best. Rasps are ideal for rough-shaping cork grips, before filing and sanding.

**Files** Coarse or bastard-cut files are also good for shaping cork grips. Best are 8 to 10 inches long.

**Sandpaper** Sandpaper, garnet paper, or emery cloth is necessary when doing the final shaping and smoothing of cork grips. Coarse, medium-fine, and extra-fine grades are needed.

**Rod Wrapper** These tools are sold by some tackle shops and mail-order houses. Usually made of wood, they consist of a base, two supports to hold the rod, and a thread-tension device. They are definitely not necessary for occasional repairs, although they do make them easier. You can make a wrapper using scrap pine shelving for a base, two 6- to 8-inch lengths tacked to the base's end with a V-cut in the top of the board as supports, and a sewing machine thread-tension device to control the thread spool.

Another tension device uses a $\frac{1}{4}$-20 bolt in the base, which holds the thread at the proper tension with a compression spring and wing nut. Plastic washers, cut from a plastic milk bottle, prevent thread from binding. Still another alternative is to use two $\frac{1}{4}$-20 eye bolts through the base, 3 inches on center, with a $\frac{1}{4}$-inch rod through the eye bolts to hold the thread. Use a spring, washer, and wing nut underneath to adjust the tension. For these rigs, you must have additional feet under the base so that the bolts clear the working table.

**Grip Seater** One of the problems with seating new synthetic grips is that they must be forced onto the blank because the hole in the grip is, by necessity, smaller than the blank. A grip seater facilitates this procedure. The seater is simply a piece of 4-inch-wide shelving with a hole drilled into its center. The hole should be slightly larger than the diameter of the blank. Use the seater to push the grip easily into place on the blank. You can also make a more elaborate grip seater, with different holes in the board that fit several sizes of grip/blank combinations.

**Cork Clamp** These clamps are used to hold cork while glue is drying, such as when replacing rings on a cork grip. Clamps can be improvised. Roger Seiders of Flex Coat suggests using a cored brick (these are for wall construction, not paving) or a 5-pound weight from a barbell set. The brick or weight is placed over the blank after the cork grip is glued, then the rod is placed vertically so that the weight presses the cork rings together. Handle the brick carefully so you won't inadvertently scratch the rod.

Cork clamps made just for gluing rod grips are available, but you can also make your own. To make one, you need two pieces of 2- or 3-inch-wide by 6- to 8-inch-long shelving, two lengths of ¼-20 All-Thread (length determined by the length of the grips made or repaired), two ¼-20 wing nuts, six washers, and four ¼-20 nuts. Drill a ¾-inch hole through the center of one board, then drill a ⅜-inch hole 1 inch from each end. Drill ¼-inch holes 1 inch from each end of the second board (so they will align with the small holes on the first board). Use four nuts and four of the washers to fasten the two lengths of All-Thread to this board. The other board is slipped over the All-Thread, followed by the washers and wing nuts. In use, a rod blank with a freshly glued grip is placed in the clamp, the rod extending through the hole in the free end. Any length can be made, based on the rod handle length.

An alternative is to use a pipe clamp to exert pressure on the grip. To do this, use a C-clamp to fasten a short length of wood shelving to each jaw of the pipe clamp. Drill a hole in the exposed end of one board. Place the rod between these temporary wood jaws, with the rod blank extending through the hole in the one board. Tighten the pipe clamp slightly to exert pressure. Do not overtighten, because these clamps could easily apply too much pressure.

**Burnisher** Burnishers smooth thread wraps after rewrapping a guide. Special burnishers are available, and the one for transferring letters in drafting, manufactured by the C-Thru Ruler Company, is ideal. Smooth plastic pens or similar items make fine substitutes.

**Rod-Curing Motor** Available from tackle shops and mail-order houses, these are slow-turning motors with a device to hold the butt end of the rod. They constantly rotate the rod so that epoxy won't sag and run. Most motors have 1- to 60-rpm speed.

Excellent home-built machines can easily be made. Attach a 2-inch PVC pipe cap to the motor shaft to hold the rod. To do this, first drill and tap three ¼-20 holes at three equal points around the edge or lip of the cap. Fit these with 2-inch-long thumbscrews or eye bolts to hold the rod. Fasten the cup (glue or use bolts on a threaded motor shaft) to the motor and mount the motor on a small stand. Use another stand with a V-cut to support the other end of the rod. Line the V with plastic from disposable bottles or cartons to protect the rod. A simpler rod support is made from a small cardboard box with a V-cut at the top.

A quick down-and-dirty rod-curing device can be made from a slow-rpm rotisserie motor. These motors have square holes for fitting the barbecue spit. A square wood plug force-fitted into the hole makes it possible to screw the PVC cup to the motor.

**Drill and Drill Bits** These are rarely needed for rod repairs, but are necessary to drill through loose reels seats to insert pins. A small variable-power drill with $\frac{1}{32}$- to $\frac{1}{8}$-inch bits works well. Exact size is determined by the pin and reel seat.

## Reel Repair Tools

As with rod repairs, the tools needed for reel repair are simple. In most cases, all you need to clean, maintain, and lightly repair a reel are the tools that came with it. Because these are simple and cheap combinations, higher-quality tools are best for extensive reel work.

**Reel Mate** This Bass Pro Shops bracket is a support stand that clamps a reel in place when repairing or lubing. It also holds a spool of line, which facilitates changing line.

**Line Winders** Line winders by Berkley, Reel Boy, and Lineminder are available to spool line on spinning, spincast, and casting reels. The Berkley mounts on a table, counter, or workbench; the Lineminder clamps to the rod to transfer line from any size of spool. A new consumer portable electric line winder, to spool line on spinning, baitcast, and fly reels, is being developed by Triangle Manufacturing Co. at this writing.

**Reel Tool** Most of these are small, flat, and a combination screwdriver and wrench. They are designed to work on the screws and fasteners on a specific reel. They are awkward to hold for extended use, so more precise tools are better. These are ideal for tacklebox and field use.

**Screwdrivers** You need small sizes for reels in both regular and Phillips heads. Get a set of these in the small sizes that fit reels. Moody, RadioShack, and many other companies make screwdrivers specifically for small, precise work. I use a RadioShack set of 16 tools, which includes regular and Phillips screwdrivers and small hex socket wrenches.

Screwdrivers are a must to remove side plates, tighten loose spinning bails, remove and replace pawls from casting reels, adjust clicks on fly reels, and so on.

**Wrenches** Wrenches are often included in screwdriver sets, but small open-end box wrenches are also available, along with tiny adjustable wrenches. Some of these are really working toys, but they are ideal for dismantling reels.

**Awls** An awl is nothing more than a point, which is handy for depositing oil in small recesses, helping to hook tension springs over holding hooks or pins, and so on. A small awl can be made from a thick darning needle fitted onto a wood dowel handle.

**Oilers** Oilers and greasers are small specialty tools that usually come with the oil or grease. Most are almost penlike—with a removable cap and a hollow needle applicator. Their small size makes them ideal for lubricating reels and other fishing tackle.

**Ring Pliers** These are small pliers with straight or angled pinpoints, used to remove and attach internal or external ring fasteners. Regular pliers, carefully used, serve the same purpose. In addition, many of the small ring fasteners used in fishing reels don't have the small end holes that allow use of these specialized pliers. So don't buy ring pliers until you need them. Good ring pliers are available from hardware and automotive-supply stores.

## Lure Repair Tools

Lure tools are needed for repainting, replacing hooks, polishing, and so on.

**Hook Sharpeners** Hook sharpeners are maintenance rather than repair tools. Hook sharpening is so important, however, that hook sharpeners are included.
   There are many styles and types of hook sharpeners available. They include:

1. Files: Large 8- to 10-inch-long files are best to quickly sharpen large hooks, because they will remove the maximum amount of metal in the shortest amount of time. Double-cut files cut better than single cut.
2. Diamond hones: Hones are available from Diamond Machining Technology, Eze-Lap, Gaines, Bass Pro Shops, and other companies. Diamond Machining Technology offers several diamond hook hones, including a long-handled hone, a small hone shaped to look like a key, and flat hones for hooks and knives. Eze-Lap has small hones in fine, medium, and coarse grits. Gaines and Bass Pro Shops sell a small pen-sized diamond hone with a penlike cap.
3. Rotary grinders: Examples of these vary greatly. There is the Point Maker by Texas Tackle, which is a bench or boat-operated, thin grinding wheel: AC for home use and DC (cigarette lighter adapter) models for boat or RV use are available. Johnson and Berkley both make battery-operated (AA or C) rotary stones.

**Brushes** Brushes are a must for most painting or touch-up jobs. The fast-drying field-use paints usually have brushes in the bottle lid. Testor's has felt-tip applicators. Other paints will require a brush. Disposable brushes are ideal.

**Pliers** Pliers are good for holding lures for painting, removing and replacing hooks, adjusting diving lips, and so on. Handy pliers include the compound-action pliers on the Sargent design, and long-nose pliers (especially for painting).

**Scale Netting** Scale netting is ideal for reproducing or replacing scale finishes on lures. Fine- and coarse-scale netting is available from tackle shops and mail-order companies. Lacking that, you can always buy tulle or similar netting in craft and fabric shops.

**Netting Frame** Netting must be held slightly against the lure when spraying a scale finish. One easy, no-mess way to do this is to hold the netting in a frame. A wood frame can be made for this, stapling the netting to it, although the spring-clamp embroidery frames, available in craft or needlepoint shops, are ideal.

**Heat Source** A heat source is needed to melt soft-plastic lures to either rejoin them or to make new lures. Disposable cigarette lighters or small alcohol lamps serve this purpose well.

**Wire Cutters** Wire cutters are handy for trimming plastic, metal, blades, lips, wires, and skirts on lures. Cutters can also be used to cut bent wires on spinner-baits and buzzbaits before repairing or converting them to short-arm lures. They can also be used to trim blades and lips on lures.

**Split-Ring Pliers** Split-ring pliers are necessary to anyone who is seriously interested in lure repair. These long-nose pliers have a small tooth at the end of one jaw, which springs open the split ring. The pliers are the only safe way to remove and replace hooks on split rings.

Knives are often suggested for opening rings, but this is dangerous because you can easily cut yourself. Split-ring pliers are available in inexpensive stamped-out styles and more sturdily constructed models.

## Tools for Tackleboxes, Accessories

Tools for repairing tackleboxes and accessories are minimal. What is broken often dictates the tool you use to fix it.

**Drill and Drill Bits** The same tool you need to repair reel seats can also be used to drill out rivets holding hinges, latches, and so on before replacing with new parts.

**Pop Rivet Tool** These are ideal for tackle repair, including replacement of parts on tackleboxes, reriveting net frames on handles, fixing bait buckets, and so on.

**Hollow Needle** A large hypodermic needle is ideal for making nail knots to connect leader butts and fly lines. Use a size 15 and file the end so it's blunt to prevent accidents.

**Clippers** Nail clippers are ideal for cutting line and trimming soft-plastic worms, plastic toothbrush-type weedguards, and other lures. Keep these and the hollow needle on a lanyard so they are readily accessible.

**Net Gauges** Not necessary but handy if you tear up nets; these usually come in sets but can be bought individually. They are nothing more than rectangular plastic sheets that ensure net loops are consistently sized. Eight sizes are available. You can make a gauge from scrap material, such as thick cardboard. The gauge should be 6 to 8 inches long; the width will be determined by the size of the net loop to repair.

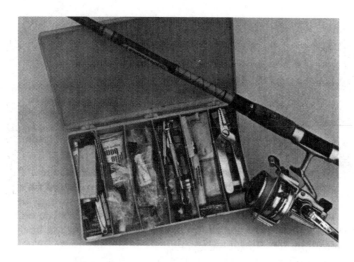

A special field repair kit.

**Net Shuttles** Net shuttles are pointed and have brackets to wrap and hold net cord used to make net loops. They come in nine sizes. Both net gauges and shuttles are available from Jann's NetCraft, Inc.

## Field Repair Kits

It would be nice to think that, barring accidents, and providing tackle is kept in good repair, field repairs are unnecessary. That's not realistic, however, because tackle does break. For longer trips, take a field kit. My practice is to carry an oiler, reel tool, and other minimal repair tools and extra tackle on local trips. On trips that might take me away from tackle supplies briefly (such as a weekend backpacking trip), I carry a repair and tool kit that fits into a 6 × 4 × 1-inch plastic lure box. On longer trips—to Alaska, abroad, or into the backwoods for a week or so—I take a more comprehensive kit that fits into a 10 × 6 × 1¾-inch box.

Suggested contents for this kit include tools and materials for simple repairs that can be easily accomplished in the field. The amount and number of items you pack depend upon the size of the kit. The following is based on the larger kit that I carry (the smaller kit is a scaled-down version) based on immediate needs and the tackle used.

Each compartment (there are usually six in these small boxes) is filled with specific parts, as follows:

**Compartment 1:** This compartment holds grease, oil, and wax. The items are kept in a small plastic sandwich bag to protect the rest of the repair kit should any of the items leak. Carry oils and grease for lubing reels, and a small piece of candle wax for assuring good fit on the ferrule. Fly-line cleaners can also be packed here.

**Compartment 2:** Glues are kept in this second section. They should include instant (Crazy) glues, Pliobond (for sealing nail knots), and five-minute epoxy.

**Compartment 3:** Many reels come with a small container filled with parts most

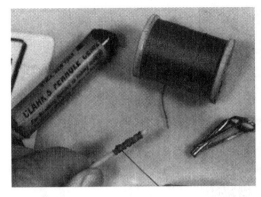

Spare tiptops should be carried in any field repair kit, but not all sizes are needed. For a temporary repair, a tiptop can be built up with thread as shown to match the size of a replacement tiptop.

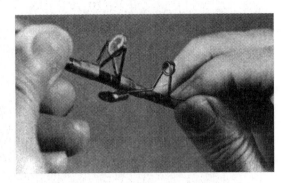

For a quick repair when everything else is lacking, a safety pin can be bent and used as a replacement guide.

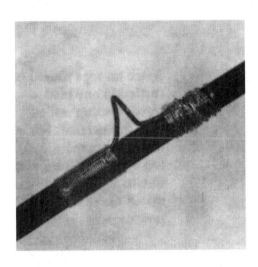

In the field, guide wraps can be done with monofilament line. Left, neat for a semipermanent job, right, quick for a one-day patch job.

often needed and most easily replaced on spinning, casting, and saltwater reels. These include springs, brake blocks, pawls, bail springs, screws, drag washers, and so on. Include these parts for all the reels that you have or are likely to take on that trip.

**Compartment 4:** Rod parts. Include replacement tiptops (such as oversize sets designed to fit almost any rod); Aetna types that are wrapped in place; and guides of several sizes and styles to fit the different rods that you carry.

**Compartment 5:** Repair materials. This section should include rod-wrapping thread, tape, sandpaper, and so on.

**Compartment 6:** Tools. This section should include the tools that came with your reels, a set of regular and Phillips-head screwdrivers, one or two small wrenches, awl, split-ring pliers, small knife, ignition file, and any other tools you need for your rod, reel, and tackle repair.